YOTSUBA&!

5

D1159416

KIYOHIKO AZUMA

TABLE OF CONTENTS

YOTSUBA&!
KIYOHIKO AZUMA

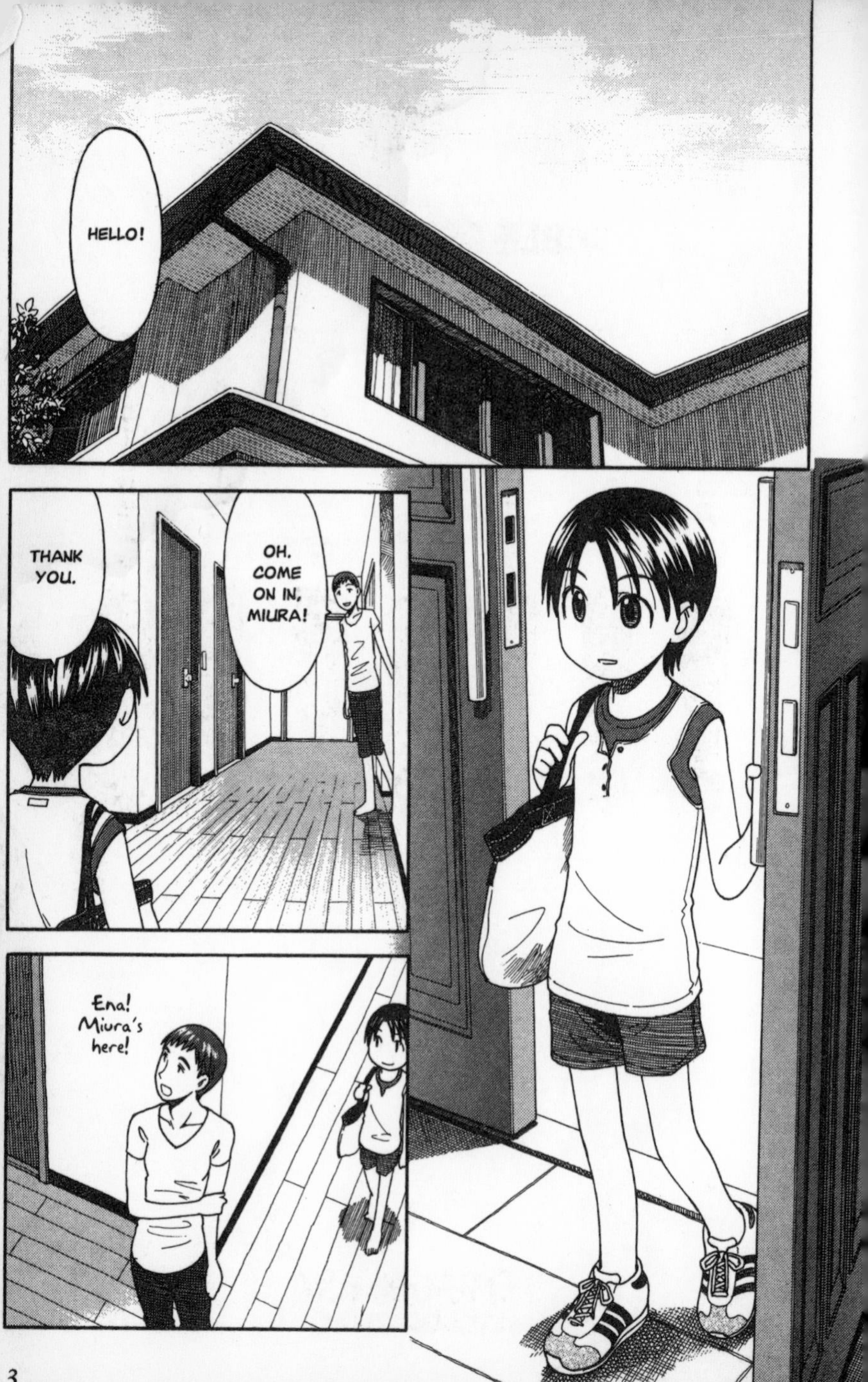
HELLO!
OH. COME ON IN, MIURA!
THANK YOU.
Ena! Miura's here!

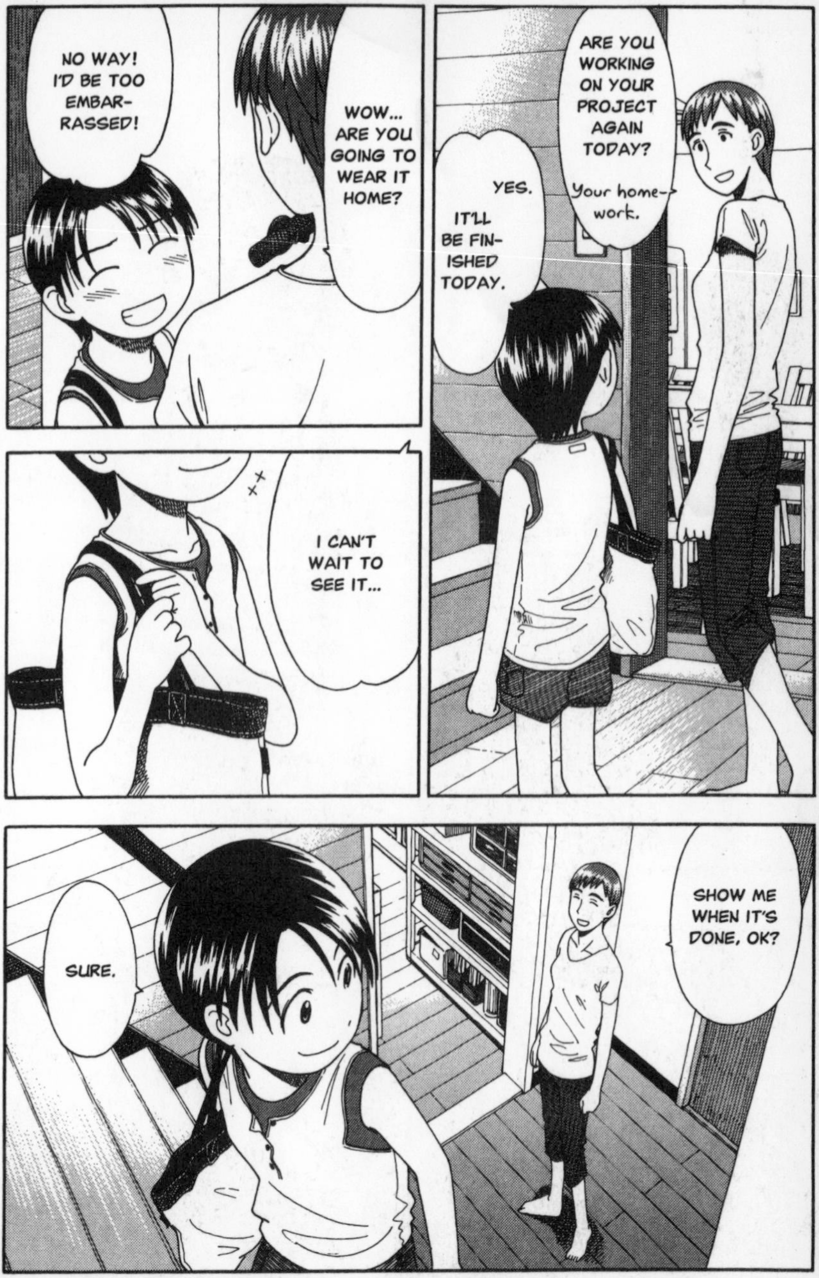
ARE YOU WORKING ON YOUR PROJECT AGAIN TODAY?
Your home-work.
YES.
IT'LL BE FIN-ISHED TODAY.
WOW... ARE YOU GOING TO WEAR IT HOME?
NO WAY! I'D BE TOO EMBAR-RASSED!
I CAN'T WAIT TO SEE IT...
SHOW ME WHEN IT'S DONE, OK?
SURE.

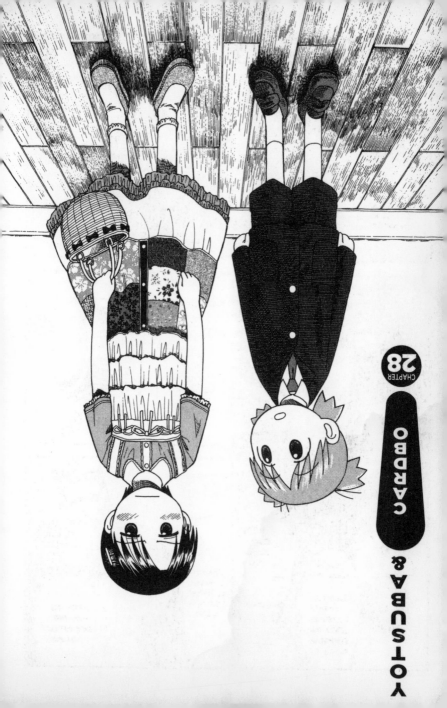

YOTSUBA&! CARDBO

CHAPTER 28

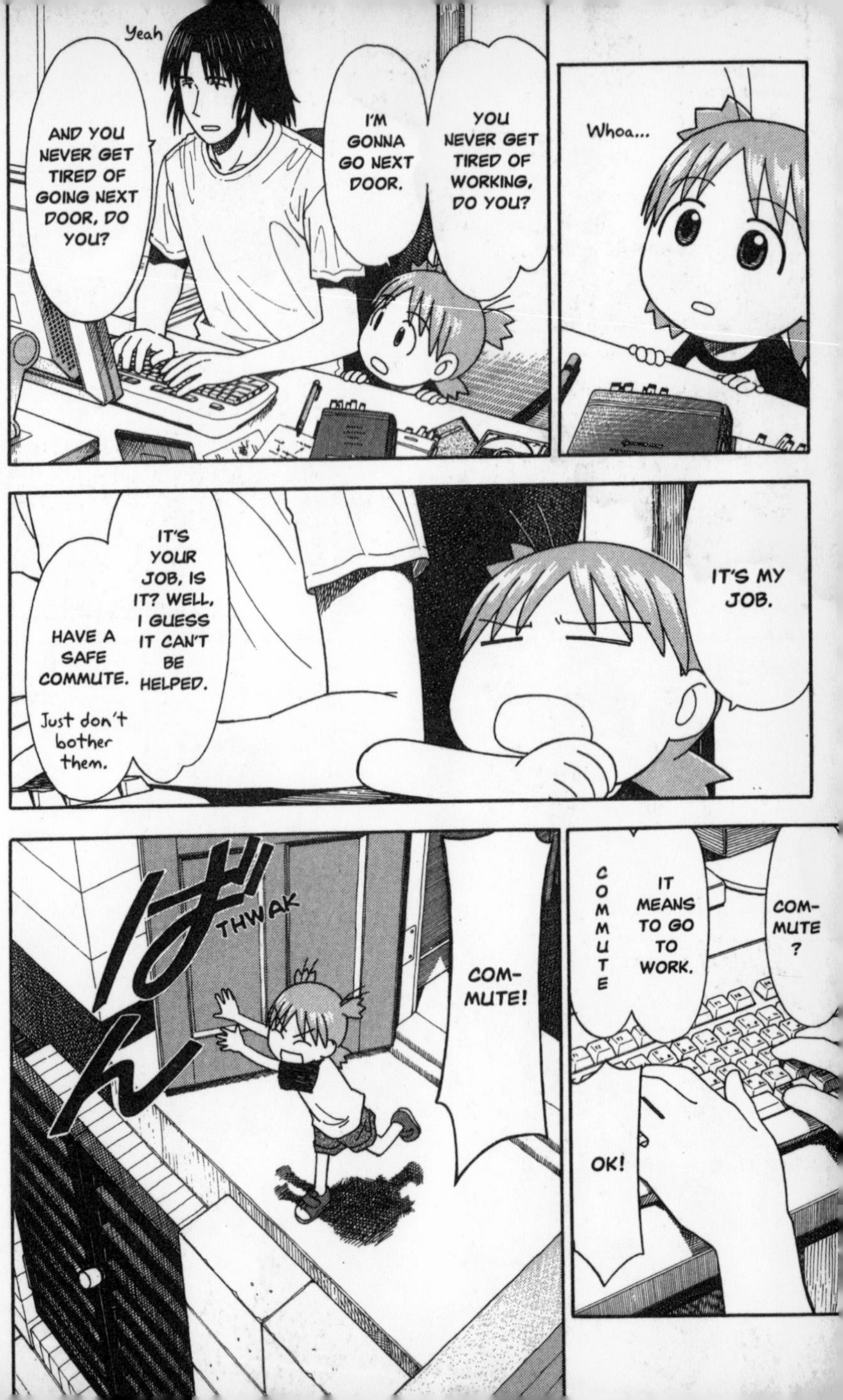
Whoa...
YOU NEVER GET TIRED OF WORKING, DO YOU?
I'M GONNA GO NEXT DOOR.
Yeah
AND YOU NEVER GET TIRED OF GOING NEXT DOOR, DO YOU?
IT'S MY JOB.
IT'S YOUR JOB, IS IT? WELL, I GUESS IT CAN'T BE HELPED.
HAVE A SAFE COMMUTE.
Just don't bother them.
COM-MUTE?
IT MEANS TO GO TO WORK.
COMMUTE
OK!
COM-MUTE!
ばん
THWAK

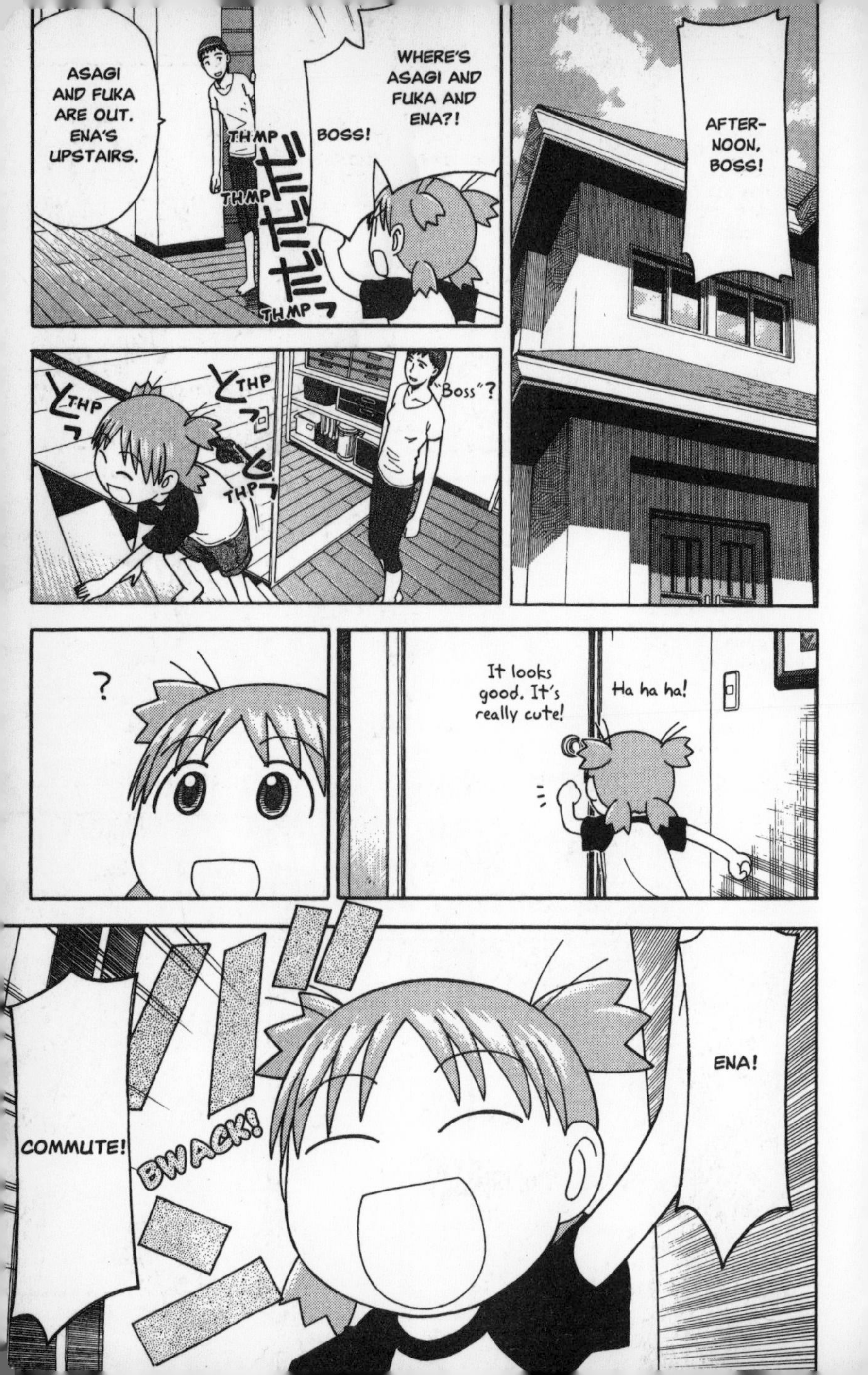
AFTER-NOON, BOSS!
WHERE'S ASAGI AND FUKA AND ENA?!
BOSS!
THMP
THMP
THMP
ASAGI AND FUKA ARE OUT. ENA'S UPSTAIRS.
"Boss"?
THP
THP
THP
Ha ha ha!
It looks good. It's really cute!
?
ENA!
BWACK!
COMMUTE!

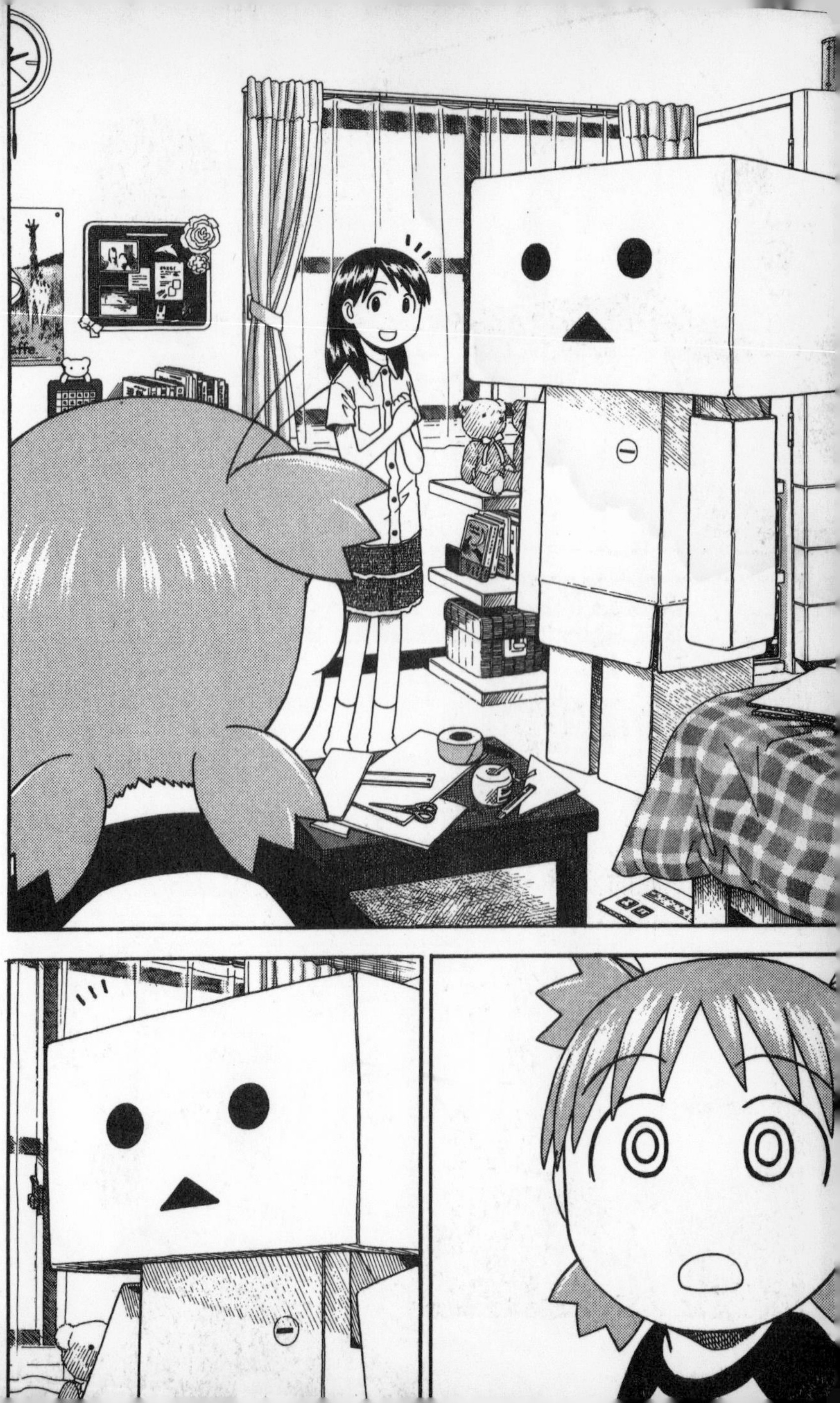

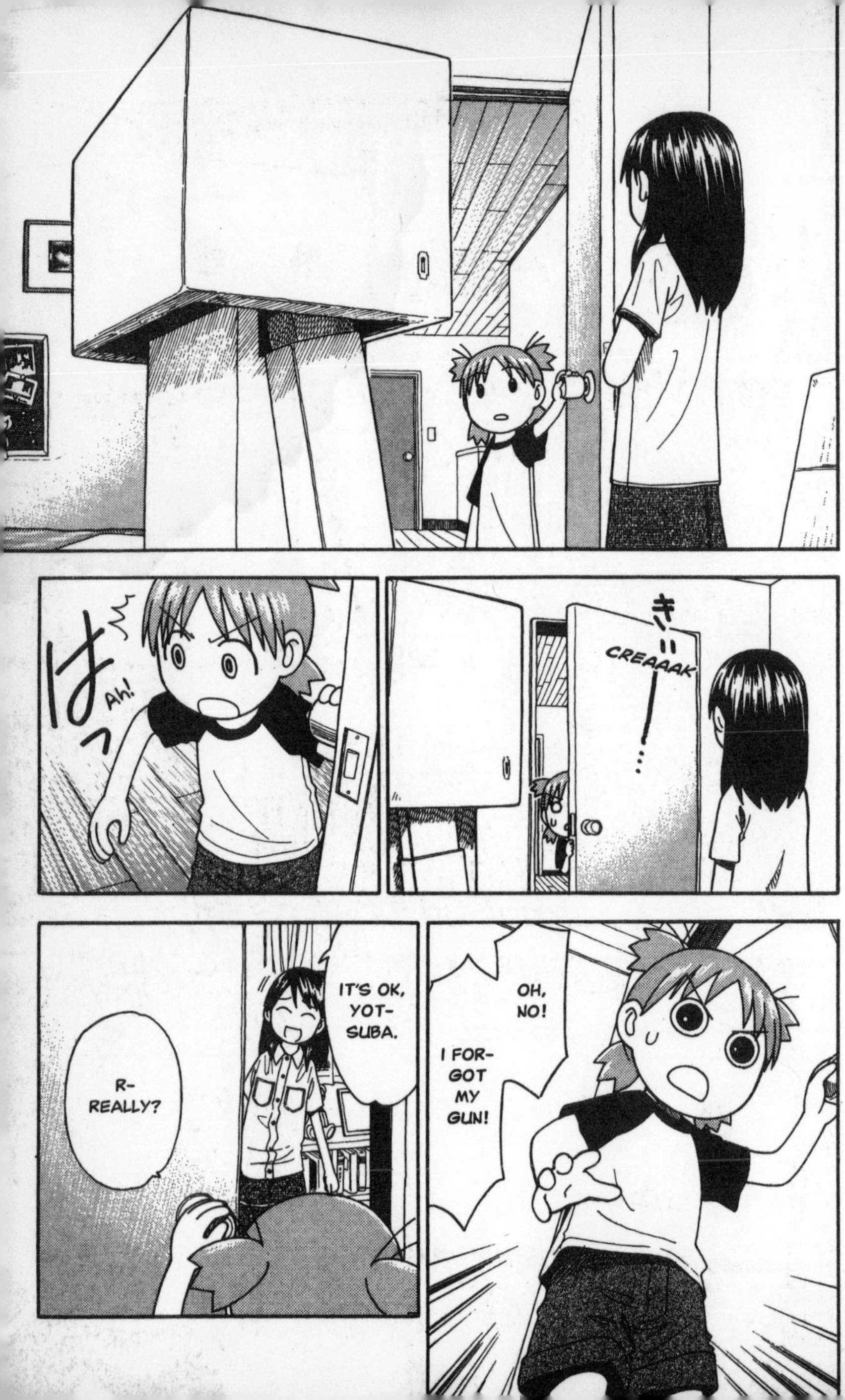
きーー
CREAAAK
—……
はっ
Ah!
OH, NO!
I FOR-GOT MY GUN!
IT'S OK, YOT-SUBA.
R-REALLY?

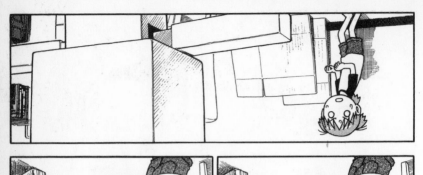

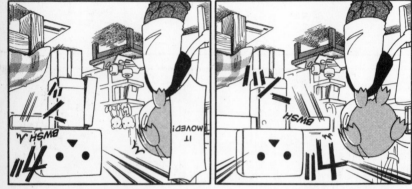

IT MOVED!

BWSH

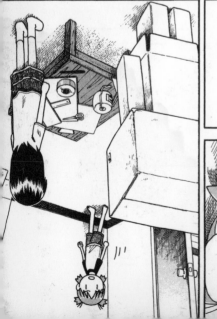

ARE YOU A ROBOT?

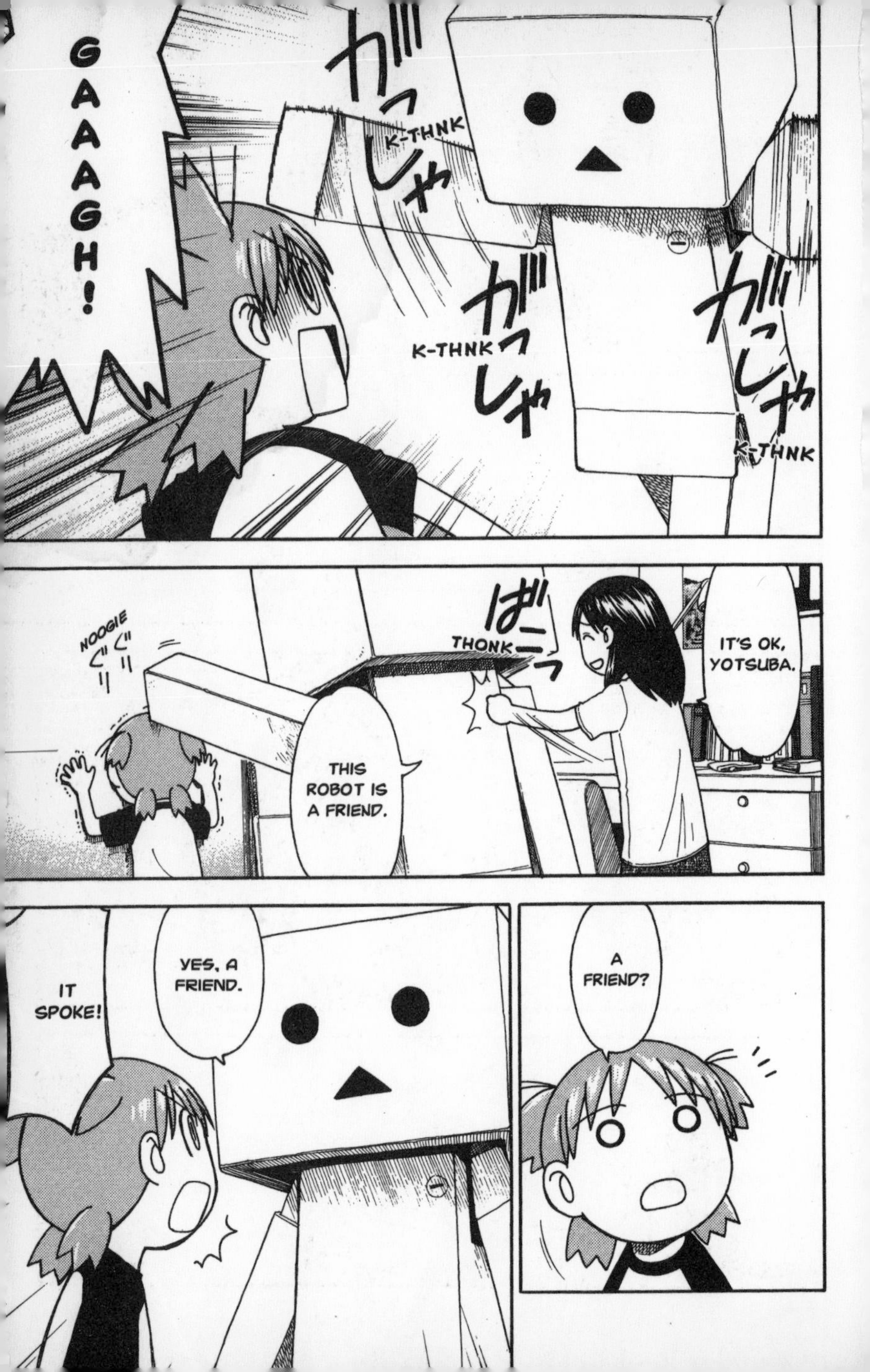

K-THNK
K-THNK
K-THNK
GAAAGH!
IT'S OK, YOTSUBA.
THONK
THIS ROBOT IS A FRIEND.
NOOGIE
A FRIEND?
YES, A FRIEND.
IT SPOKE!

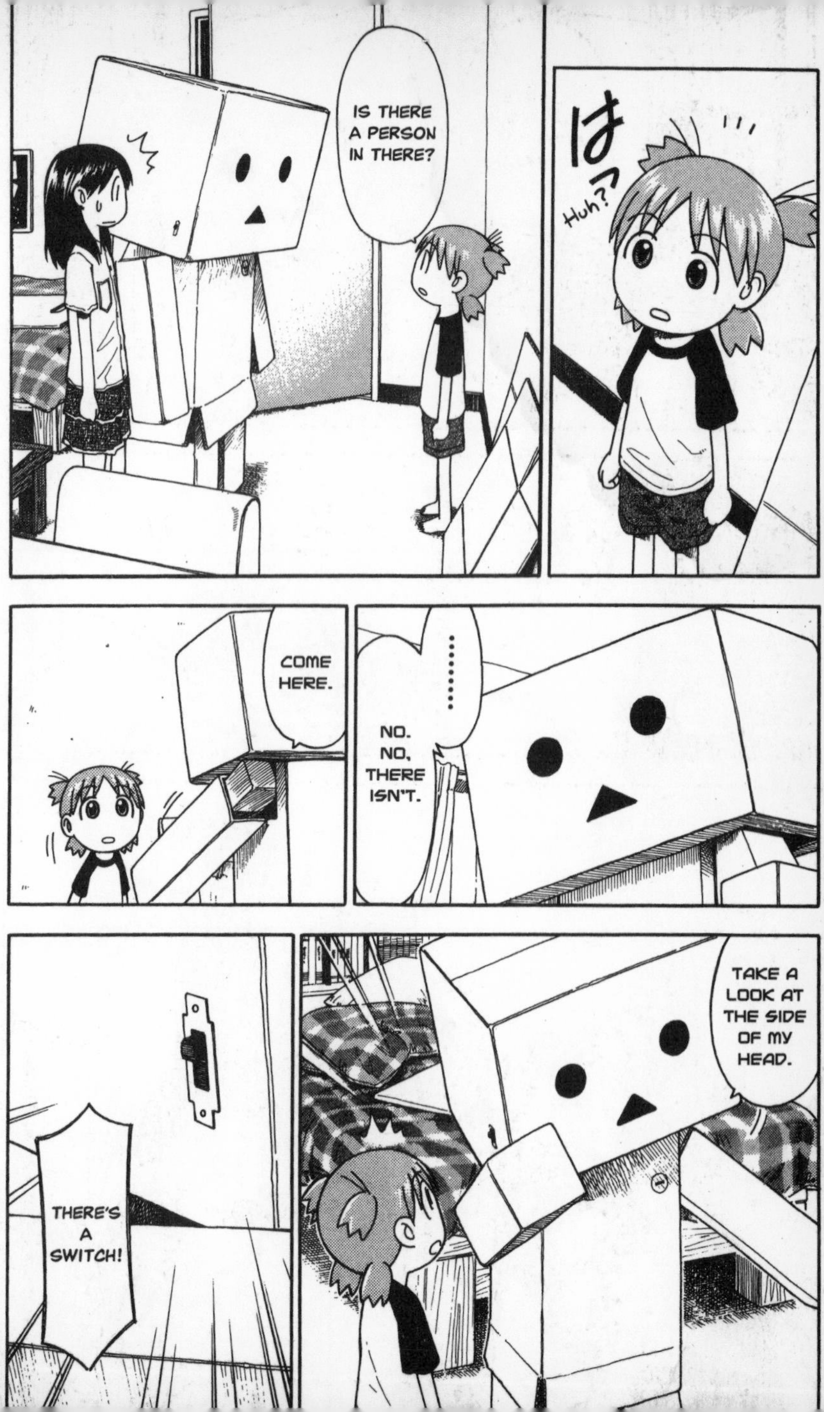
は
Huh??
IS THERE A PERSON IN THERE?
......
NO. NO, THERE ISN'T.
COME HERE.
TAKE A LOOK AT THE SIDE OF MY HEAD.
THERE'S A SWITCH!

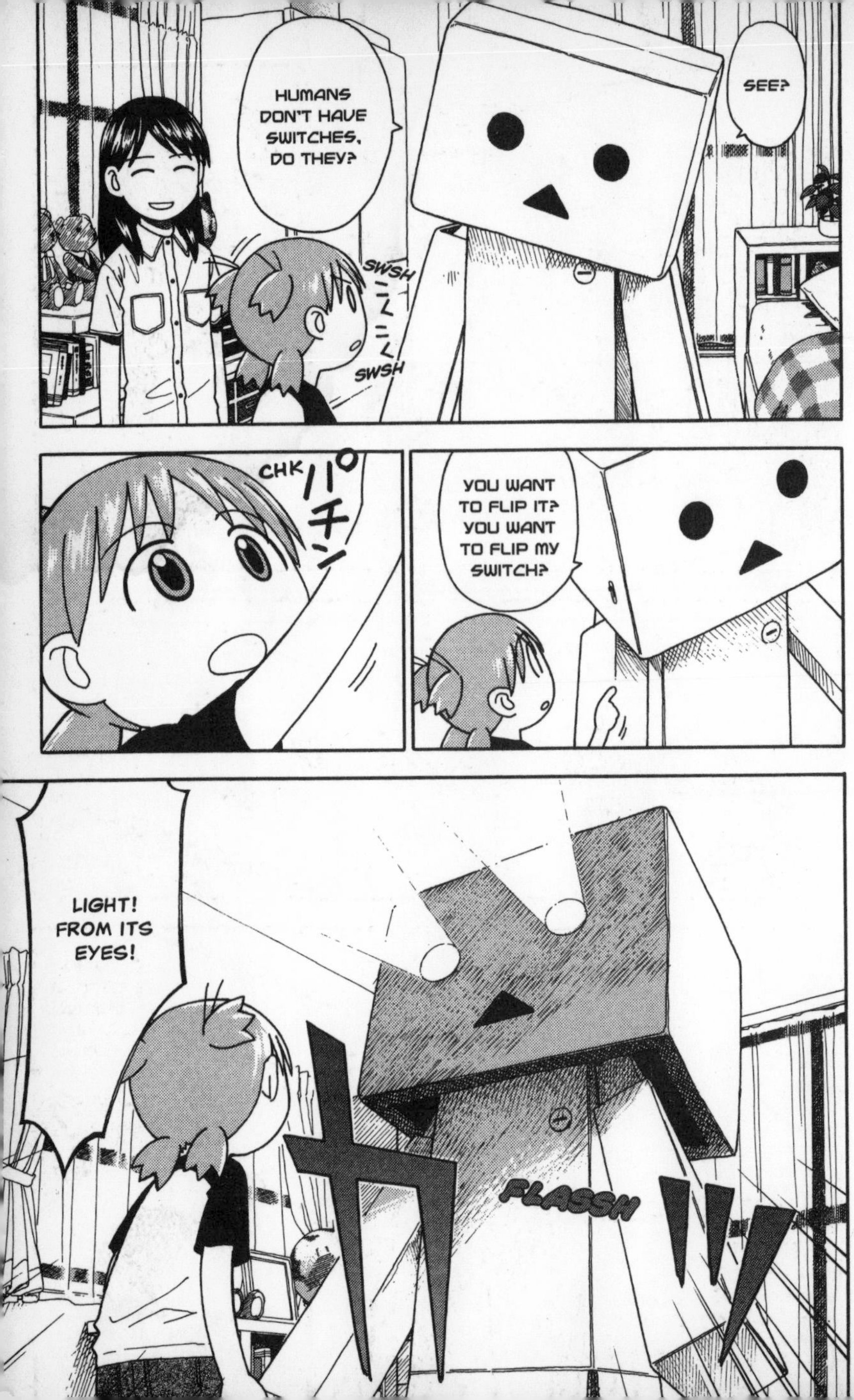
HUMANS DON'T HAVE SWITCHES, DO THEY?
SWSH SWSH
SEE?
YOU WANT TO FLIP IT? YOU WANT TO FLIP MY SWITCH?
CHK
パチン
LIGHT! FROM ITS EYES!
FLASSH

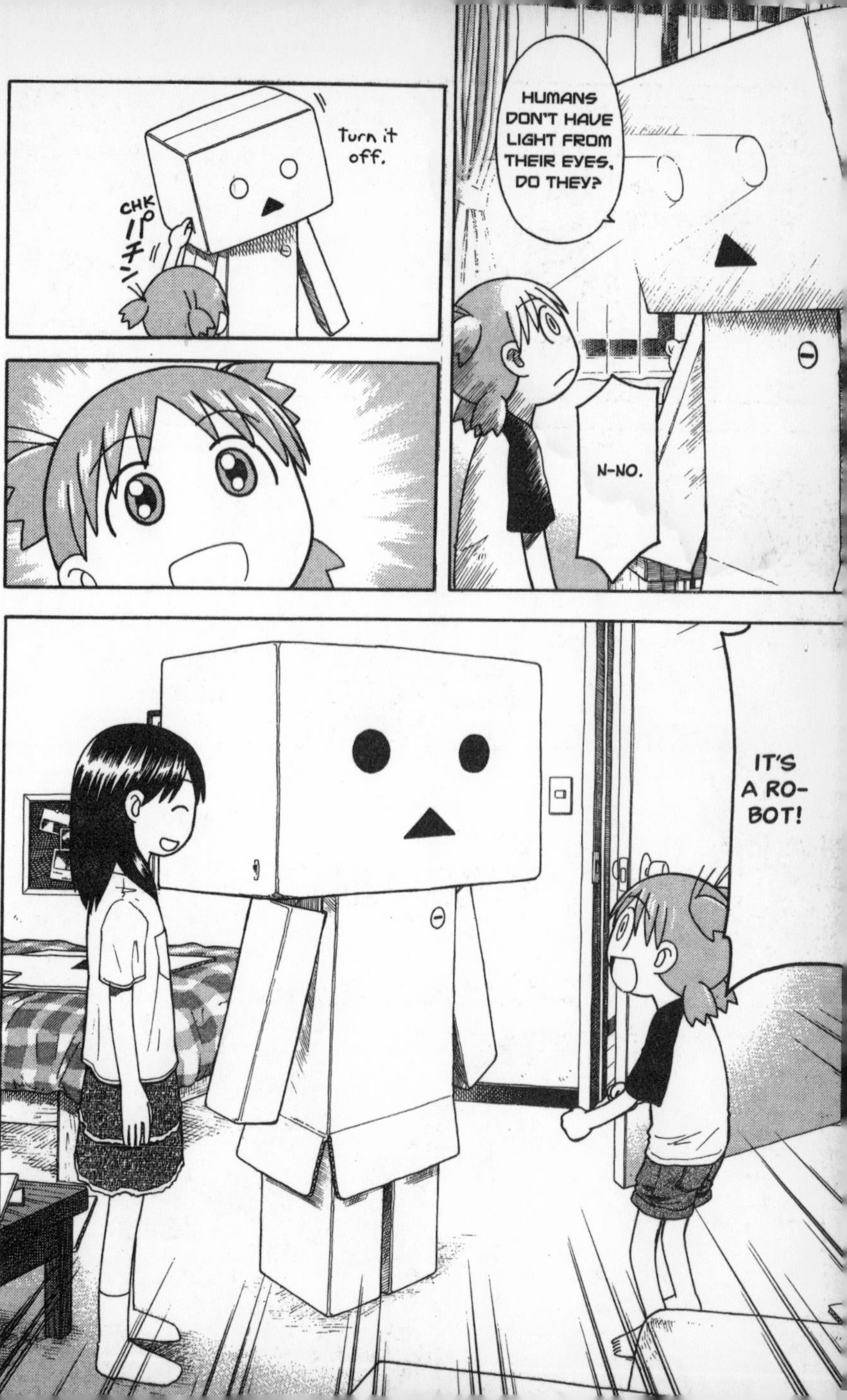
HUMANS DON'T HAVE LIGHT FROM THEIR EYES, DO THEY?
N-NO.
turn it off.
CHK
パチン
IT'S A RO-BOT!

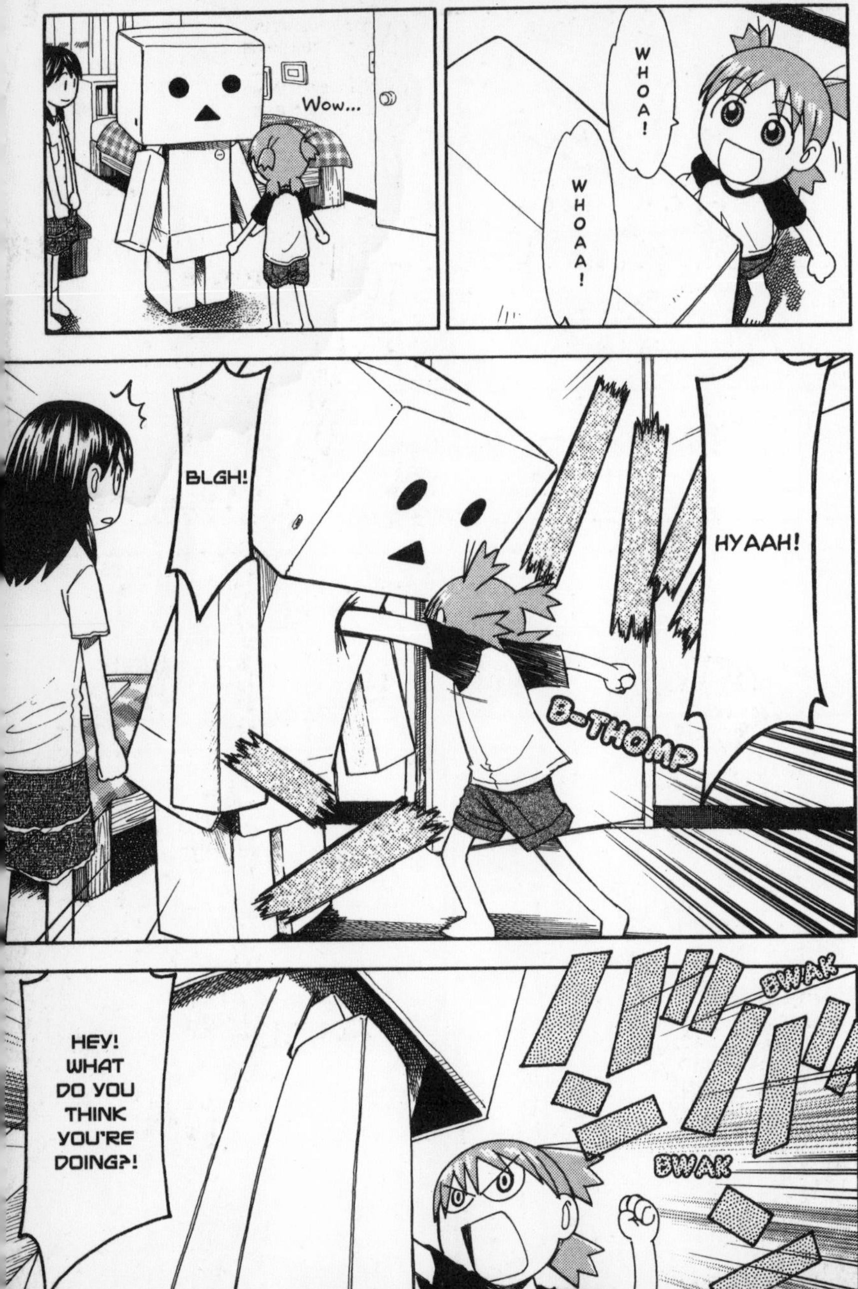
WHOA!
WHOAA!
Wow...
HYAAH!
B-THOMP
BLGH!
BWAK
BWAK
HEY! WHAT DO YOU THINK YOU'RE DOING?!

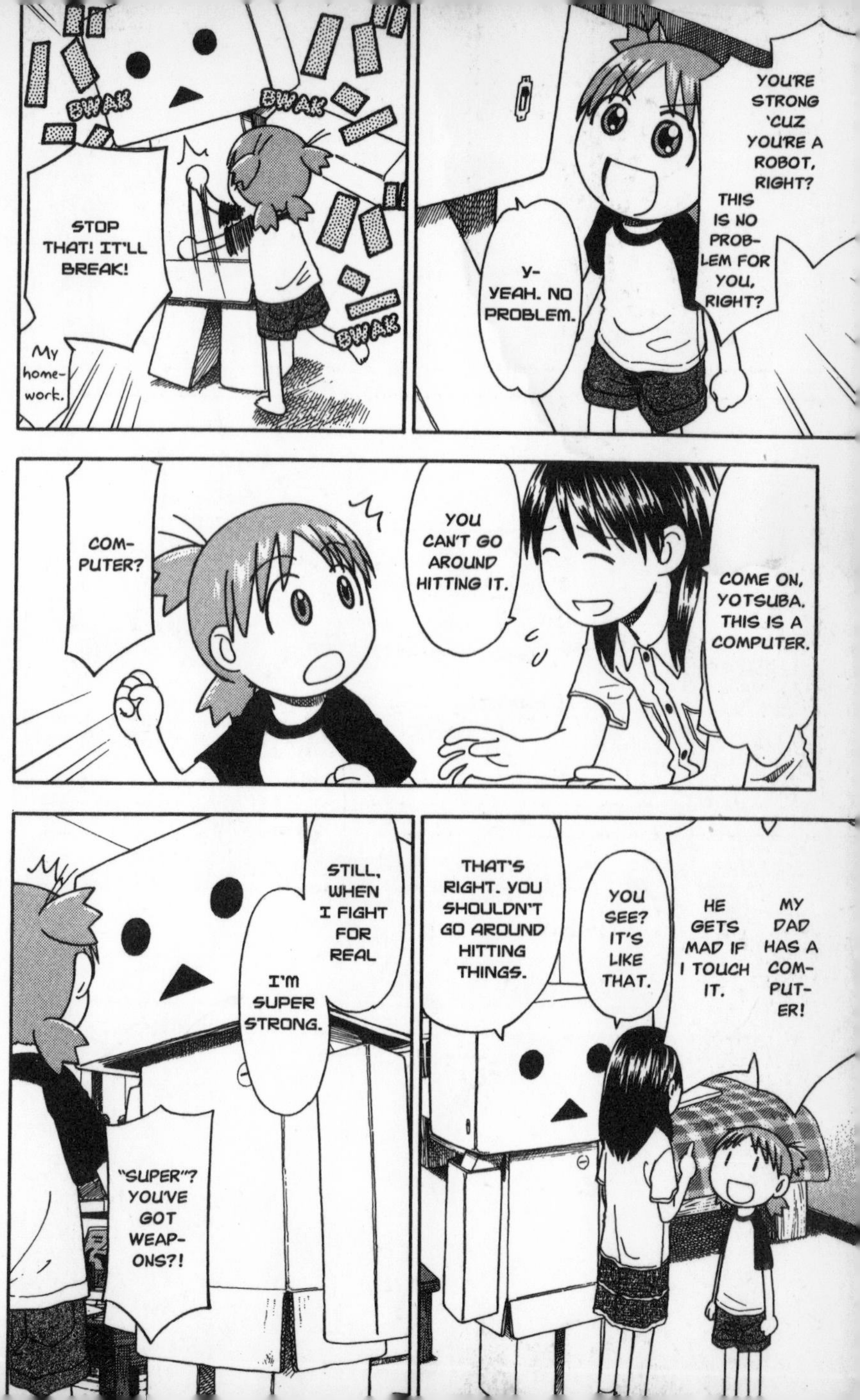
YOU'RE STRONG 'CUZ YOU'RE A ROBOT, RIGHT?
THIS IS NO PROBLEM FOR YOU, RIGHT?
Y- YEAH. NO PROBLEM.
STOP THAT! IT'LL BREAK!
BWAK
BWAK
BWAK
My homework.
COME ON, YOTSUBA. THIS IS A COMPUTER.
YOU CAN'T GO AROUND HITTING IT.
COMPUTER?
MY DAD HAS A COMPUTER!
HE GETS MAD IF I TOUCH IT.
YOU SEE? IT'S LIKE THAT.
THAT'S RIGHT. YOU SHOULDN'T GO AROUND HITTING THINGS.
STILL, WHEN I FIGHT FOR REAL
I'M SUPER STRONG.
"SUPER"? YOU'VE GOT WEAPONS?!

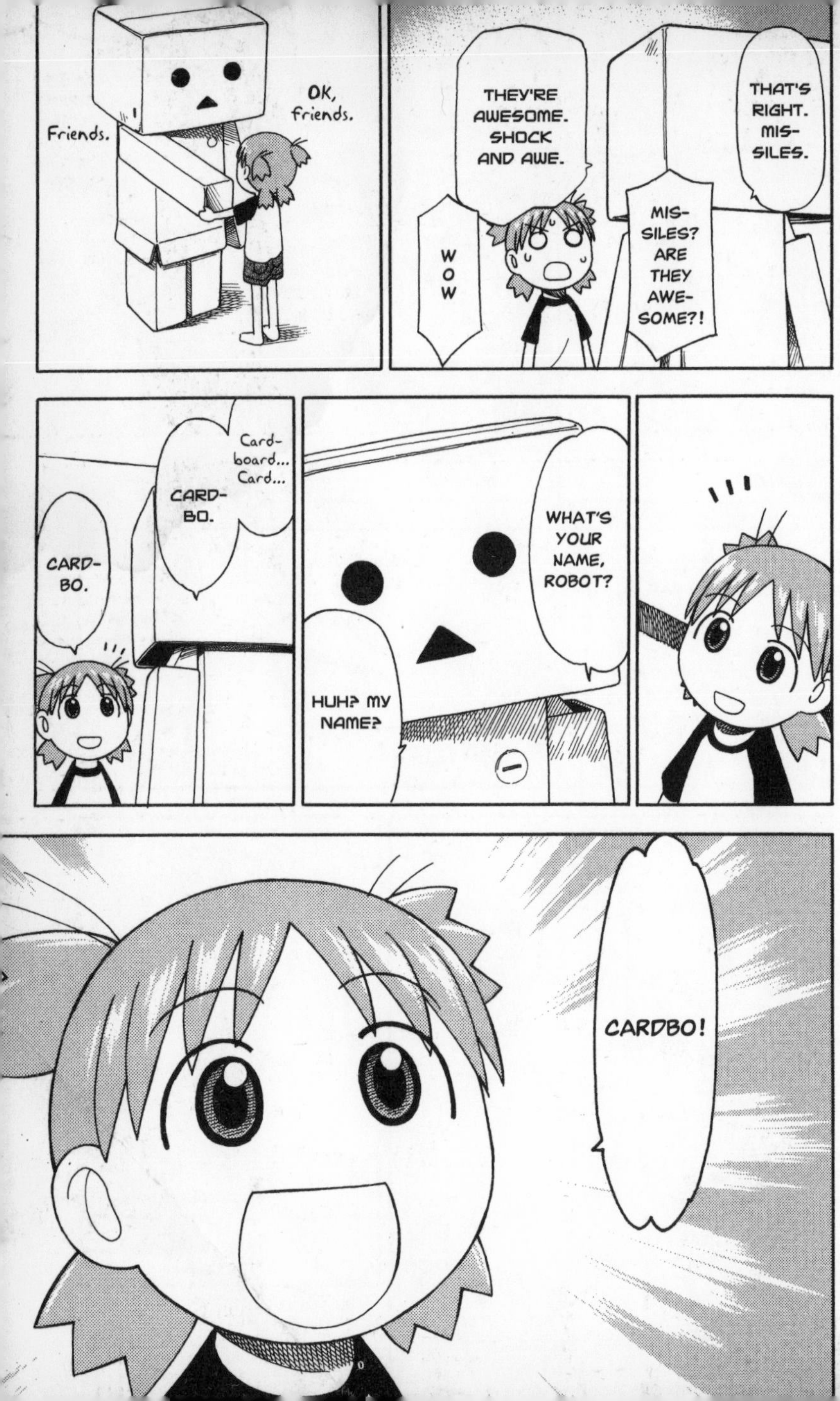
THAT'S RIGHT. MIS-SILES.
MIS-SILES? ARE THEY AWE-SOME?!
THEY'RE AWESOME. SHOCK AND AWE.
WOW
OK, friends.
Friends.
WHAT'S YOUR NAME, ROBOT?
HUH? MY NAME?
Card-board... Card...
CARD-BO.
CARD-BO.
CARDBO!

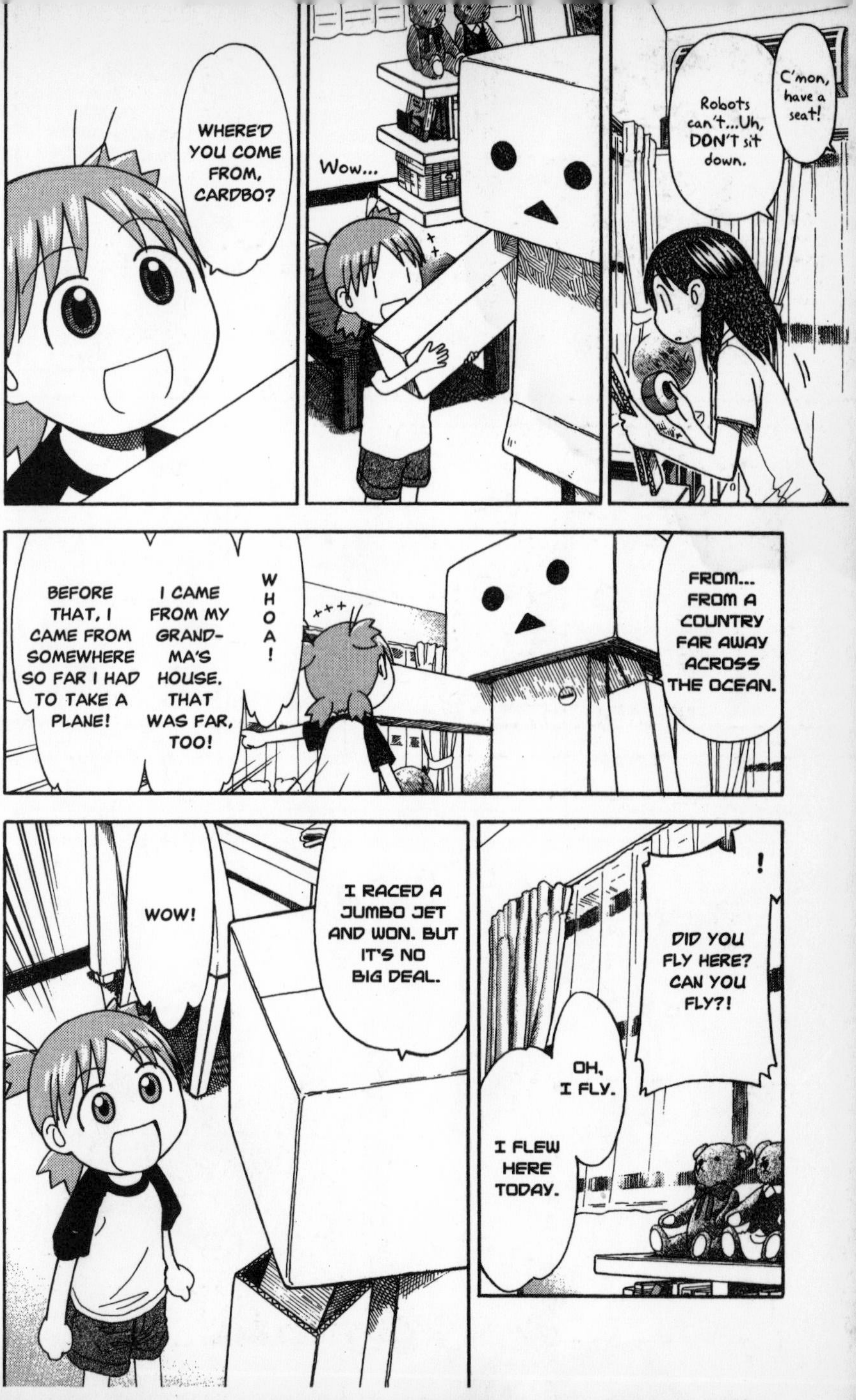
C'mon, have a seat!
Robots can't...Uh, DON'T sit down.
Wow...
WHERE'D YOU COME FROM, CARDBO?
FROM... FROM A COUNTRY FAR AWAY ACROSS THE OCEAN.
WHOA!
I CAME FROM MY GRAND-MA'S HOUSE. THAT WAS FAR, TOO!
BEFORE THAT, I CAME FROM SOMEWHERE SO FAR I HAD TO TAKE A PLANE!
!
DID YOU FLY HERE? CAN YOU FLY?!
OH, I FLY.
I FLEW HERE TODAY.
I RACED A JUMBO JET AND WON. BUT IT'S NO BIG DEAL.
WOW!

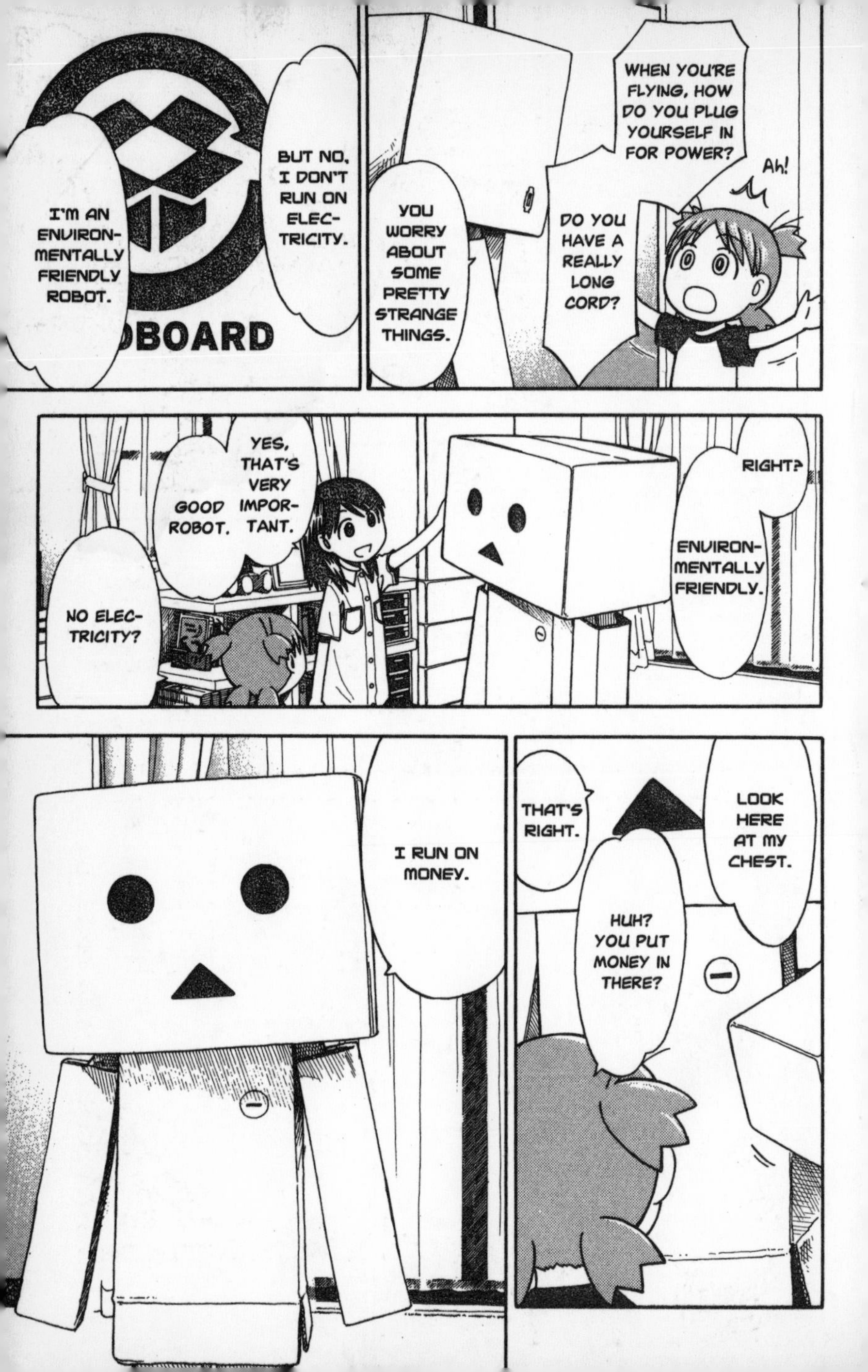
WHEN YOU'RE FLYING, HOW DO YOU PLUG YOURSELF IN FOR POWER?
Ah!
DO YOU HAVE A REALLY LONG CORD?
YOU WORRY ABOUT SOME PRETTY STRANGE THINGS.
BUT NO, I DON'T RUN ON ELEC-TRICITY.
I'M AN ENVIRON-MENTALLY FRIENDLY ROBOT.
DBOARD
RIGHT?
ENVIRON-MENTALLY FRIENDLY.
YES, THAT'S VERY IMPOR-TANT.
GOOD ROBOT.
NO ELEC-TRICITY?
LOOK HERE AT MY CHEST.
THAT'S RIGHT.
HUH? YOU PUT MONEY IN THERE?
I RUN ON MONEY.

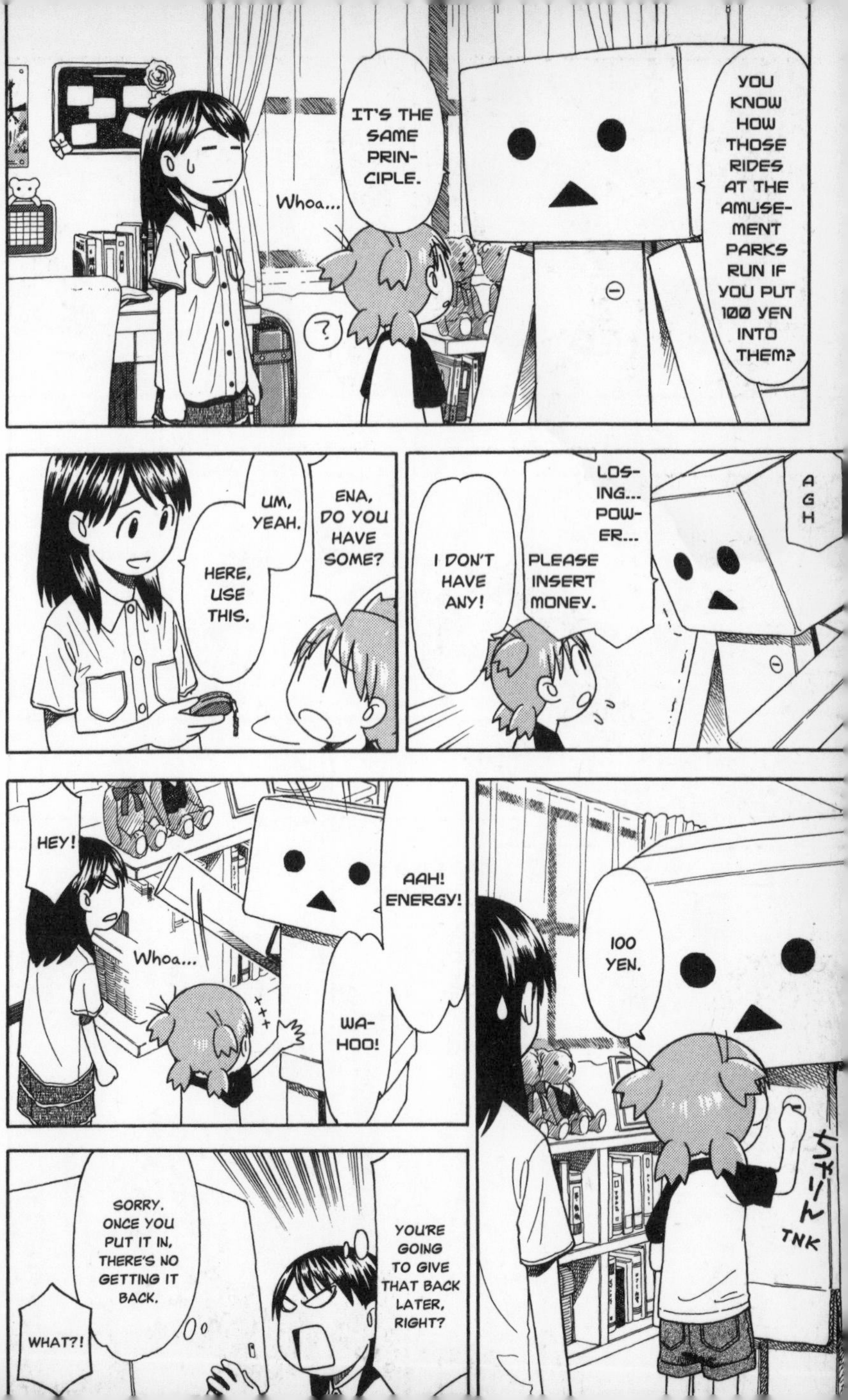
YOU KNOW HOW THOSE RIDES AT THE AMUSEMENT PARKS RUN IF YOU PUT 100 YEN INTO THEM?
IT'S THE SAME PRINCIPLE.
Whoa...
?
AGH
LOSING... POWER...
PLEASE INSERT MONEY.
I DON'T HAVE ANY!
ENA, DO YOU HAVE SOME?
UM, YEAH.
HERE, USE THIS.
100 YEN.
ちゃりん
TNK
AAH! ENERGY!
WA-HOO!
Whoa...
HEY!
YOU'RE GOING TO GIVE THAT BACK LATER, RIGHT?
SORRY. ONCE YOU PUT IT IN, THERE'S NO GETTING IT BACK.
WHAT?!

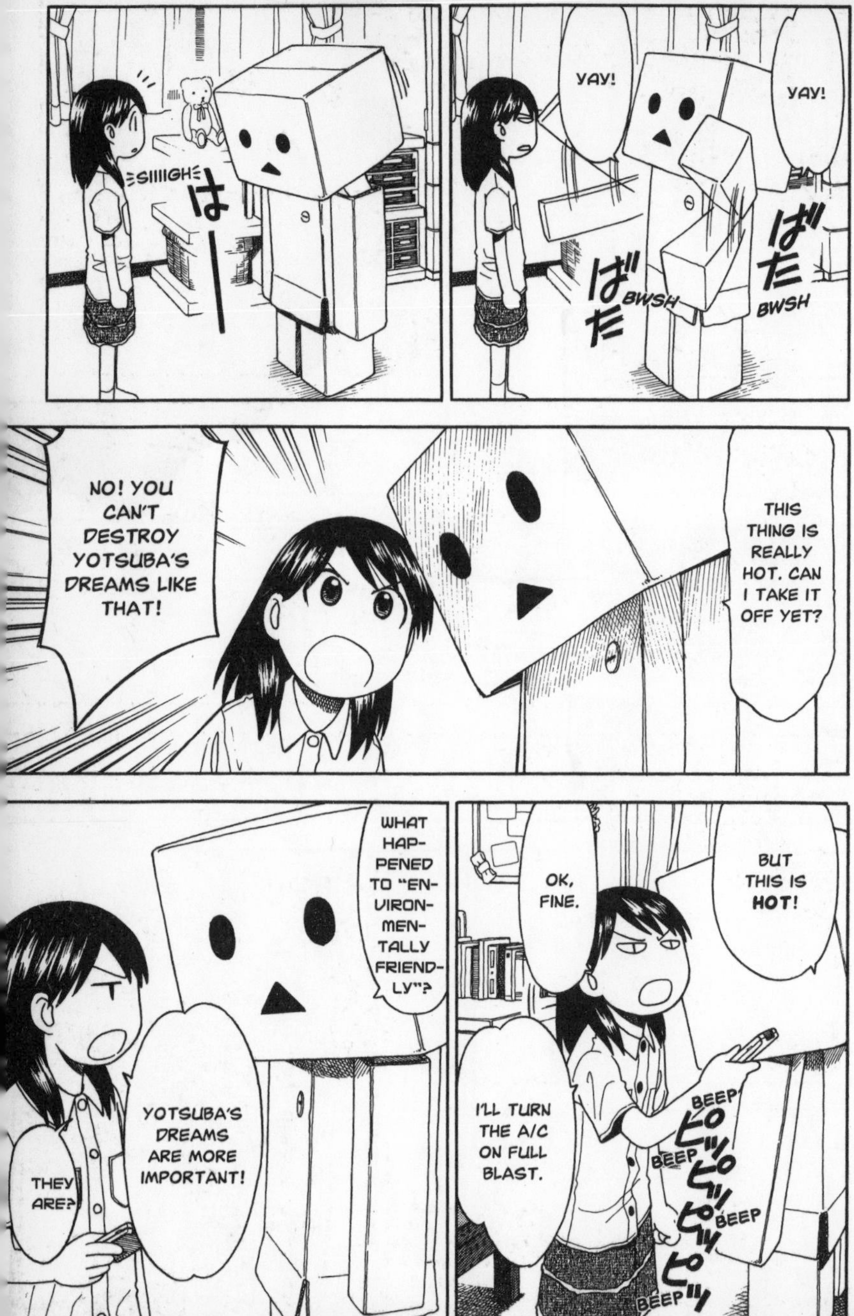

YAY!
ばた BWSH
YAY!
ばた BWSH
SIIIIGH
は—
THIS THING IS REALLY HOT. CAN I TAKE IT OFF YET?
NO! YOU CAN'T DESTROY YOTSUBA'S DREAMS LIKE THAT!
BUT THIS IS HOT!
OK, FINE.
I'LL TURN THE A/C ON FULL BLAST.
ピッ BEEP
ピッ BEEP
ピッ BEEP
ピッ BEEP
WHAT HAP-PENED TO "EN-VIRON-MEN-TALLY FRIEND-LY"?
YOTSUBA'S DREAMS ARE MORE IMPORTANT!
THEY ARE?

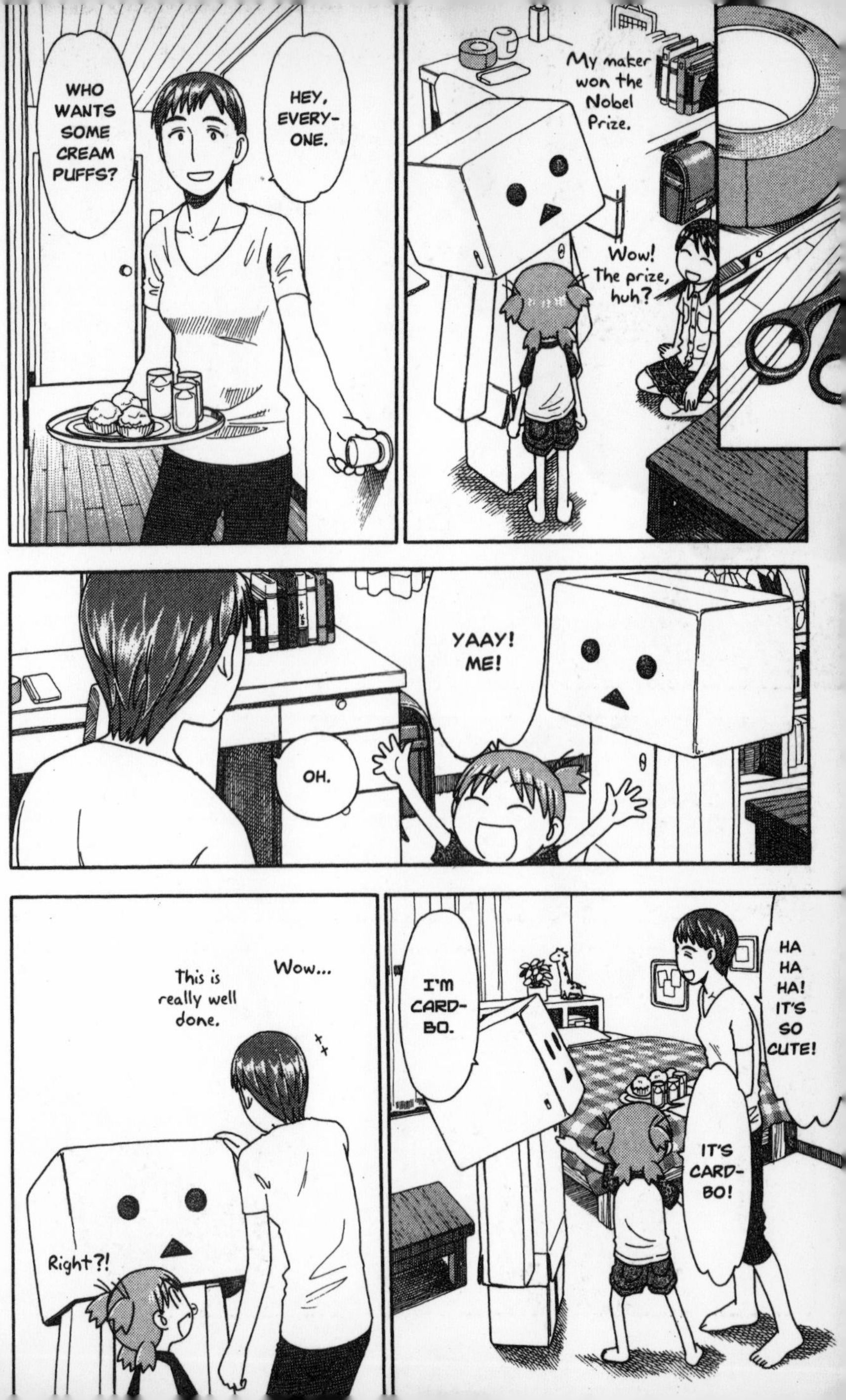
My maker won the Nobel Prize.
Wow! The prize, huh?
HEY, EVERYONE.
WHO WANTS SOME CREAM PUFFS?
YAAY! ME!
OH.
HA HA HA! IT'S SO CUTE!
IT'S CARD-BO!
I'M CARD-BO.
Wow...
This is really well done.
Right?!

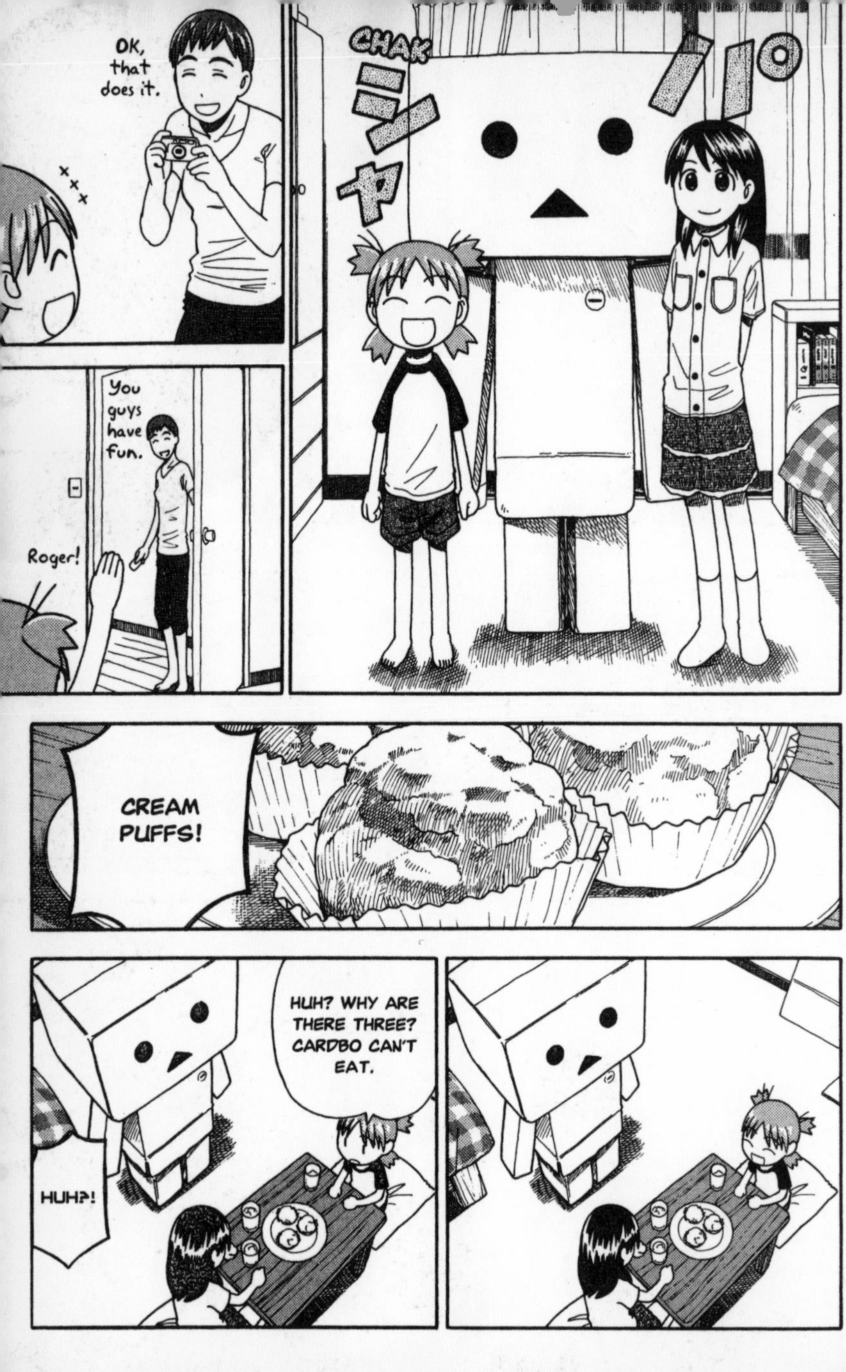
CHAK
OK, that does it.
You guys have fun.
Roger!
CREAM PUFFS!
HUH? WHY ARE THERE THREE? CARDBO CAN'T EAT.
HUH?!

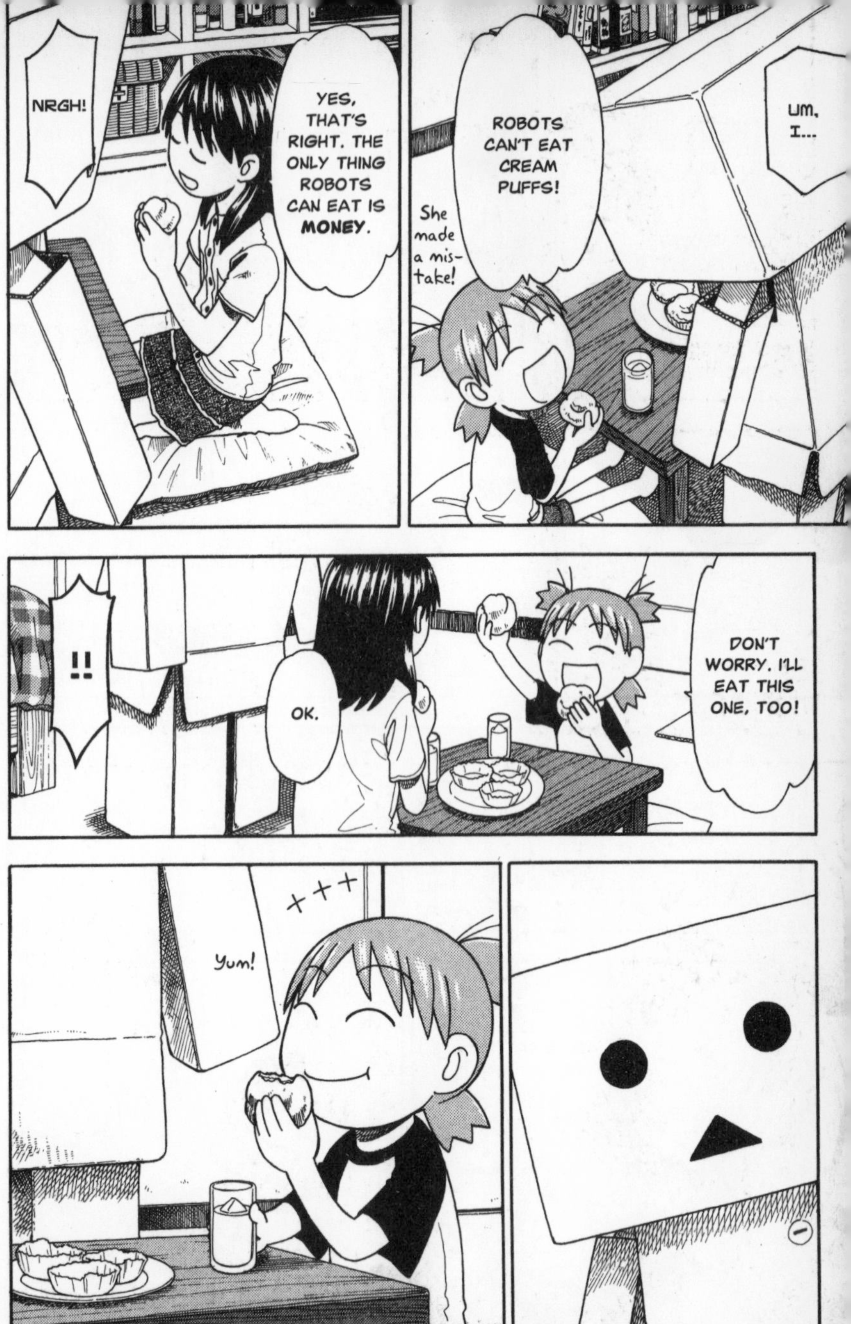
Um, I...
ROBOTS CAN'T EAT CREAM PUFFS!
She made a mis-take!
YES, THAT'S RIGHT. THE ONLY THING ROBOTS CAN EAT IS **MONEY**.
NRGH!
DON'T WORRY. I'LL EAT THIS ONE, TOO!
OK.
!!
Yum!

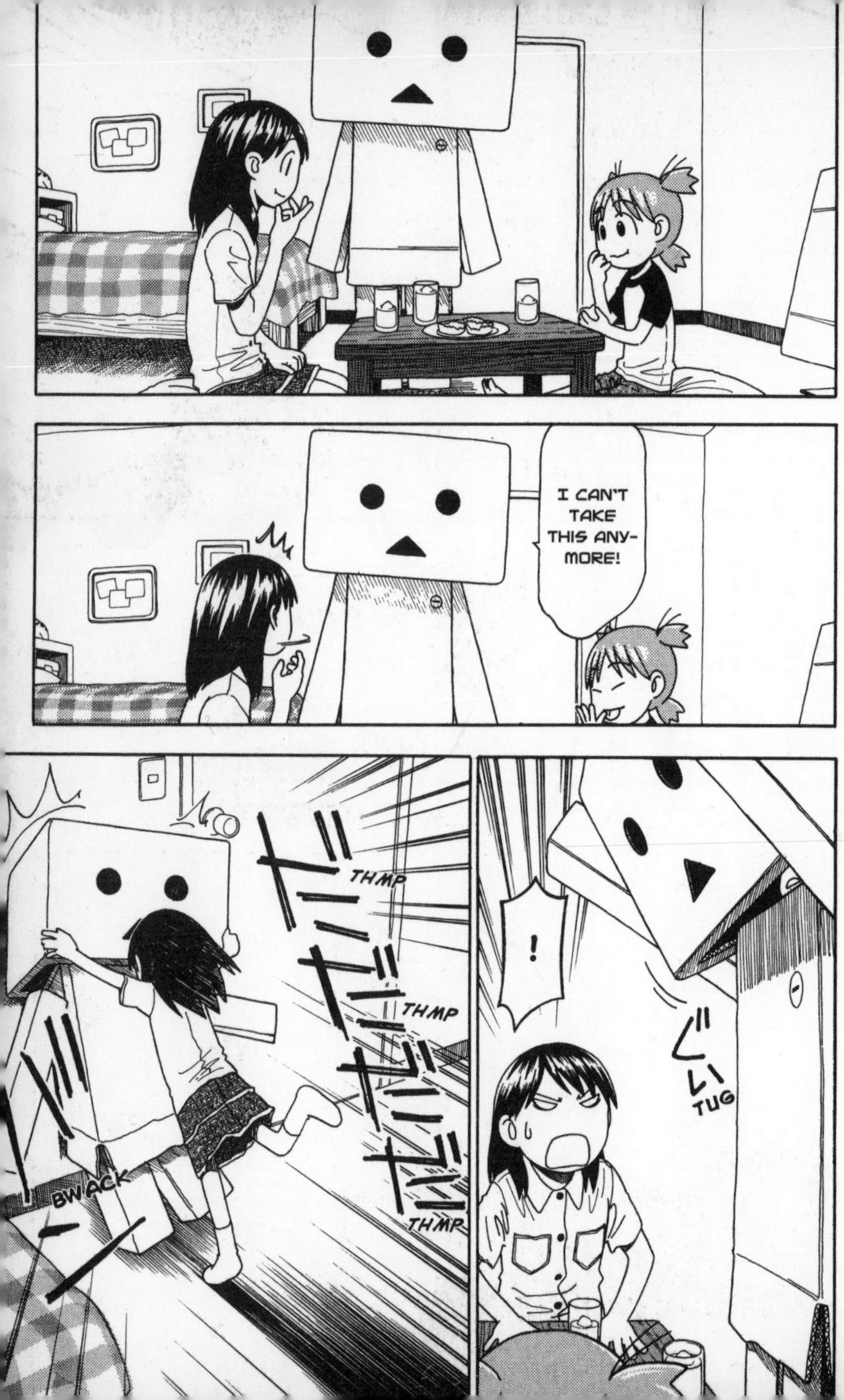
I CAN'T TAKE THIS ANY-MORE!
TUG
!
THMP
THMP
THMP
BWACK

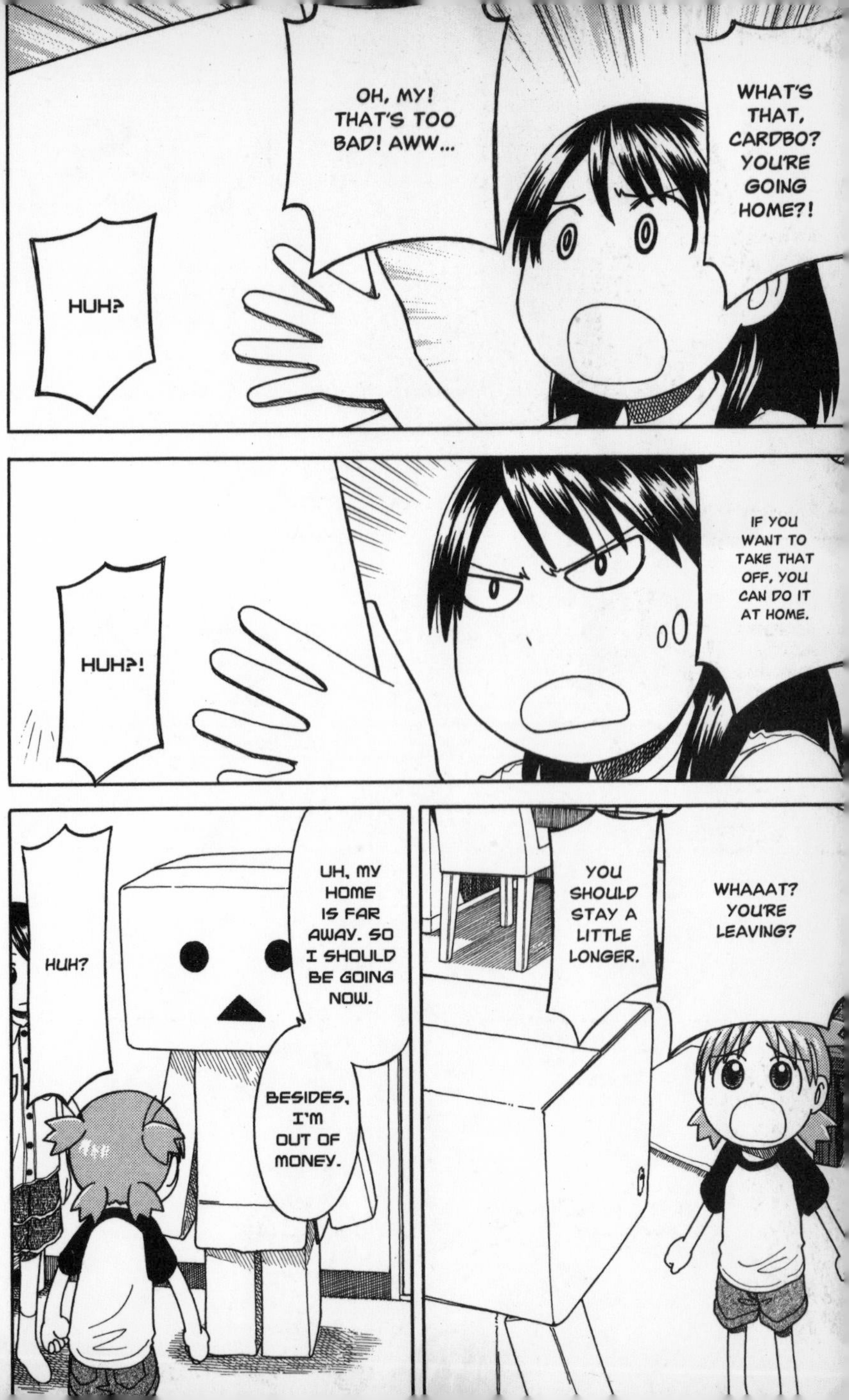
WHAT'S THAT, CARDBO? YOU'RE GOING HOME?!
OH, MY! THAT'S TOO BAD! AWW...
HUH?
IF YOU WANT TO TAKE THAT OFF, YOU CAN DO IT AT HOME.
HUH?!
WHAAAT? YOU'RE LEAVING?
YOU SHOULD STAY A LITTLE LONGER.
UH, MY HOME IS FAR AWAY. SO I SHOULD BE GOING NOW.
BESIDES, I'M OUT OF MONEY.
HUH?

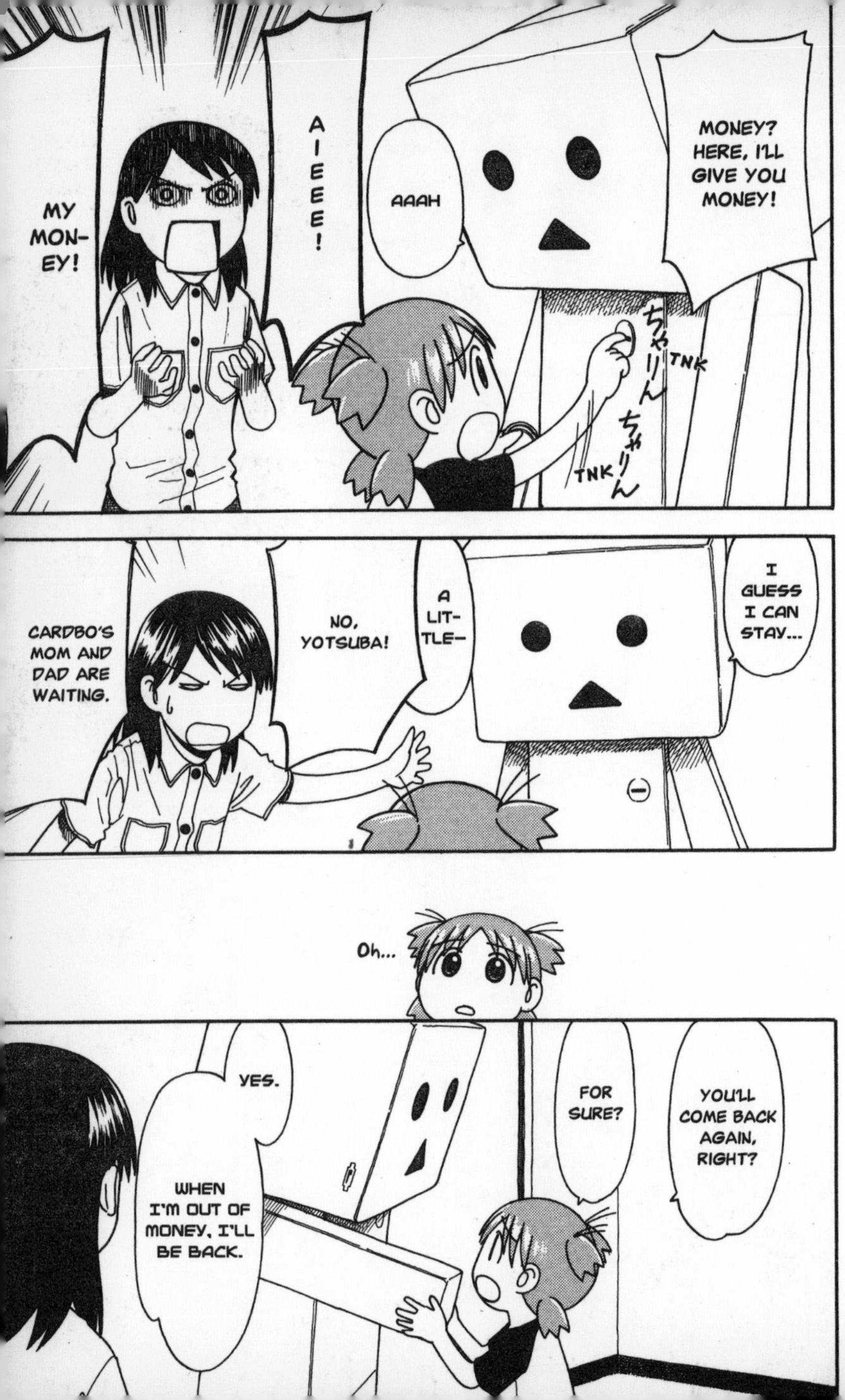
MONEY? HERE, I'LL GIVE YOU MONEY!
AAAH
ちゃりん TNK
ちゃりん TNK
AIEEE!
MY MON-EY!
I GUESS I CAN STAY...
A LIT-TLE-
NO, YOTSUBA!
CARDBO'S MOM AND DAD ARE WAITING.
Oh...
YOU'LL COME BACK AGAIN, RIGHT?
FOR SURE?
YES.
WHEN I'M OUT OF MONEY, I'LL BE BACK.

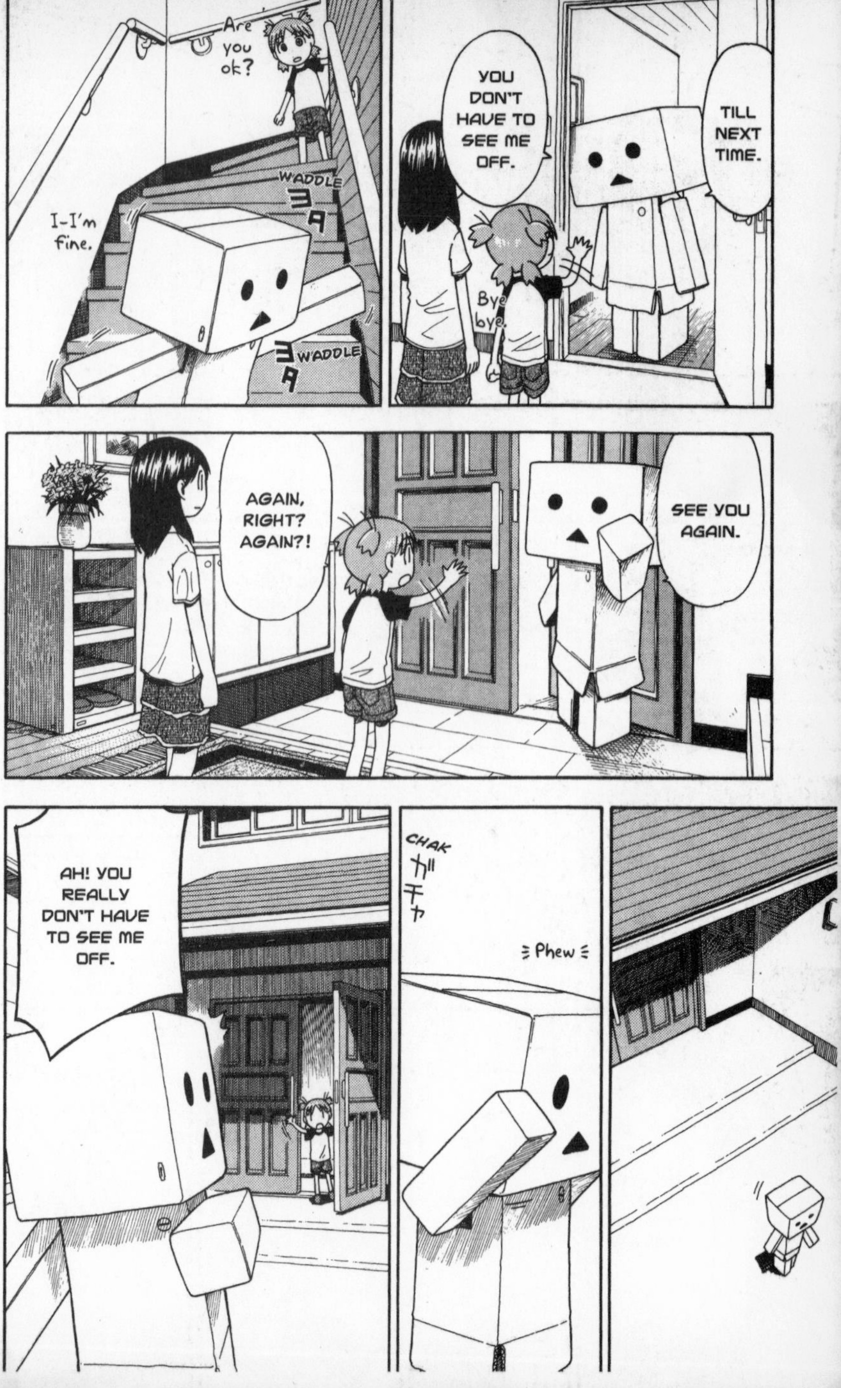
TILL NEXT TIME.
YOU DON'T HAVE TO SEE ME OFF.
Bye bye.
Are you ok?
I-I'm fine.
WADDLE
WADDLE
SEE YOU AGAIN.
AGAIN, RIGHT? AGAIN?!
CHAK
ガチャ
Phew
AH! YOU REALLY DON'T HAVE TO SEE ME OFF.

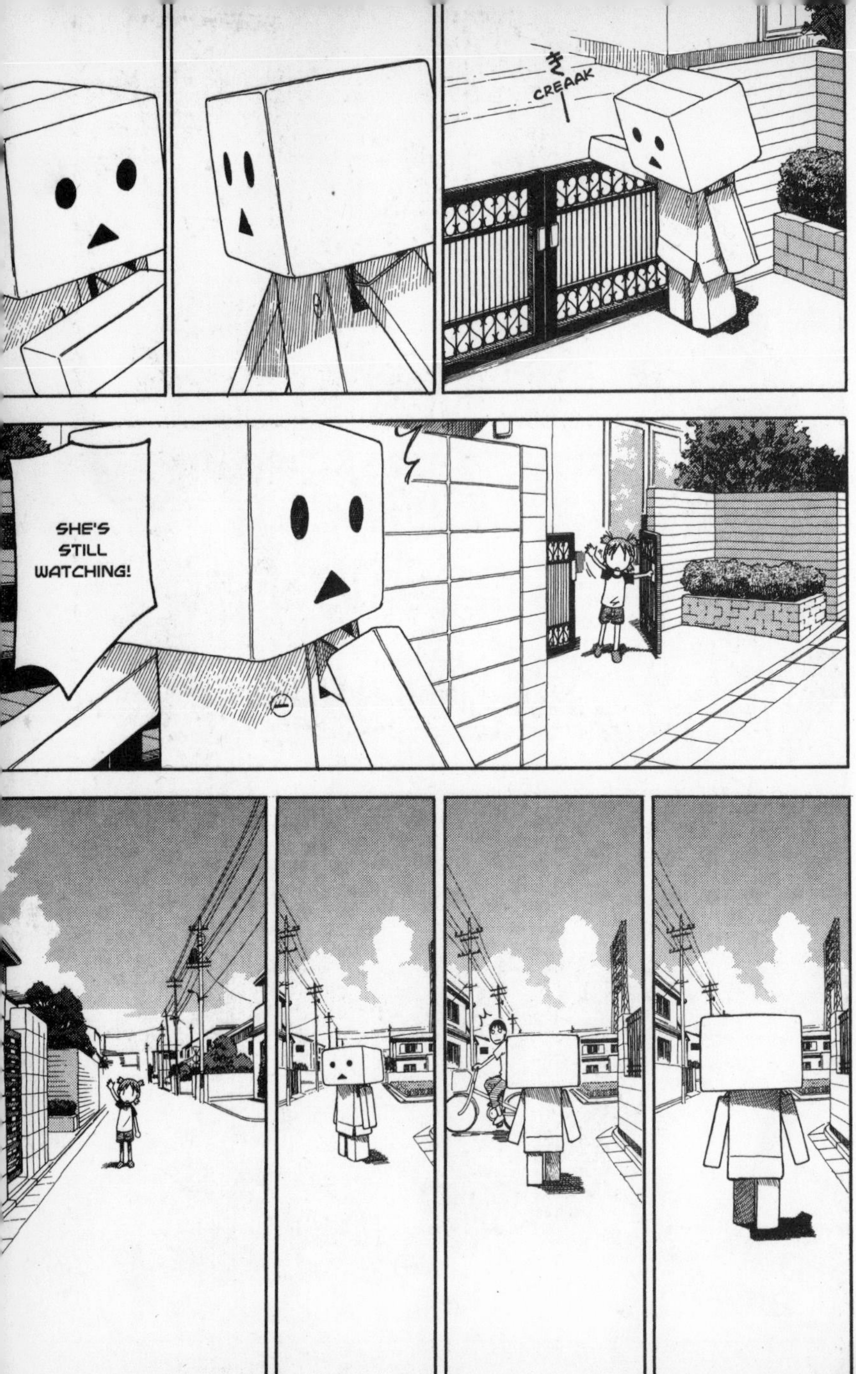
き
CREAAK
SHE'S STILL WATCHING!

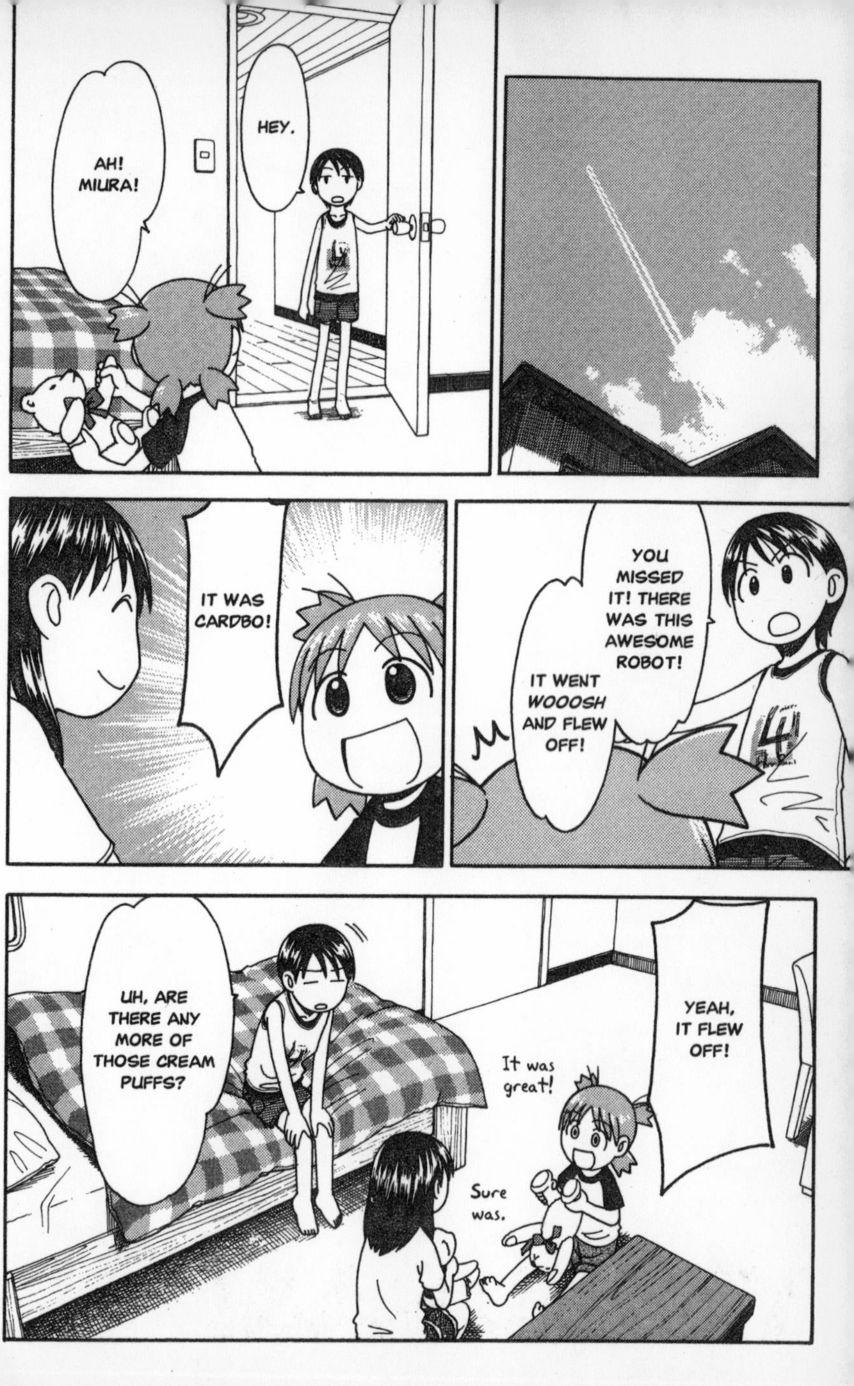
HEY.
AH! MIURA!
YOU MISSED IT! THERE WAS THIS AWESOME ROBOT!
IT WENT WOOOSH AND FLEW OFF!
IT WAS CARDBO!
YEAH, IT FLEW OFF!
It was great!
Sure was.
UH, ARE THERE ANY MORE OF THOSE CREAM PUFFS?

YOTSUBA&!

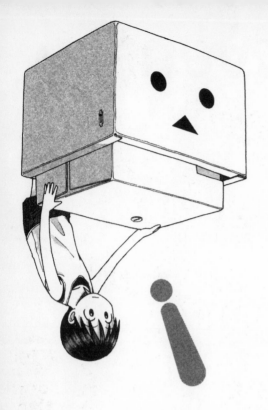

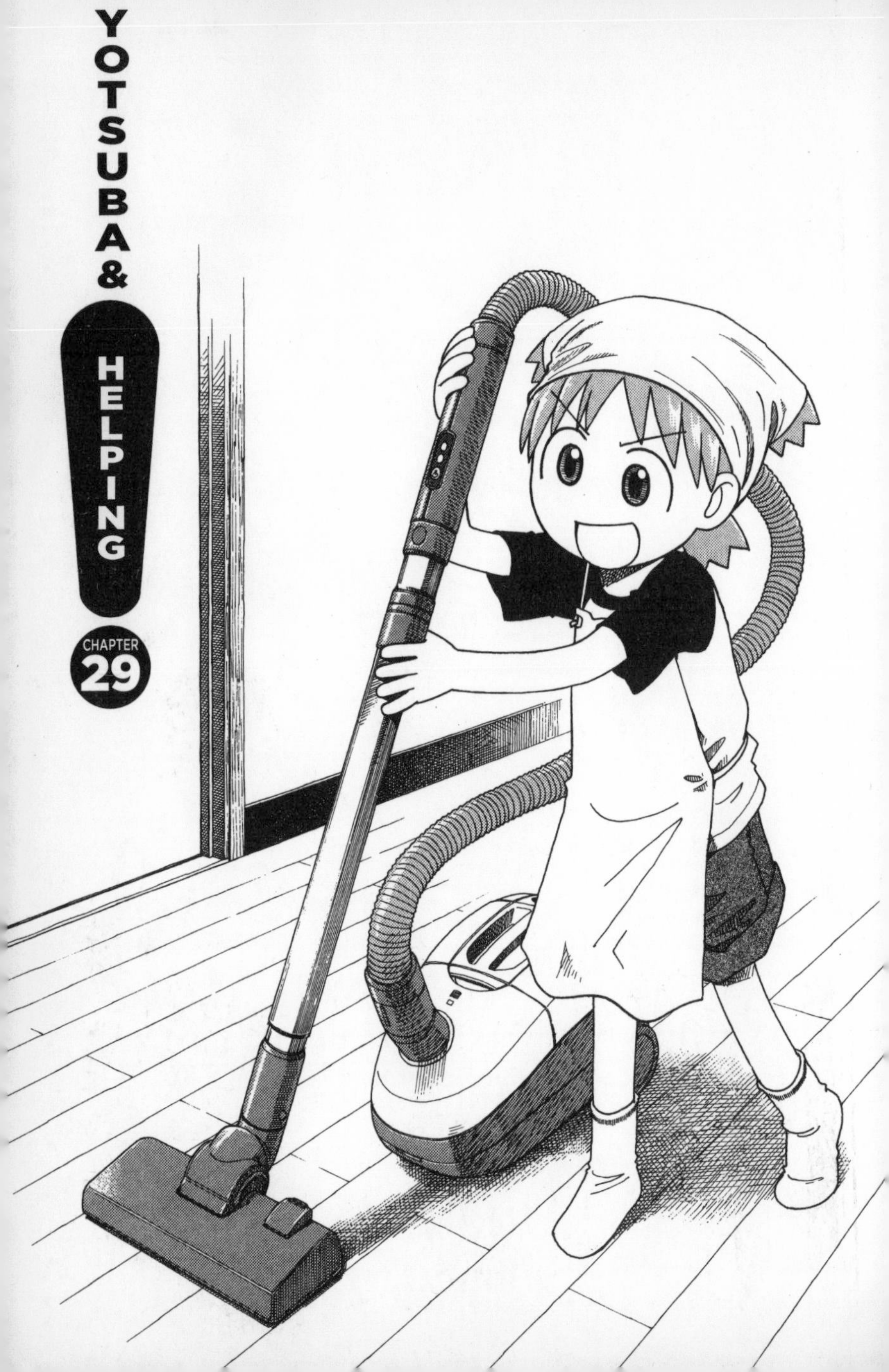
YOTSUBA&
HELPING
CHAPTER 29

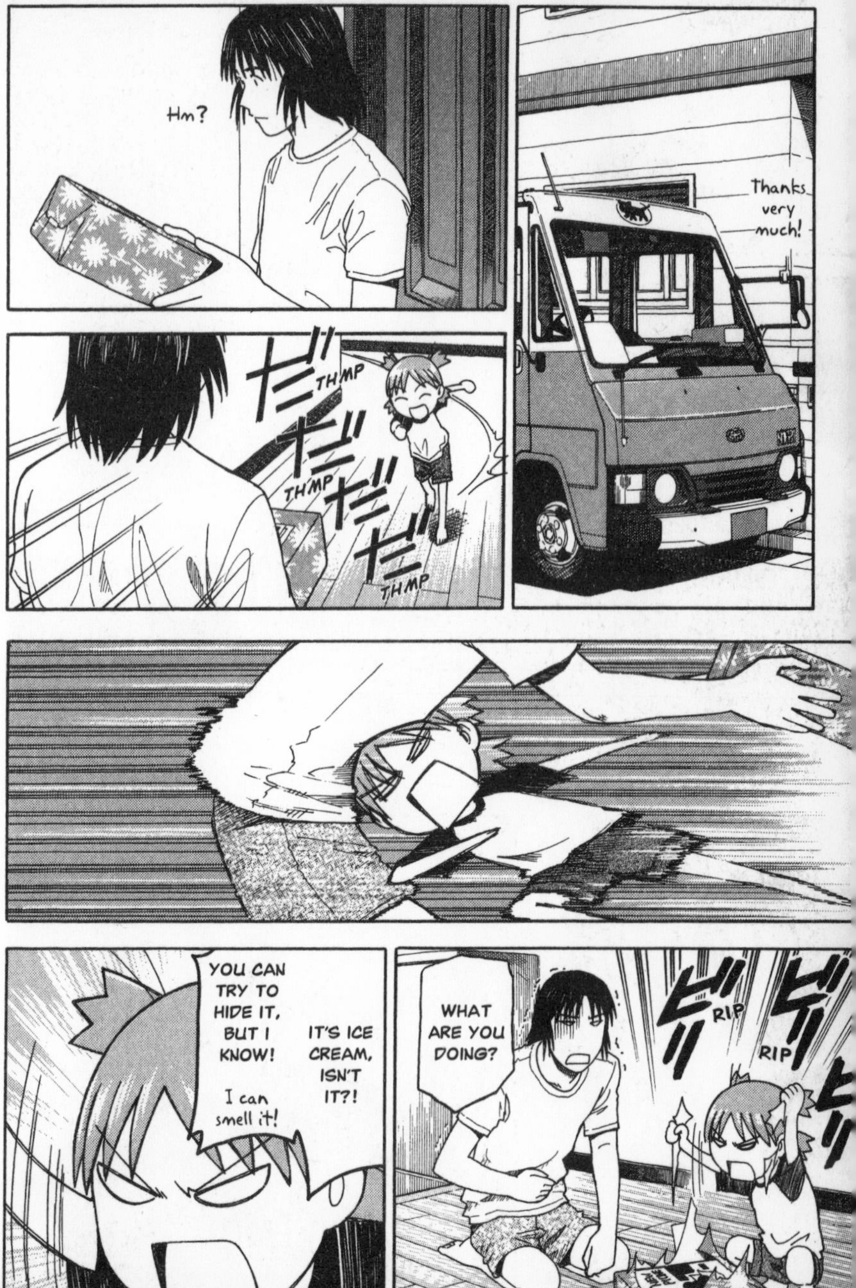
Thanks very much!
Hm?
THMP
THMP
THMP
RIP
RIP
WHAT ARE YOU DOING?
YOU CAN TRY TO HIDE IT, BUT I KNOW!
IT'S ICE CREAM, ISN'T IT?!
I can smell it!

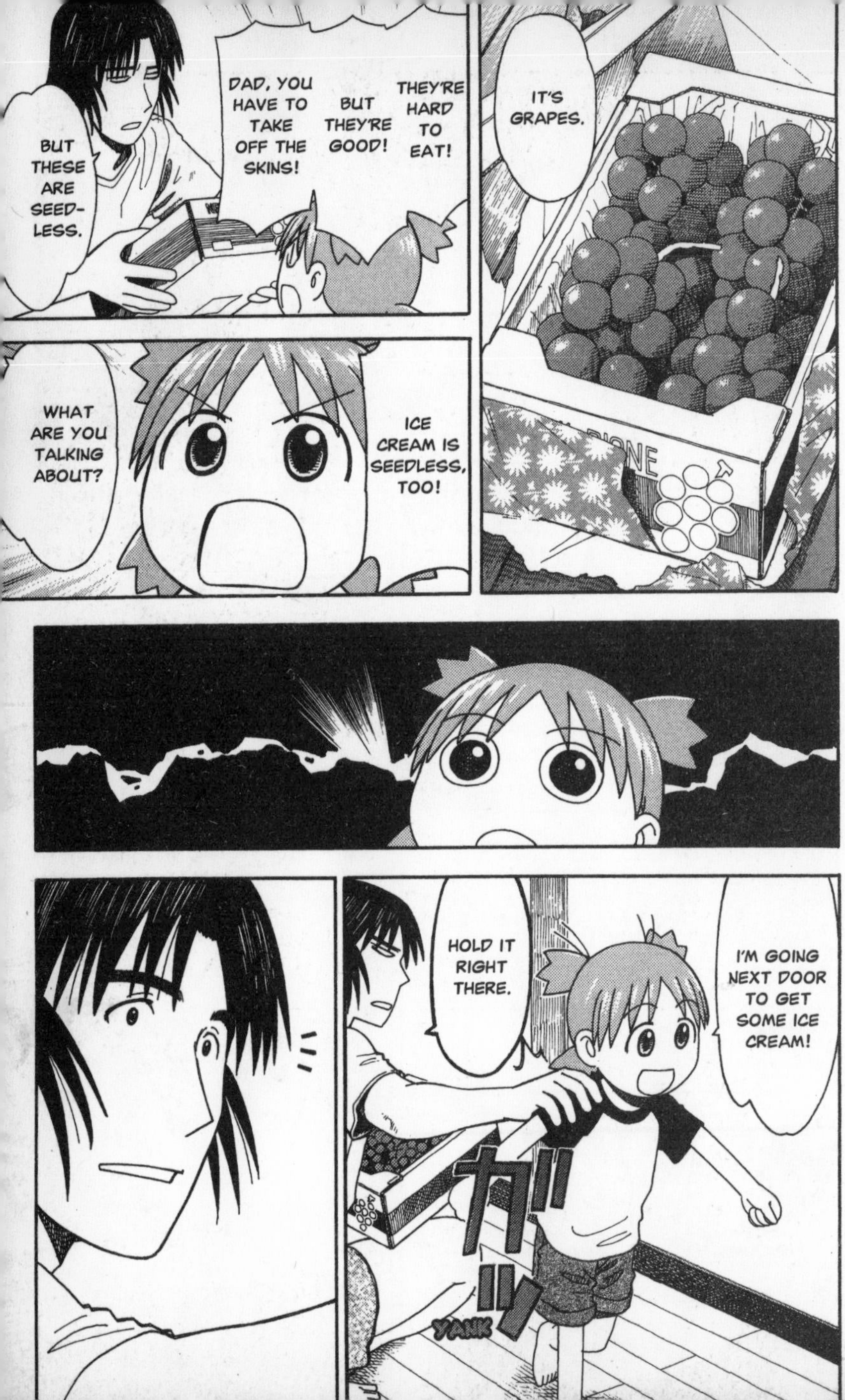
IT'S GRAPES.
DAD, YOU HAVE TO TAKE OFF THE SKINS!
BUT THEY'RE GOOD!
THEY'RE HARD TO EAT!
BUT THESE ARE SEED-LESS.
ICE CREAM IS SEEDLESS, TOO!
WHAT ARE YOU TALKING ABOUT?
I'M GOING NEXT DOOR TO GET SOME ICE CREAM!
HOLD IT RIGHT THERE.
YANK

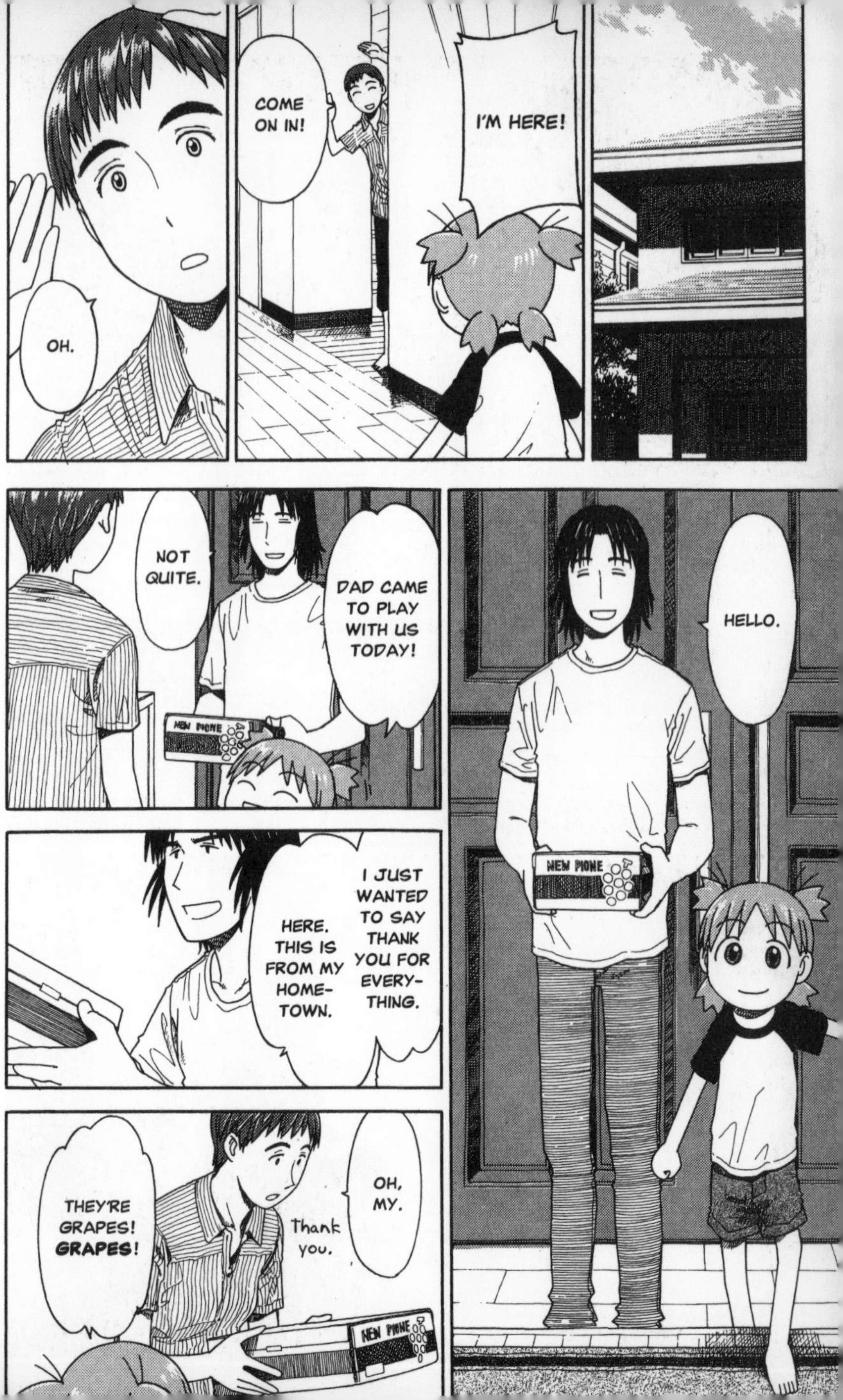
I'M HERE!
COME ON IN!
OH.
HELLO.
DAD CAME TO PLAY WITH US TODAY!
NOT QUITE.
I JUST WANTED TO SAY THANK YOU FOR EVERY-THING.
HERE. THIS IS FROM MY HOME-TOWN.
NEW PIONE
OH, MY.
Thank you.
THEY'RE GRAPES! GRAPES!
NEW PIONE

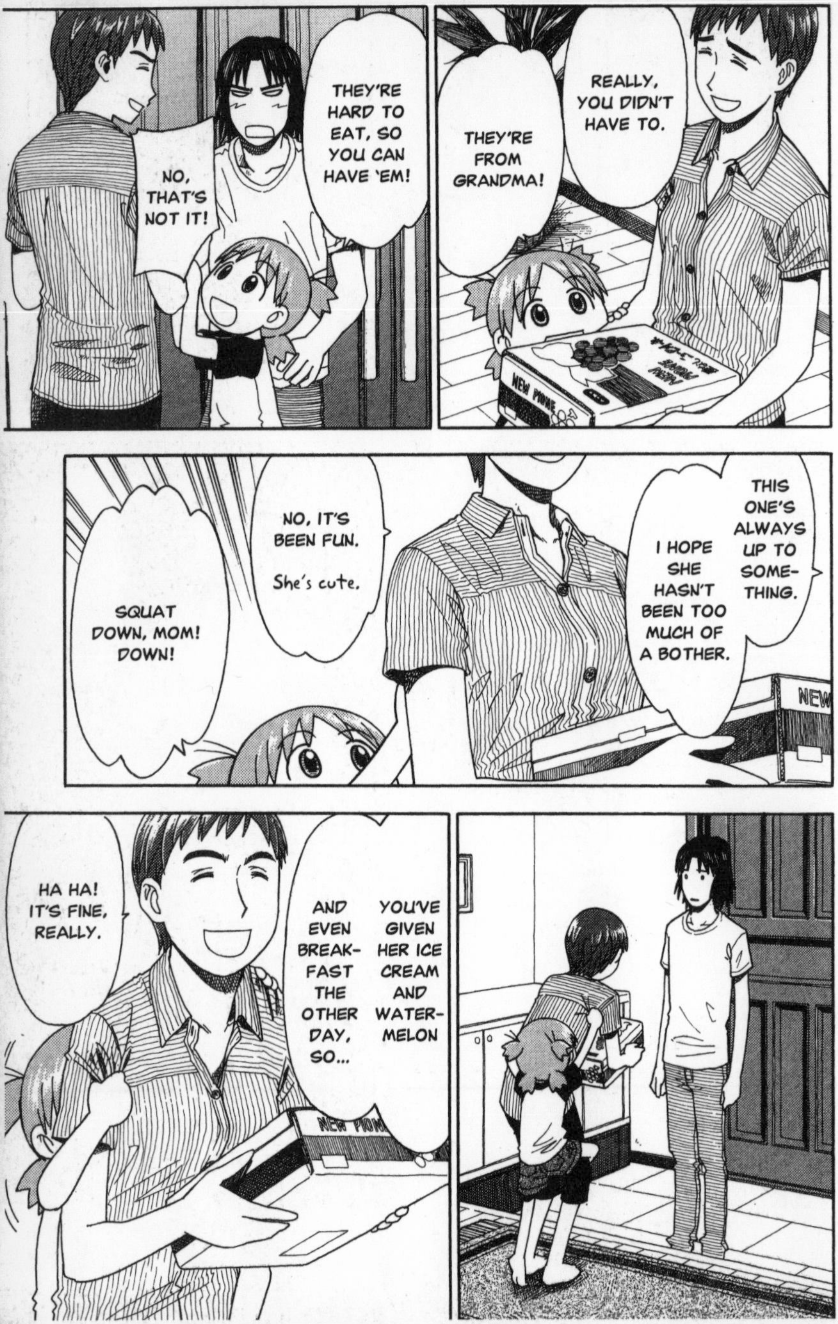
REALLY, YOU DIDN'T HAVE TO.
THEY'RE FROM GRANDMA!
THEY'RE HARD TO EAT, SO YOU CAN HAVE 'EM!
NO, THAT'S NOT IT!
THIS ONE'S ALWAYS UP TO SOME-THING.
I HOPE SHE HASN'T BEEN TOO MUCH OF A BOTHER.
NO, IT'S BEEN FUN.
She's cute.
SQUAT DOWN, MOM! DOWN!
YOU'VE GIVEN HER ICE CREAM AND WATER-MELON
AND EVEN BREAK-FAST THE OTHER DAY, SO...
HA HA! IT'S FINE, REALLY.

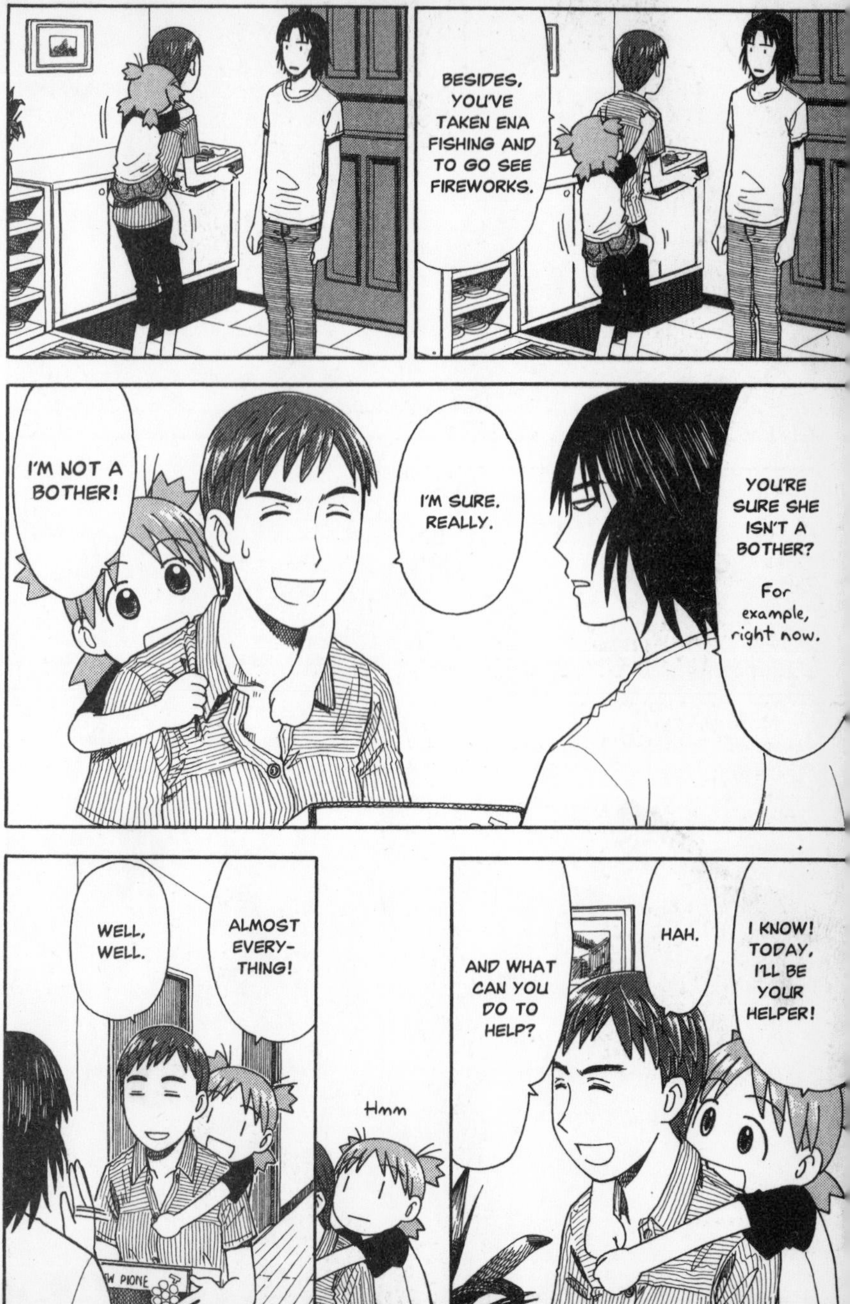
BESIDES, YOU'VE TAKEN ENA FISHING AND TO GO SEE FIREWORKS.
YOU'RE SURE SHE ISN'T A BOTHER?
For example, right now.
I'M SURE. REALLY.
I'M NOT A BOTHER!
I KNOW! TODAY, I'LL BE YOUR HELPER!
HAH.
AND WHAT CAN YOU DO TO HELP?
Hmm
ALMOST EVERY-THING!
WELL, WELL.
W PIONE

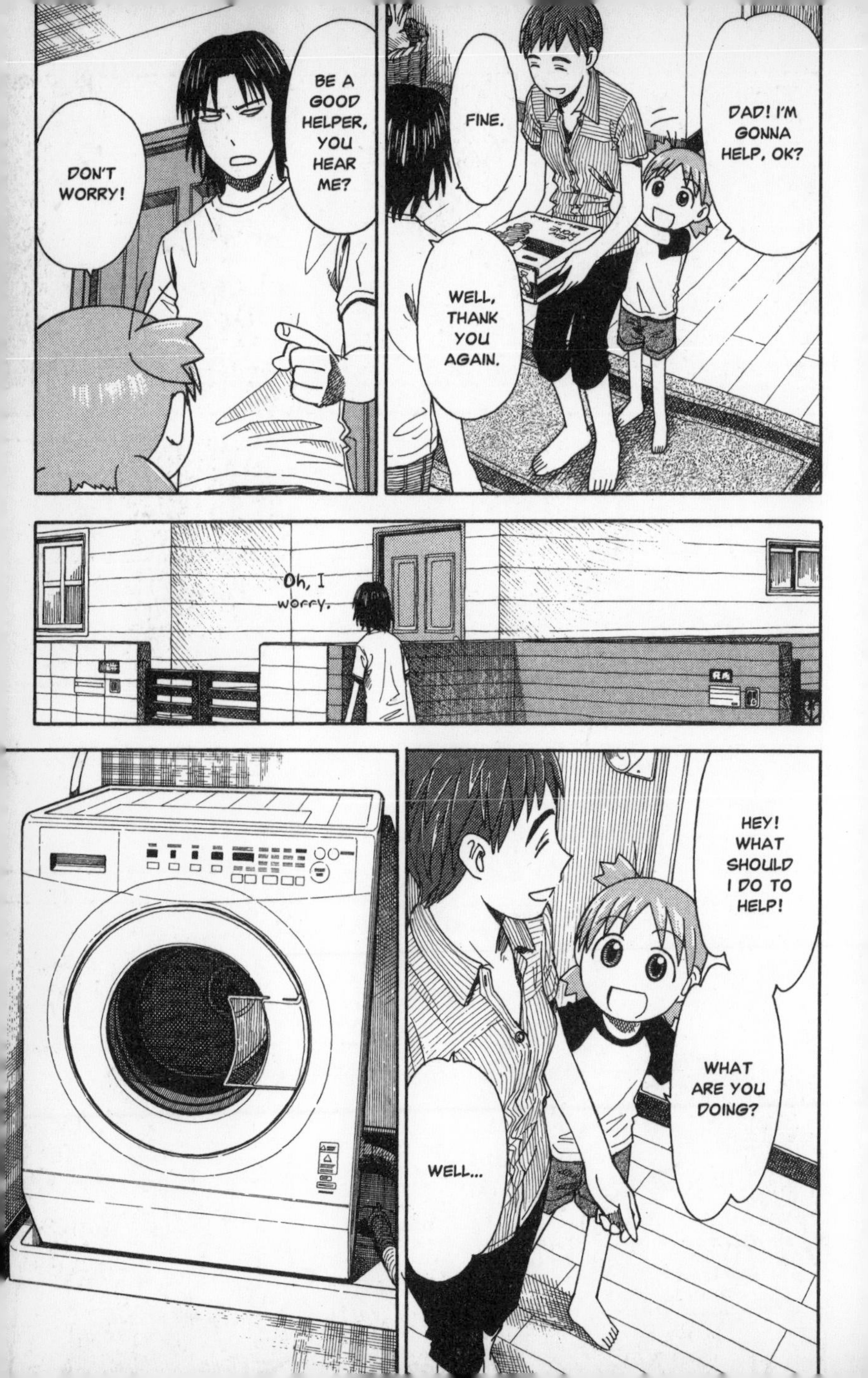
DAD! I'M GONNA HELP, OK?
FINE.
WELL, THANK YOU AGAIN.
BE A GOOD HELPER, YOU HEAR ME?
DON'T WORRY!
Oh, I worry.
HEY! WHAT SHOULD I DO TO HELP!
WHAT ARE YOU DOING?
WELL...

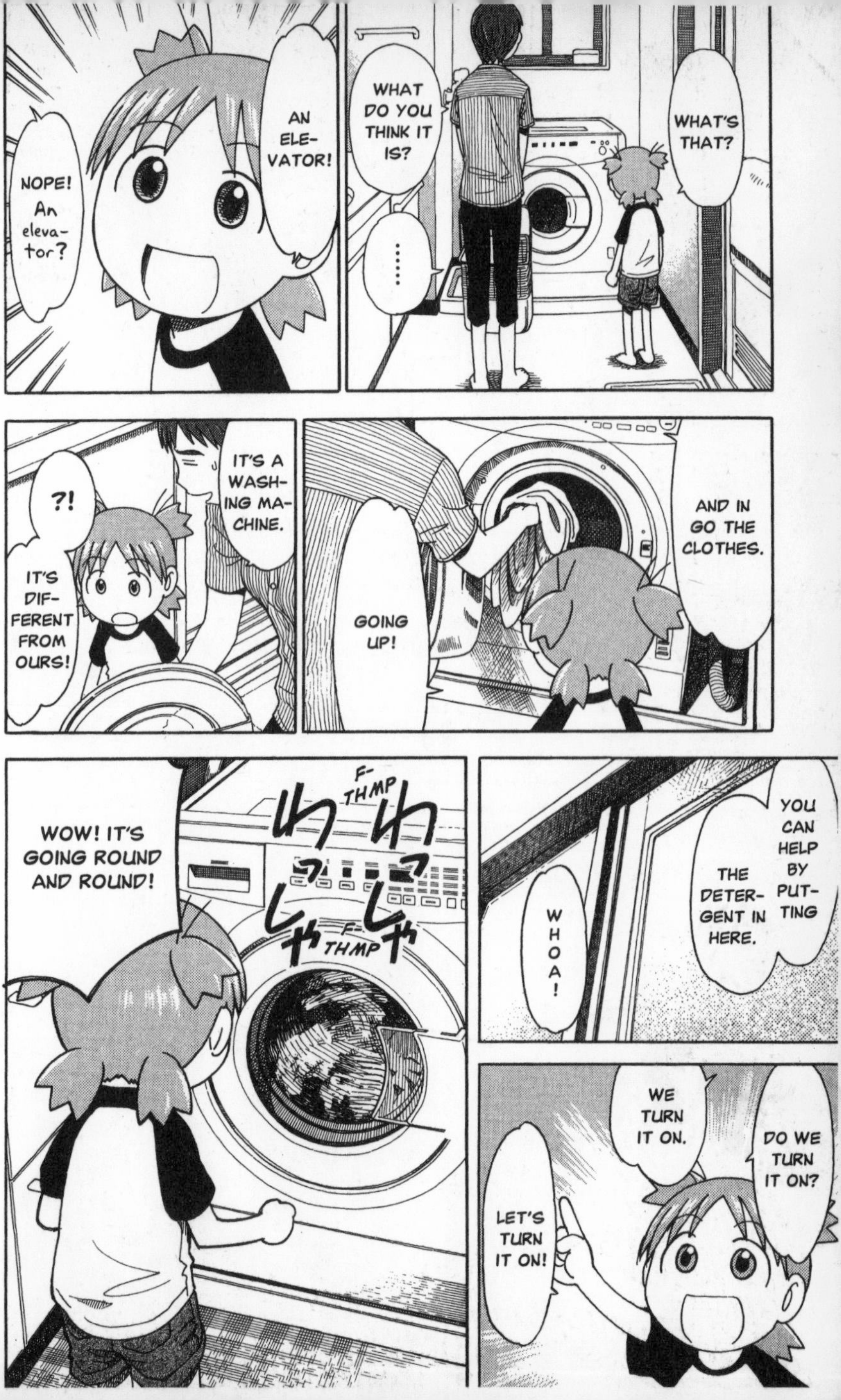
WHAT'S THAT?
WHAT DO YOU THINK IT IS?
......
AN ELE-VATOR!
NOPE! An eleva-tor?
AND IN GO THE CLOTHES.
GOING UP!
IT'S A WASH-ING MA-CHINE.
?!
IT'S DIF-FERENT FROM OURS!
YOU CAN HELP BY PUT-TING THE DETER-GENT IN HERE.
WHOA!
DO WE TURN IT ON?
WE TURN IT ON.
LET'S TURN IT ON!
WOW! IT'S GOING ROUND AND ROUND!
わっしゃ F-THMP
わっしゃ F-THMP

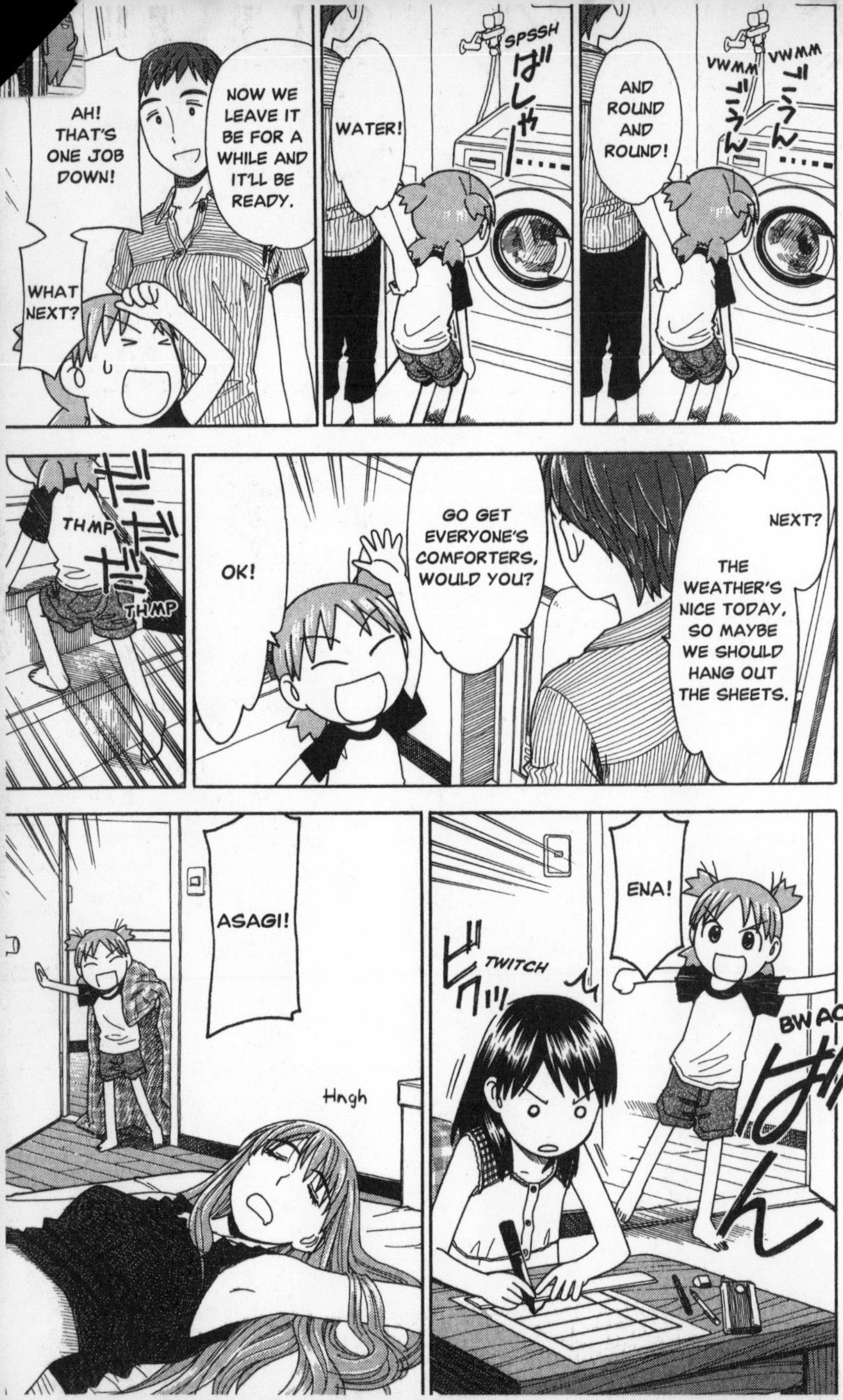
AND ROUND AND ROUND!
VWMM
VWMM
WATER!
SPSSH
NOW WE LEAVE IT BE FOR A WHILE AND IT'LL BE READY.
AH! THAT'S ONE JOB DOWN!
WHAT NEXT?
NEXT?
THE WEATHER'S NICE TODAY, SO MAYBE WE SHOULD HANG OUT THE SHEETS.
GO GET EVERYONE'S COMFORTERS, WOULD YOU?
OK!
THMP
THMP
ENA!
BWACK
TWITCH
ASAGI!
Hngh

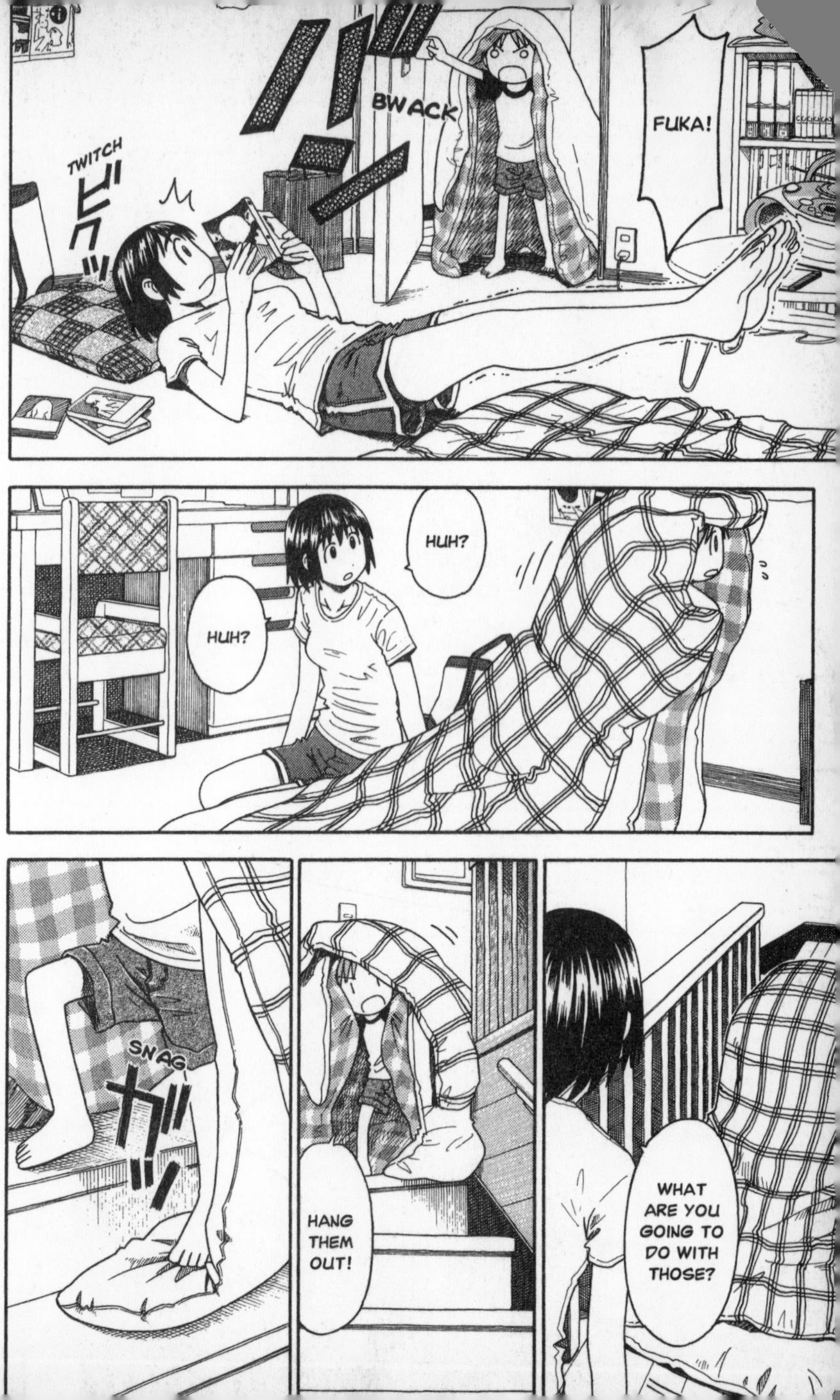
FUKA!
BWACK
TWITCH
HUH?
HUH?
WHAT ARE YOU GOING TO DO WITH THOSE?
HANG THEM OUT!
SNAG

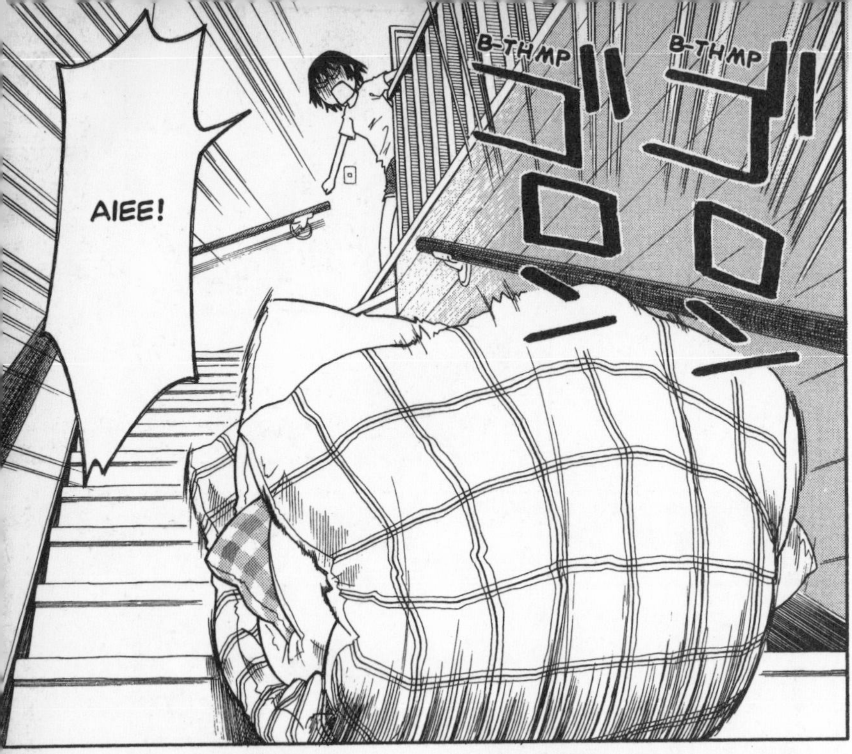
B-THMP
B-THMP
AIEE!
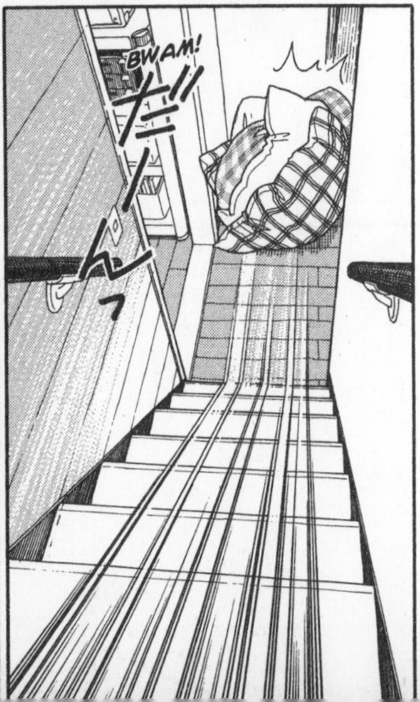
BWAM!
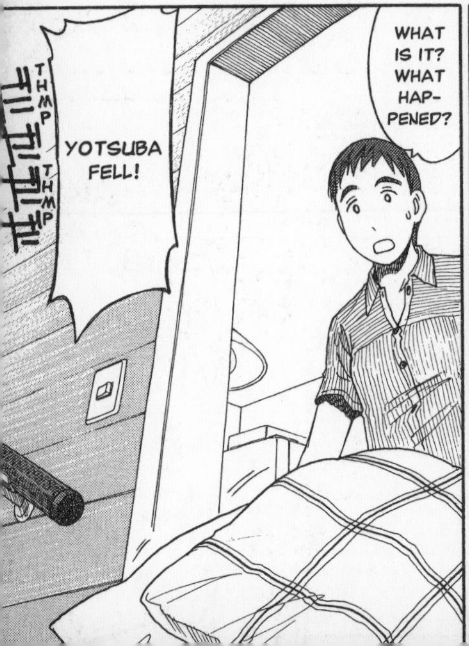
WHAT IS IT? WHAT HAP-PENED?
THMP THMP
YOTSUBA FELL!

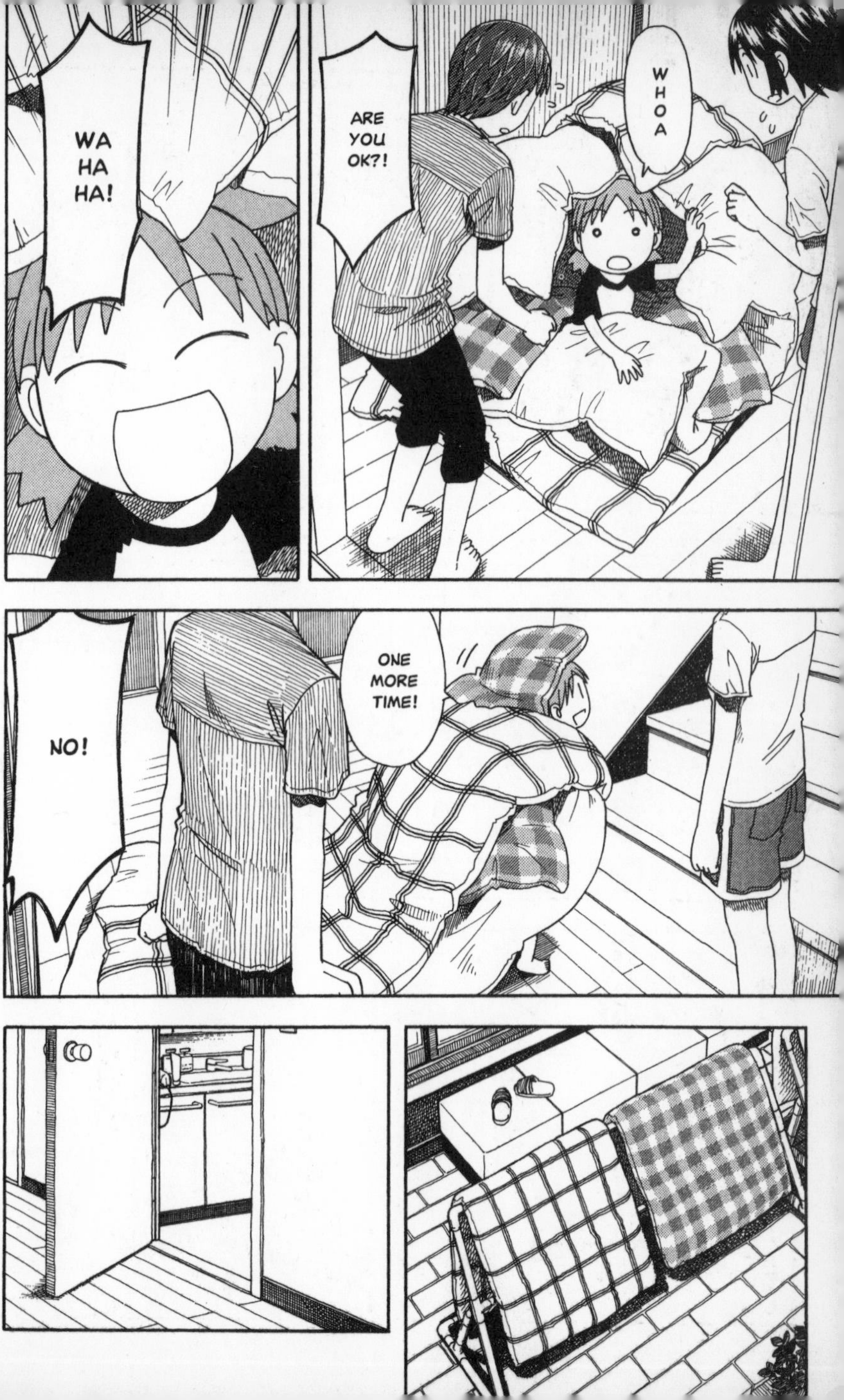
WHOA
ARE YOU OK?!
WA HA HA!
ONE MORE TIME!
NO!

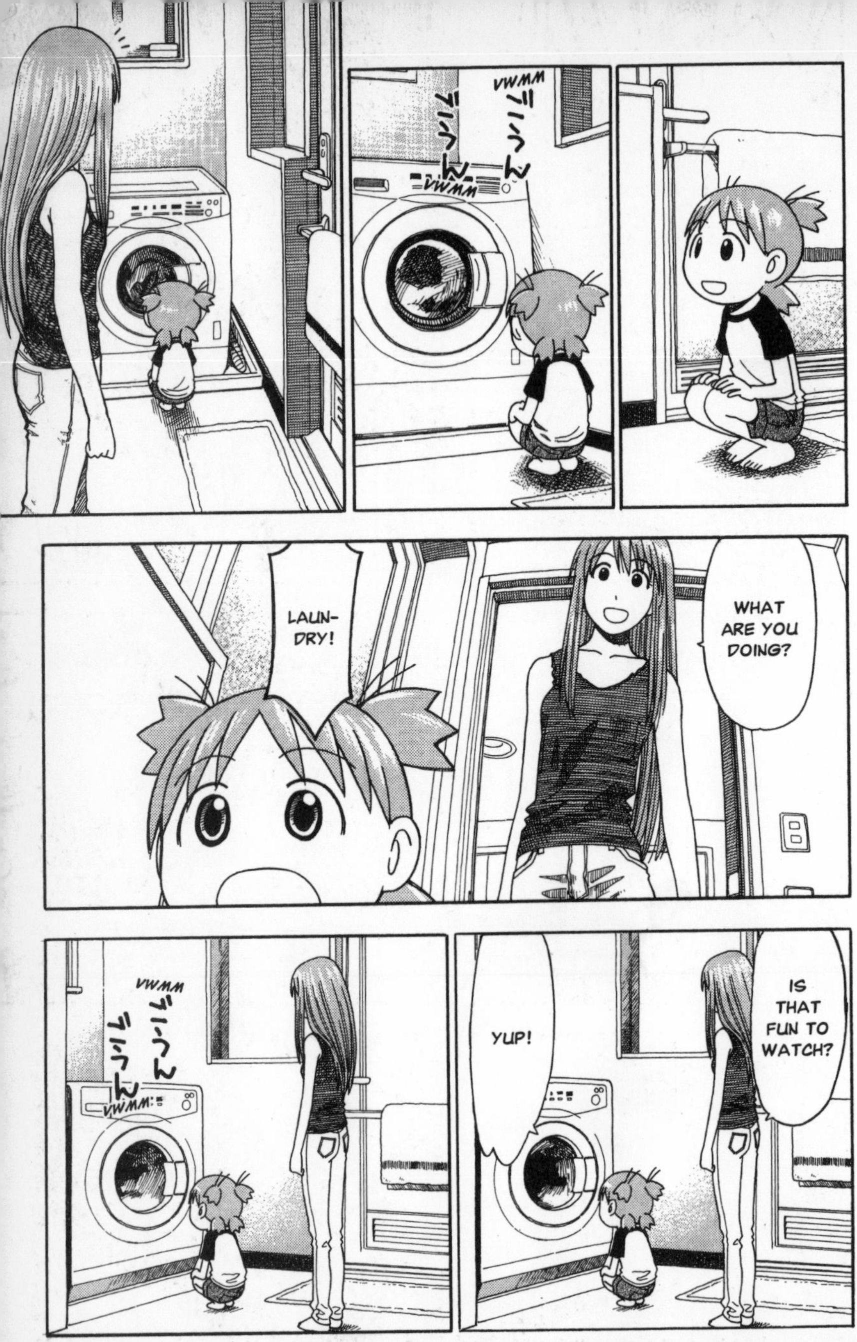

ごうんごうん
VWMM
VWMM
WHAT ARE YOU DOING?
LAUN-DRY!
IS THAT FUN TO WATCH?
YUP!
ごうんごうん
VWMM
VWMM

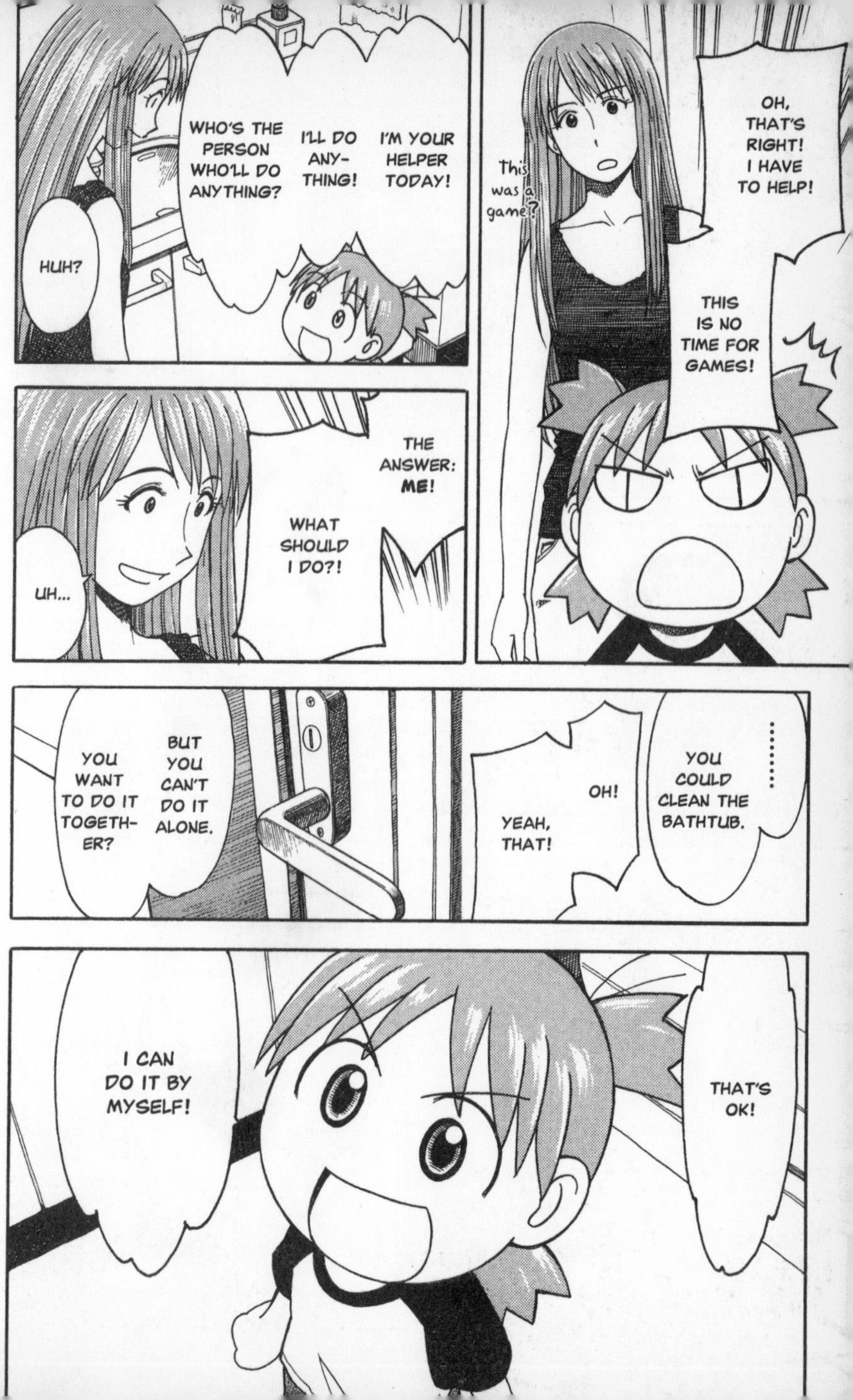
OH, THAT'S RIGHT! I HAVE TO HELP!
This was a game?
THIS IS NO TIME FOR GAMES!
WHO'S THE PERSON WHO'LL DO ANYTHING?
I'LL DO ANY-THING!
I'M YOUR HELPER TODAY!
HUH?
THE ANSWER: ME!
WHAT SHOULD I DO?!
UH...
....
YOU COULD CLEAN THE BATHTUB.
OH!
YEAH, THAT!
BUT YOU CAN'T DO IT ALONE.
YOU WANT TO DO IT TOGETH-ER?
THAT'S OK!
I CAN DO IT BY MYSELF!

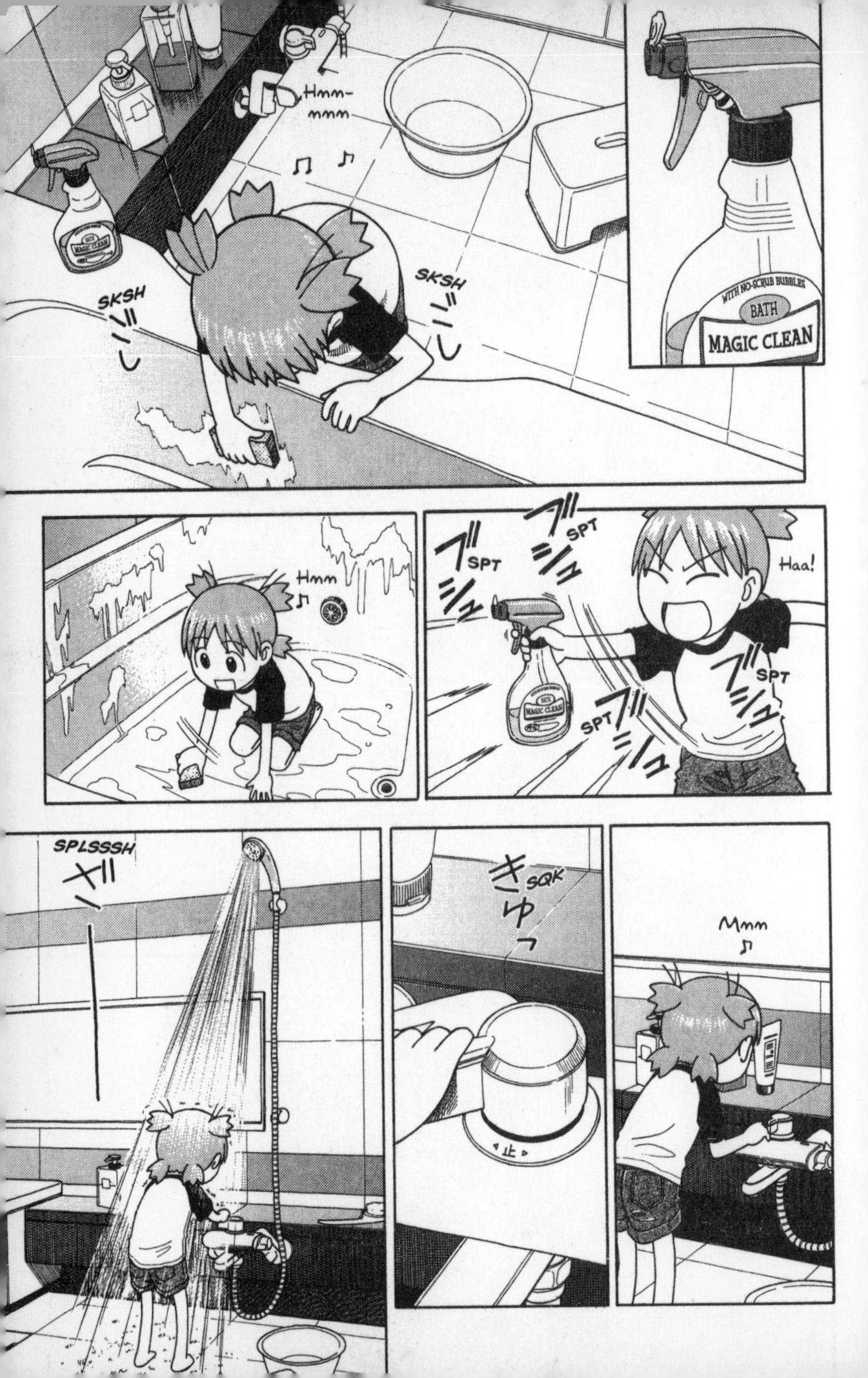
WITH NO-SCRUB BUBBLES
BATH
MAGIC CLEAN
Hmm-
mmm
♫ ♪
SKSH
SKSH
Haa!
SPT
SPT
SPT
SPT
Hmm ♪
Mmm ♪
SQK
SPLSSSH

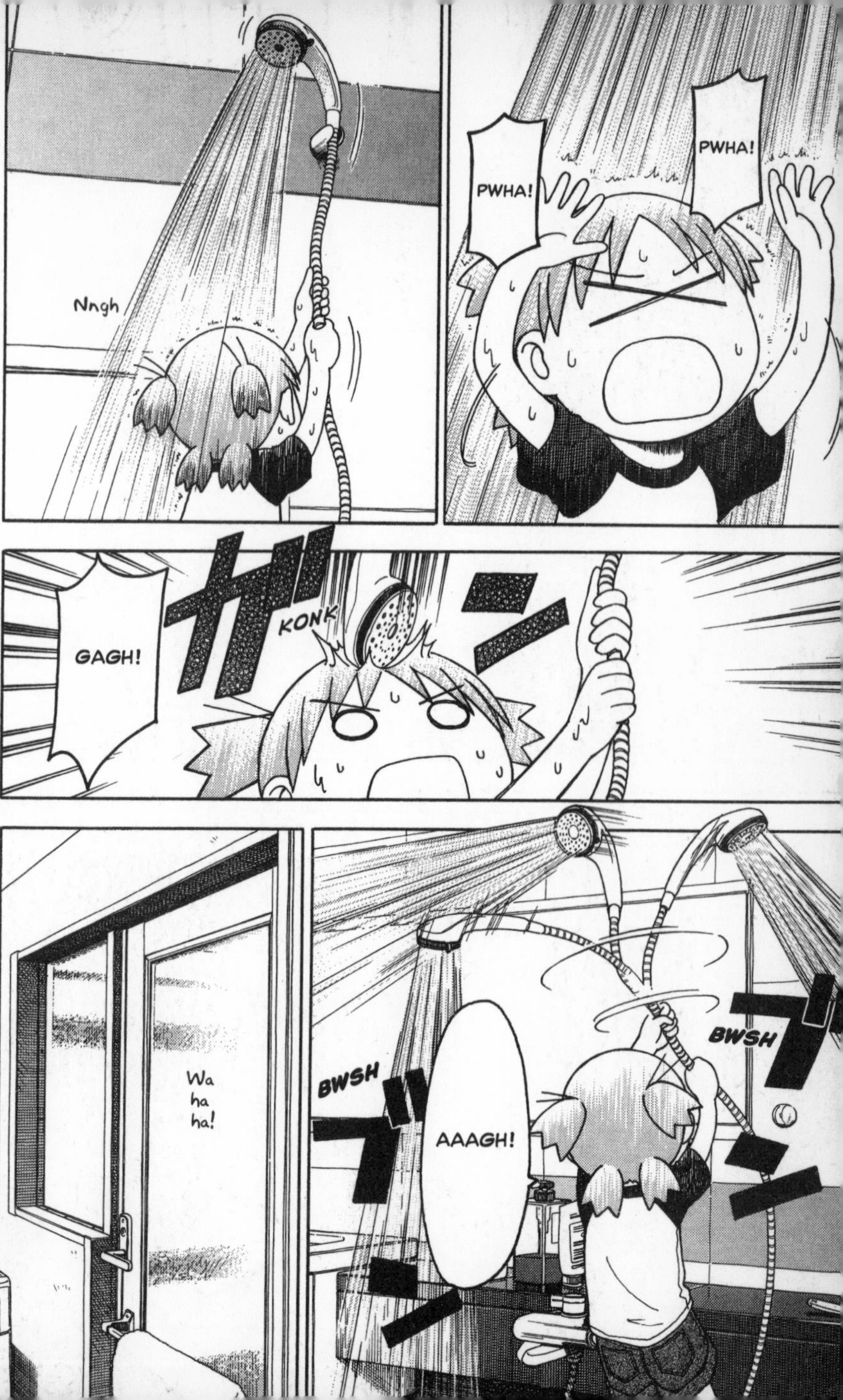
PWHA!
PWHA!
Nngh
GAGH!
KONK
BWSH
BWSH
AAAGH!
Wa ha ha!

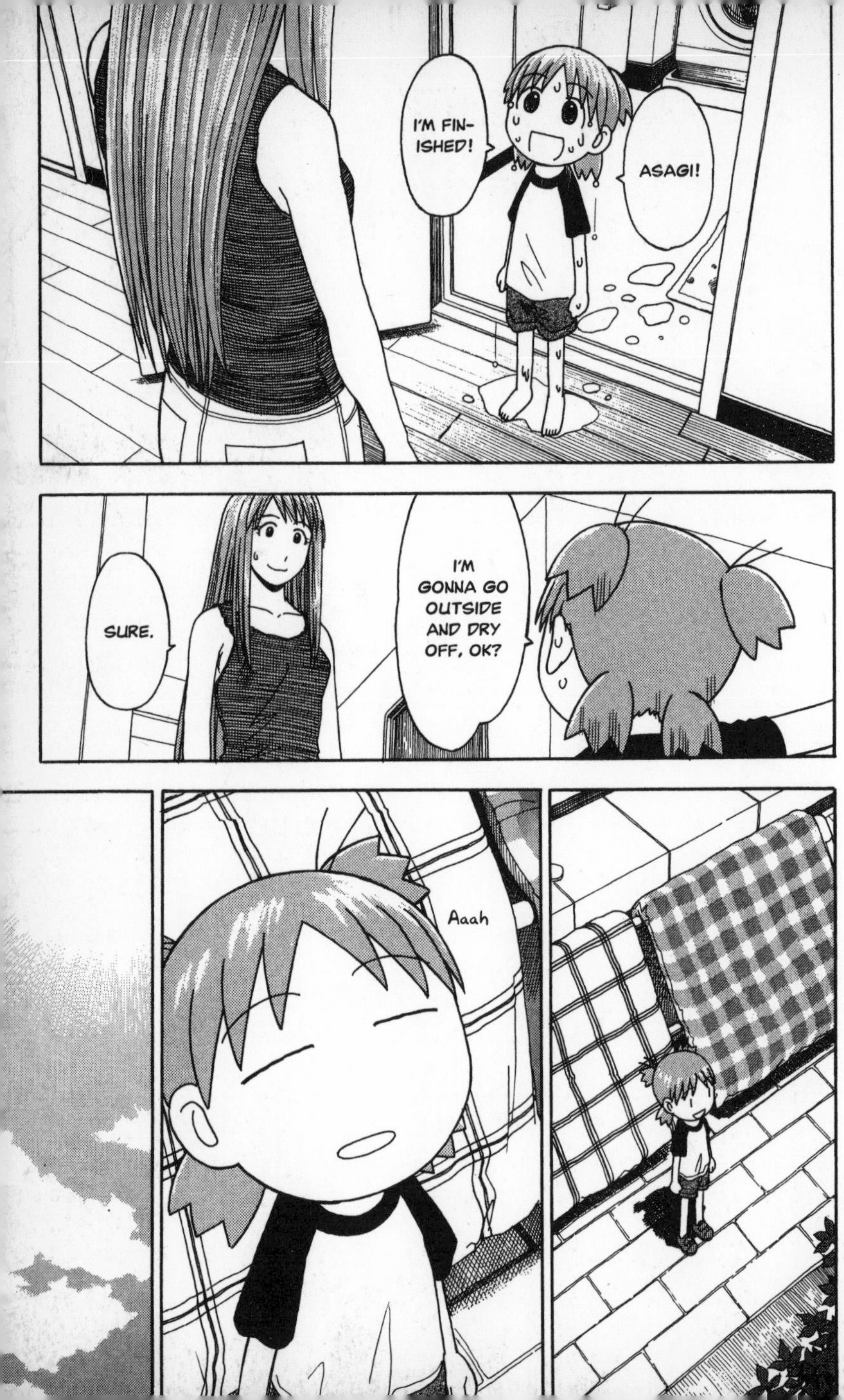
ASAGI!
I'M FIN-ISHED!
I'M GONNA GO OUTSIDE AND DRY OFF, OK?
SURE.
Aaah

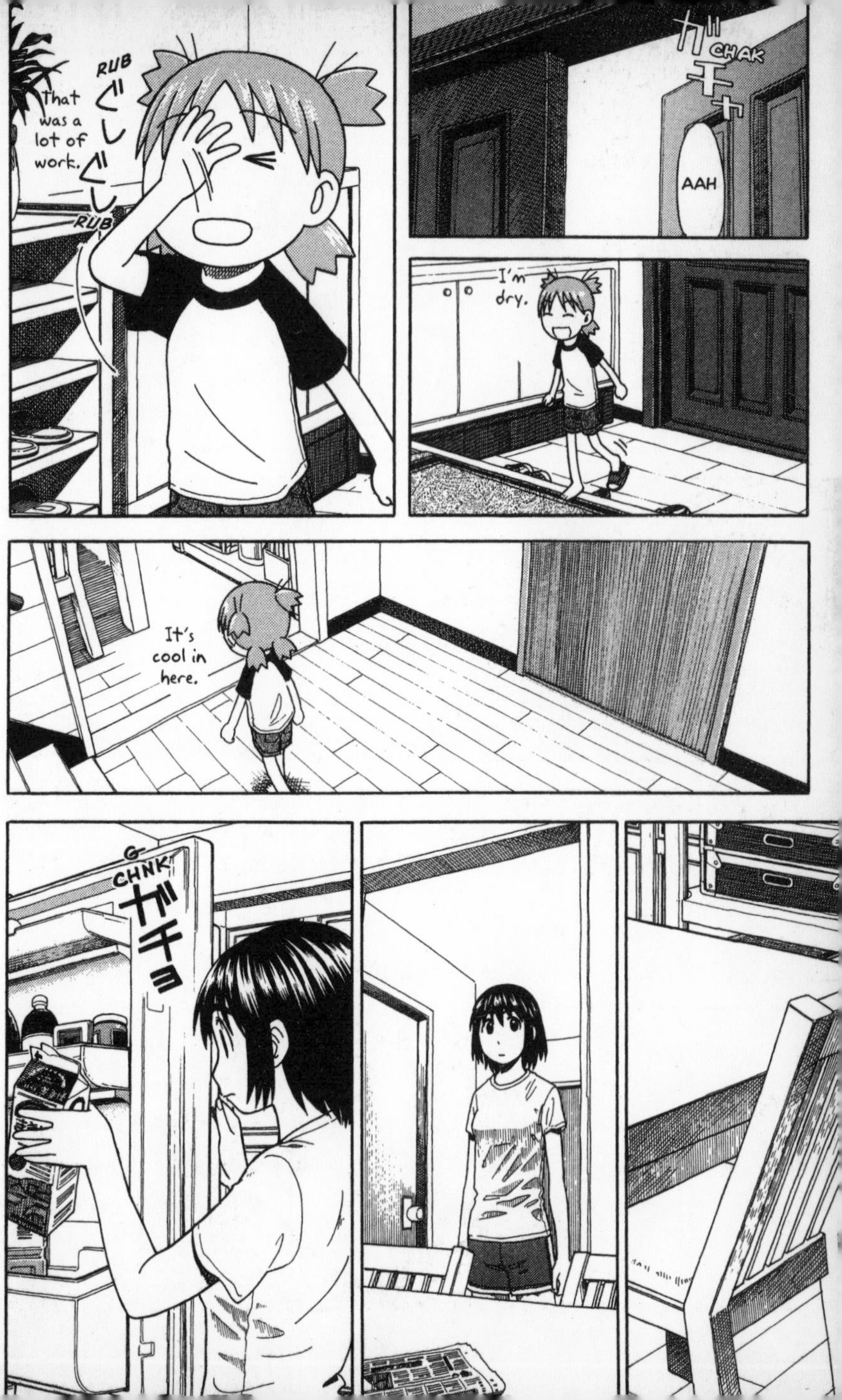
ガチャ
CHAK
AAH
I'm dry.
RUB
ぐしぐし
RUB
That was a lot of work.
It's cool in here.
ガチョ
G-CHNK

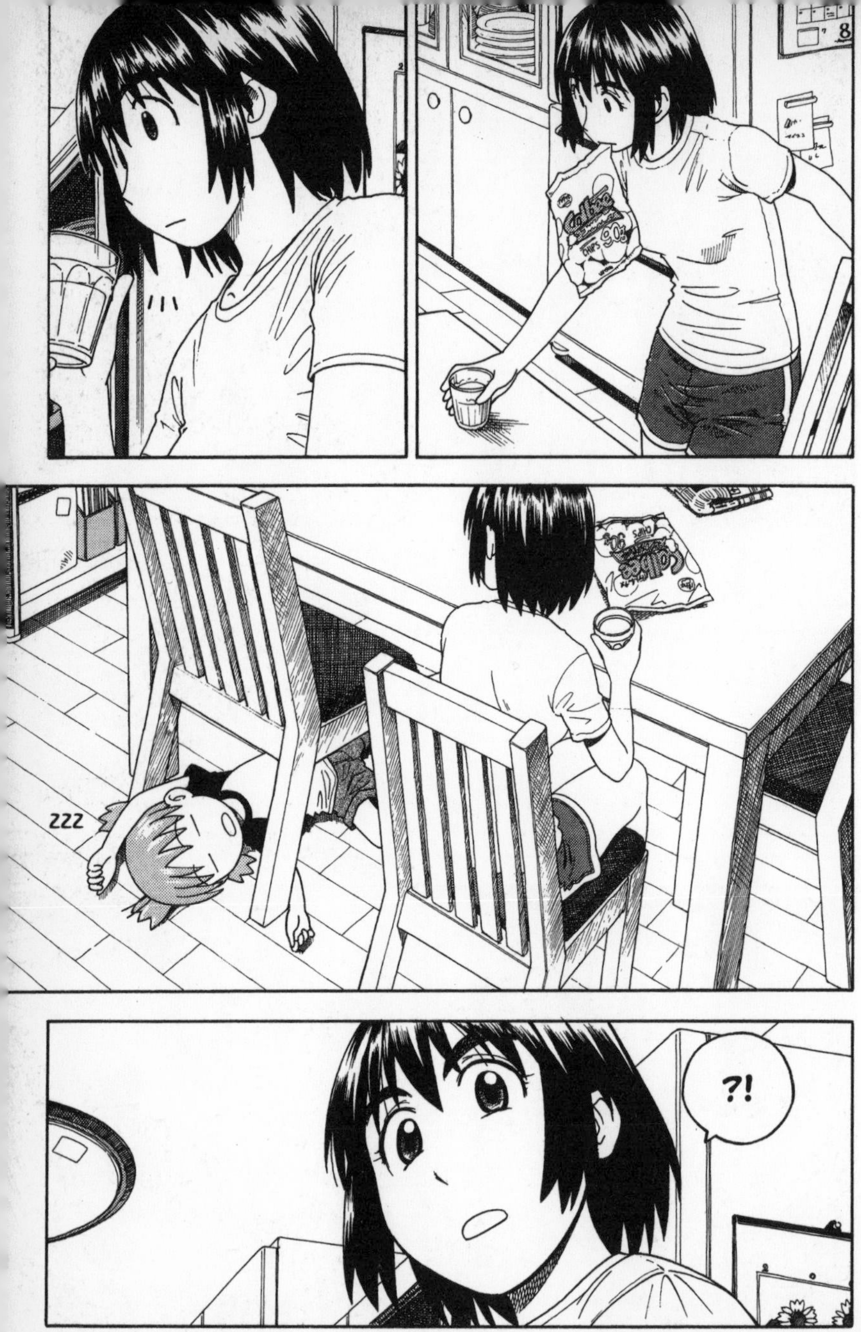

ZZZ
?!

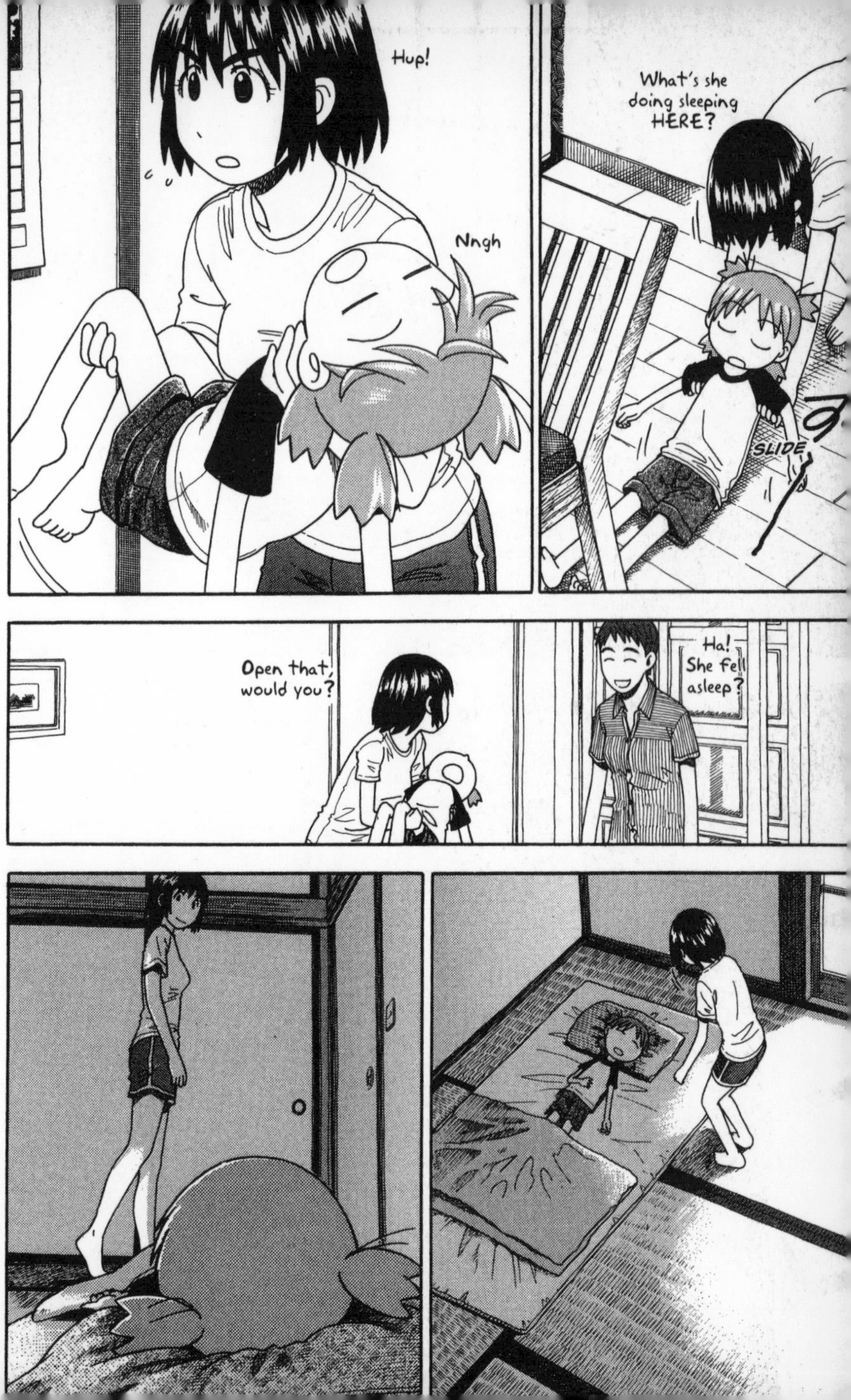
What's she doing sleeping HERE?
SLIDE
Hup!
Nngh
Ha! She fell asleep?
Open that, would you?

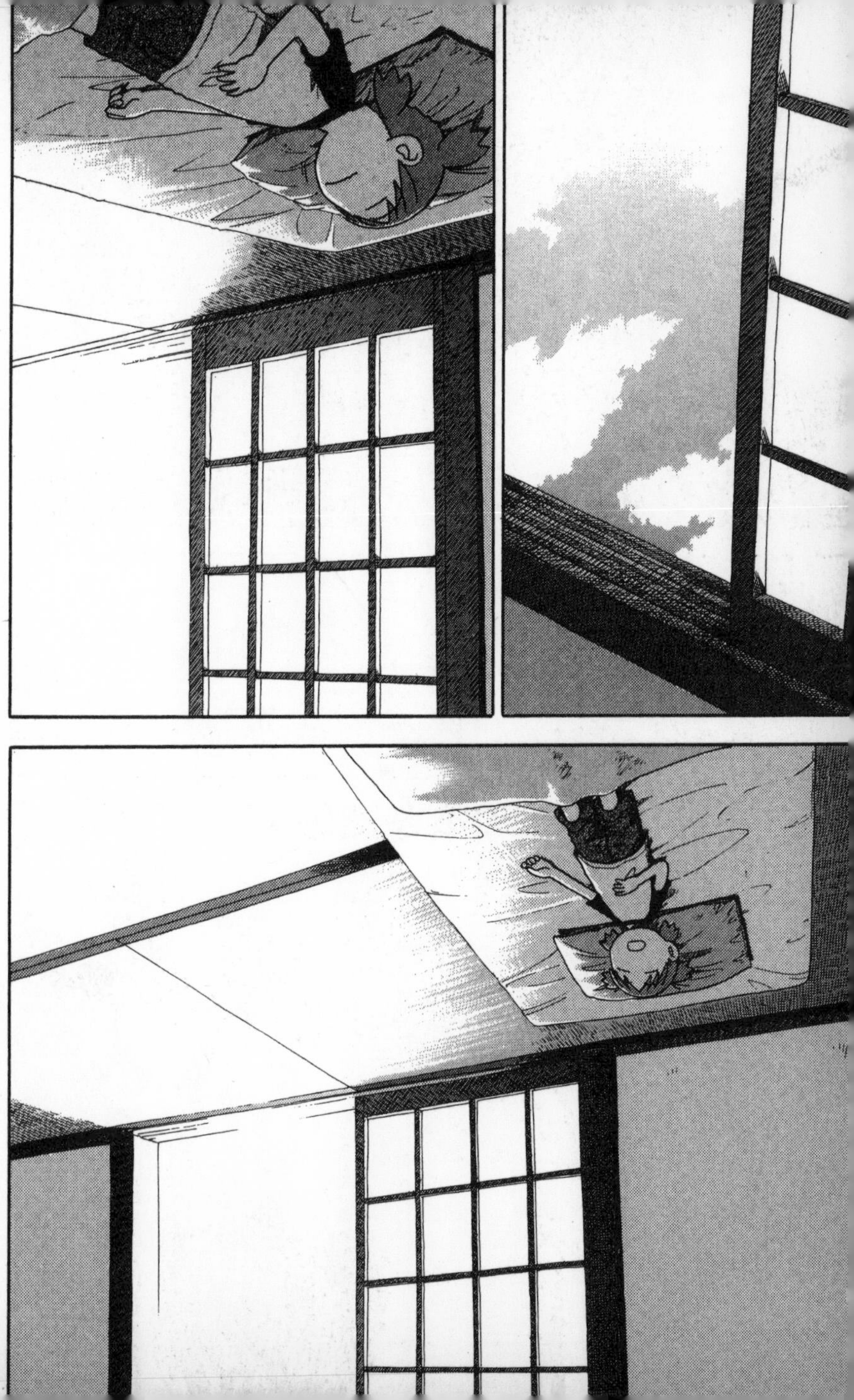

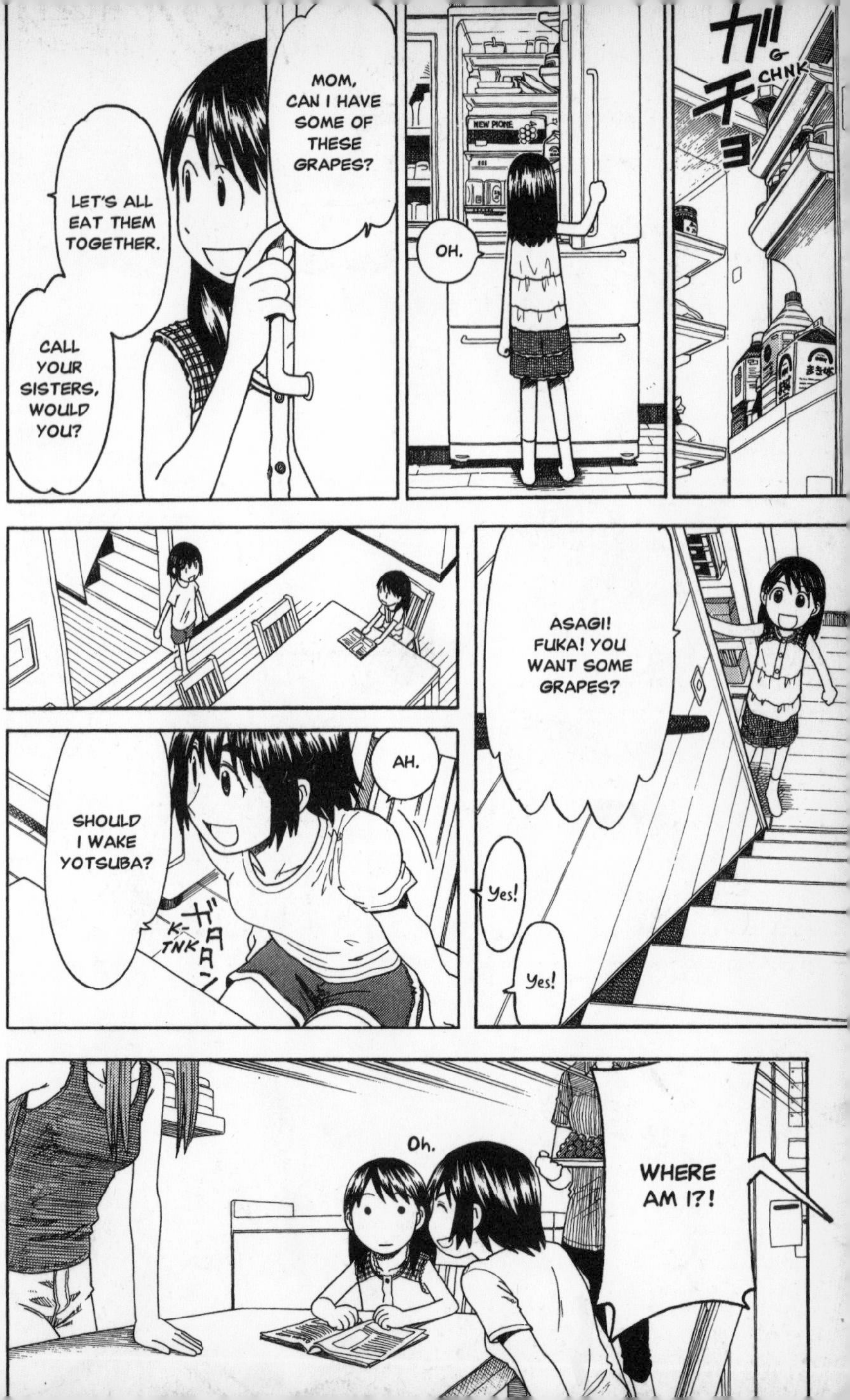
GCHNK
OH.
MOM, CAN I HAVE SOME OF THESE GRAPES?
LET'S ALL EAT THEM TOGETHER.
CALL YOUR SISTERS, WOULD YOU?
ASAGI! FUKA! YOU WANT SOME GRAPES?
Yes!
Yes!
AH.
SHOULD I WAKE YOTSUBA?
K-TNK
WHERE AM I?!
Oh.

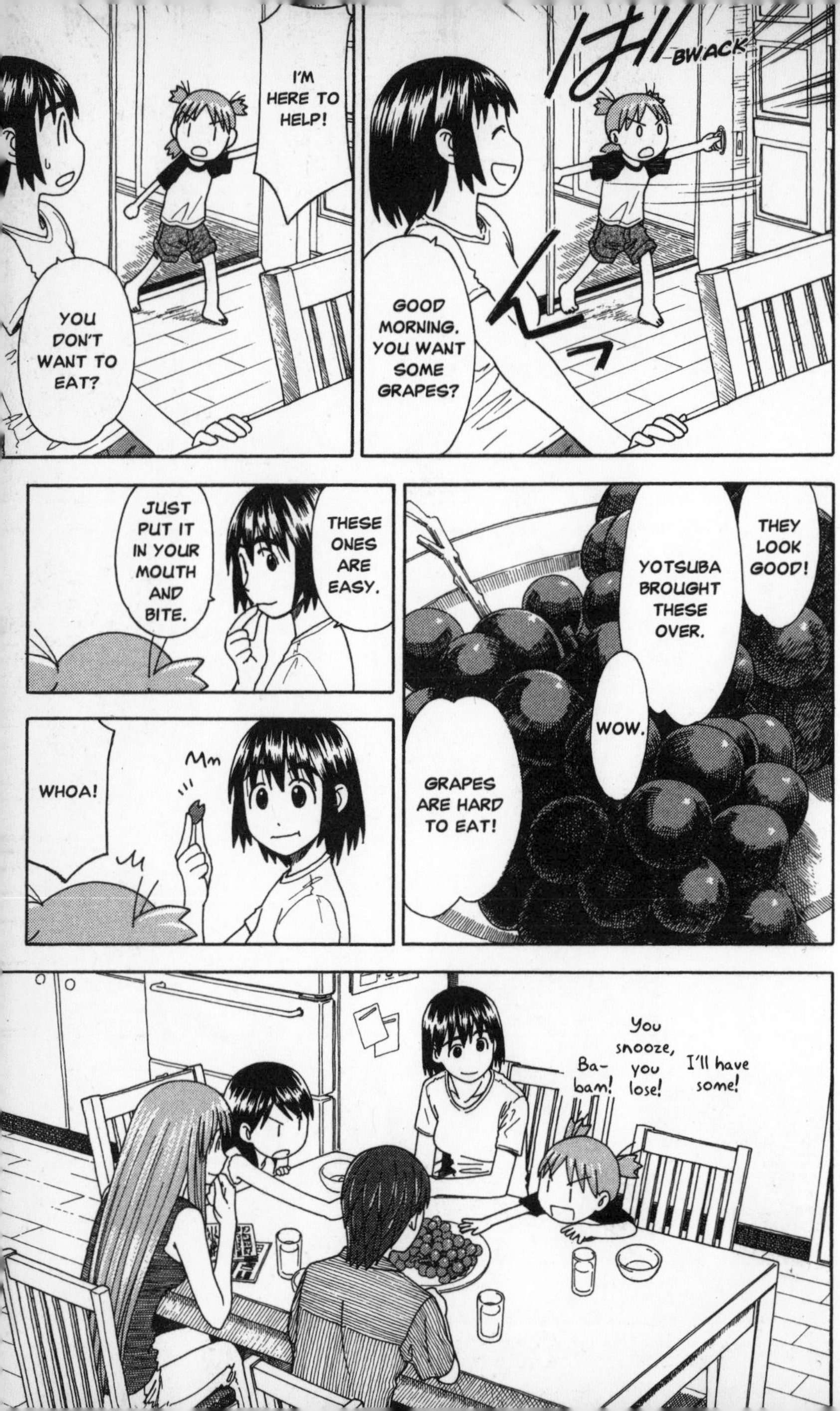
BWACK
GOOD MORNING. YOU WANT SOME GRAPES?
I'M HERE TO HELP!
YOU DON'T WANT TO EAT?
THEY LOOK GOOD!
YOTSUBA BROUGHT THESE OVER.
WOW.
GRAPES ARE HARD TO EAT!
THESE ONES ARE EASY.
JUST PUT IT IN YOUR MOUTH AND BITE.
Mm
WHOA!
I'll have some!
You snooze, you lose!
Ba-bam!

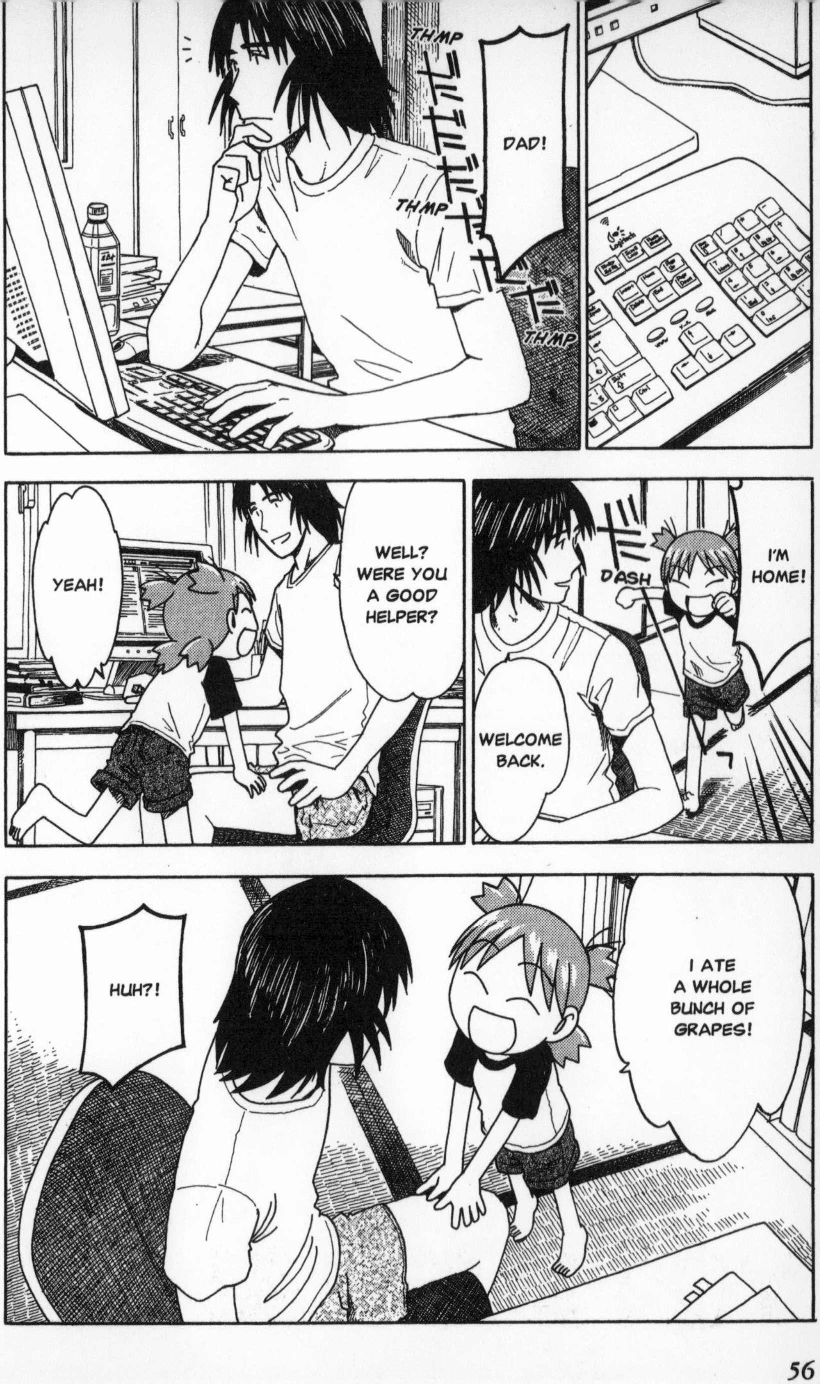
THMP
DAD!
THMP
THMP
I'M HOME!
DASH
WELCOME BACK.
WELL? WERE YOU A GOOD HELPER?
YEAH!
I ATE A WHOLE BUNCH OF GRAPES!
HUH?!

YOTSUBA&!

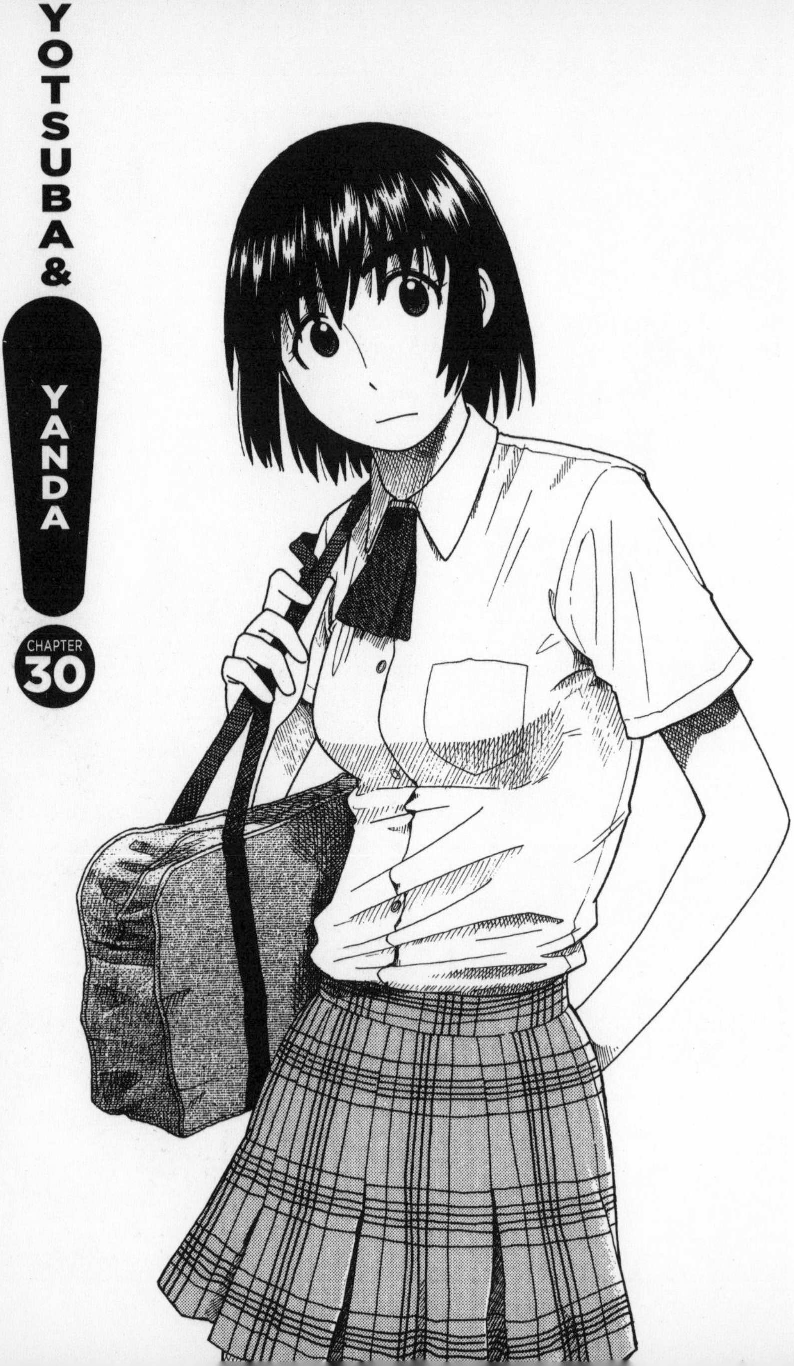
YOTSUBA&
YANDA
CHAPTER 30

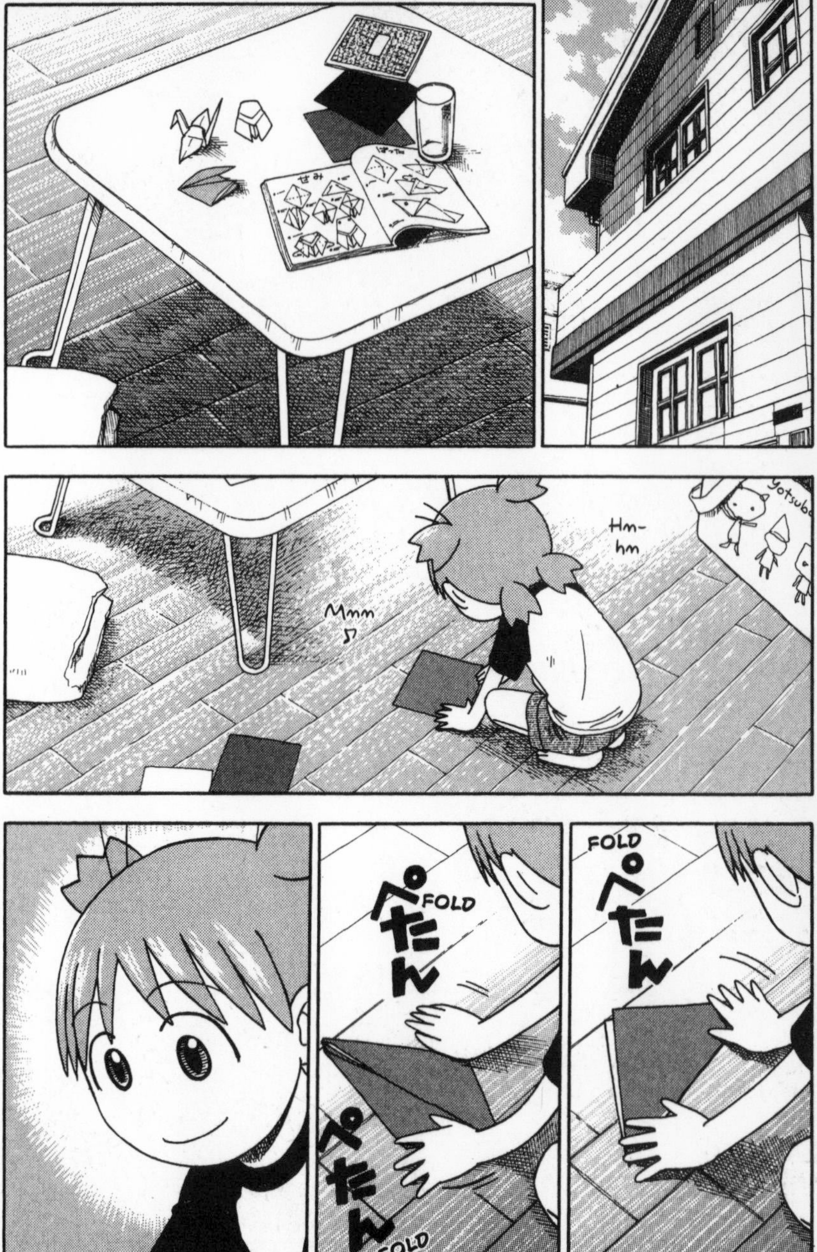
Yotsuba
Hm-
hm
Mnm ♪
FOLD
ぺたん
ぺたん
FOLD
ぺたん
FOLD

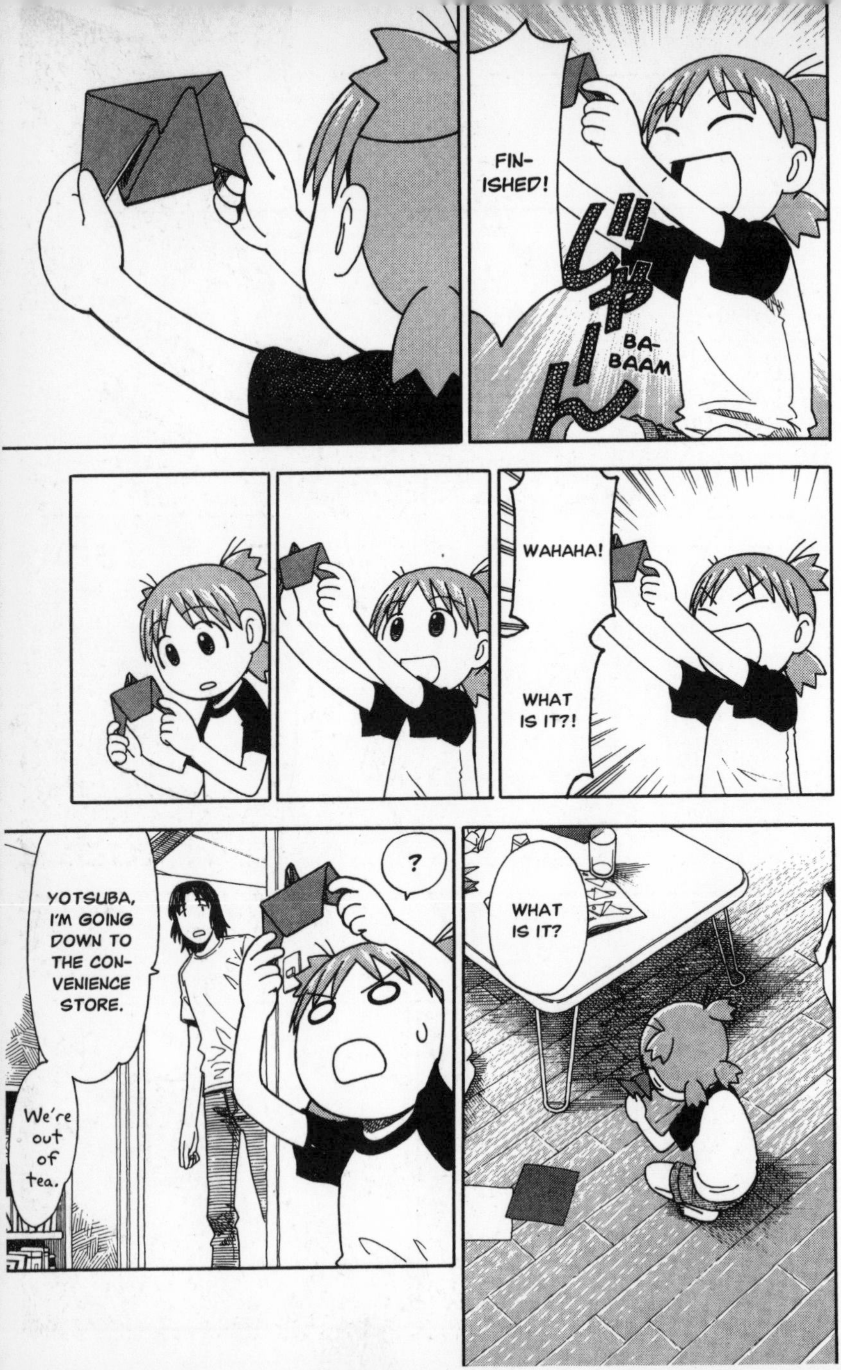
FIN-
ISHED!
じゃーん
BA-
BAAM
WAHAHA!
WHAT
IS IT?!
WHAT
IS IT?
?
YOTSUBA,
I'M GOING
DOWN TO
THE CON-
VENIENCE
STORE.
We're
out
of
tea.

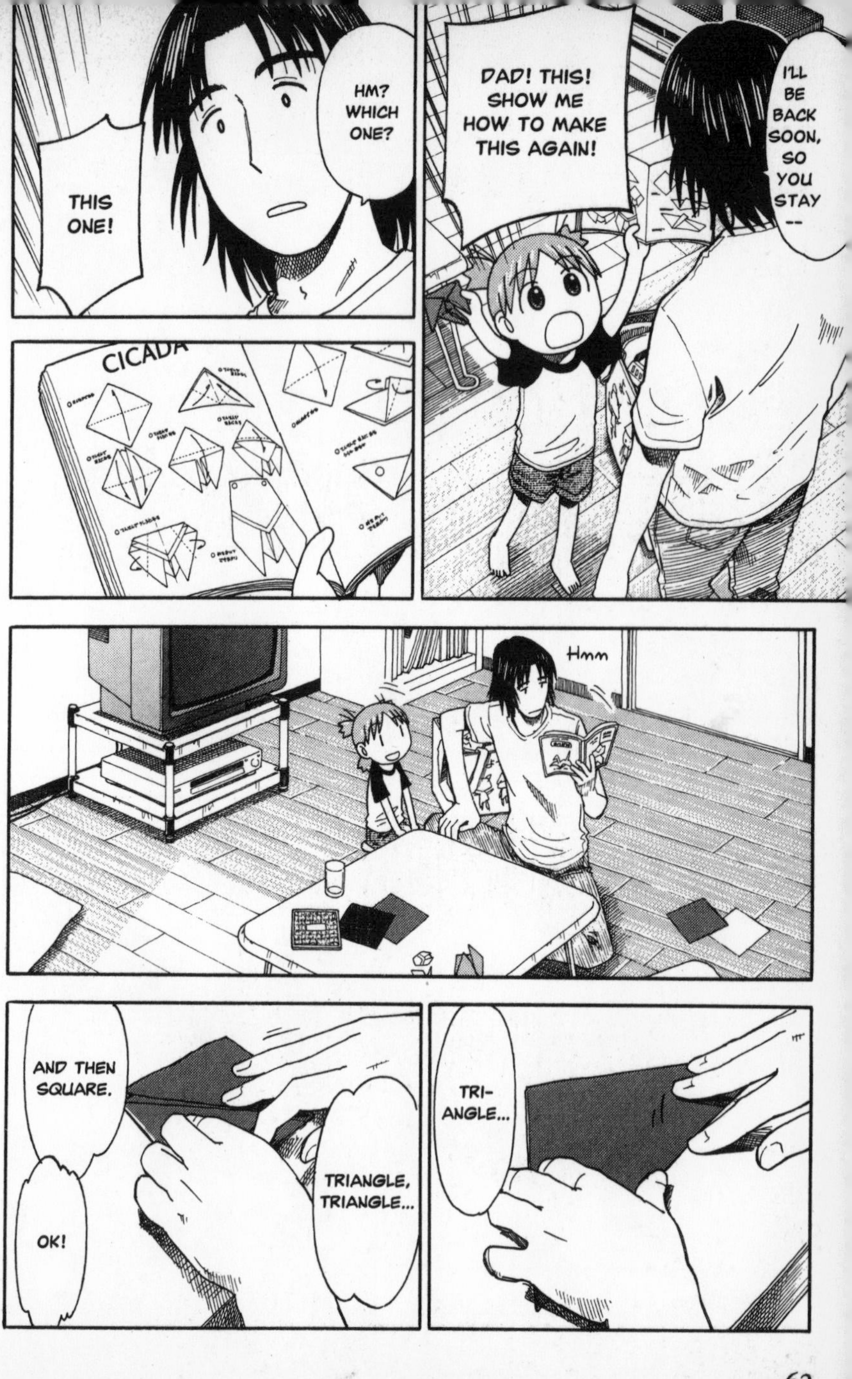
I'LL BE BACK SOON, SO YOU STAY --
DAD! THIS! SHOW ME HOW TO MAKE THIS AGAIN!
HM? WHICH ONE?
THIS ONE!
CICADA
Hmm
TRI-ANGLE...
TRIANGLE, TRIANGLE...
AND THEN SQUARE.
OK!

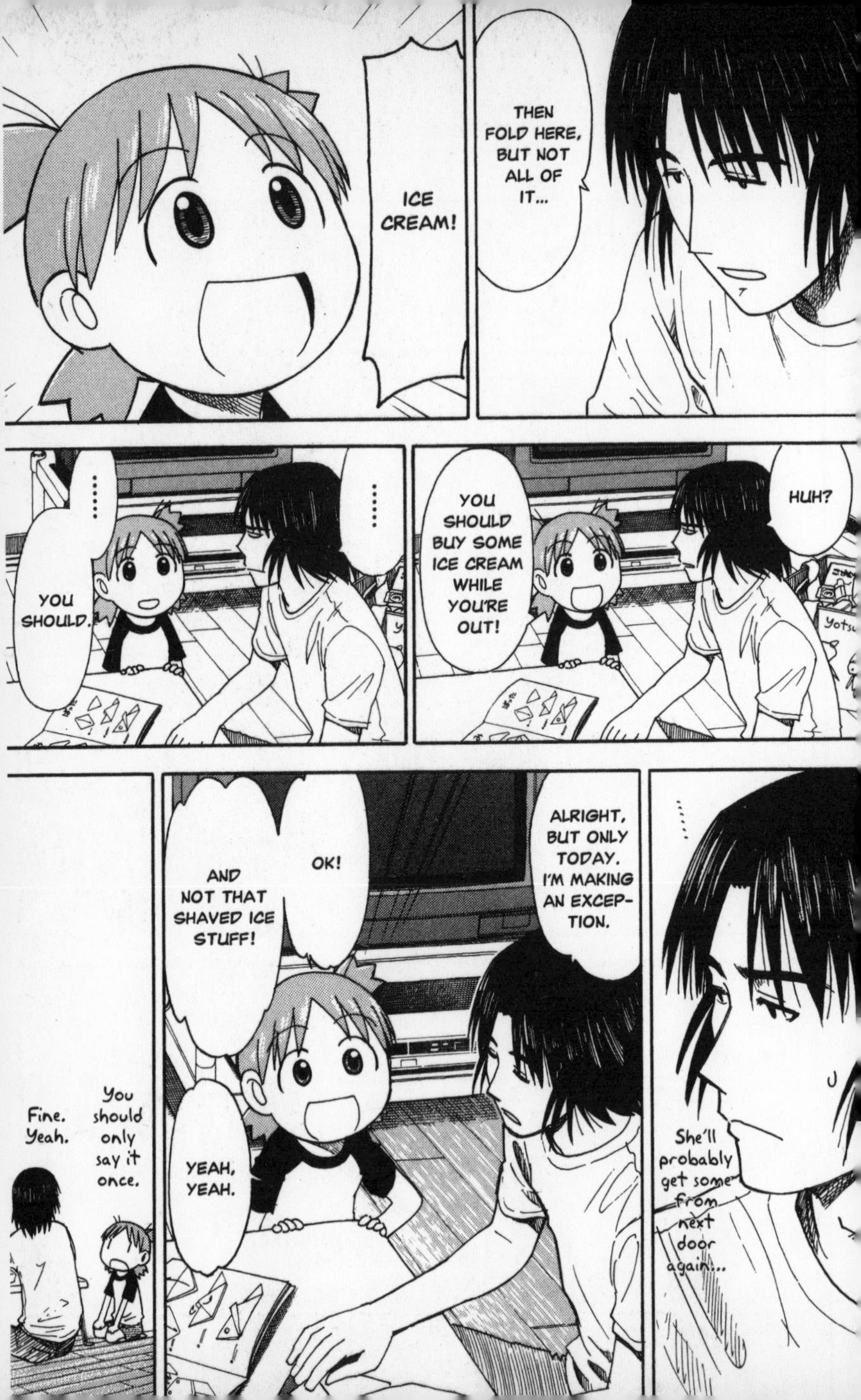
THEN FOLD HERE, BUT NOT ALL OF IT...
ICE CREAM!
HUH?
YOU SHOULD BUY SOME ICE CREAM WHILE YOU'RE OUT!
......
......
YOU SHOULD.
......
She'll probably get some from next door again...
ALRIGHT, BUT ONLY TODAY. I'M MAKING AN EXCEPTION.
OK!
AND NOT THAT SHAVED ICE STUFF!
YEAH, YEAH.
You should only say it once.
Fine. Yeah.

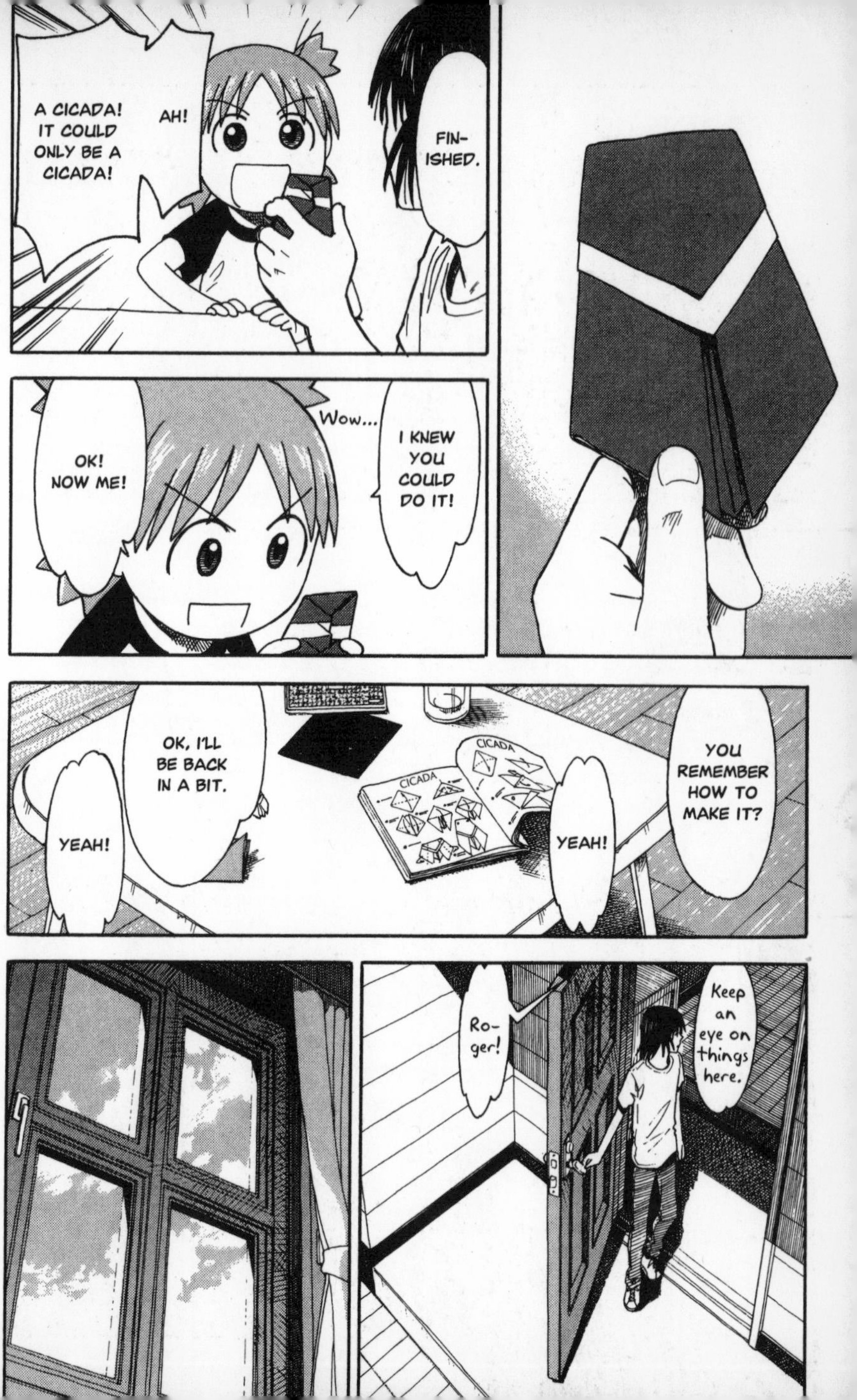
FIN-ISHED.
AH!
A CICADA! IT COULD ONLY BE A CICADA!
Wow...
I KNEW YOU COULD DO IT!
OK! NOW ME!
YOU REMEMBER HOW TO MAKE IT?
YEAH!
CICADA
CICADA
OK, I'LL BE BACK IN A BIT.
YEAH!
Keep an eye on things here.
Ro-ger!

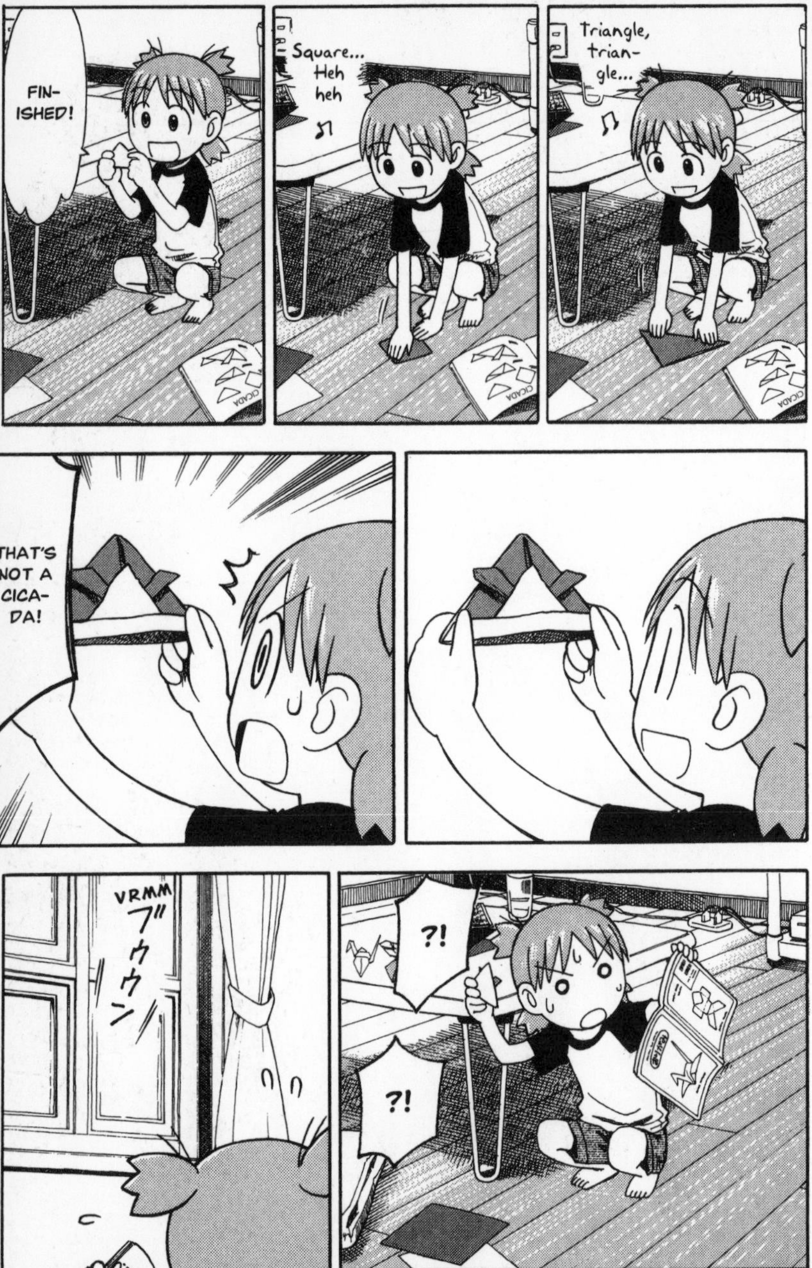
Triangle, triangle...
Square... Heh heh
FINISHED!
THAT'S NOT A CICADA!
CICADA
?!
?!
VRMM
ブゥウン

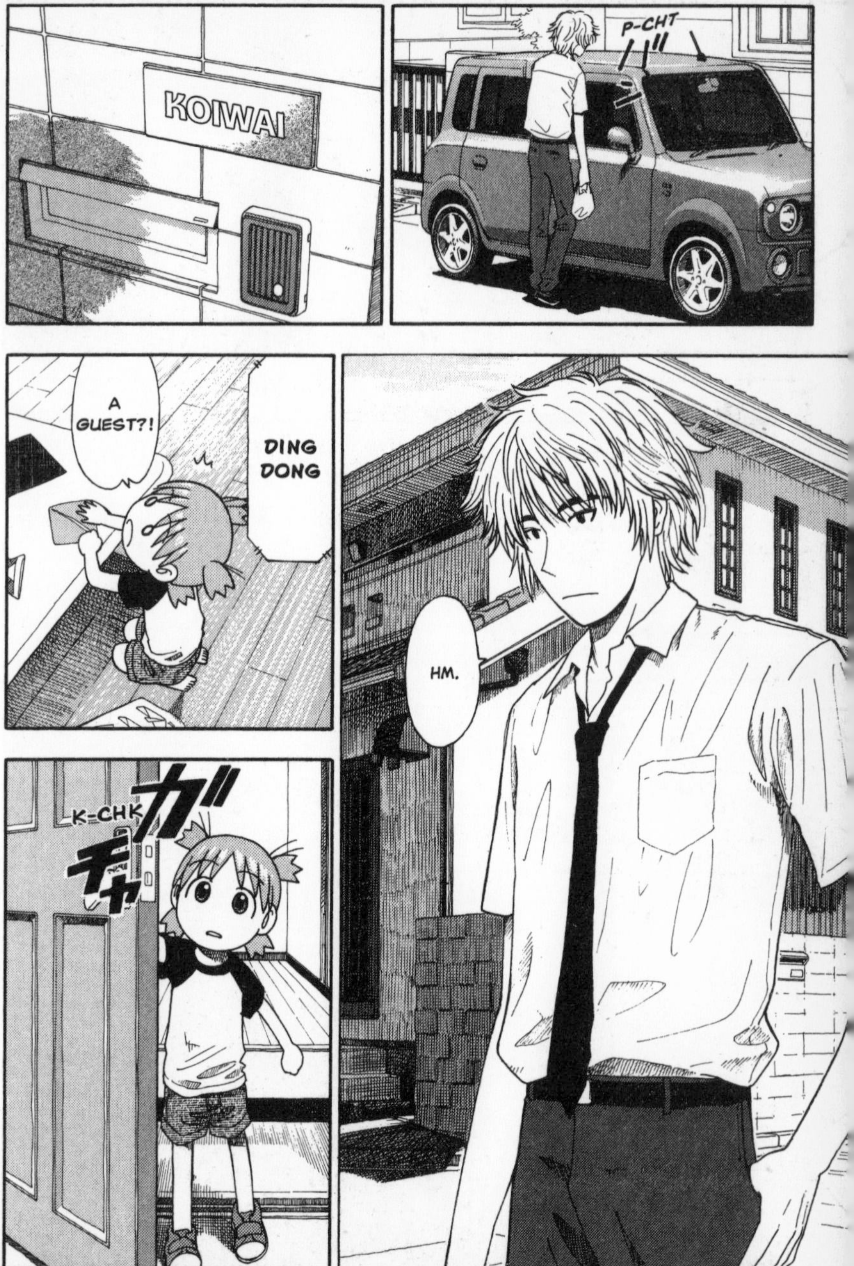
P-CHT
KOIWAI
HM.
DING DONG
A GUEST?!
K-CHK
ガチャ

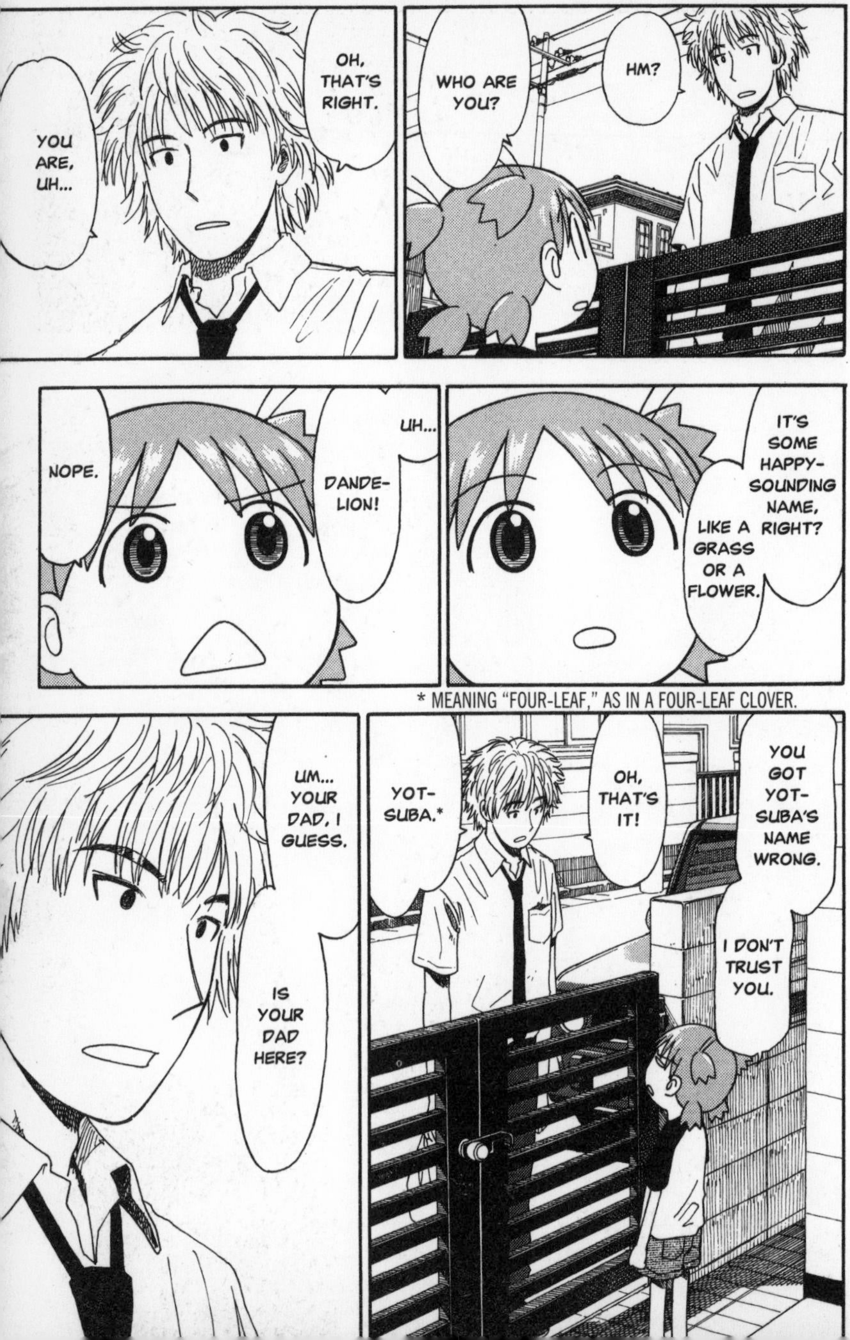
HM?
WHO ARE YOU?
OH, THAT'S RIGHT.
YOU ARE, UH...
IT'S SOME HAPPY-SOUNDING NAME, RIGHT?
LIKE A GRASS OR A FLOWER.
UH...
DANDE-LION!
NOPE.
YOU GOT YOT-SUBA'S NAME WRONG.
OH, THAT'S IT!
YOT-SUBA.*
I DON'T TRUST YOU.
UM... YOUR DAD, I GUESS.
IS YOUR DAD HERE?

* MEANING "FOUR-LEAF," AS IN A FOUR-LEAF CLOVER.

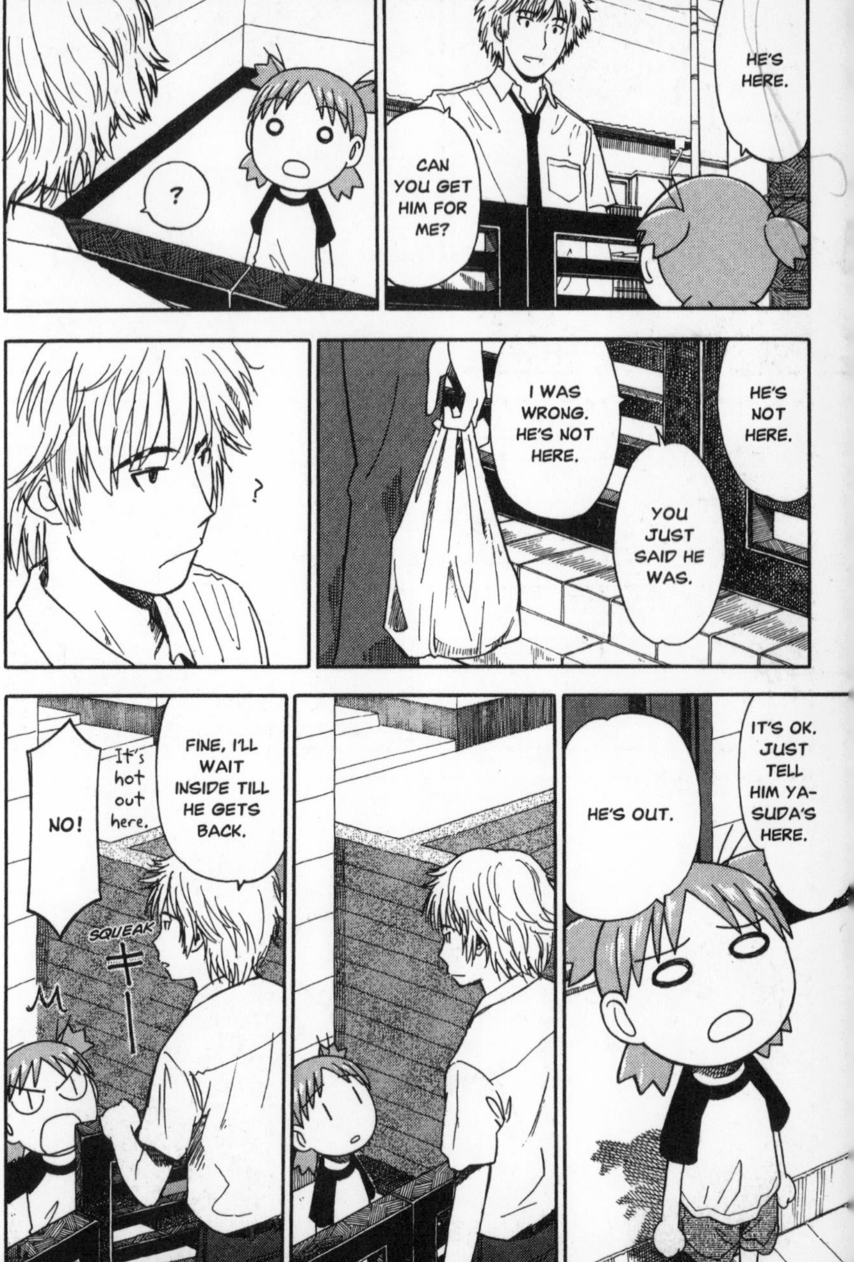
HE'S HERE.
CAN YOU GET HIM FOR ME?
?
HE'S NOT HERE.
I WAS WRONG. HE'S NOT HERE.
YOU JUST SAID HE WAS.
?
IT'S OK. JUST TELL HIM YA-SUDA'S HERE.
HE'S OUT.
FINE, I'LL WAIT INSIDE TILL HE GETS BACK.
It's hot out here.
NO!
SQUEAK

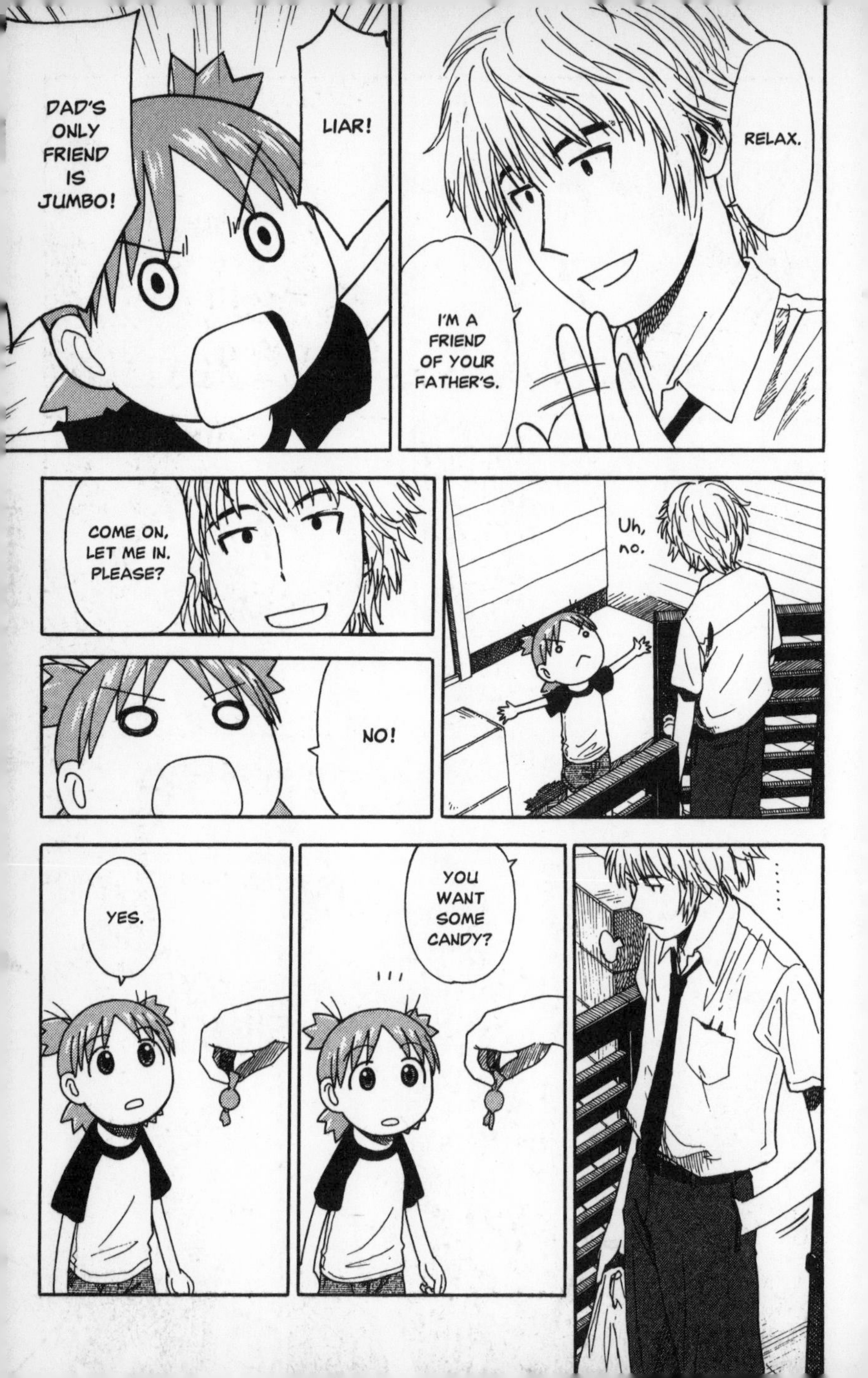
RELAX.
I'M A FRIEND OF YOUR FATHER'S.
LIAR!
DAD'S ONLY FRIEND IS JUMBO!
Uh, no.
COME ON, LET ME IN. PLEASE?
NO!
......
YOU WANT SOME CANDY?
YES.

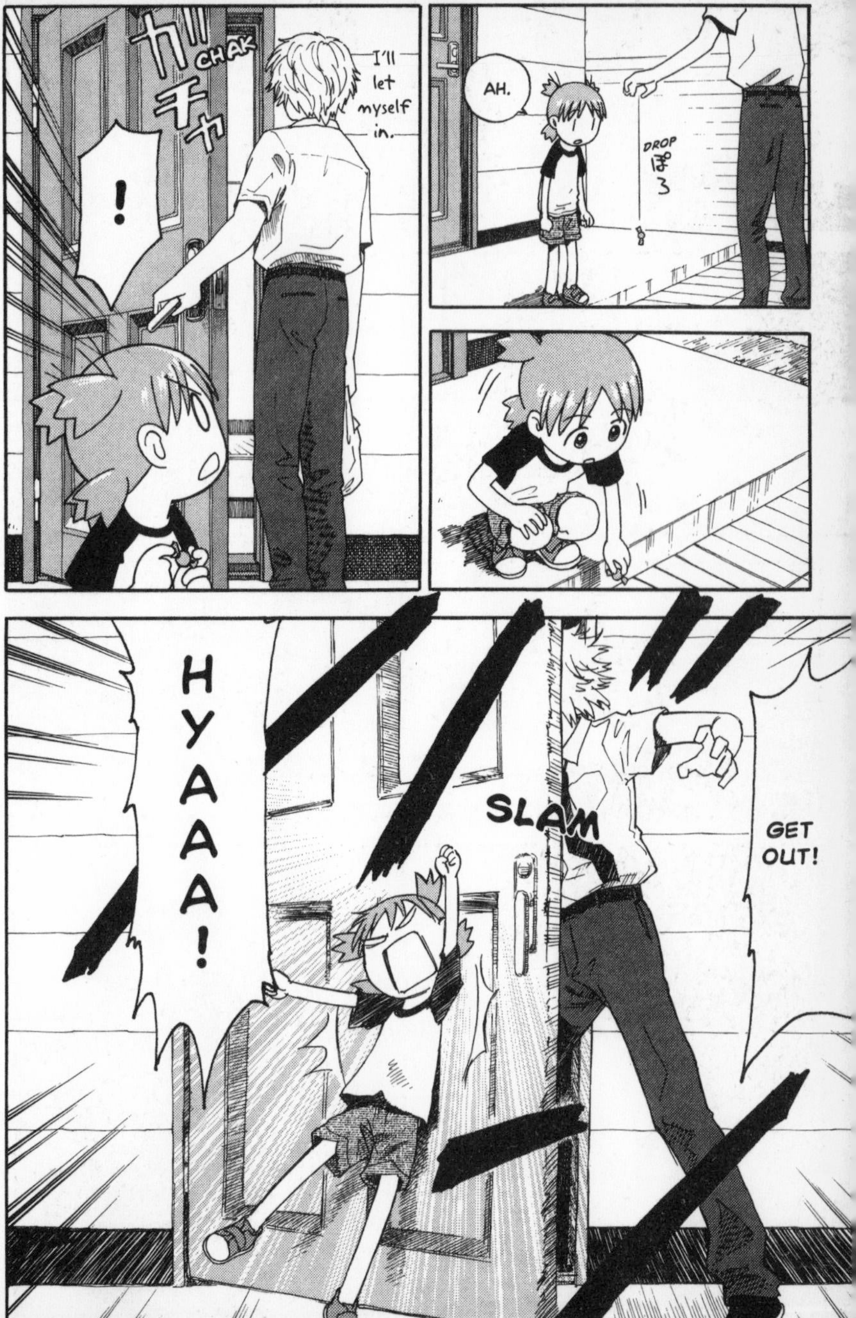
AH.
DROP
ぽろ
I'll let myself in.
カチャ
CHAK
!
GET OUT!
SLAM
HYAAA!

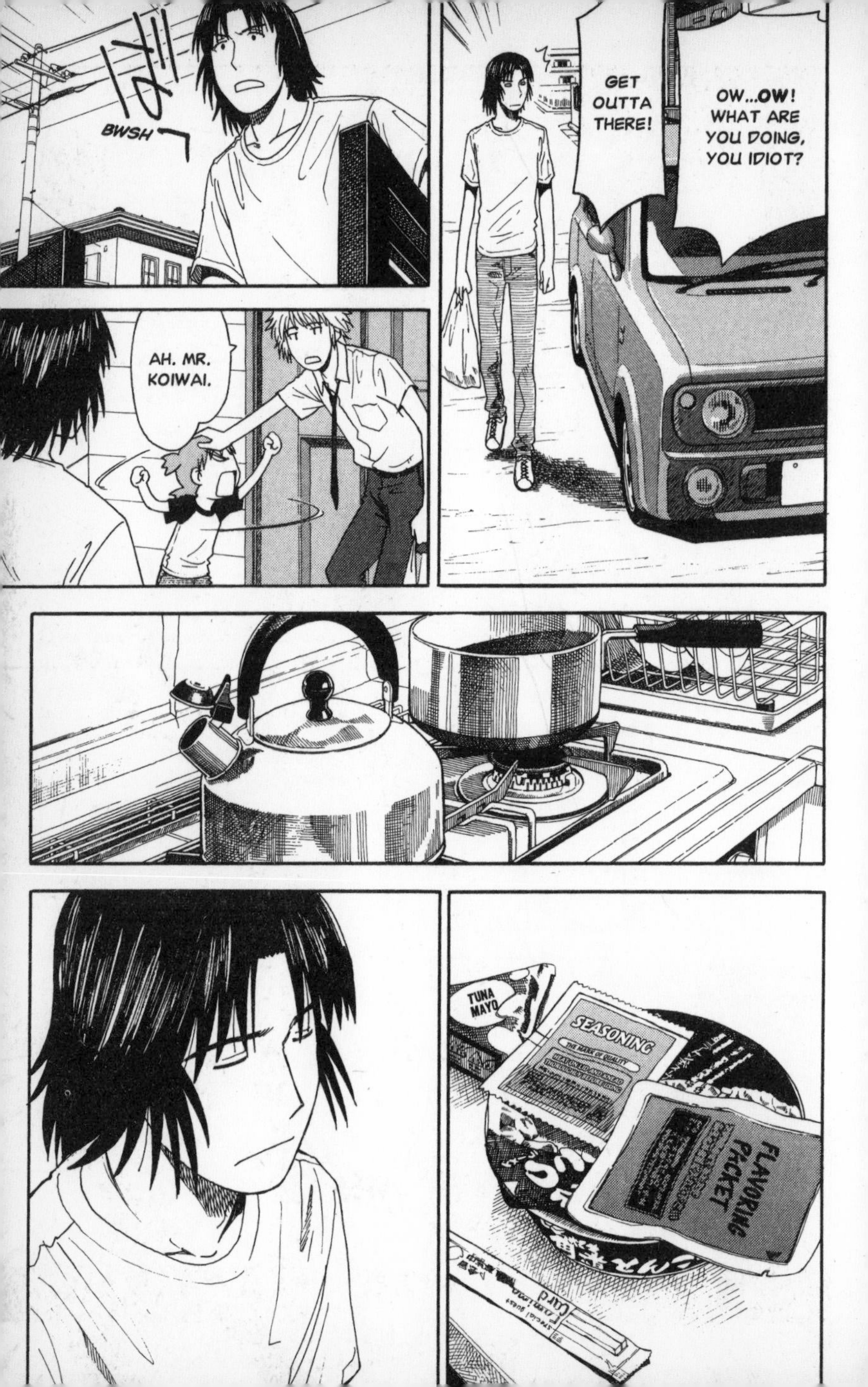
OW...OW! WHAT ARE YOU DOING, YOU IDIOT?
GET OUTTA THERE!
BWSH
AH. MR. KOIWAI.
FLAVORING PACKET
SEASONING
THE MARK OF QUALITY
TUNA MAYO

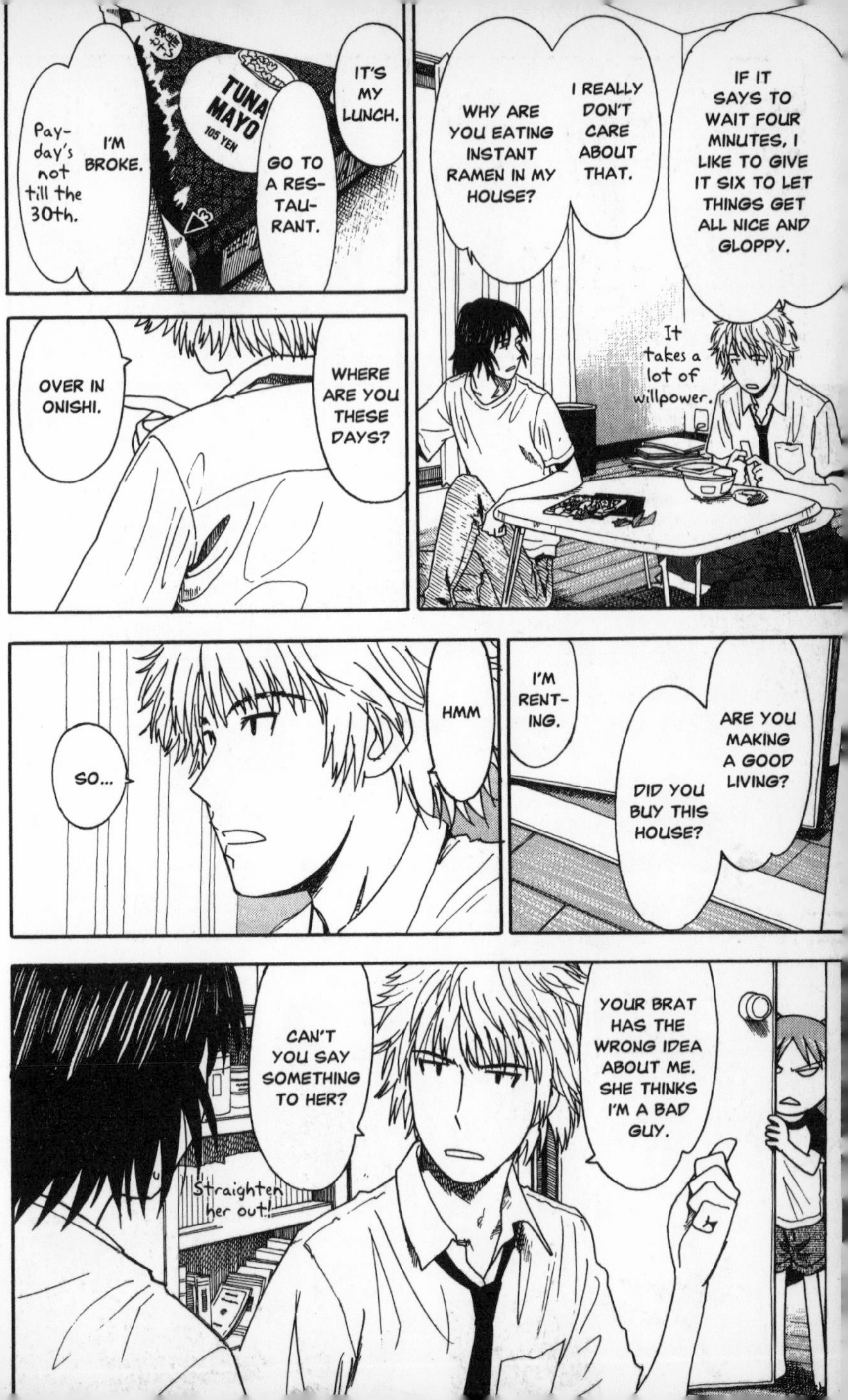
IF IT SAYS TO WAIT FOUR MINUTES, I LIKE TO GIVE IT SIX TO LET THINGS GET ALL NICE AND GLOPPY.
I REALLY DON'T CARE ABOUT THAT.
WHY ARE YOU EATING INSTANT RAMEN IN MY HOUSE?
It takes a lot of willpower.
IT'S MY LUNCH.
GO TO A RES-TAU-RANT.
TUNA MAYO
105 YEN
I'M BROKE.
Pay-day's not till the 30th.
WHERE ARE YOU THESE DAYS?
OVER IN ONISHI.
ARE YOU MAKING A GOOD LIVING?
DID YOU BUY THIS HOUSE?
I'M RENT-ING.
HMM
SO...
YOUR BRAT HAS THE WRONG IDEA ABOUT ME. SHE THINKS I'M A BAD GUY.
CAN'T YOU SAY SOMETHING TO HER?
Straighten her out!

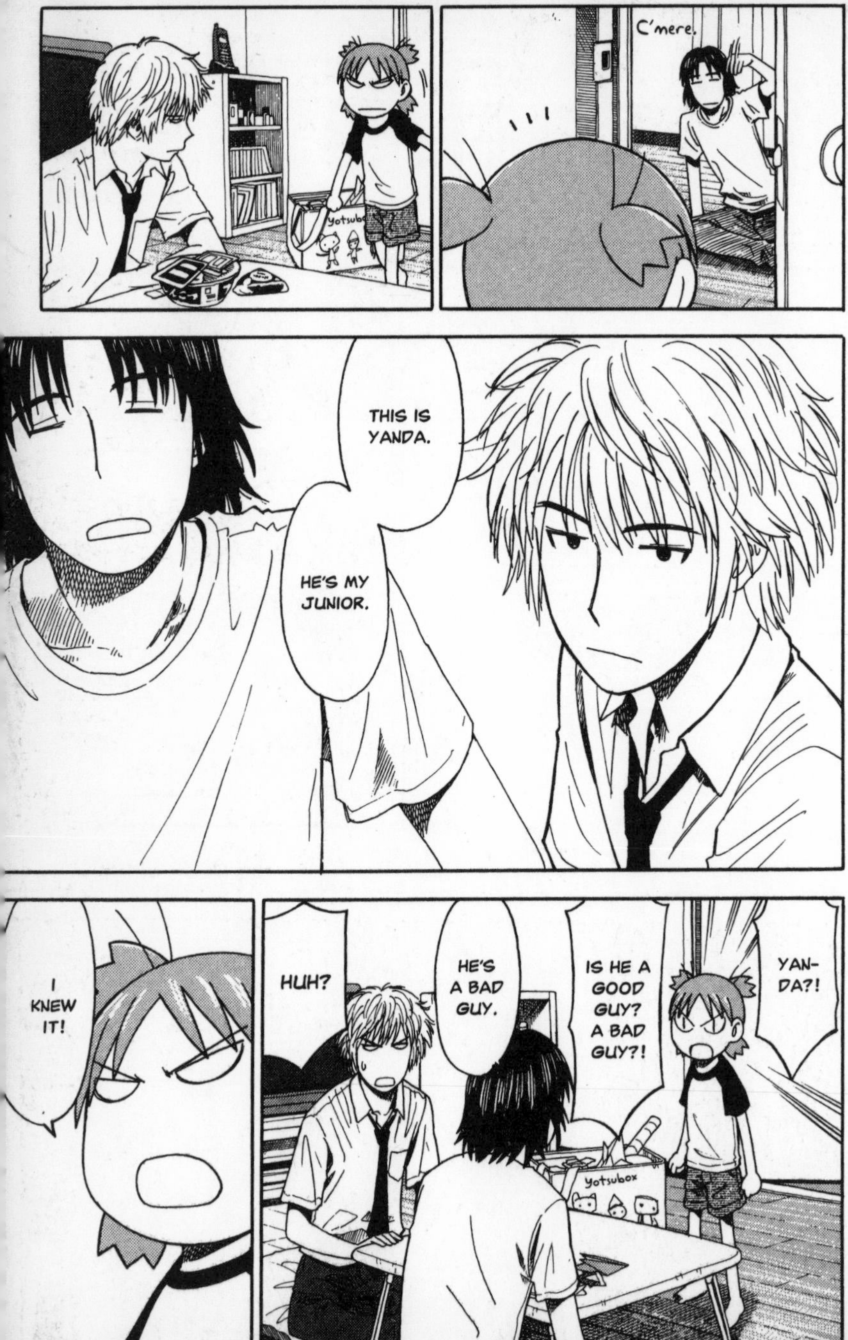
C'mere.
THIS IS YANDA.
HE'S MY JUNIOR.
YAN-DA?!
IS HE A GOOD GUY? A BAD GUY?!
HE'S A BAD GUY.
HUH?
yotsubox
I KNEW IT!

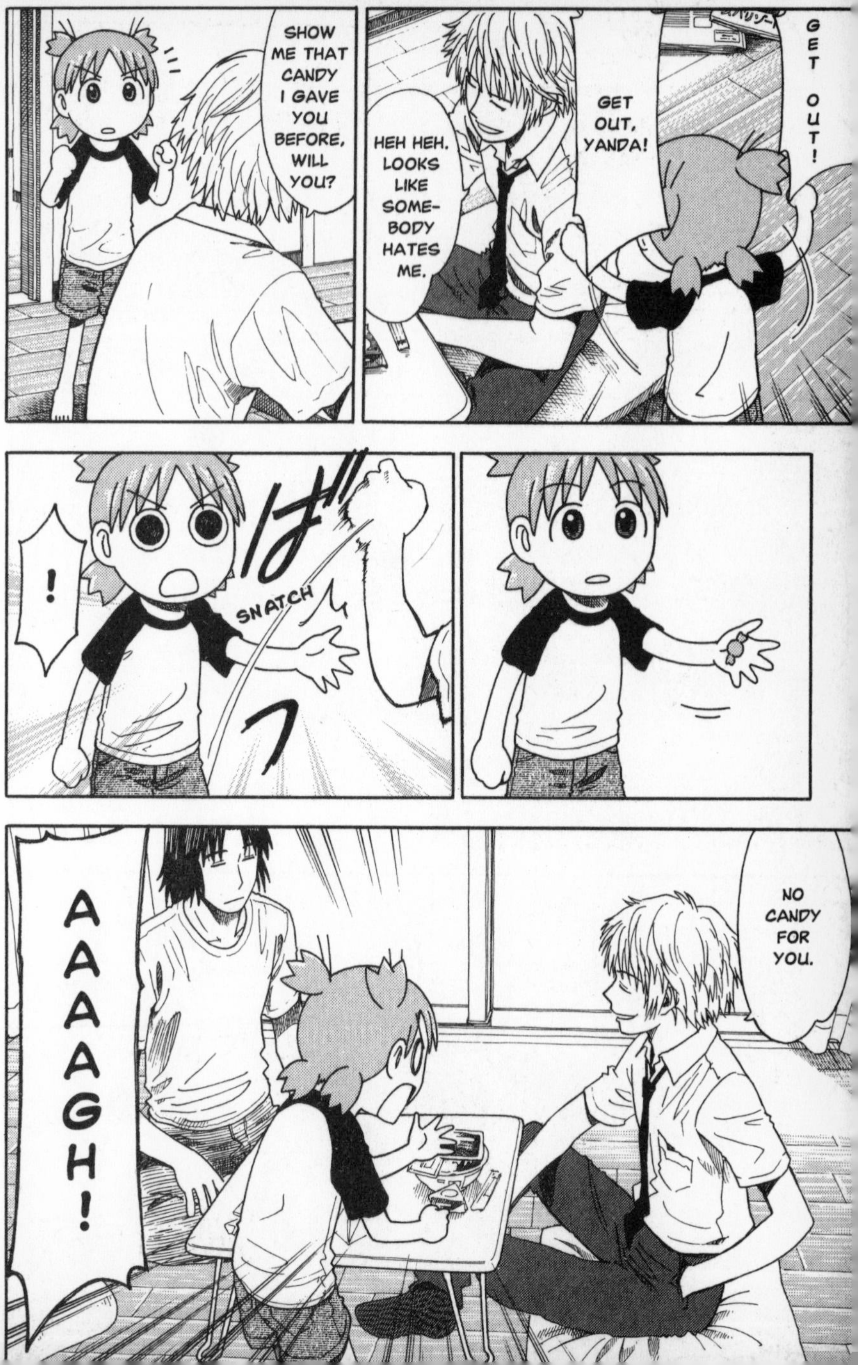
GET OUT!
GET OUT, YANDA!
HEH HEH. LOOKS LIKE SOME-BODY HATES ME.
SHOW ME THAT CANDY I GAVE YOU BEFORE, WILL YOU?
!
SNATCH
NO CANDY FOR YOU.
AAAAGH!

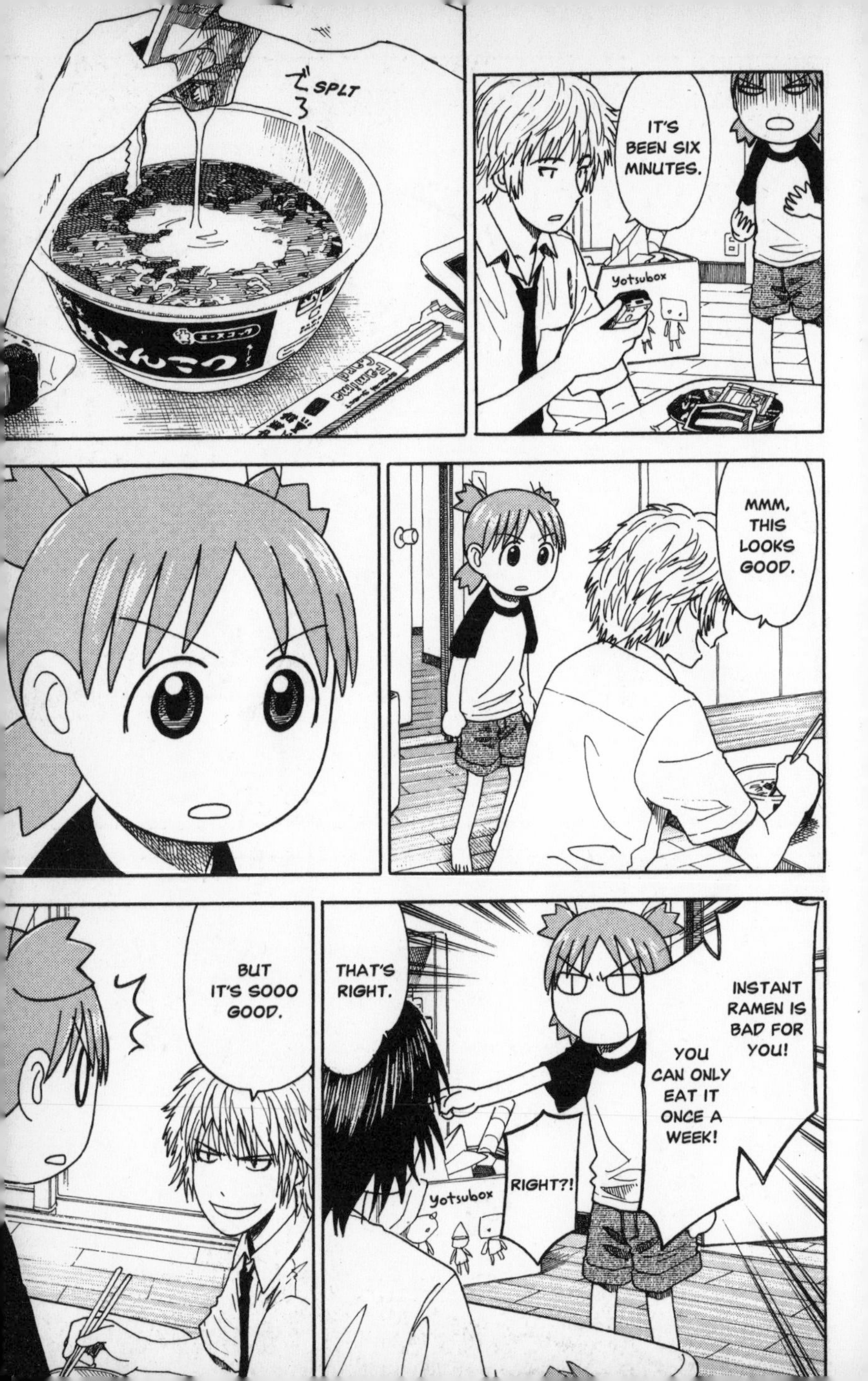
IT'S BEEN SIX MINUTES.
yotsubox
SPLT
MMM, THIS LOOKS GOOD.
INSTANT RAMEN IS BAD FOR YOU!
YOU CAN ONLY EAT IT ONCE A WEEK!
RIGHT?!
yotsubox
THAT'S RIGHT.
BUT IT'S SOOO GOOD.

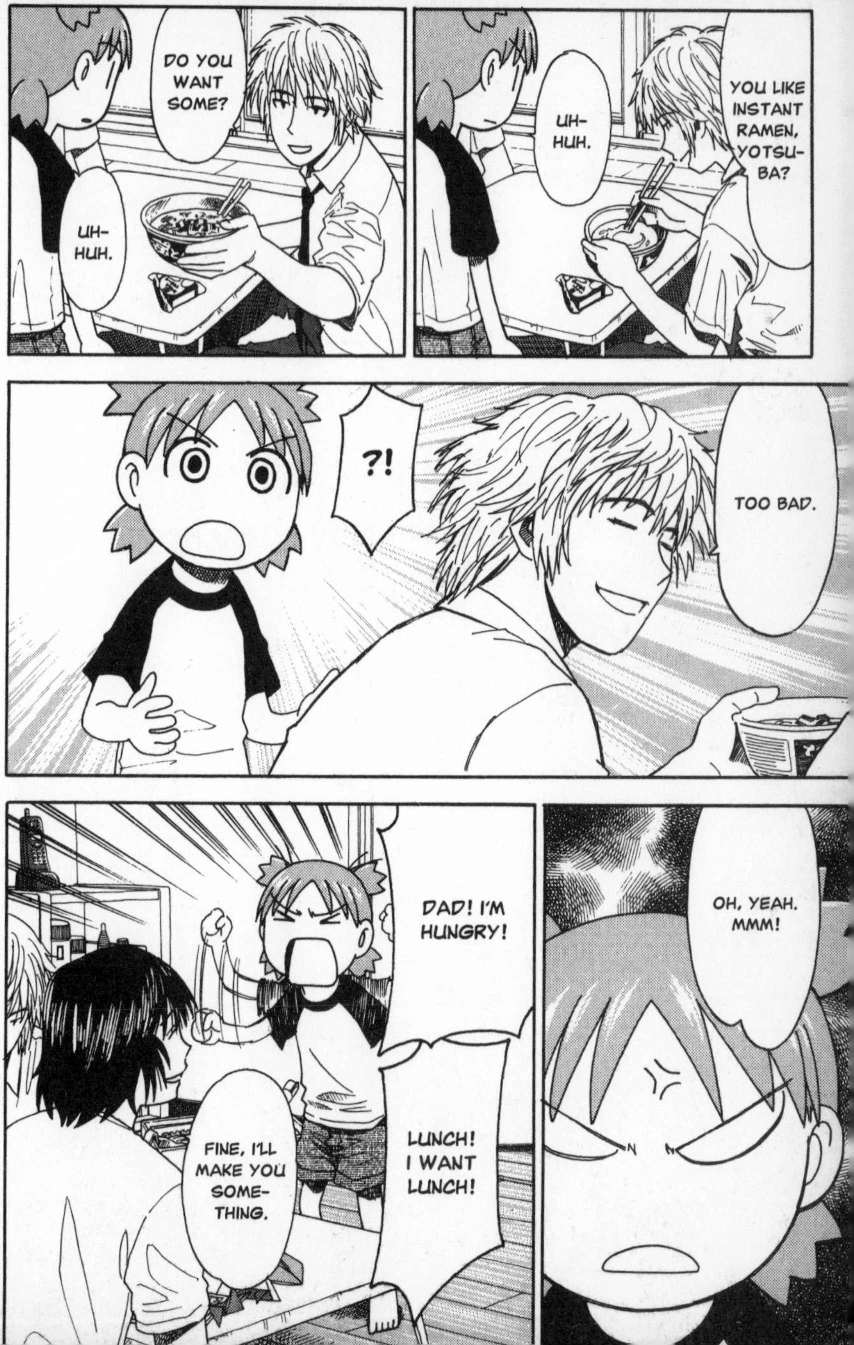
YOU LIKE INSTANT RAMEN, YOTSUBA?
UH-HUH.
DO YOU WANT SOME?
UH-HUH.
TOO BAD.
?!
OH, YEAH. MMM!
DAD! I'M HUNGRY!
LUNCH! I WANT LUNCH!
FINE, I'LL MAKE YOU SOMETHING.

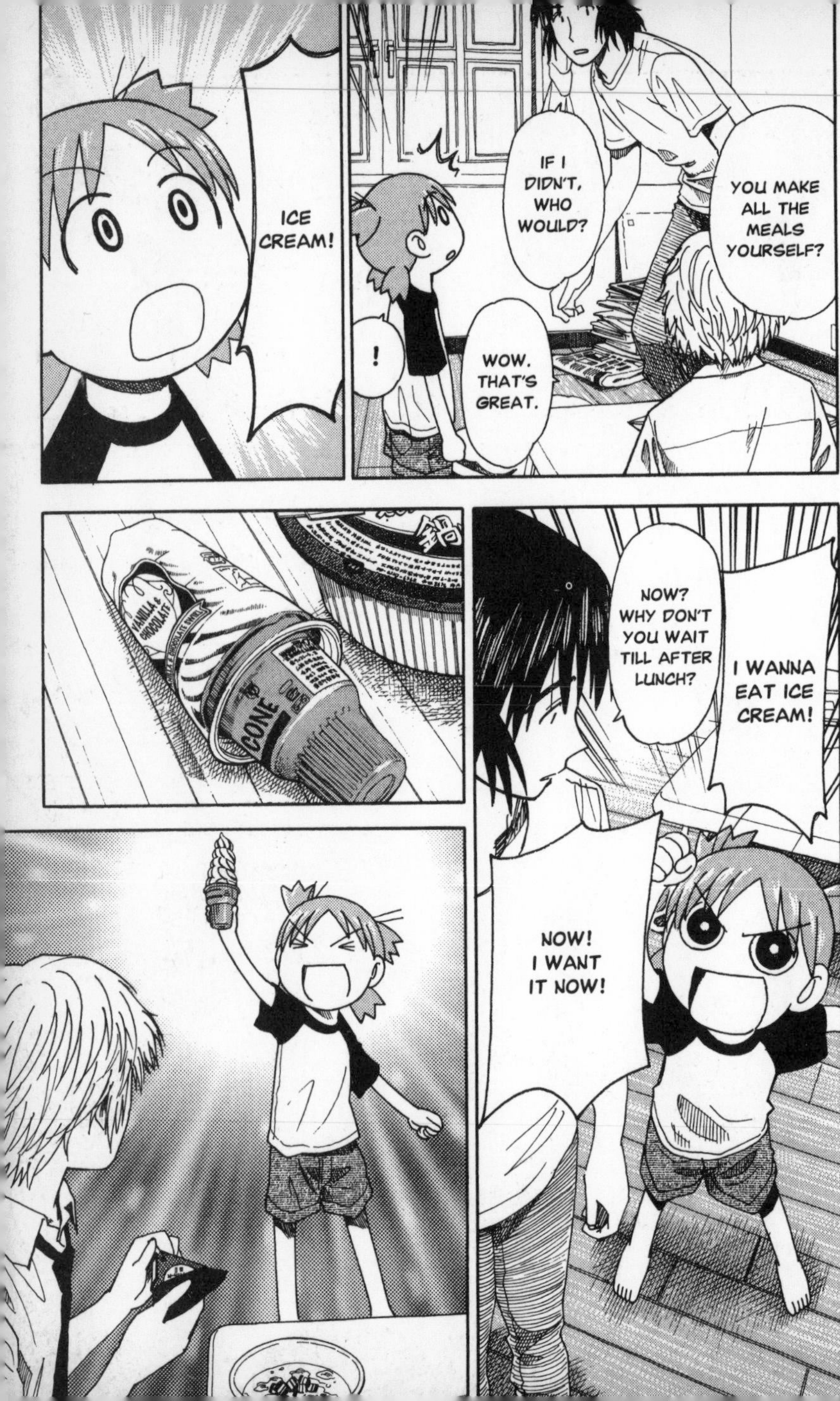
YOU MAKE ALL THE MEALS YOURSELF?
IF I DIDN'T, WHO WOULD?
WOW. THAT'S GREAT.
!
ICE CREAM!
I WANNA EAT ICE CREAM!
NOW? WHY DON'T YOU WAIT TILL AFTER LUNCH?
NOW! I WANT IT NOW!
VANILLA & CHOCOLATE
CONE

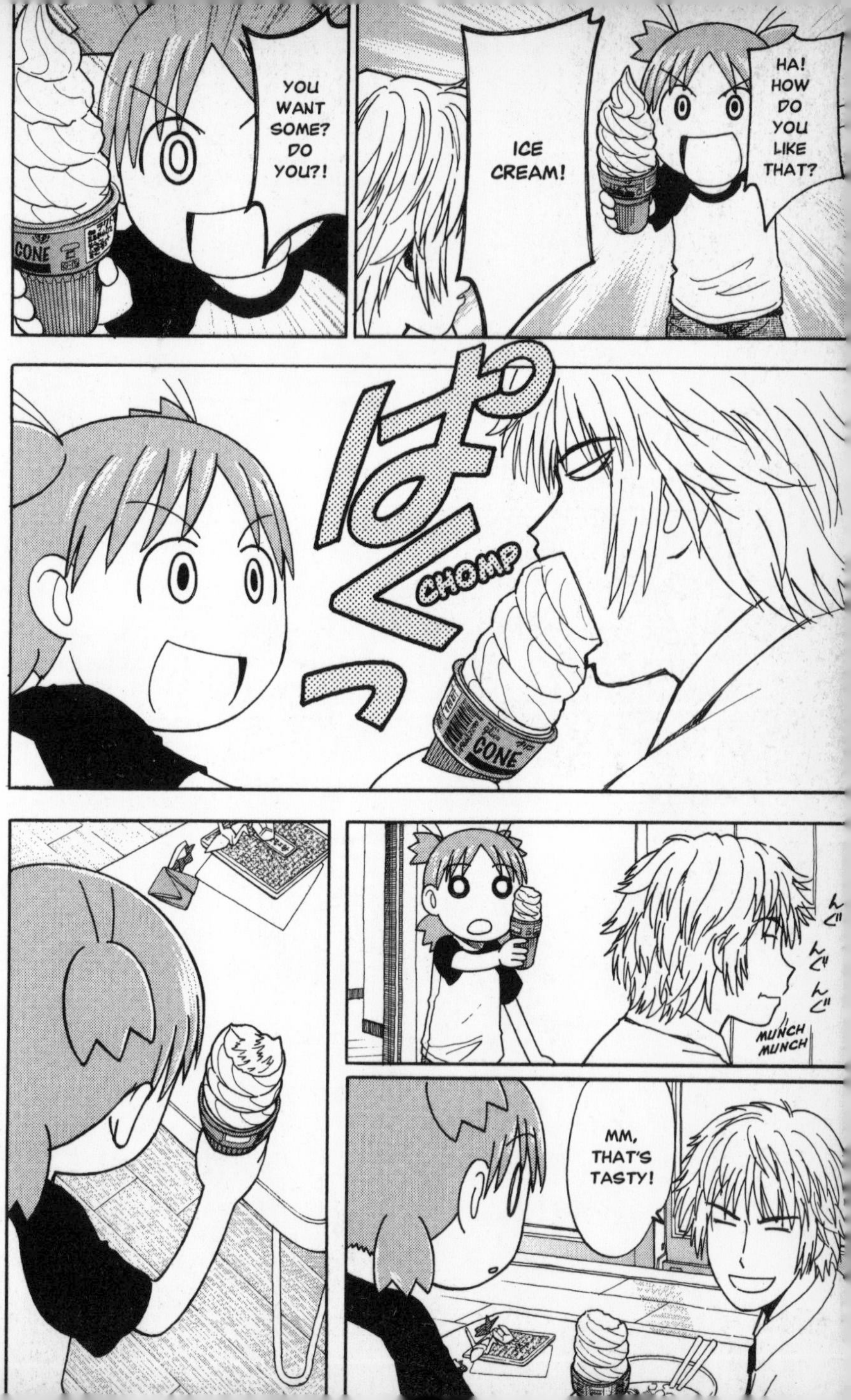
HA! HOW DO YOU LIKE THAT?
ICE CREAM!
YOU WANT SOME? DO YOU?!
ぱくっ
CHOMP
んぐ んぐ んぐ
MUNCH MUNCH
MM, THAT'S TASTY!

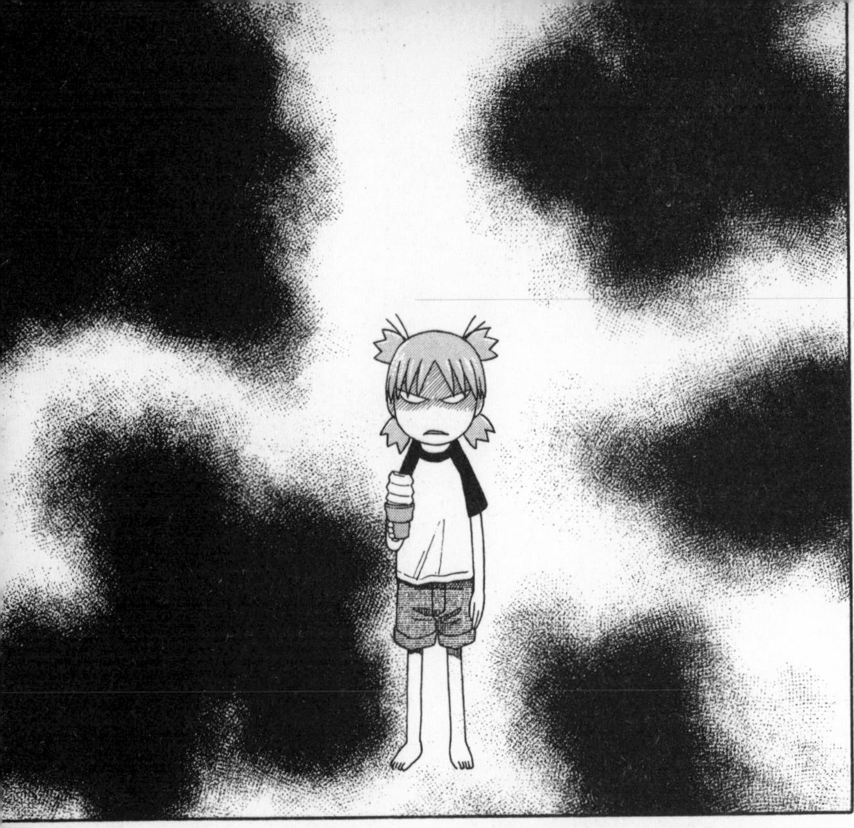

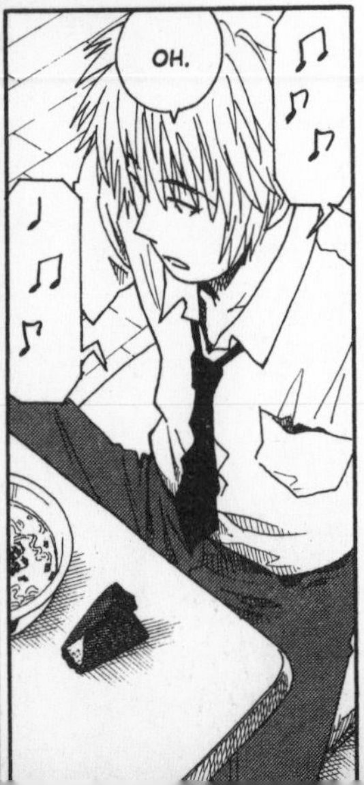
OH.

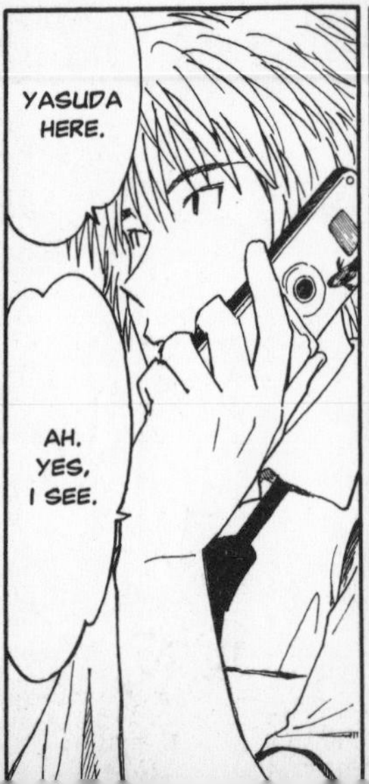
YASUDA HERE.
AH. YES, I SEE.

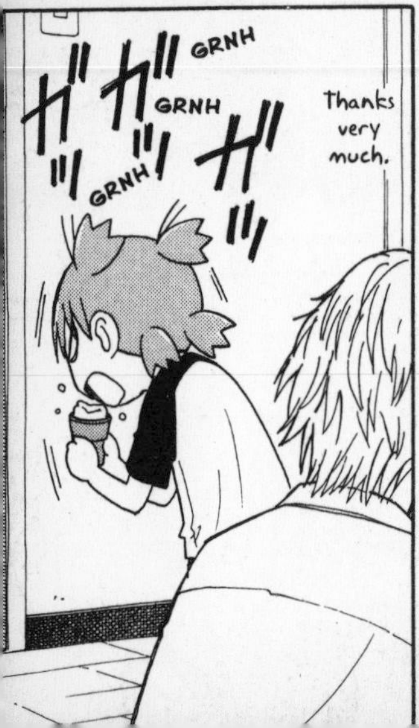
Thanks very much.
GRNH
GRNH
GRNH

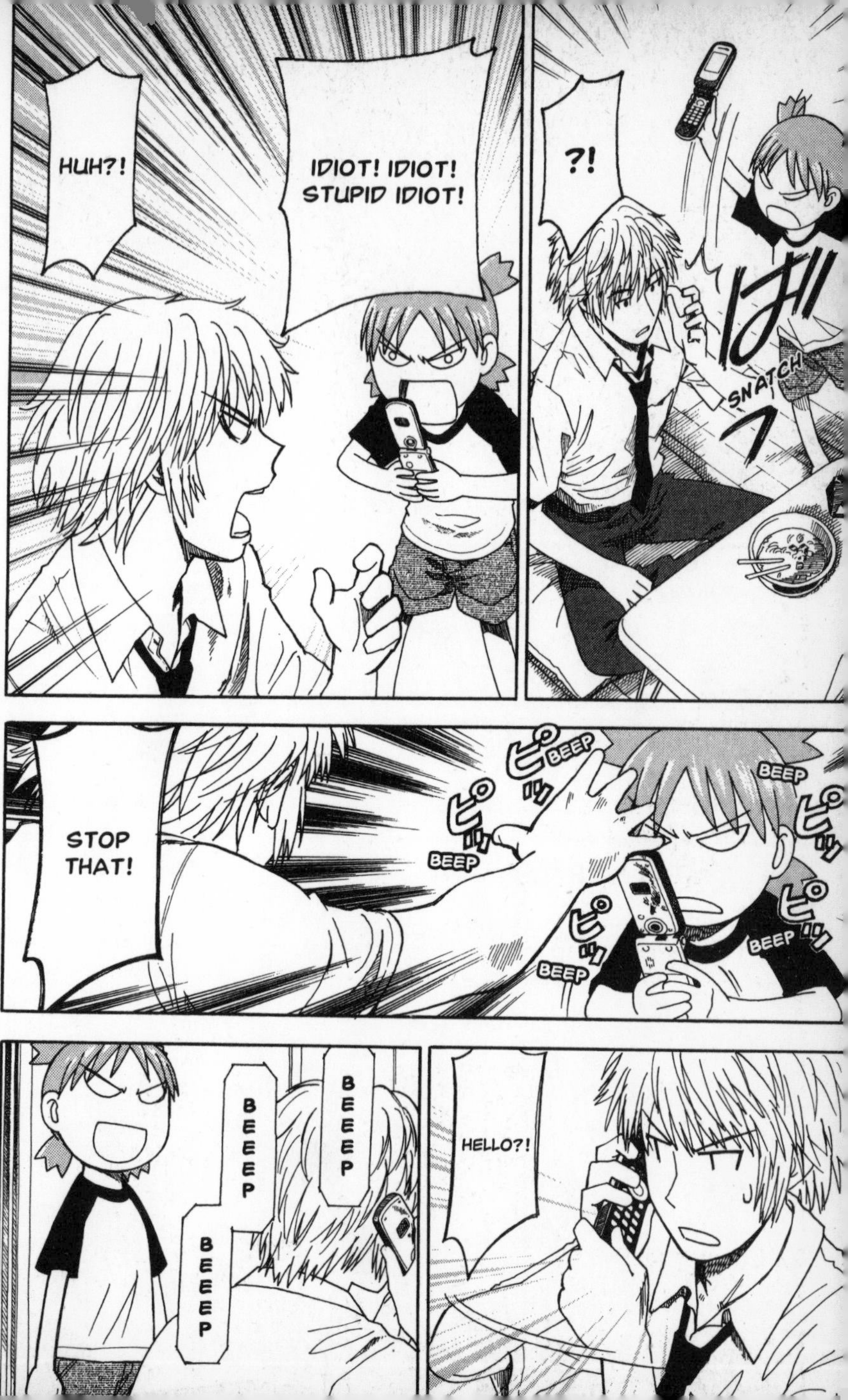
?!
SNATCH
HUH?!
IDIOT! IDIOT!
STUPID IDIOT!
BEEP
BEEP
BEEP
BEEP
BEEP
STOP THAT!
HELLO?!
BEEEP
BEEEP

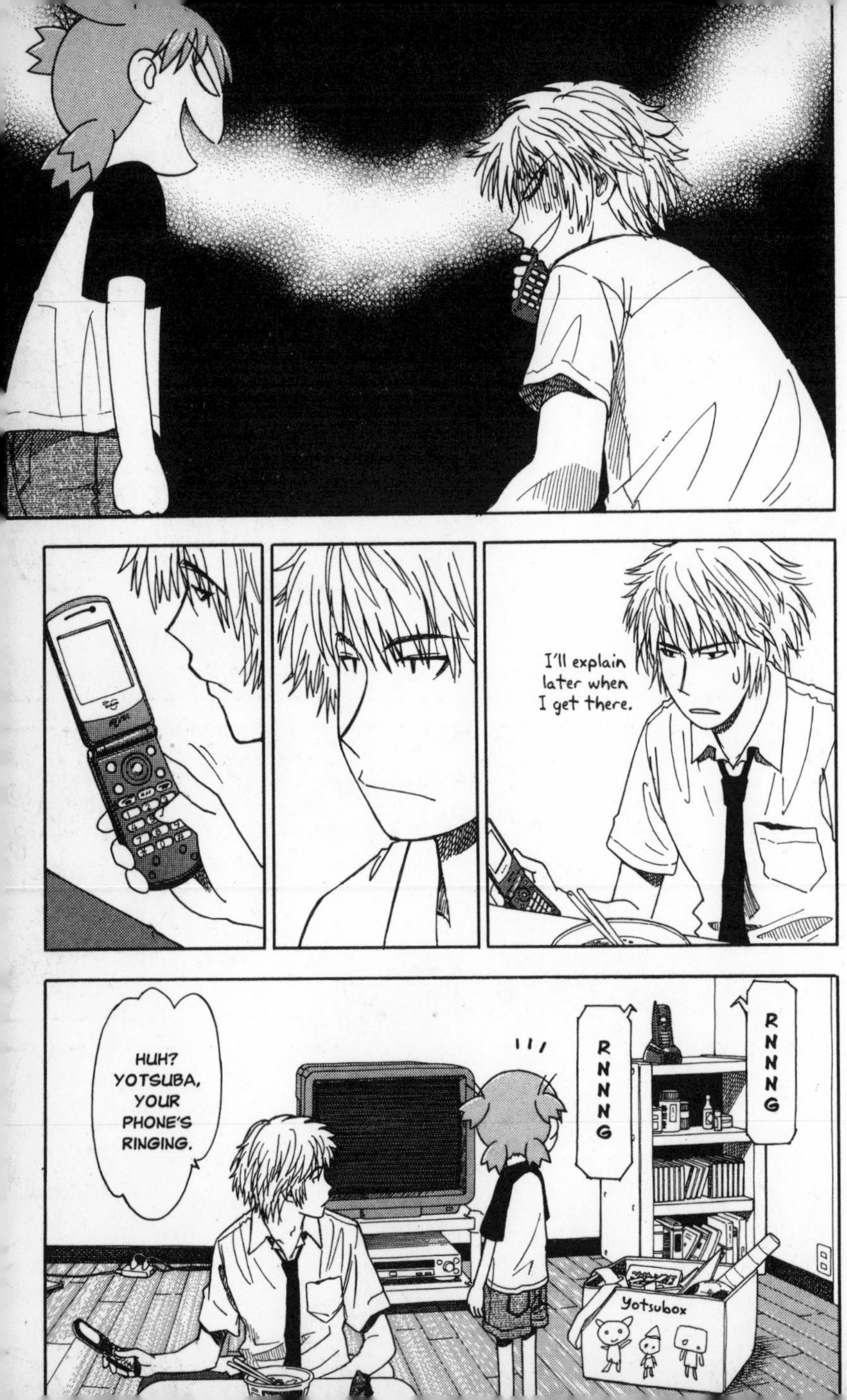
I'll explain later when I get there.
RNNNG
RNNNG
HUH? YOTSUBA, YOUR PHONE'S RINGING.
yotsubox

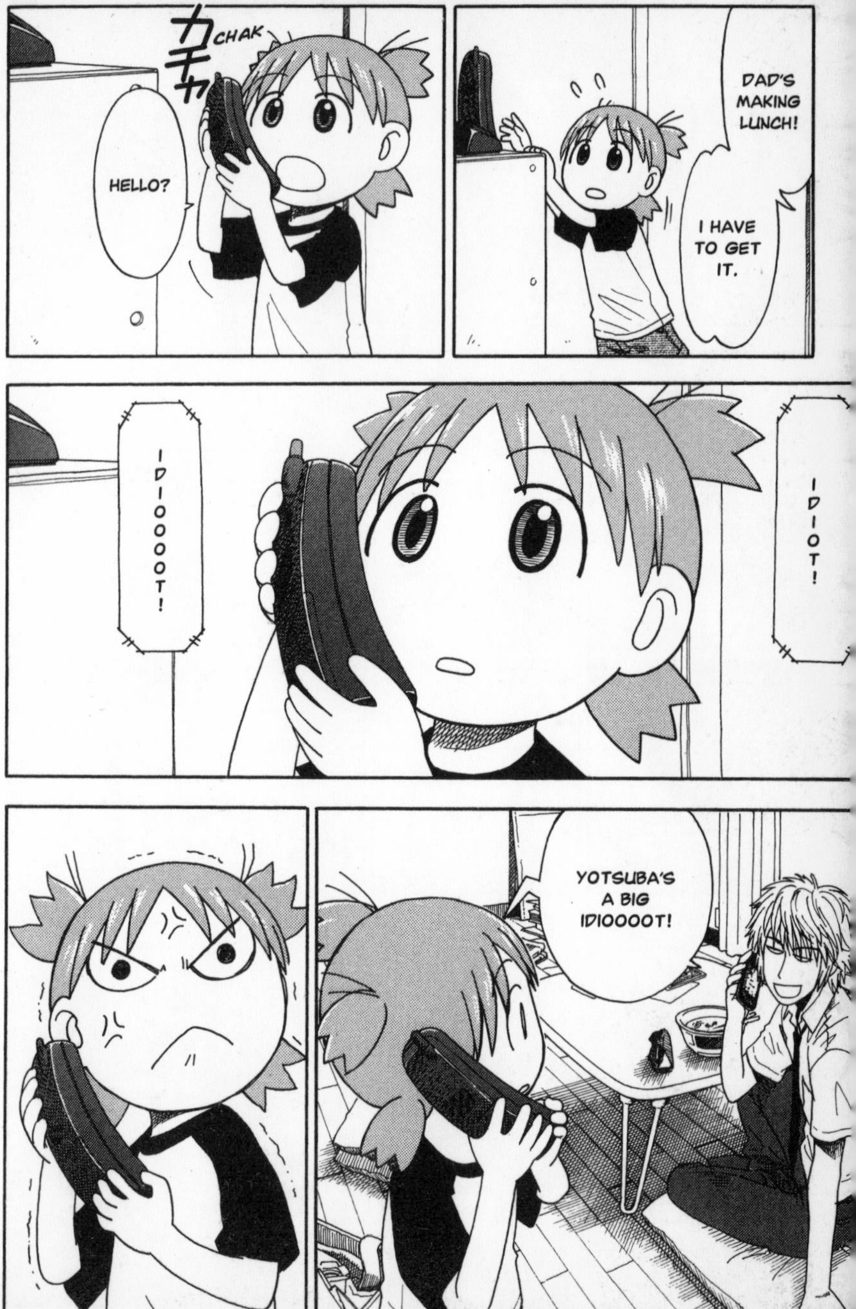
DAD'S MAKING LUNCH!
I HAVE TO GET IT.
CHAK
HELLO?
IDIOT!
IDIOOOOT!
YOTSUBA'S A BIG IDIOOOOT!

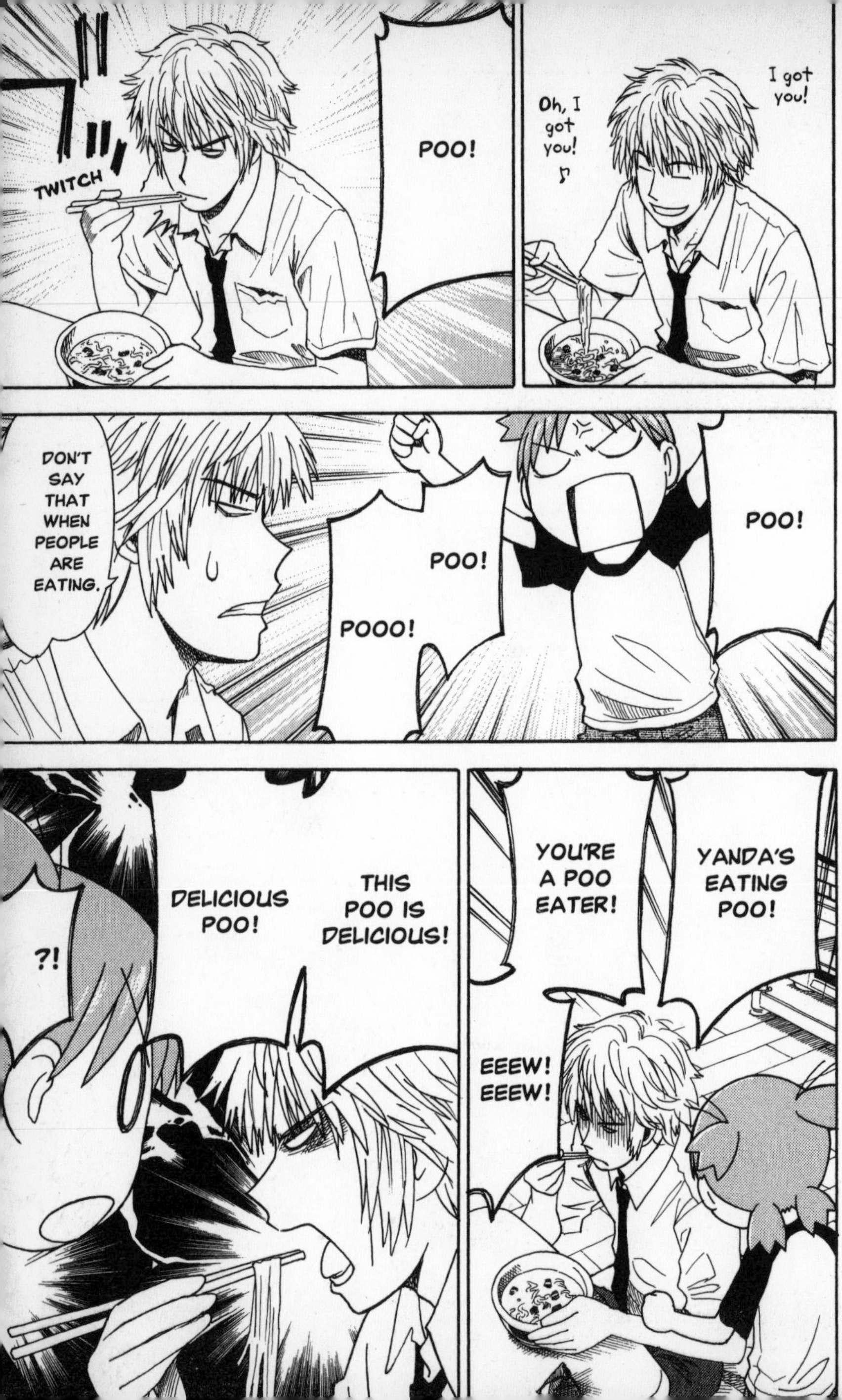
I got you!
Oh, I got you! ♪
POO!
TWITCH
POO!
POO!
POOO!
DON'T SAY THAT WHEN PEOPLE ARE EATING.
YANDA'S EATING POO!
YOU'RE A POO EATER!
EEEW! EEEW!
THIS POO IS DELICIOUS!
DELICIOUS POO!
?!

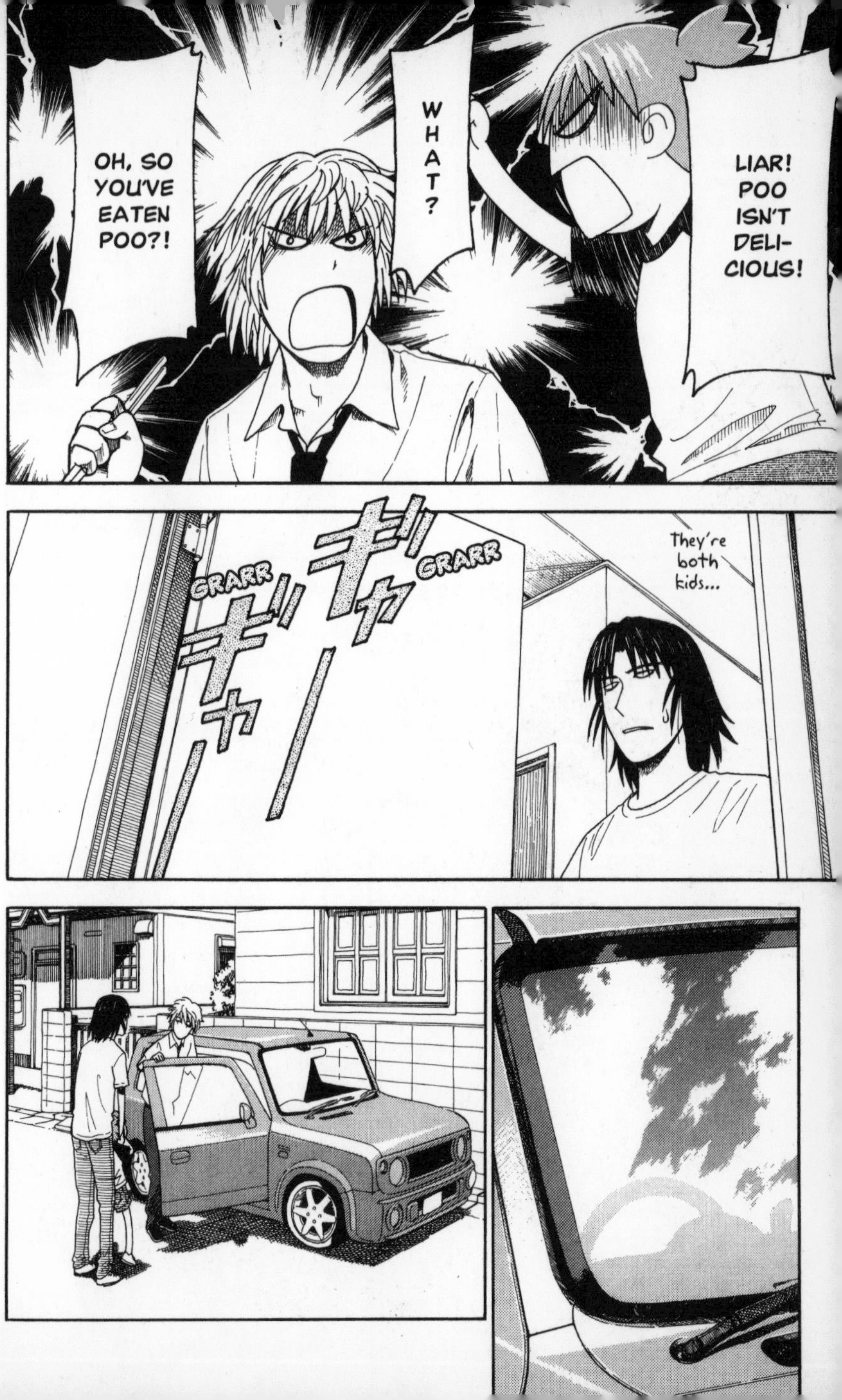
LIAR! POO ISN'T DELI- CIOUS!
WHAT?
OH, SO YOU'VE EATEN POO?!
They're both kids...
GRARR
GRARR

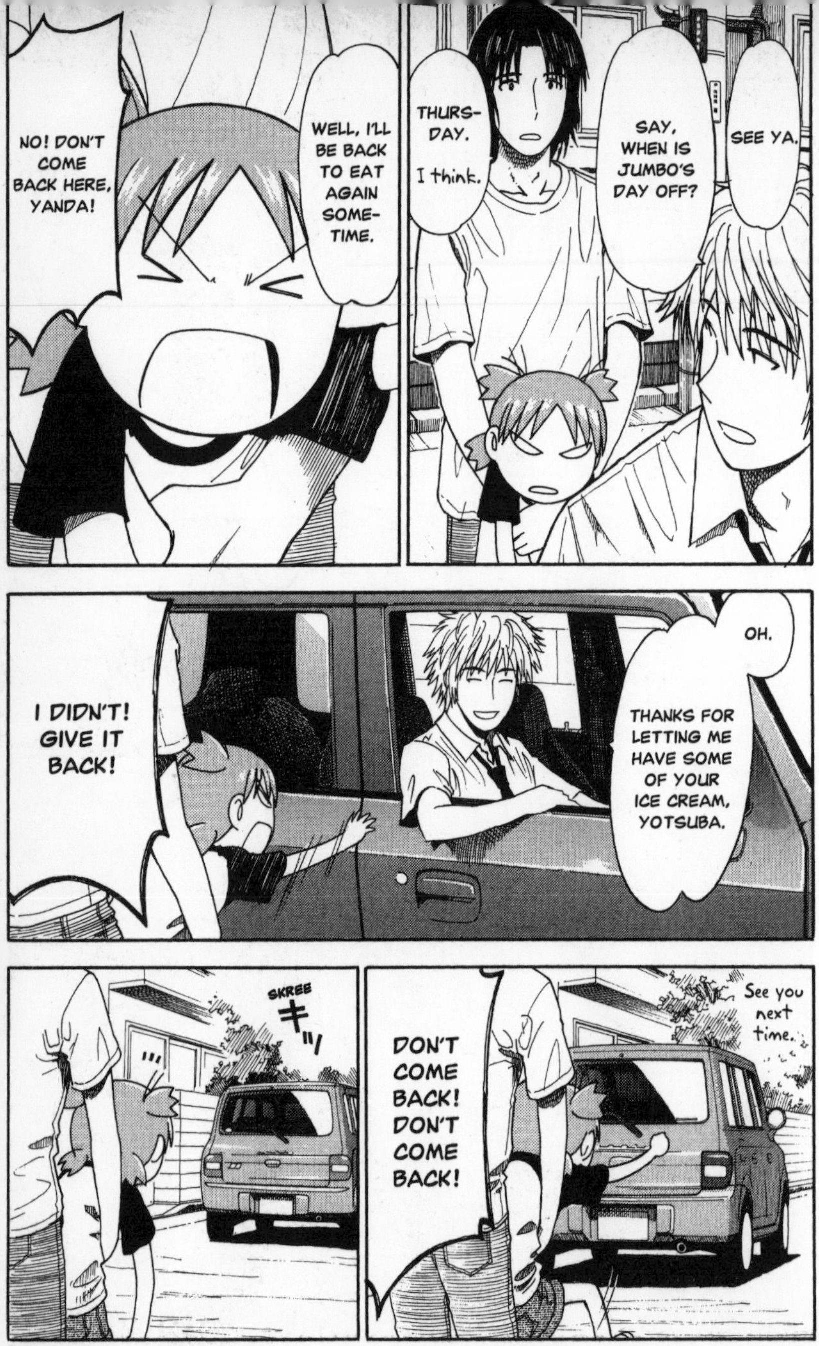
SEE YA.
SAY, WHEN IS JUMBO'S DAY OFF?
THURS-DAY.
I think.
WELL, I'LL BE BACK TO EAT AGAIN SOME-TIME.
NO! DON'T COME BACK HERE, YANDA!
OH.
THANKS FOR LETTING ME HAVE SOME OF YOUR ICE CREAM, YOTSUBA.
I DIDN'T! GIVE IT BACK!
See you next time.
DON'T COME BACK! DON'T COME BACK!
SKREE
...

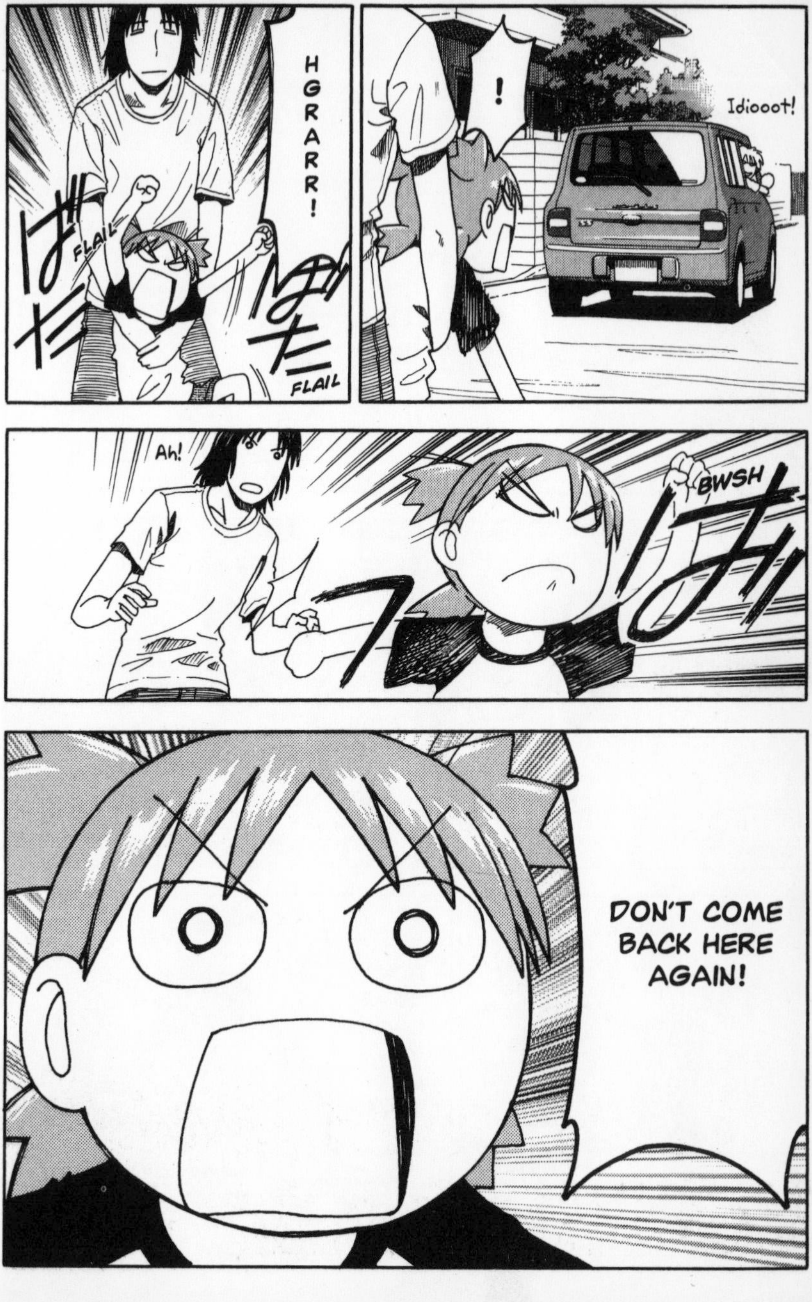
Idiooot!
!
HGRARR!
FLAIL
FLAIL
Ah!
BWSH
DON'T COME BACK HERE AGAIN!

YOTSUBA&!

YOTSUBA & STARS

CHAPTER 31

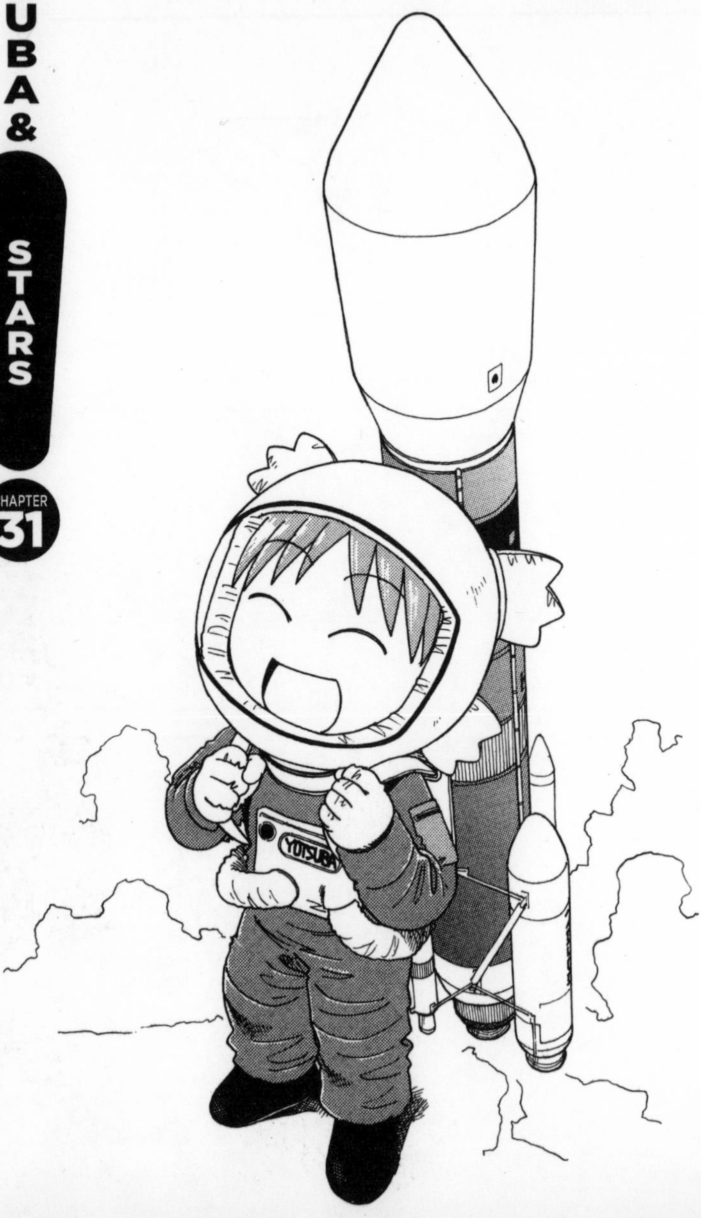
YOTSUBA

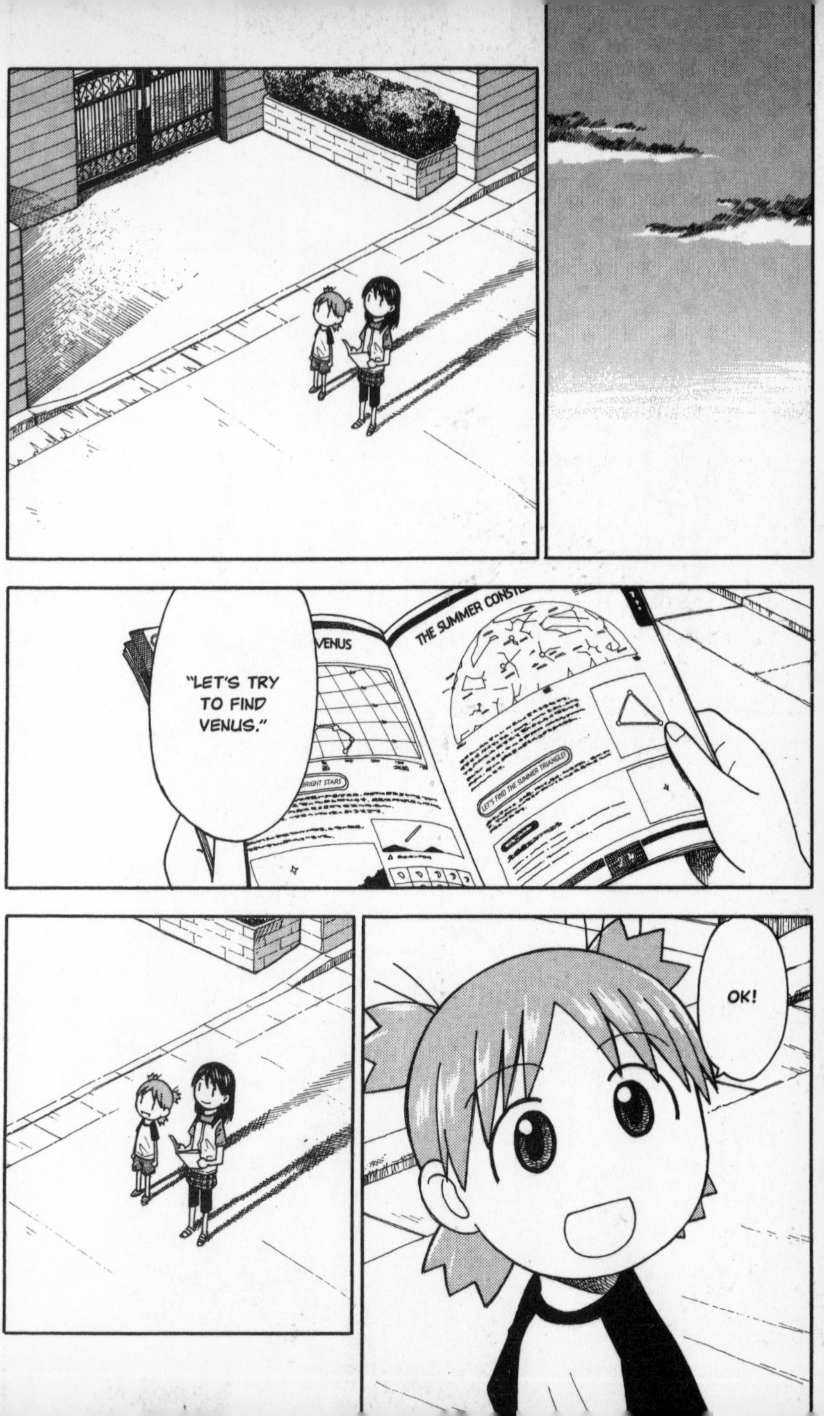
THE SUMMER CONSTE
VENUS
BRIGHT STARS
LET'S FIND THE SUMMER TRIANGLE!
"LET'S TRY TO FIND VENUS."
OK!

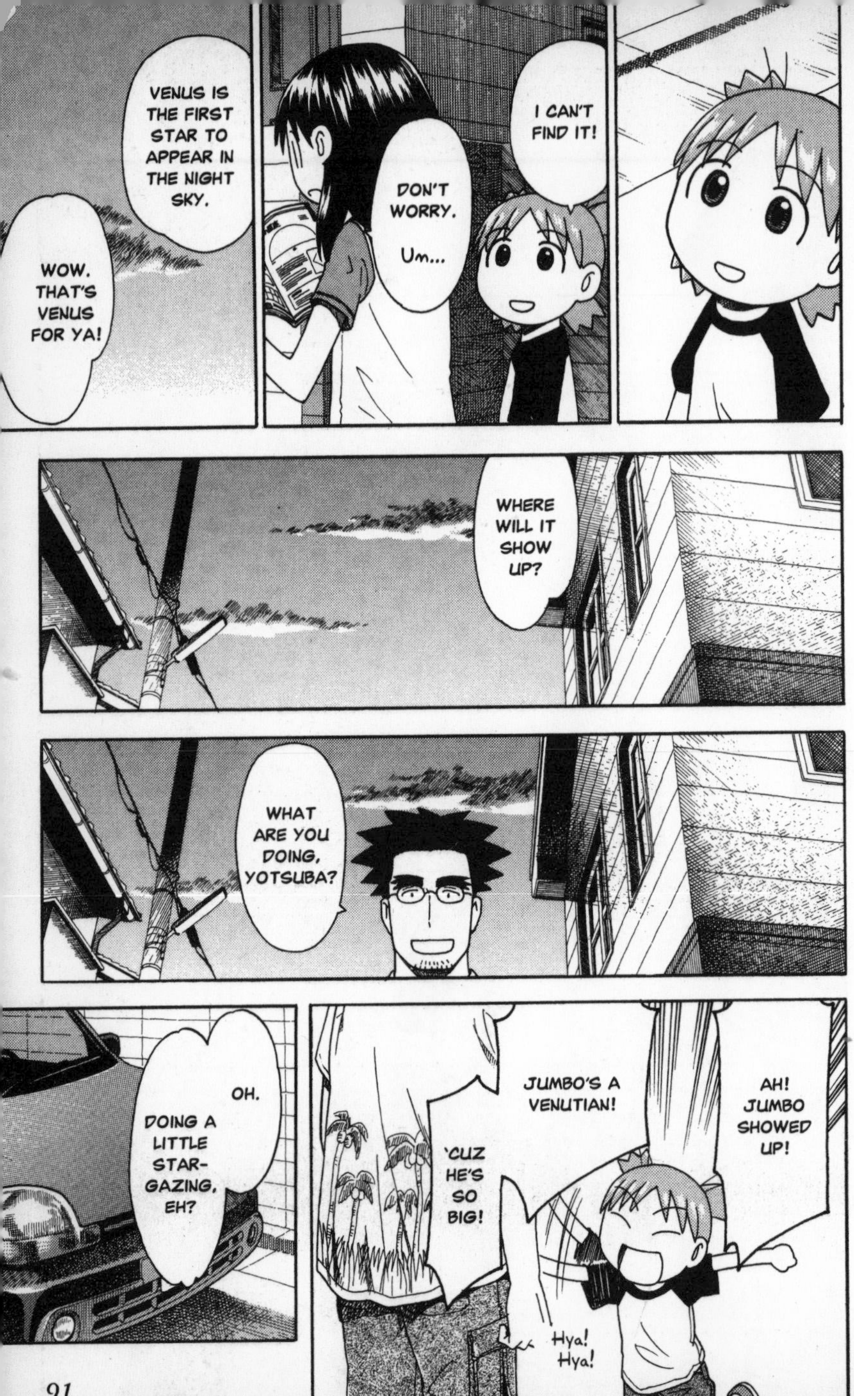
I CAN'T FIND IT!
DON'T WORRY.
Um...
VENUS IS THE FIRST STAR TO APPEAR IN THE NIGHT SKY.
WOW. THAT'S VENUS FOR YA!
WHERE WILL IT SHOW UP?
WHAT ARE YOU DOING, YOTSUBA?
AH! JUMBO SHOWED UP!
JUMBO'S A VENUTIAN!
'CUZ HE'S SO BIG!
Hya! Hya!
OH.
DOING A LITTLE STAR-GAZING, EH?

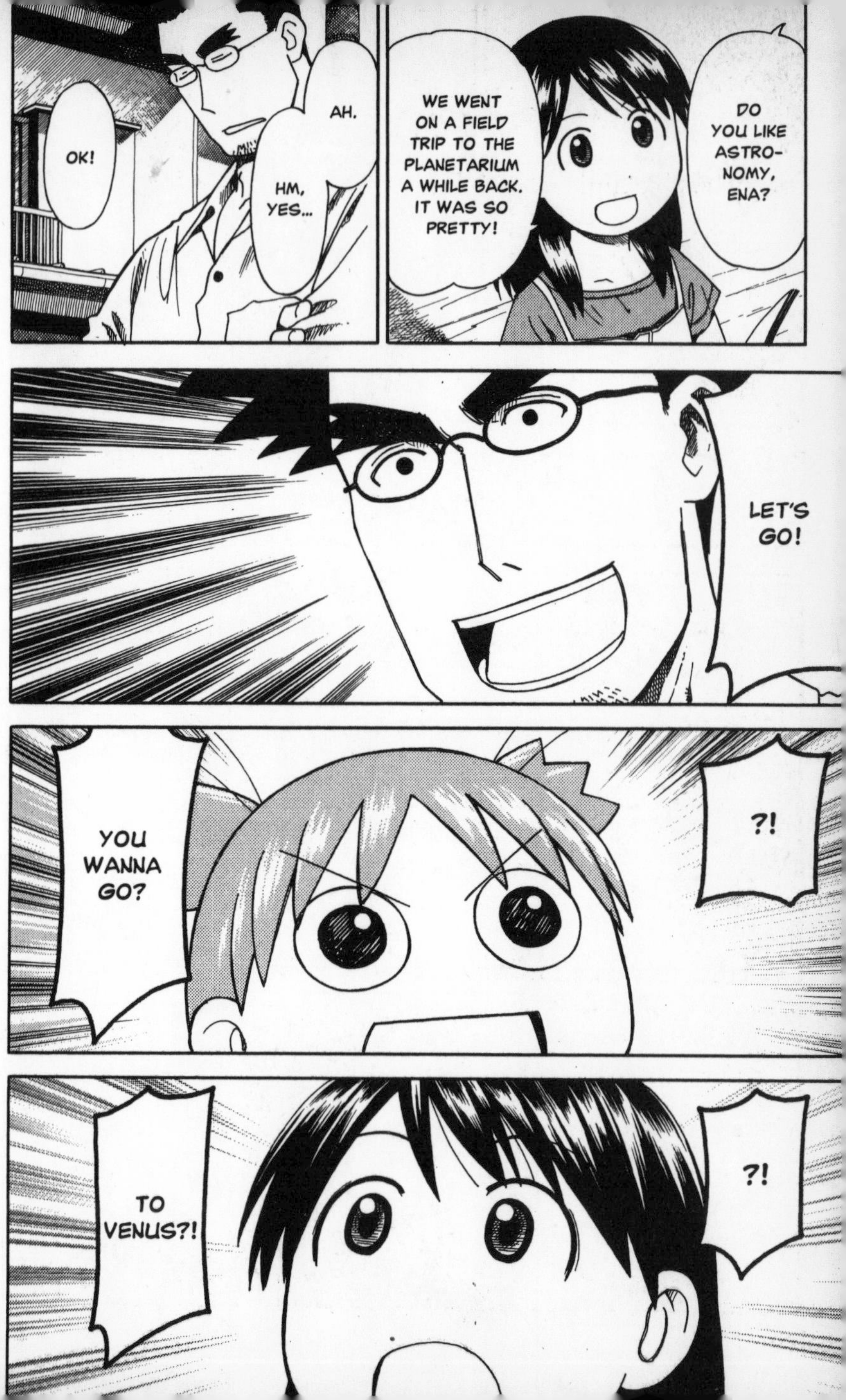
DO YOU LIKE ASTRO-NOMY, ENA?
WE WENT ON A FIELD TRIP TO THE PLANETARIUM A WHILE BACK. IT WAS SO PRETTY!
AH.
HM, YES...
OK!
LET'S GO!
?!
YOU WANNA GO?
?!
TO VENUS?!

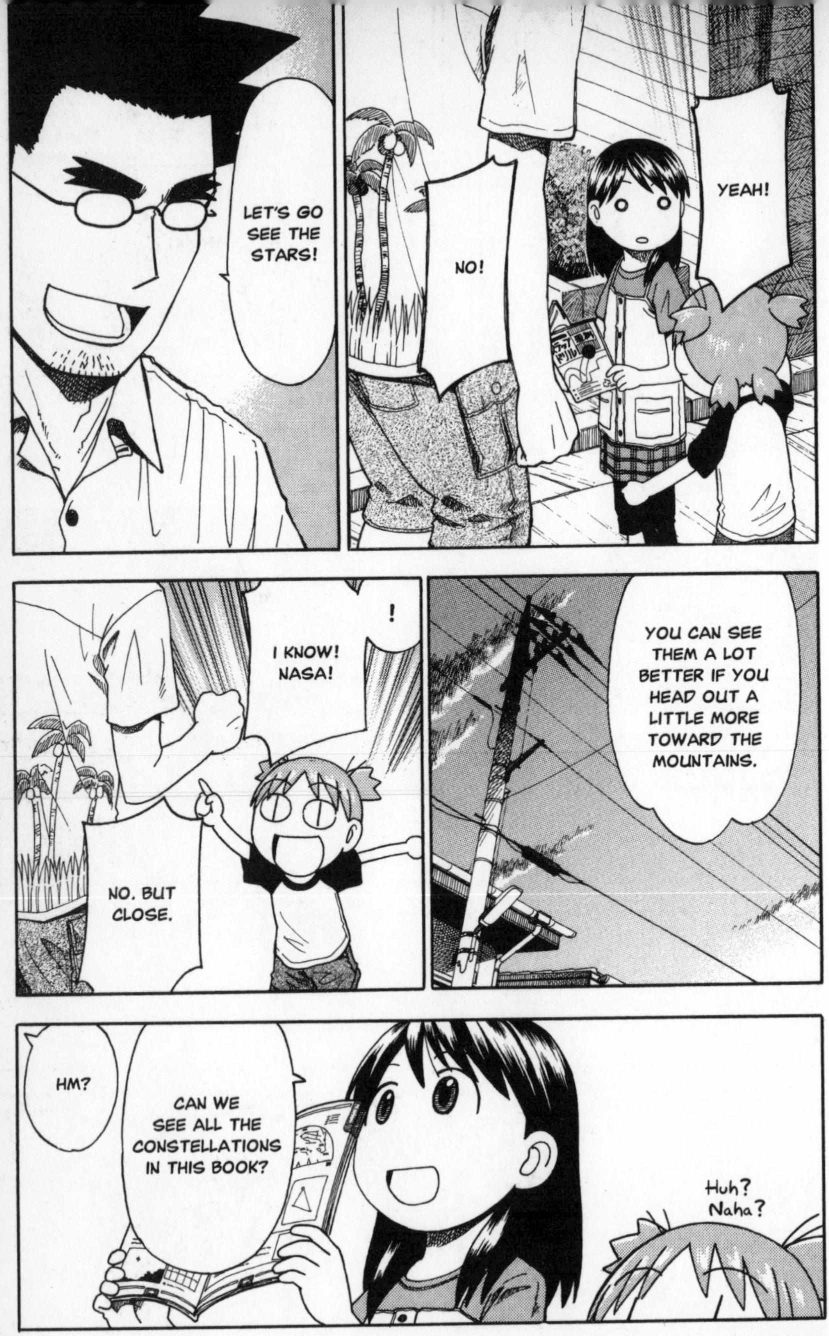
LET'S GO SEE THE STARS!
NO!
YEAH!
!
I KNOW! NASA!
NO. BUT CLOSE.
YOU CAN SEE THEM A LOT BETTER IF YOU HEAD OUT A LITTLE MORE TOWARD THE MOUNTAINS.
HM?
CAN WE SEE ALL THE CONSTELLATIONS IN THIS BOOK?
Huh? Naha?

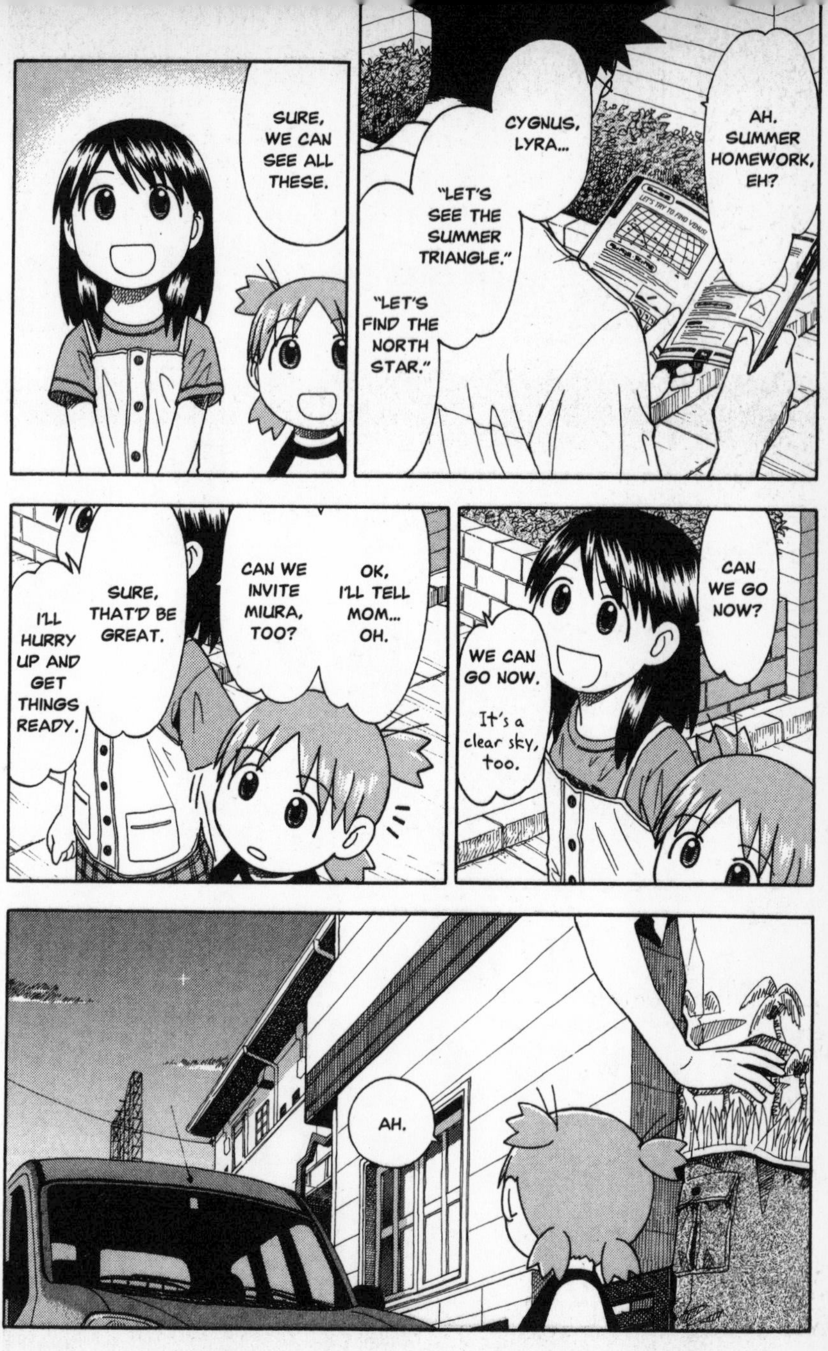
AH. SUMMER HOMEWORK, EH?
CYGNUS, LYRA...
"LET'S SEE THE SUMMER TRIANGLE."
"LET'S FIND THE NORTH STAR."
LET'S TRY TO FIND VENUS!
SURE, WE CAN SEE ALL THESE.
CAN WE GO NOW?
WE CAN GO NOW.
It's a clear sky, too.
OK, I'LL TELL MOM... OH.
CAN WE INVITE MIURA, TOO?
SURE, THAT'D BE GREAT.
I'LL HURRY UP AND GET THINGS READY.
AH.

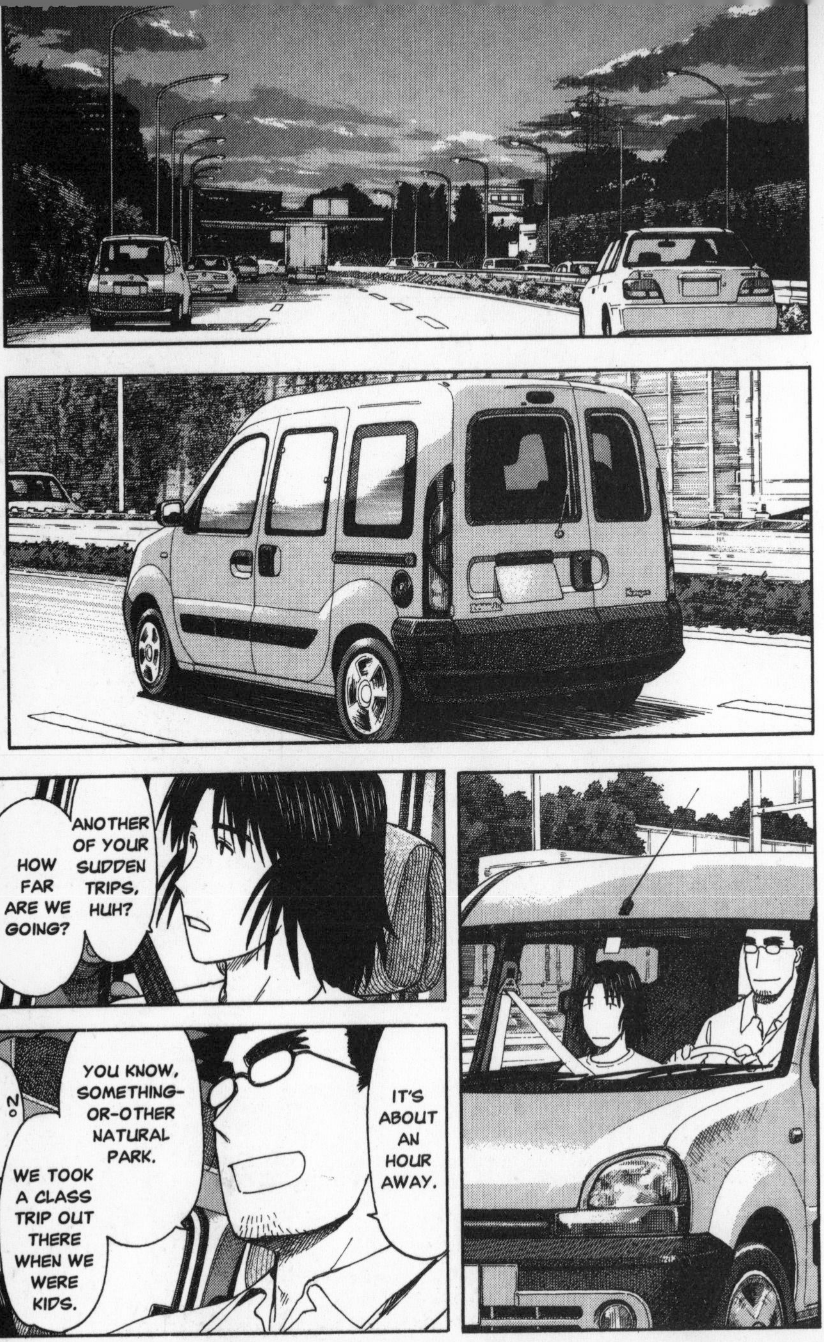
ANOTHER OF YOUR SUDDEN TRIPS, HUH?
HOW FAR ARE WE GOING?
IT'S ABOUT AN HOUR AWAY.
YOU KNOW, SOMETHING-OR-OTHER NATURAL PARK.
WE TOOK A CLASS TRIP OUT THERE WHEN WE WERE KIDS.
No

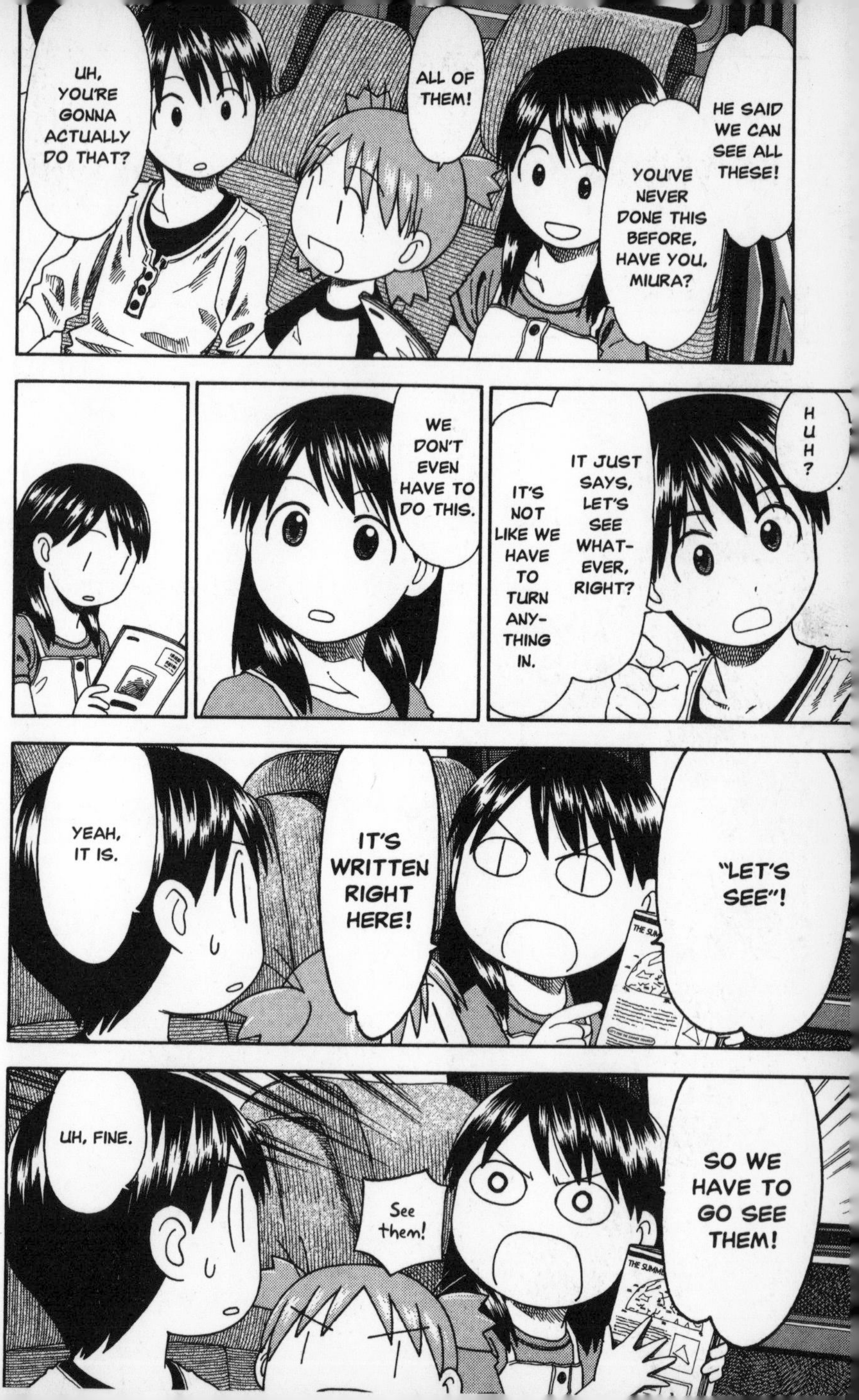
HE SAID WE CAN SEE ALL THESE!
YOU'VE NEVER DONE THIS BEFORE, HAVE YOU, MIURA?
ALL OF THEM!
UH, YOU'RE GONNA ACTUALLY DO THAT?
HUH?
IT JUST SAYS, LET'S SEE WHAT-EVER, RIGHT?
IT'S NOT LIKE WE HAVE TO TURN ANY-THING IN.
WE DON'T EVEN HAVE TO DO THIS.
"LET'S SEE"!
IT'S WRITTEN RIGHT HERE!
YEAH, IT IS.
SO WE HAVE TO GO SEE THEM!
See them!
UH, FINE.

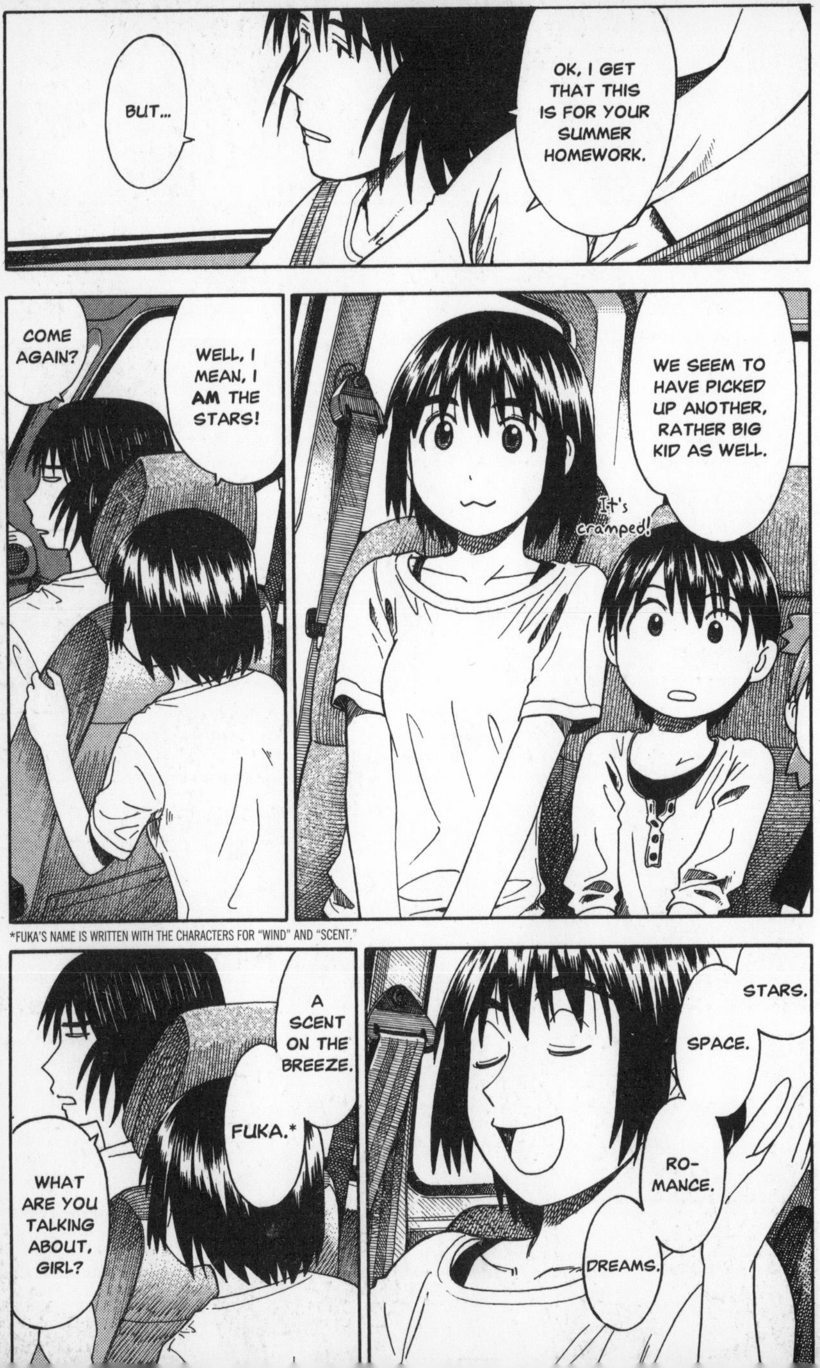
OK, I GET THAT THIS IS FOR YOUR SUMMER HOMEWORK.
BUT...
WE SEEM TO HAVE PICKED UP ANOTHER, RATHER BIG KID AS WELL.
It's cramped!
WELL, I MEAN, I AM THE STARS!
COME AGAIN?
STARS.
SPACE.
RO-MANCE.
DREAMS.
A SCENT ON THE BREEZE.
FUKA.*
WHAT ARE YOU TALKING ABOUT, GIRL?

*FUKA'S NAME IS WRITTEN WITH THE CHARACTERS FOR "WIND" AND "SCENT."

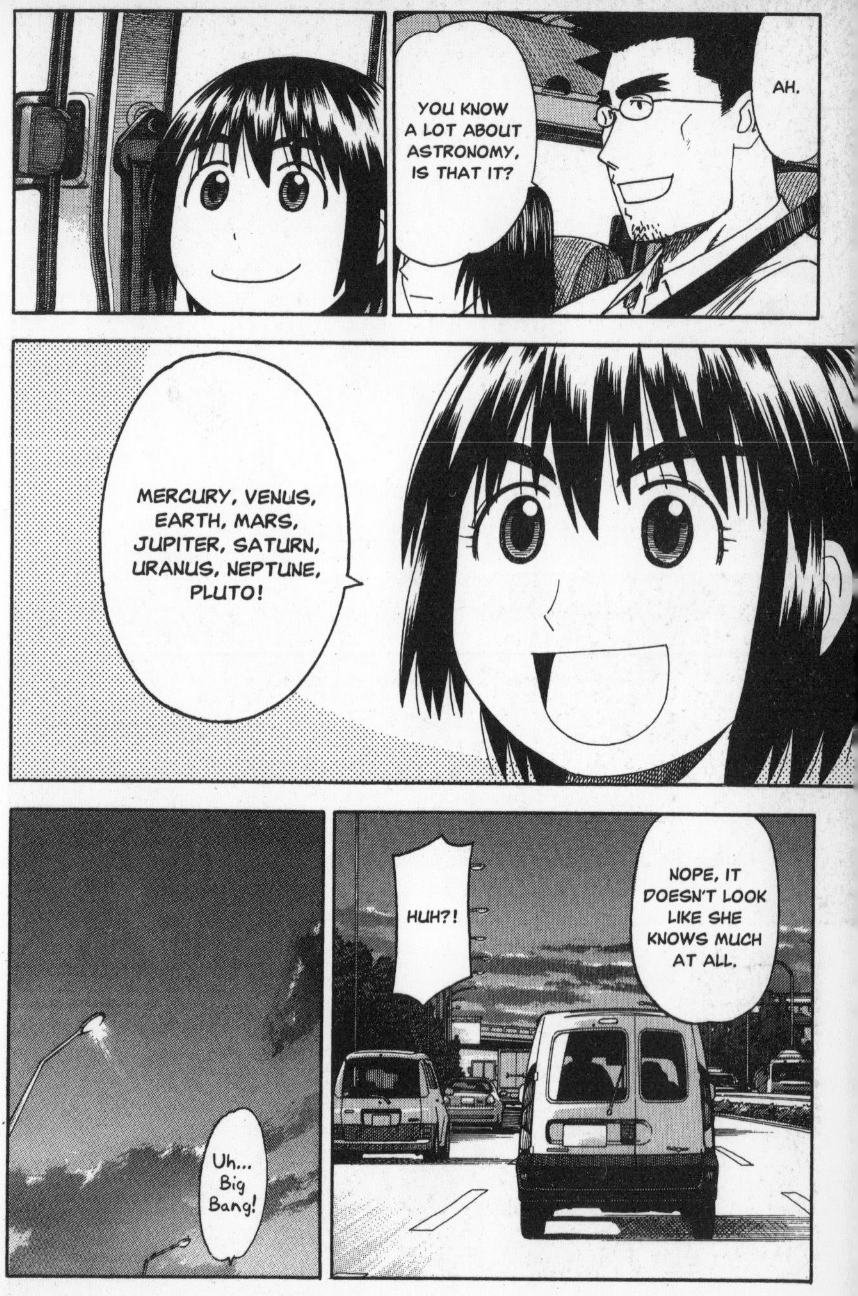
YOU KNOW A LOT ABOUT ASTRONOMY, IS THAT IT?
AH.
MERCURY, VENUS, EARTH, MARS, JUPITER, SATURN, URANUS, NEPTUNE, PLUTO!
Uh... Big Bang!
HUH?!
NOPE, IT DOESN'T LOOK LIKE SHE KNOWS MUCH AT ALL.

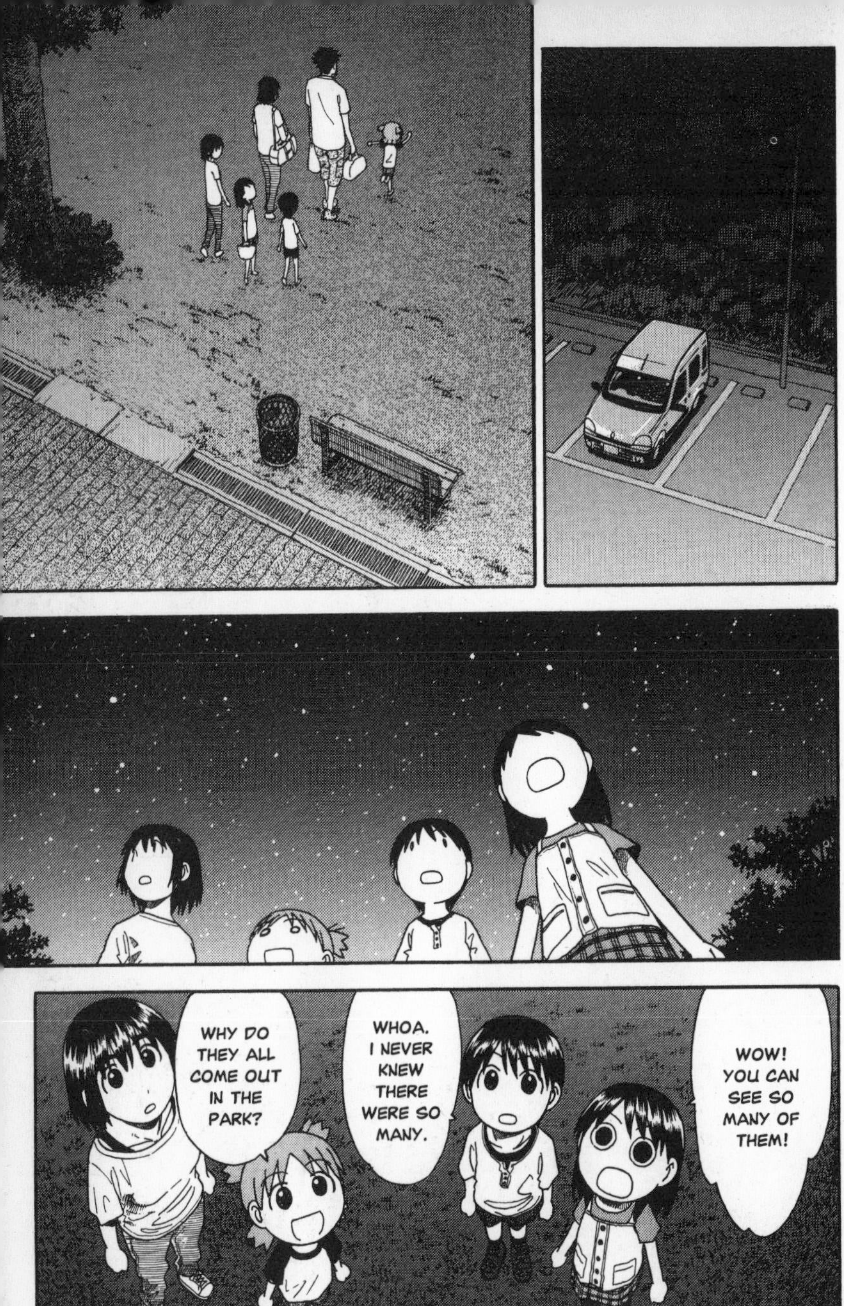
WOW! YOU CAN SEE SO MANY OF THEM!
WHOA. I NEVER KNEW THERE WERE SO MANY.
WHY DO THEY ALL COME OUT IN THE PARK?

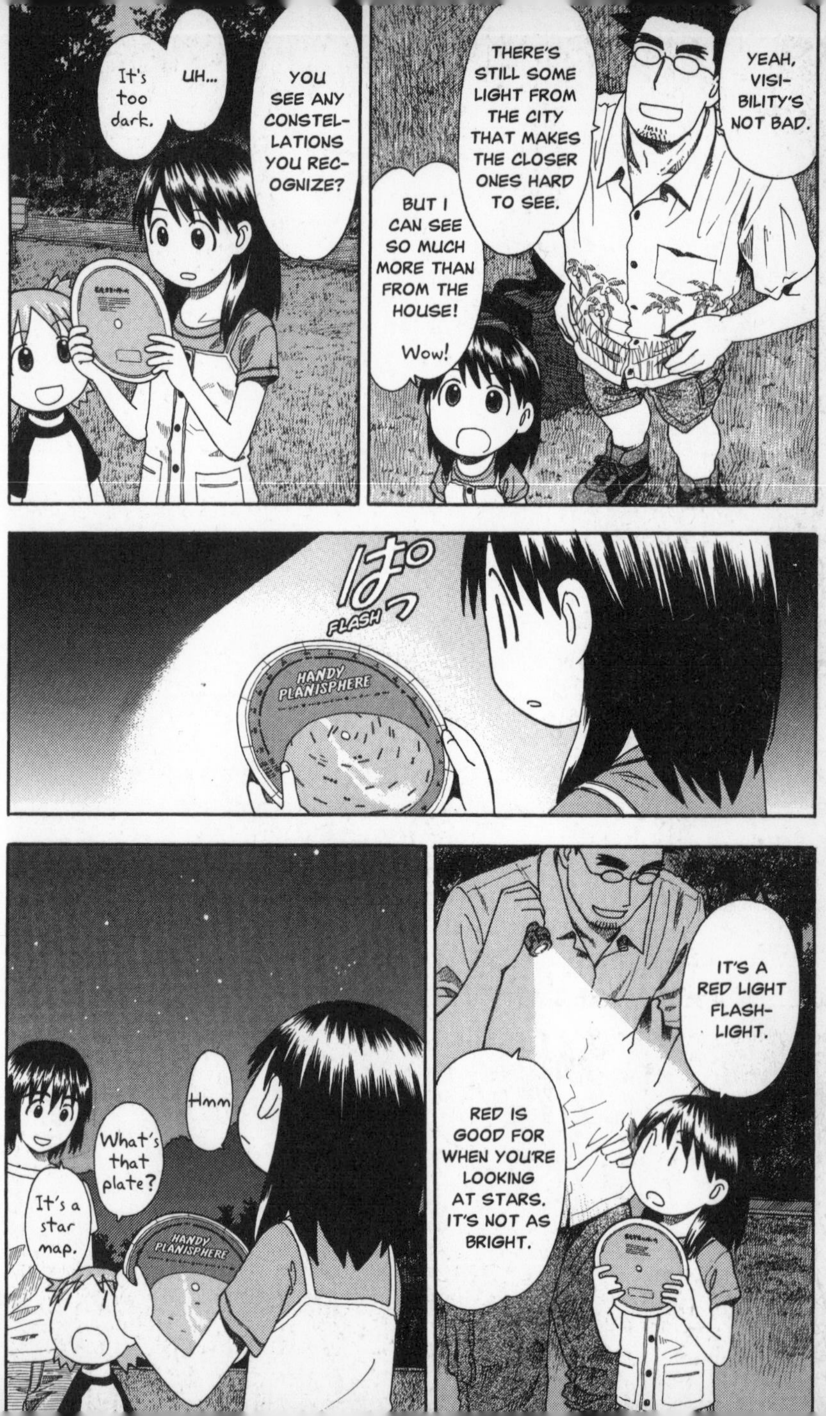
YEAH, VISIBILITY'S NOT BAD.
THERE'S STILL SOME LIGHT FROM THE CITY THAT MAKES THE CLOSER ONES HARD TO SEE.
BUT I CAN SEE SO MUCH MORE THAN FROM THE HOUSE!
Wow!
YOU SEE ANY CONSTELLATIONS YOU RECOGNIZE?
UH...
It's too dark.
ぱっ
FLASH
HANDY PLANISPHERE
IT'S A RED LIGHT FLASHLIGHT.
RED IS GOOD FOR WHEN YOU'RE LOOKING AT STARS. IT'S NOT AS BRIGHT.
Hmm
What's that plate?
It's a star map.
HANDY PLANISPHERE

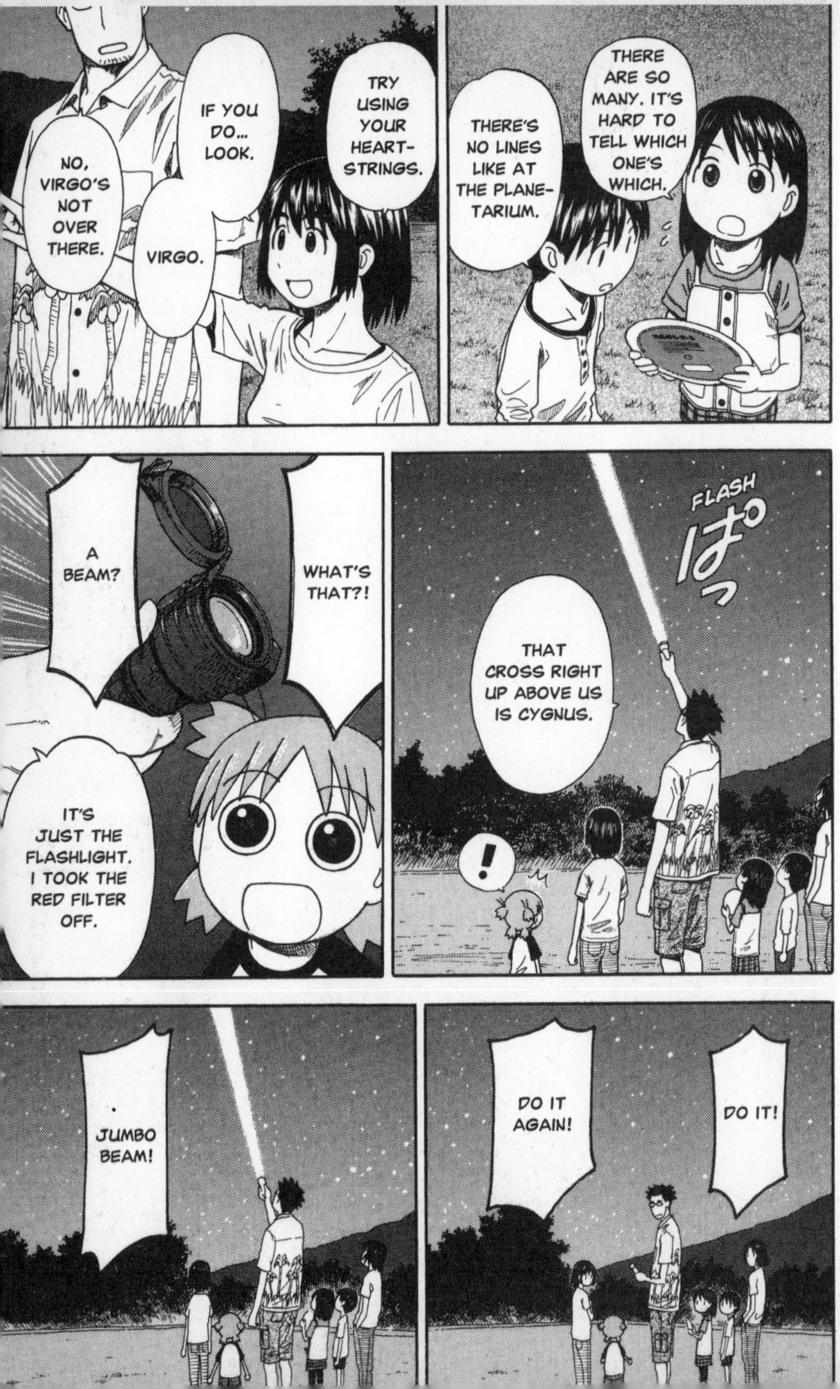
THERE ARE SO MANY. IT'S HARD TO TELL WHICH ONE'S WHICH.
THERE'S NO LINES LIKE AT THE PLANETARIUM.
TRY USING YOUR HEART-STRINGS.
IF YOU DO... LOOK.
VIRGO.
NO, VIRGO'S NOT OVER THERE.
FLASH
ぱっ
THAT CROSS RIGHT UP ABOVE US IS CYGNUS.
!
WHAT'S THAT?!
A BEAM?
IT'S JUST THE FLASHLIGHT. I TOOK THE RED FILTER OFF.
DO IT!
DO IT AGAIN!
JUMBO BEAM!

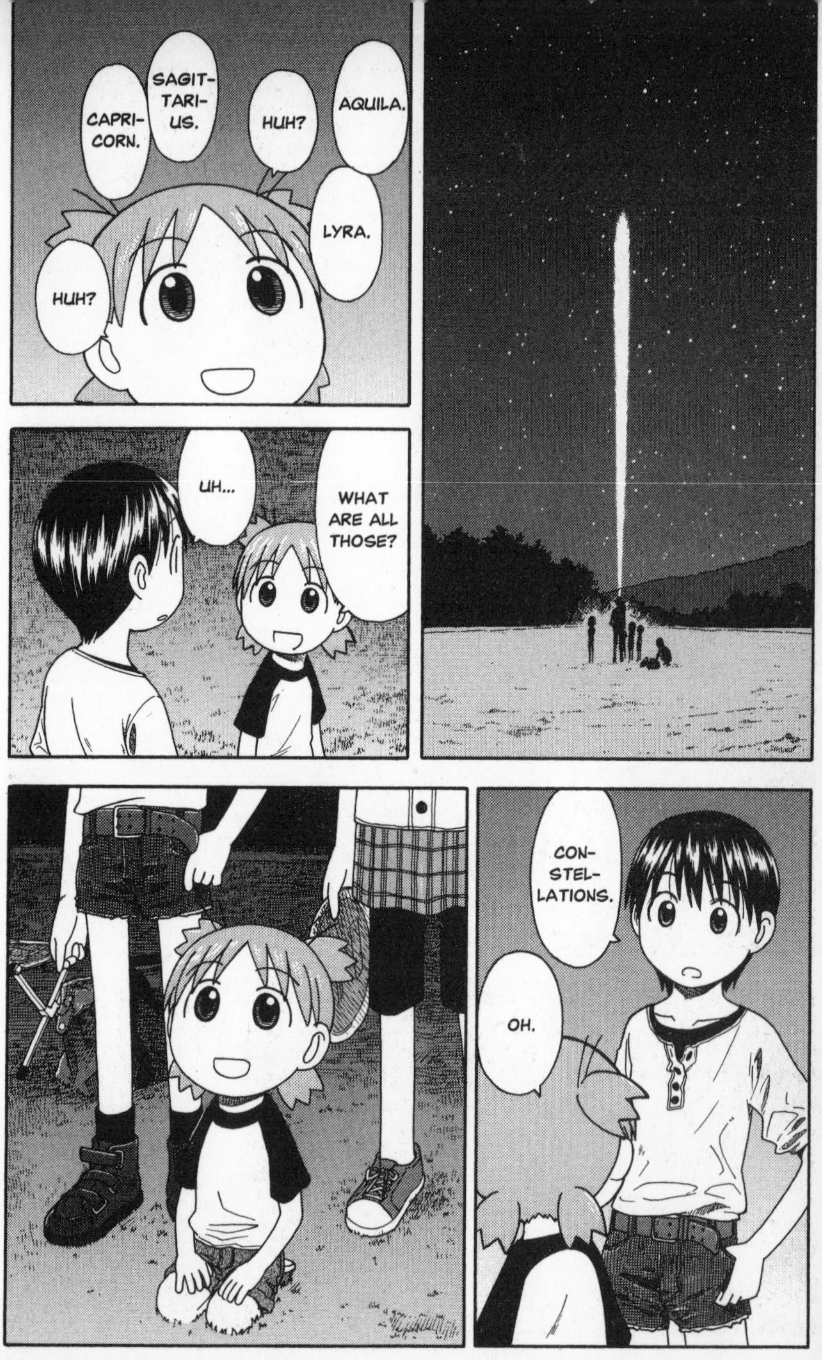
AQUILA.
HUH?
SAGIT-TARI-US.
CAPRI-CORN.
LYRA.
HUH?
WHAT ARE ALL THOSE?
UH...
CON-STEL-LATIONS.
OH.

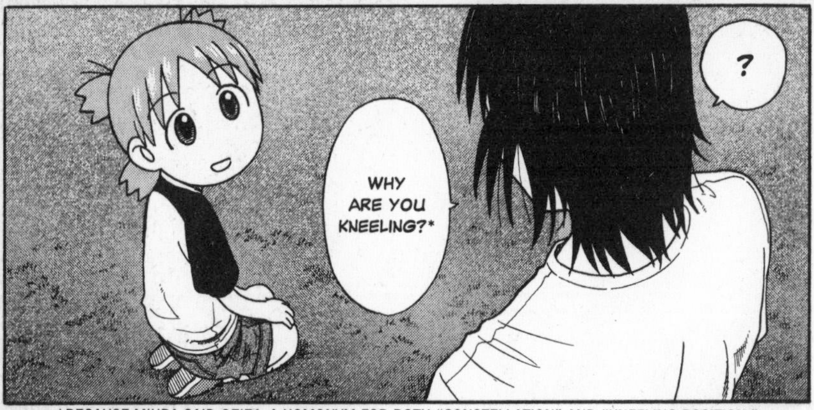
?
WHY ARE YOU KNEELING?*

*BECAUSE MIURA SAID *SEIZA*, A HOMONYM FOR BOTH "CONSTELLATION" AND "KNEELING POSITION."

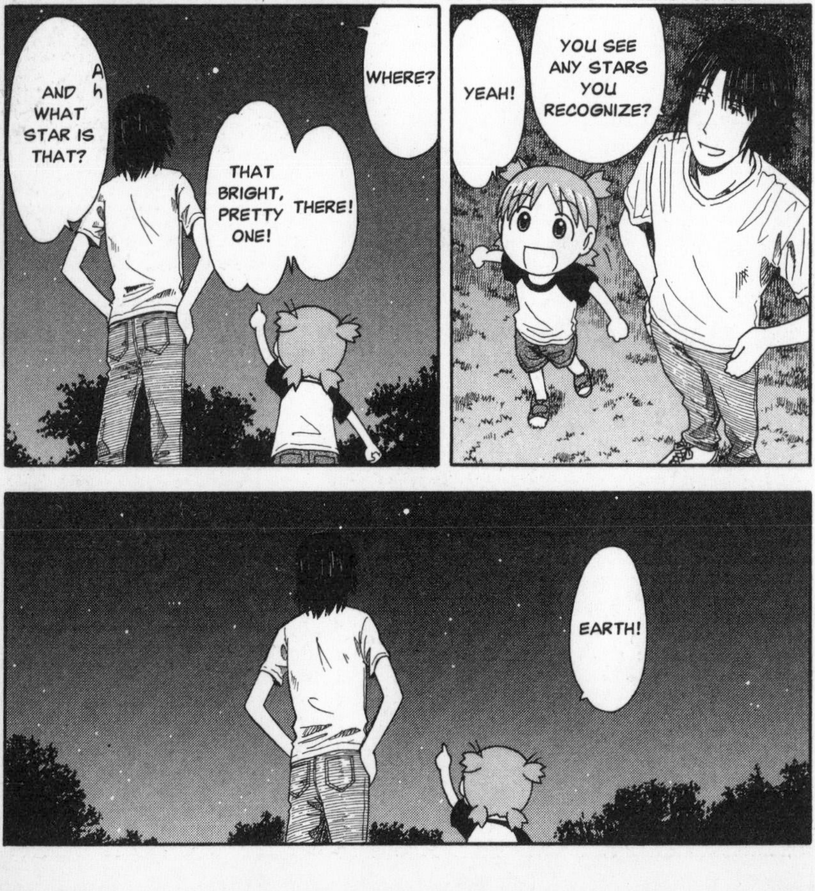
YOU SEE ANY STARS YOU RECOGNIZE?
YEAH!
WHERE?
THERE!
THAT BRIGHT, PRETTY ONE!
Ah
AND WHAT STAR IS THAT?
EARTH!

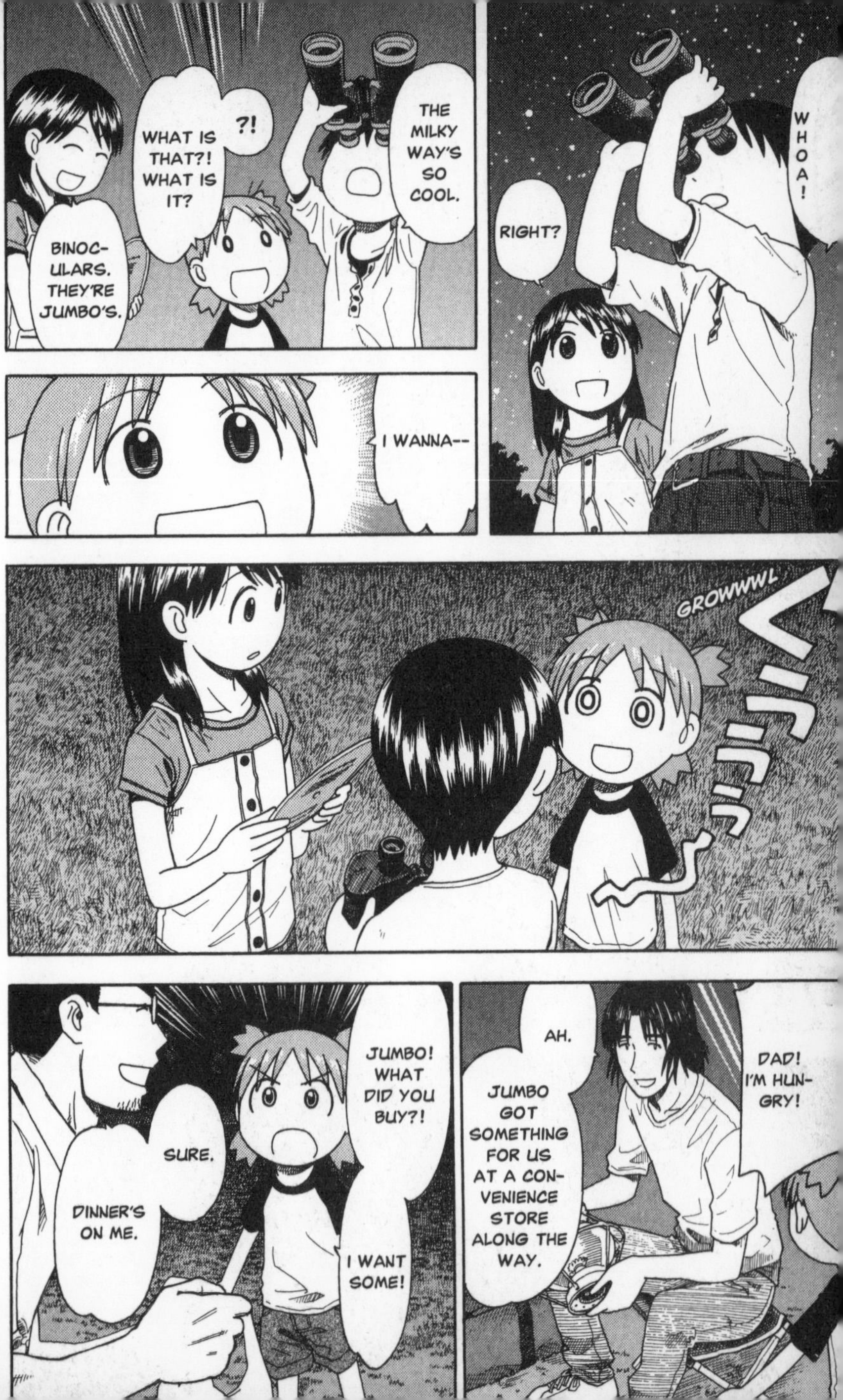
WHOA!
RIGHT?
THE MILKY WAY'S SO COOL.
?!
WHAT IS THAT?! WHAT IS IT?
BINOC-ULARS. THEY'RE JUMBO'S.
I WANNA--
GROWWWL
DAD! I'M HUN-GRY!
AH.
JUMBO GOT SOMETHING FOR US AT A CON-VENIENCE STORE ALONG THE WAY.
JUMBO! WHAT DID YOU BUY?!
I WANT SOME!
SURE.
DINNER'S ON ME.

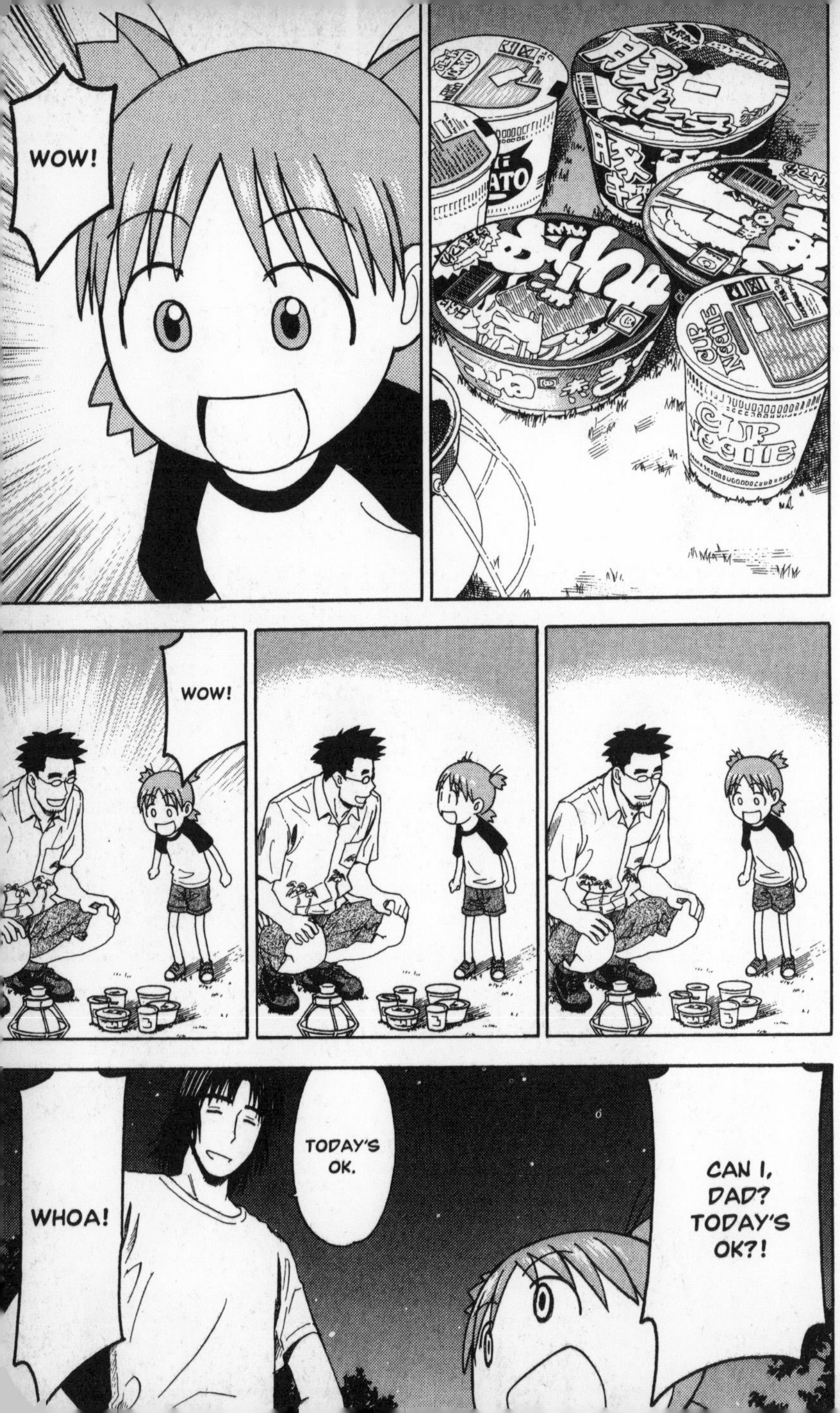
WOW!
WOW!
CAN I, DAD? TODAY'S OK?!
TODAY'S OK.
WHOA!

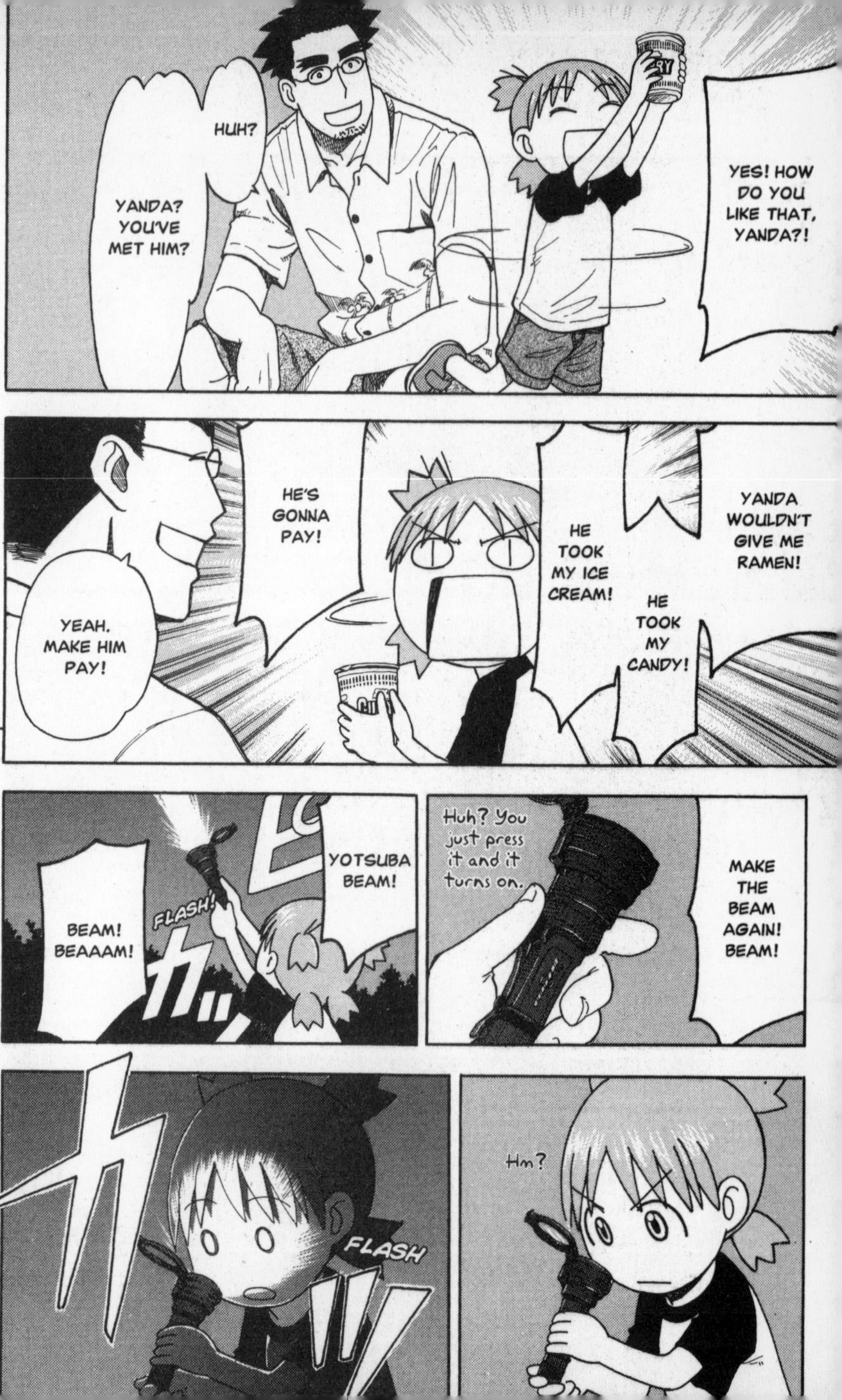
YES! HOW DO YOU LIKE THAT, YANDA?!
HUH?
YANDA? YOU'VE MET HIM?
YANDA WOULDN'T GIVE ME RAMEN!
HE TOOK MY ICE CREAM!
HE TOOK MY CANDY!
HE'S GONNA PAY!
YEAH. MAKE HIM PAY!
MAKE THE BEAM AGAIN! BEAM!
Huh? You just press it and it turns on.
YOTSUBA BEAM!
FLASH!
カッ
BEAM! BEAAAM!
Hm?
カッ
FLASH

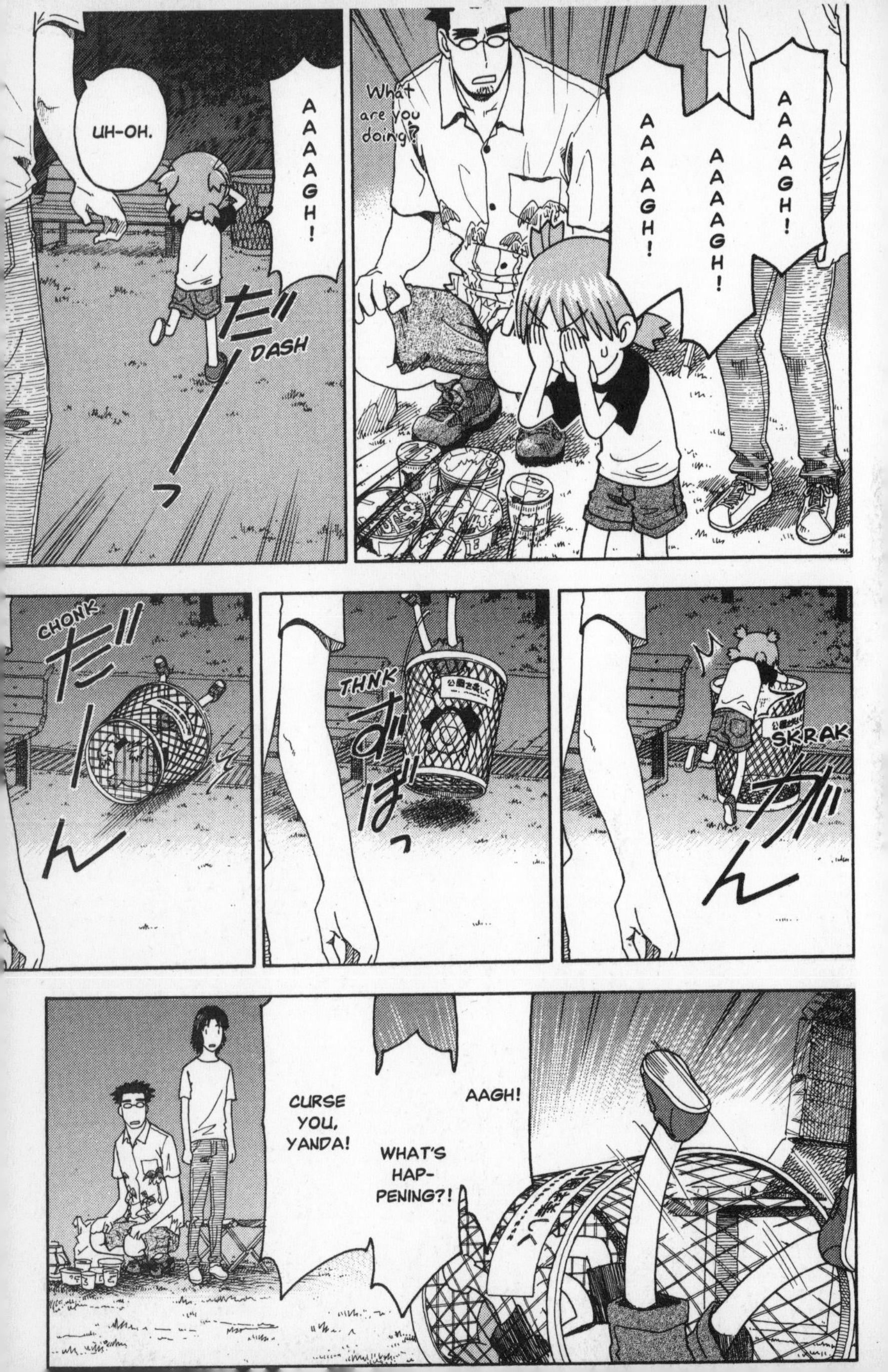
AAAAAGH!
AAAAAGH!
AAAAAGH!
What are you doing?
AAAAAGH!
UH-OH.
DASH
SKRAK
THNK
CHONK
AAGH!
CURSE YOU, YANDA!
WHAT'S HAP-PENING?!

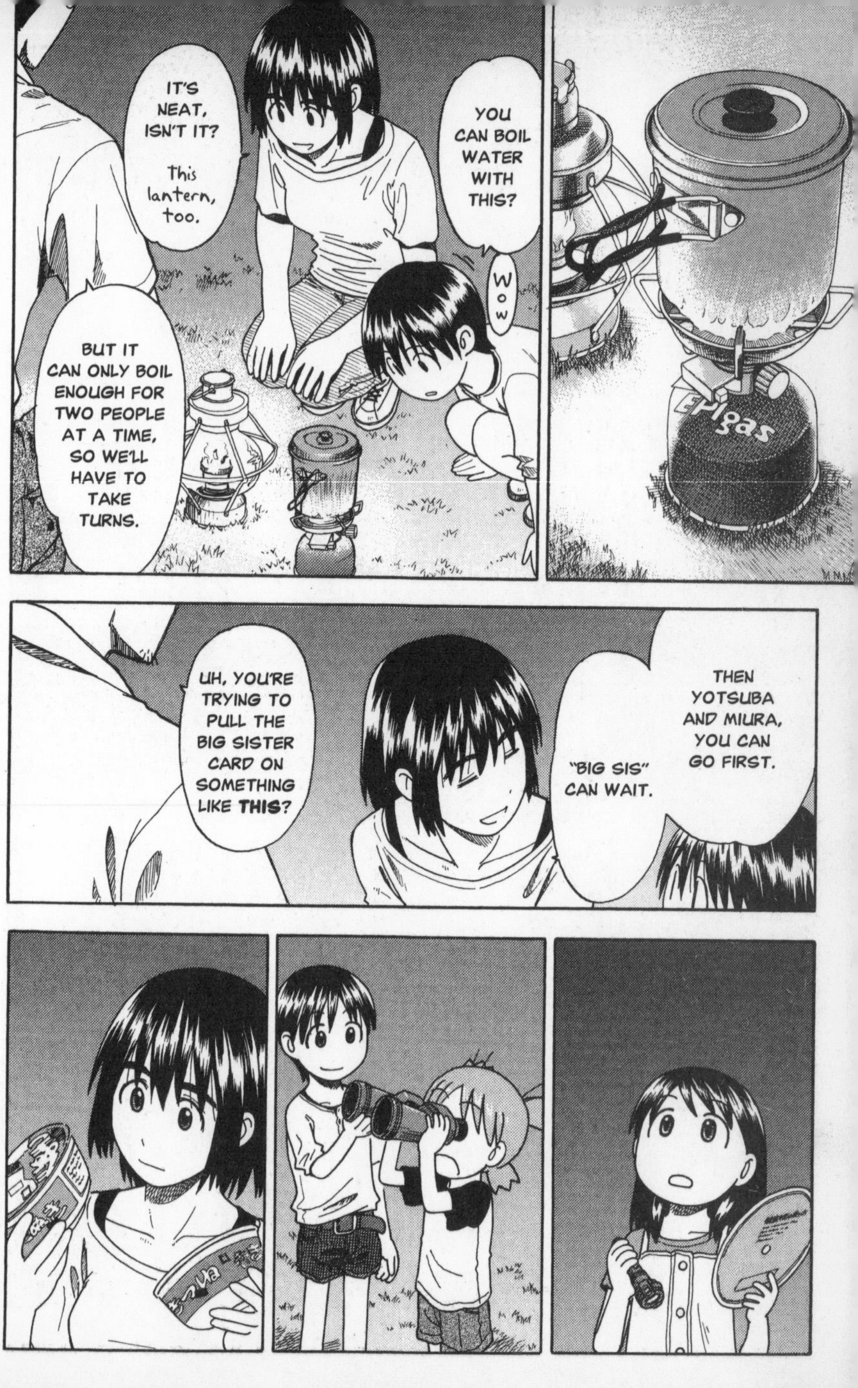
YOU CAN BOIL WATER WITH THIS?
IT'S NEAT, ISN'T IT? This lantern, too.
Wow
BUT IT CAN ONLY BOIL ENOUGH FOR TWO PEOPLE AT A TIME, SO WE'LL HAVE TO TAKE TURNS.
THEN YOTSUBA AND MIURA, YOU CAN GO FIRST.
"BIG SIS" CAN WAIT.
UH, YOU'RE TRYING TO PULL THE BIG SISTER CARD ON SOMETHING LIKE **THIS**?

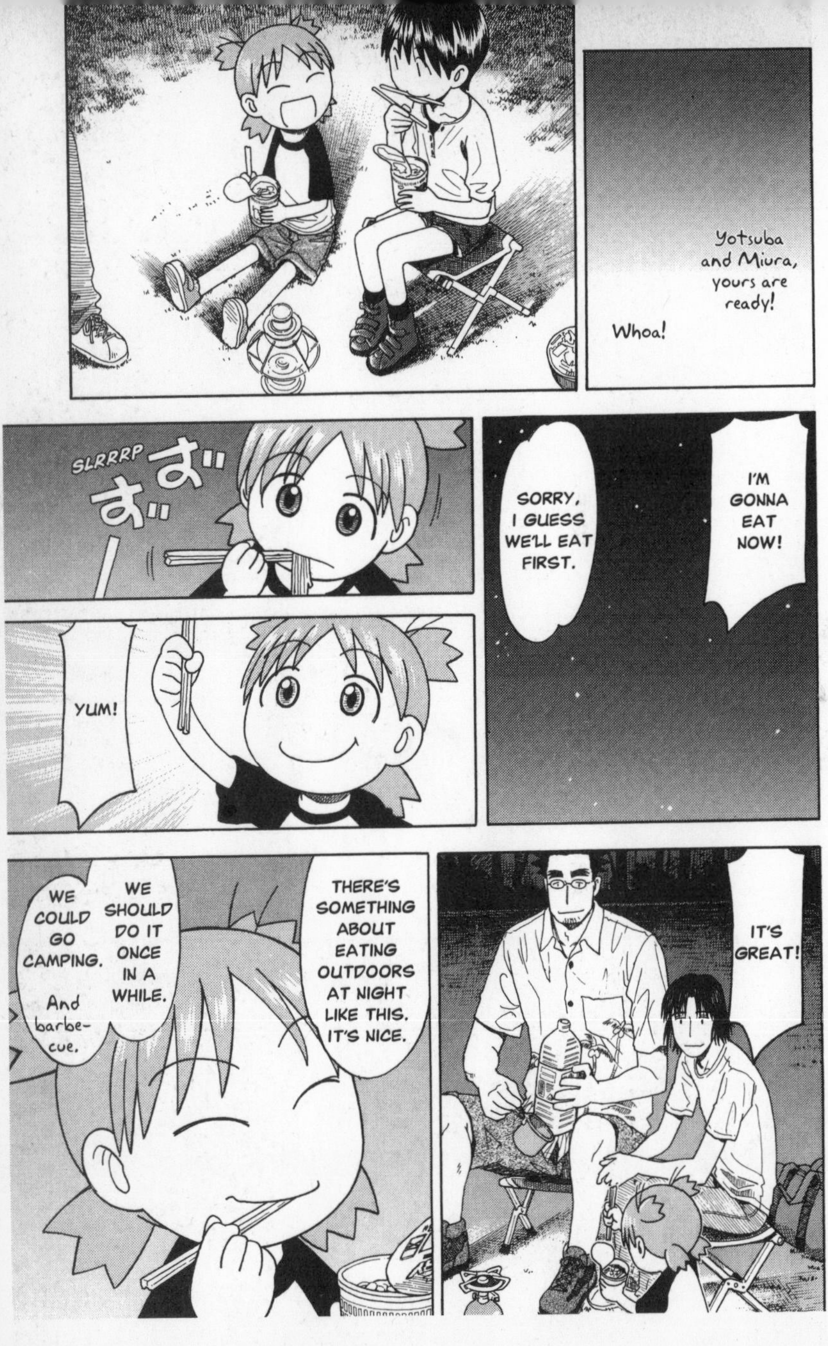
Yotsuba and Miura, yours are ready!
Whoa!
I'M GONNA EAT NOW!
SORRY, I GUESS WE'LL EAT FIRST.
SLRRRP
ずず
YUM!
IT'S GREAT!
THERE'S SOMETHING ABOUT EATING OUTDOORS AT NIGHT LIKE THIS. IT'S NICE.
WE SHOULD DO IT ONCE IN A WHILE.
WE COULD GO CAMPING.
And barbe-cue.

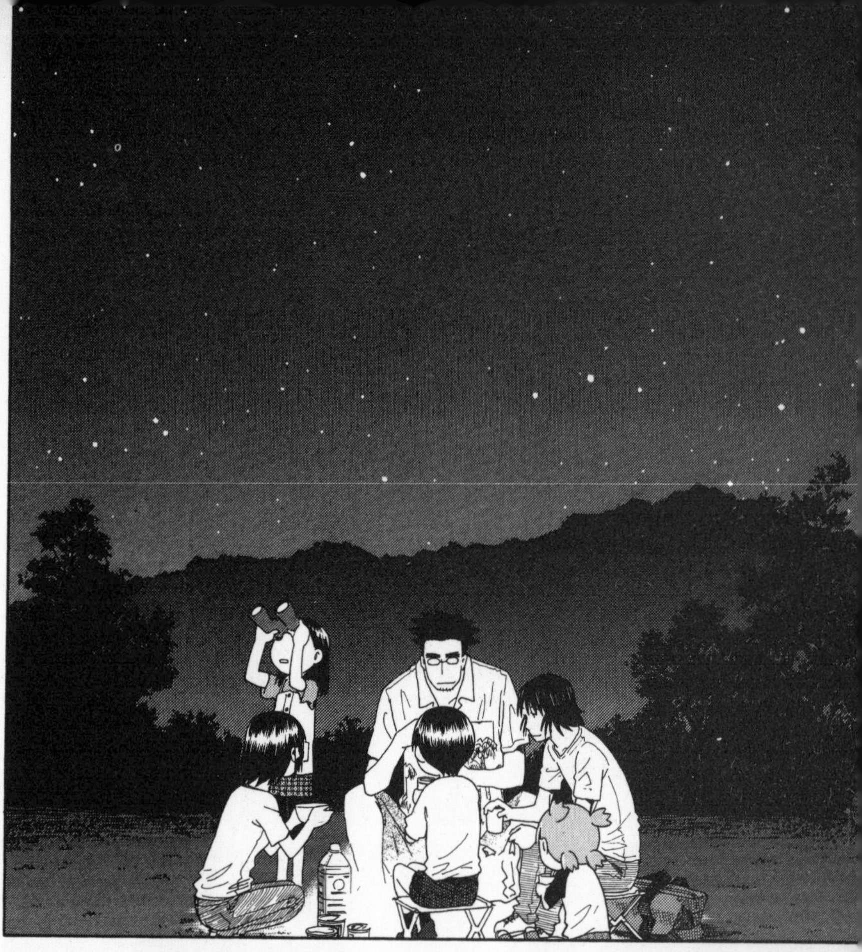

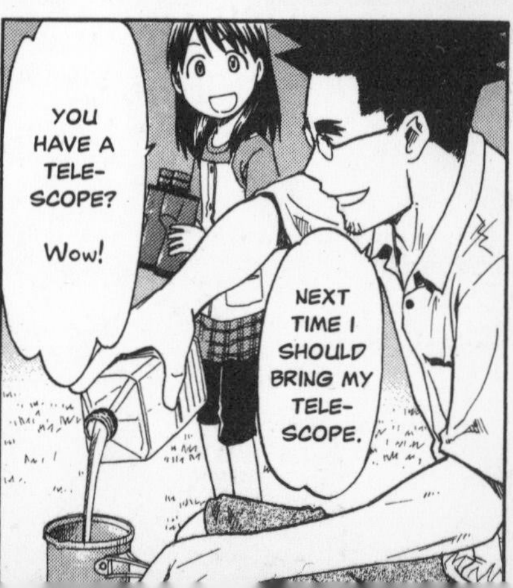
YOU HAVE A TELE-SCOPE?
Wow!
NEXT TIME I SHOULD BRING MY TELE-SCOPE.

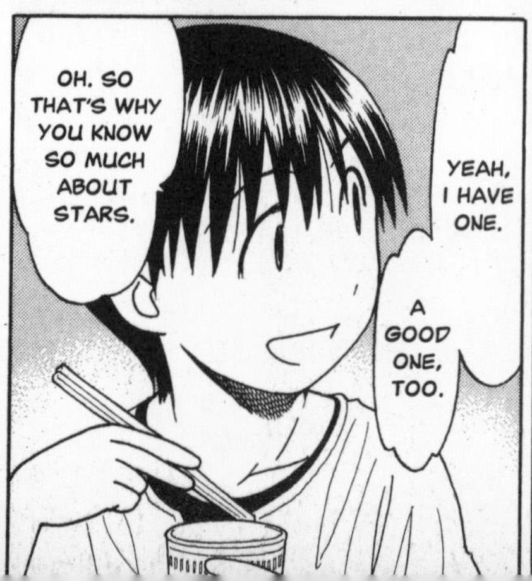
YEAH, I HAVE ONE.
A GOOD ONE, TOO.
OH. SO THAT'S WHY YOU KNOW SO MUCH ABOUT STARS.

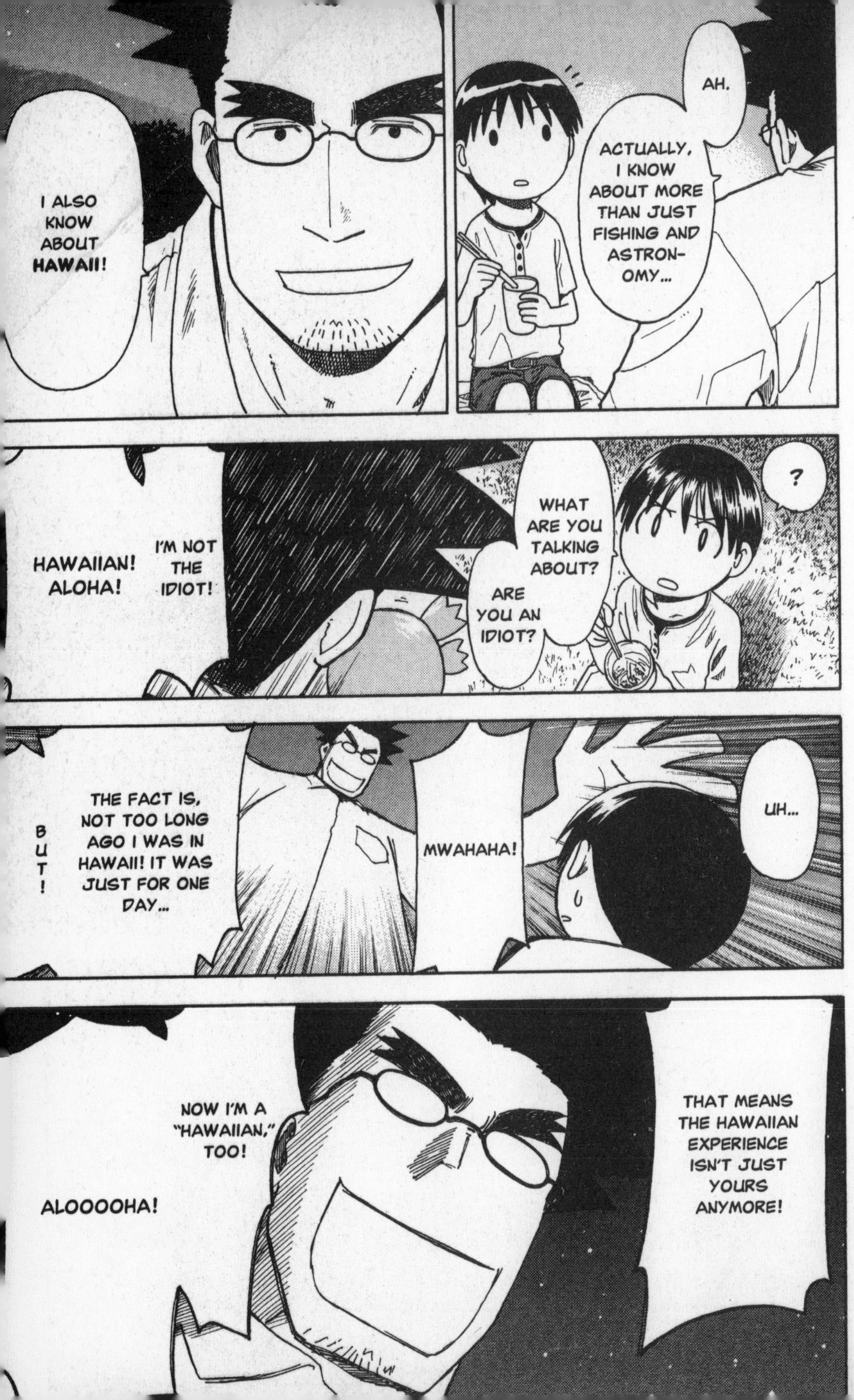
AH.
ACTUALLY, I KNOW ABOUT MORE THAN JUST FISHING AND ASTRON-OMY...
I ALSO KNOW ABOUT HAWAII!
?
WHAT ARE YOU TALKING ABOUT?
ARE YOU AN IDIOT?
I'M NOT THE IDIOT!
HAWAIIAN! ALOHA!
UH...
MWAHAHA!
THE FACT IS, NOT TOO LONG AGO I WAS IN HAWAII! IT WAS JUST FOR ONE DAY...
BUT!
THAT MEANS THE HAWAIIAN EXPERIENCE ISN'T JUST YOURS ANYMORE!
NOW I'M A "HAWAIIAN," TOO!
ALOOOOHA!

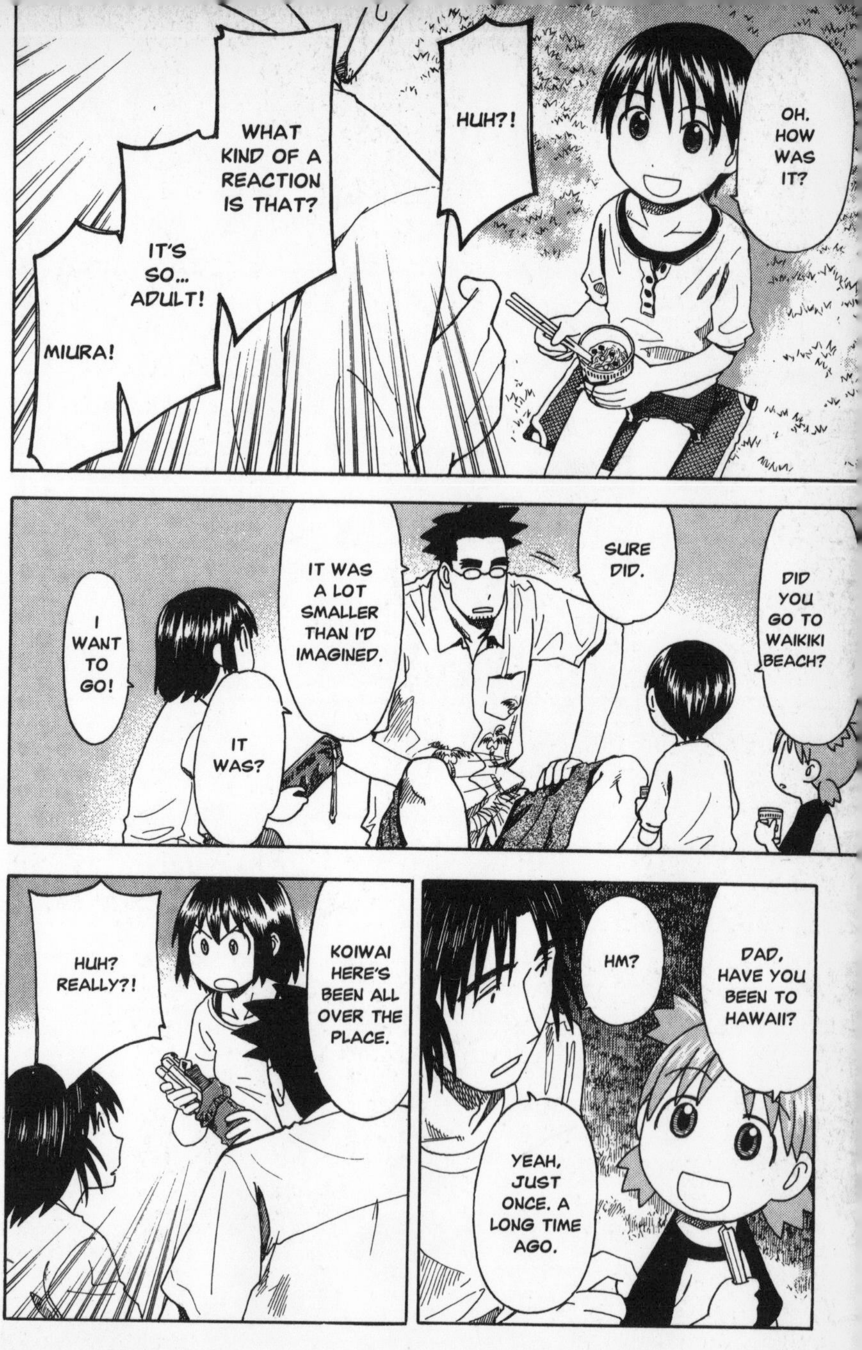
OH. HOW WAS IT?
HUH?!
WHAT KIND OF A REACTION IS THAT?
IT'S SO... ADULT!
MIURA!
DID YOU GO TO WAIKIKI BEACH?
SURE DID.
IT WAS A LOT SMALLER THAN I'D IMAGINED.
IT WAS?
I WANT TO GO!
DAD, HAVE YOU BEEN TO HAWAII?
HM?
YEAH, JUST ONCE. A LONG TIME AGO.
KOIWAI HERE'S BEEN ALL OVER THE PLACE.
HUH? REALLY?!

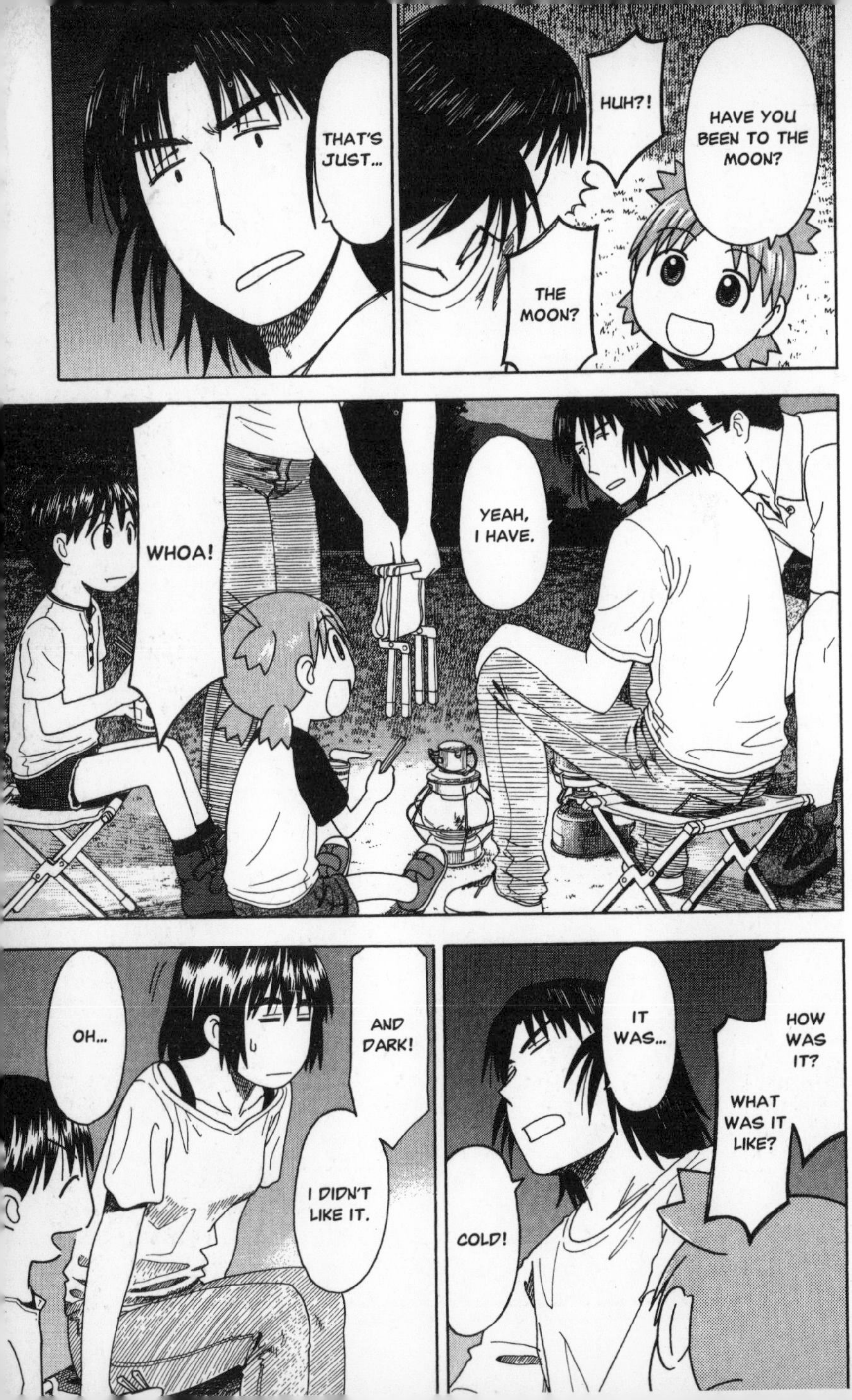
HAVE YOU BEEN TO THE MOON?
HUH?!
THE MOON?
THAT'S JUST...
YEAH, I HAVE.
WHOA!
HOW WAS IT?
WHAT WAS IT LIKE?
IT WAS...
COLD!
AND DARK!
I DIDN'T LIKE IT.
OH...

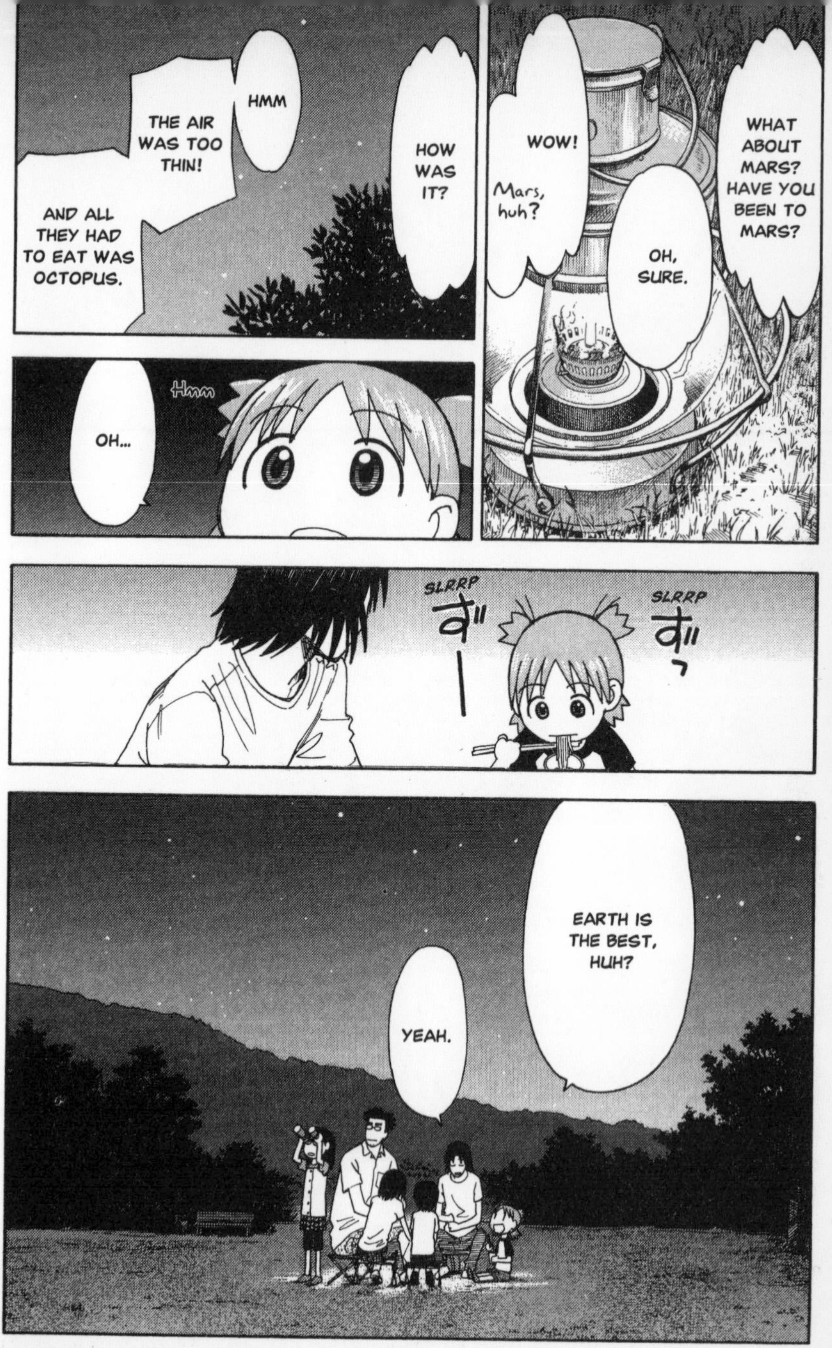
WHAT ABOUT MARS? HAVE YOU BEEN TO MARS?
OH, SURE.
WOW!
Mars, huh?
HOW WAS IT?
HMM
THE AIR WAS TOO THIN!
AND ALL THEY HAD TO EAT WAS OCTOPUS.
Hmm
OH...
SLRRP
ずっ
SLRRP
ずー
EARTH IS THE BEST, HUH?
YEAH.

YOTSUBA&!

YOTSUBA&!

CHAPTER 32

RAIN

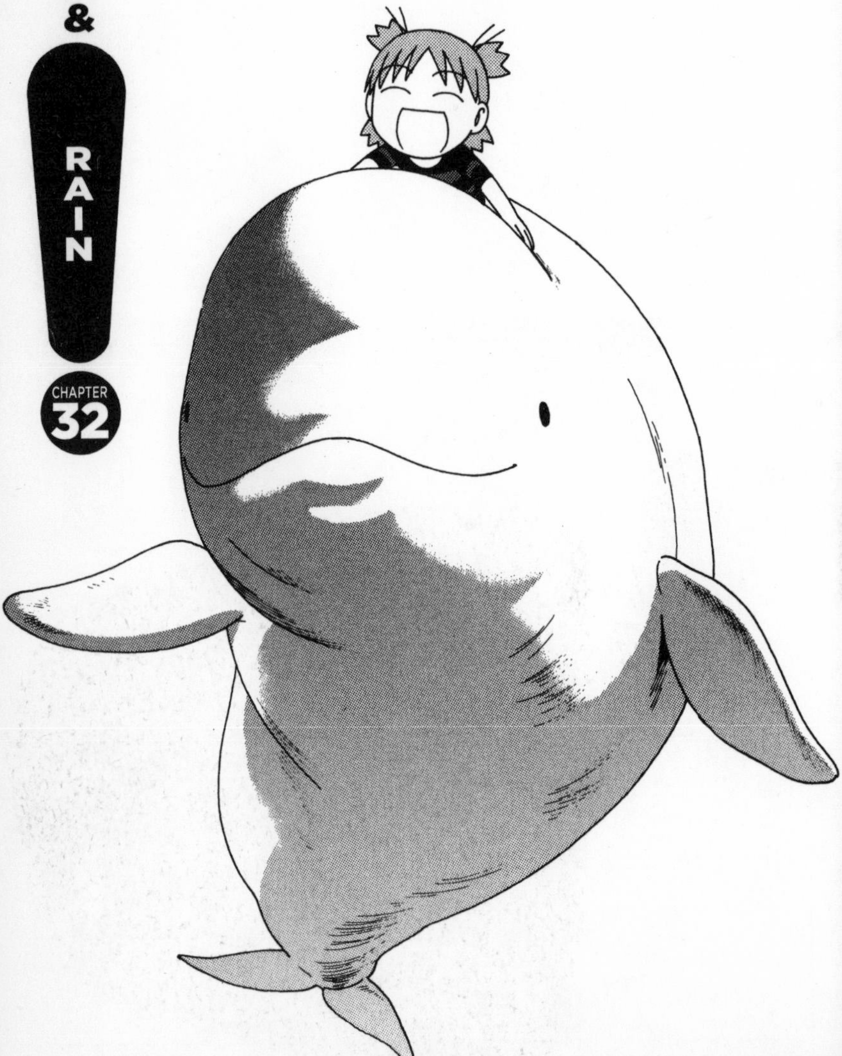

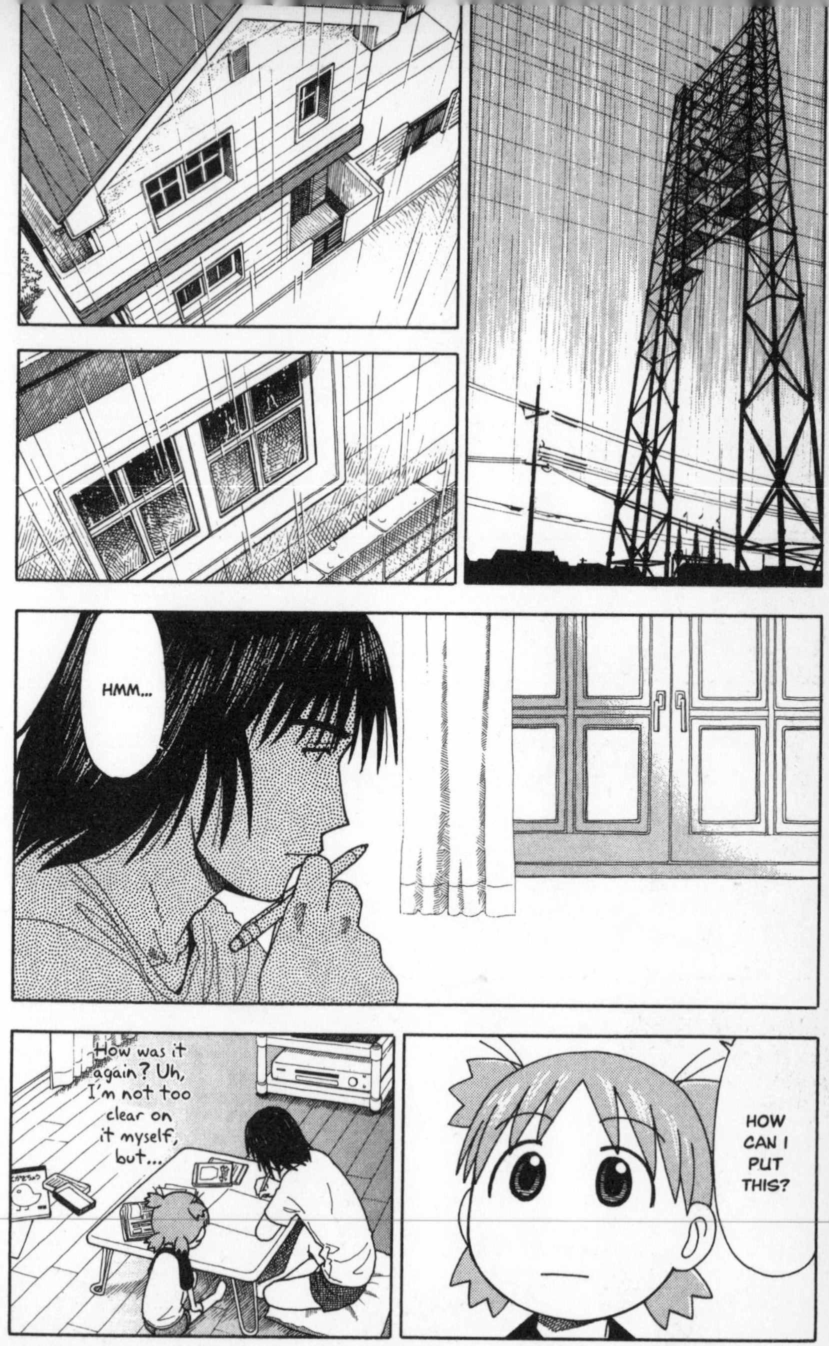
HMM...
HOW CAN I PUT THIS?
How was it again? Uh, I'm not too clear on it myself, but...

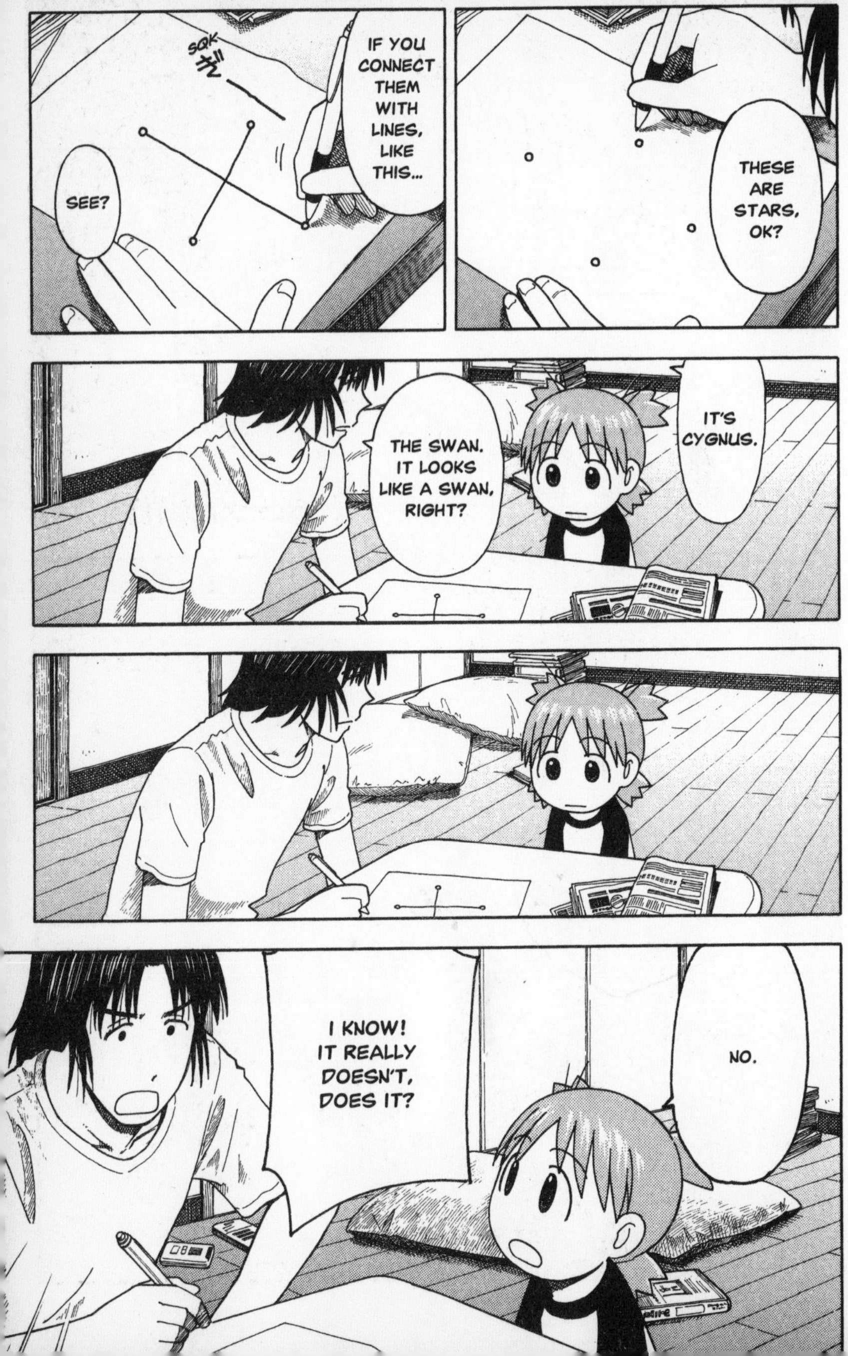
THESE ARE STARS, OK?
IF YOU CONNECT THEM WITH LINES, LIKE THIS...
SQK
SEE?
IT'S CYGNUS.
THE SWAN. IT LOOKS LIKE A SWAN, RIGHT?
NO.
I KNOW! IT REALLY DOESN'T, DOES IT?

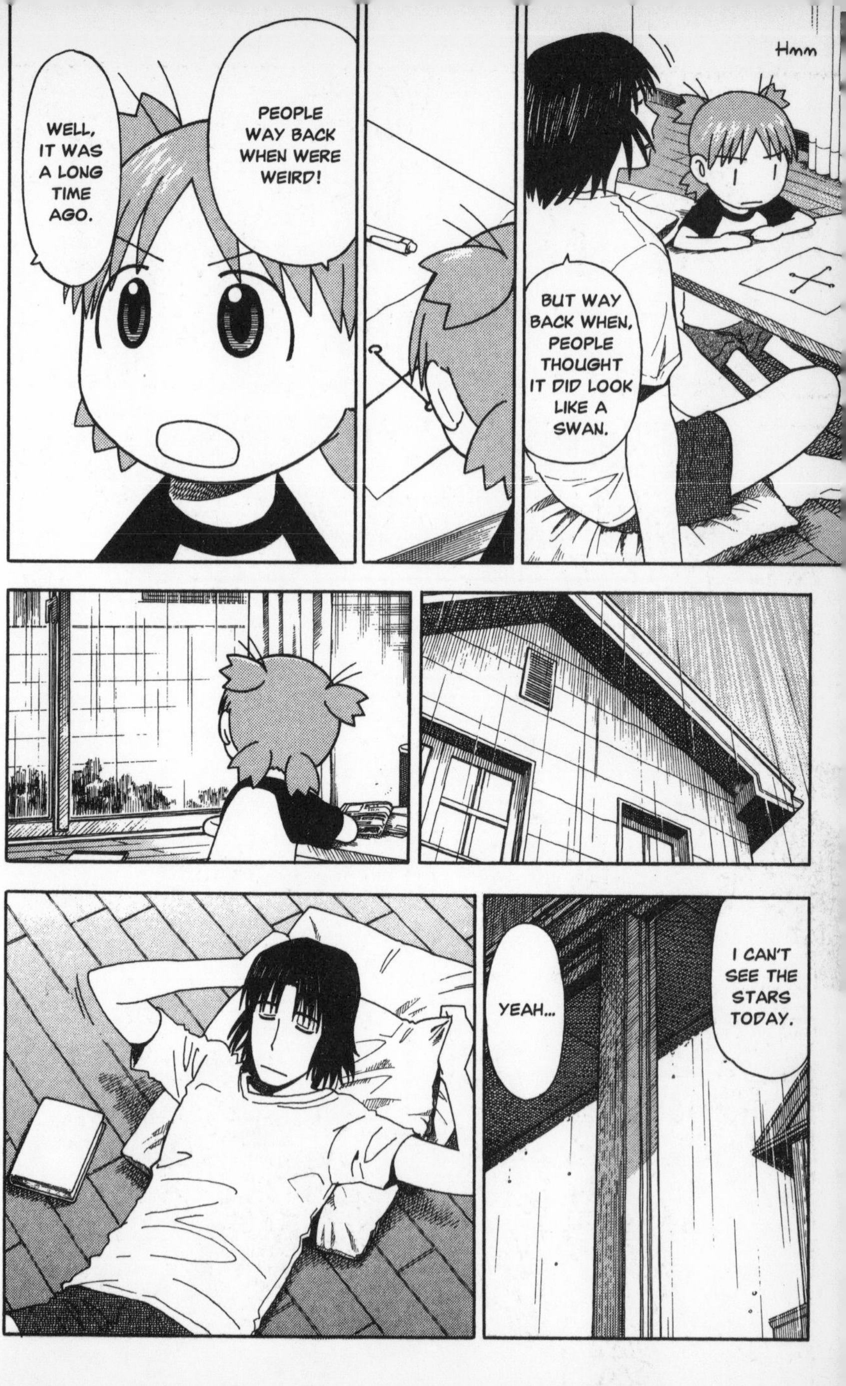
Hmm
BUT WAY BACK WHEN, PEOPLE THOUGHT IT DID LOOK LIKE A SWAN.
PEOPLE WAY BACK WHEN WERE WEIRD!
WELL, IT WAS A LONG TIME AGO.
I CAN'T SEE THE STARS TODAY.
YEAH...

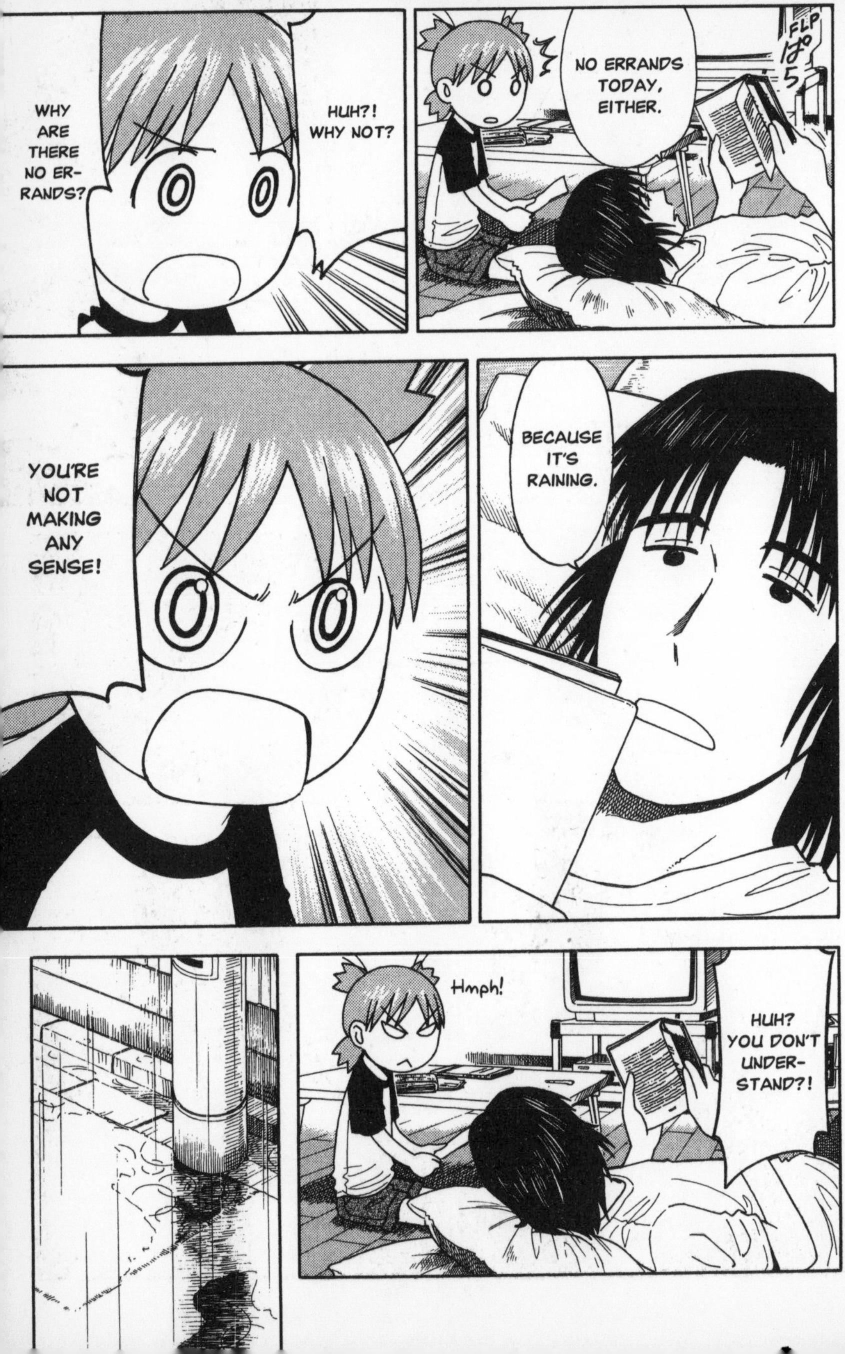
FLP ぱら
NO ERRANDS TODAY, EITHER.
HUH?! WHY NOT?
WHY ARE THERE NO ER-RANDS?
BECAUSE IT'S RAINING.
YOU'RE NOT MAKING ANY SENSE!
HUH? YOU DON'T UNDER-STAND?!
Hmph!

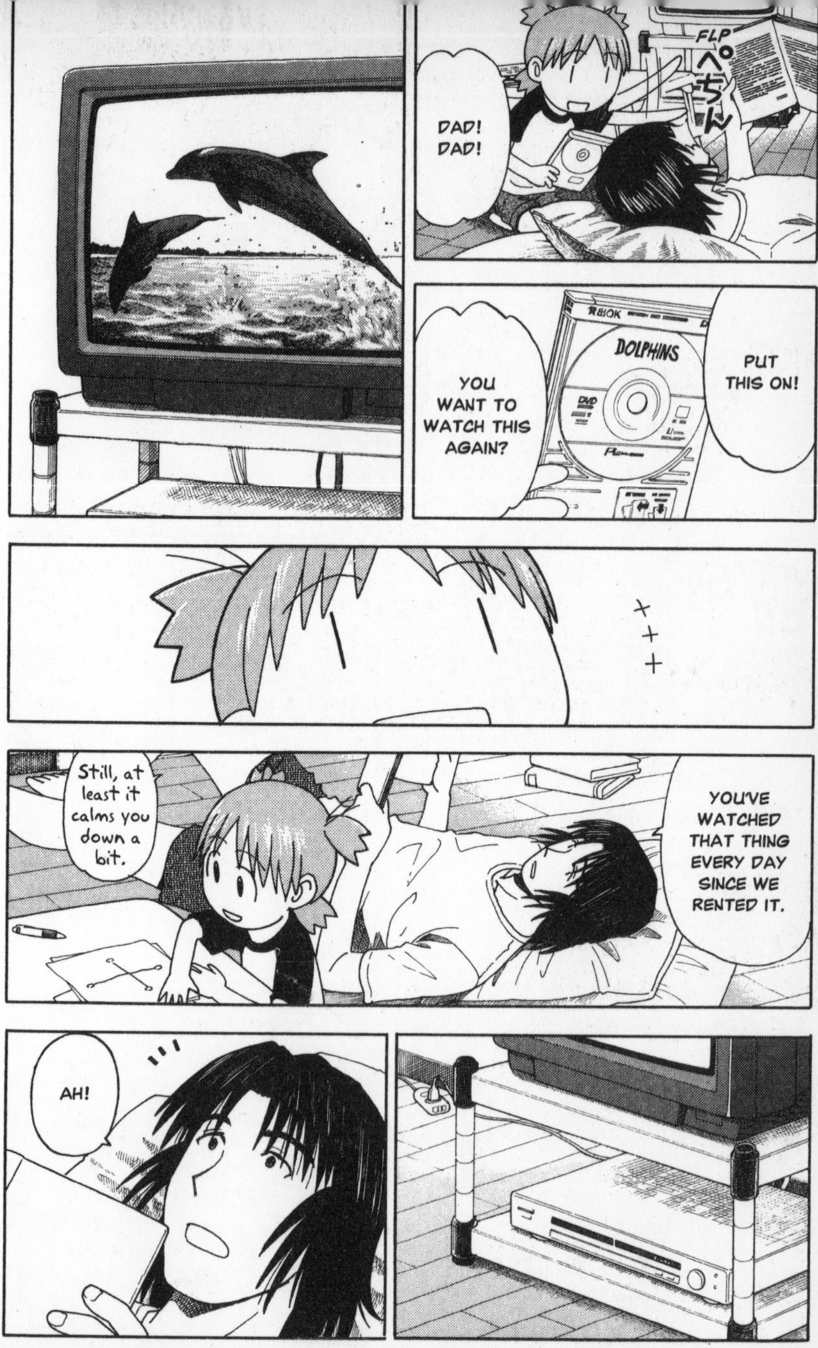
FLP
ぺちん
DAD! DAD!
PUT THIS ON!
貸出OK
DOLPHINS
YOU WANT TO WATCH THIS AGAIN?
YOU'VE WATCHED THAT THING EVERY DAY SINCE WE RENTED IT.
Still, at least it calms you down a bit.
AH!

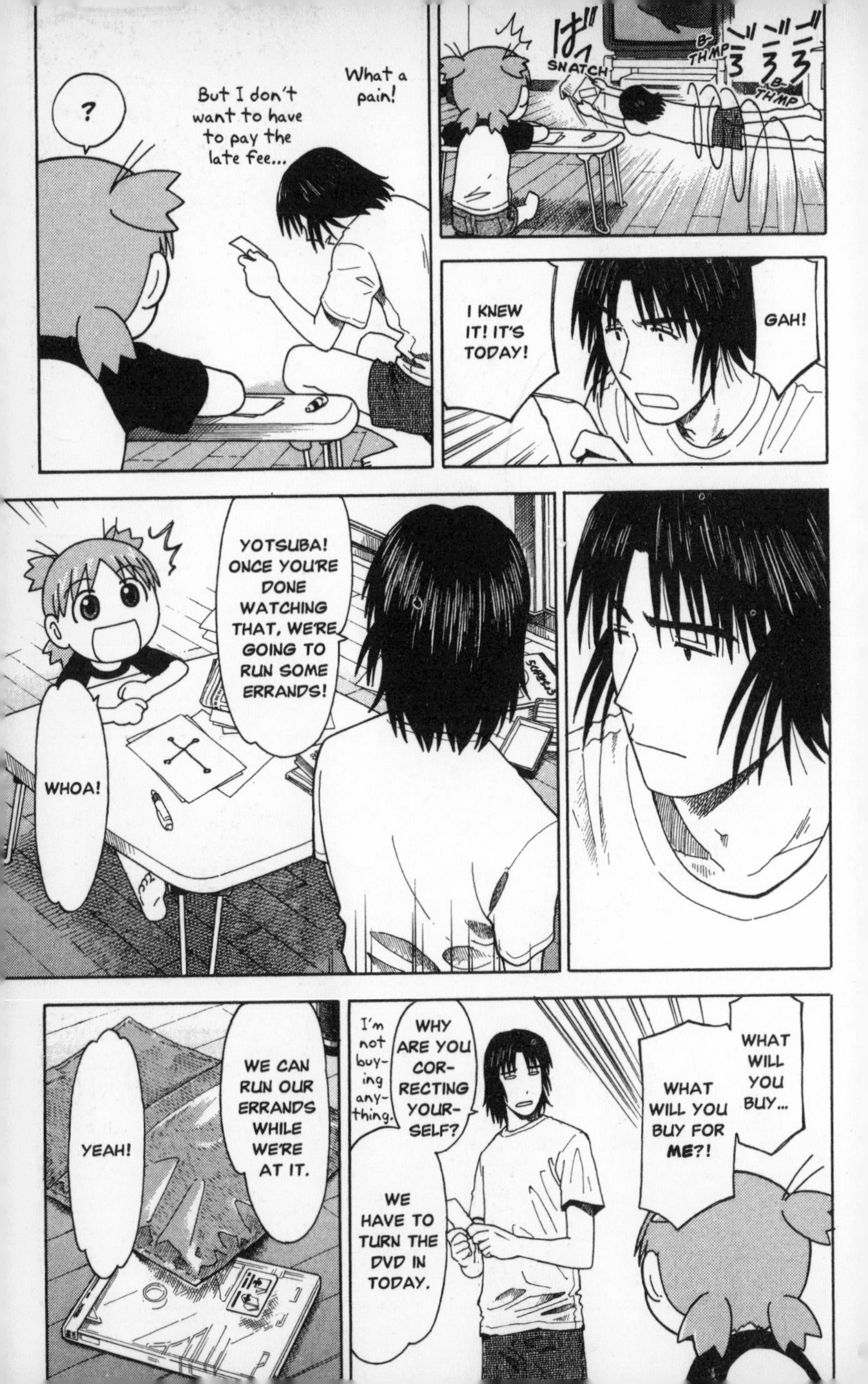
B-THMP
B-THMP
SNATCH
GAH!
I KNEW IT! IT'S TODAY!
What a pain!
But I don't want to have to pay the late fee...
?
YOTSUBA! ONCE YOU'RE DONE WATCHING THAT, WE'RE GOING TO RUN SOME ERRANDS!
WHOA!
WHAT WILL YOU BUY...
WHAT WILL YOU BUY FOR ME?!
WHY ARE YOU COR-RECTING YOUR-SELF?
I'm not buy-ing any-thing.
WE HAVE TO TURN THE DVD IN TODAY.
WE CAN RUN OUR ERRANDS WHILE WE'RE AT IT.
YEAH!

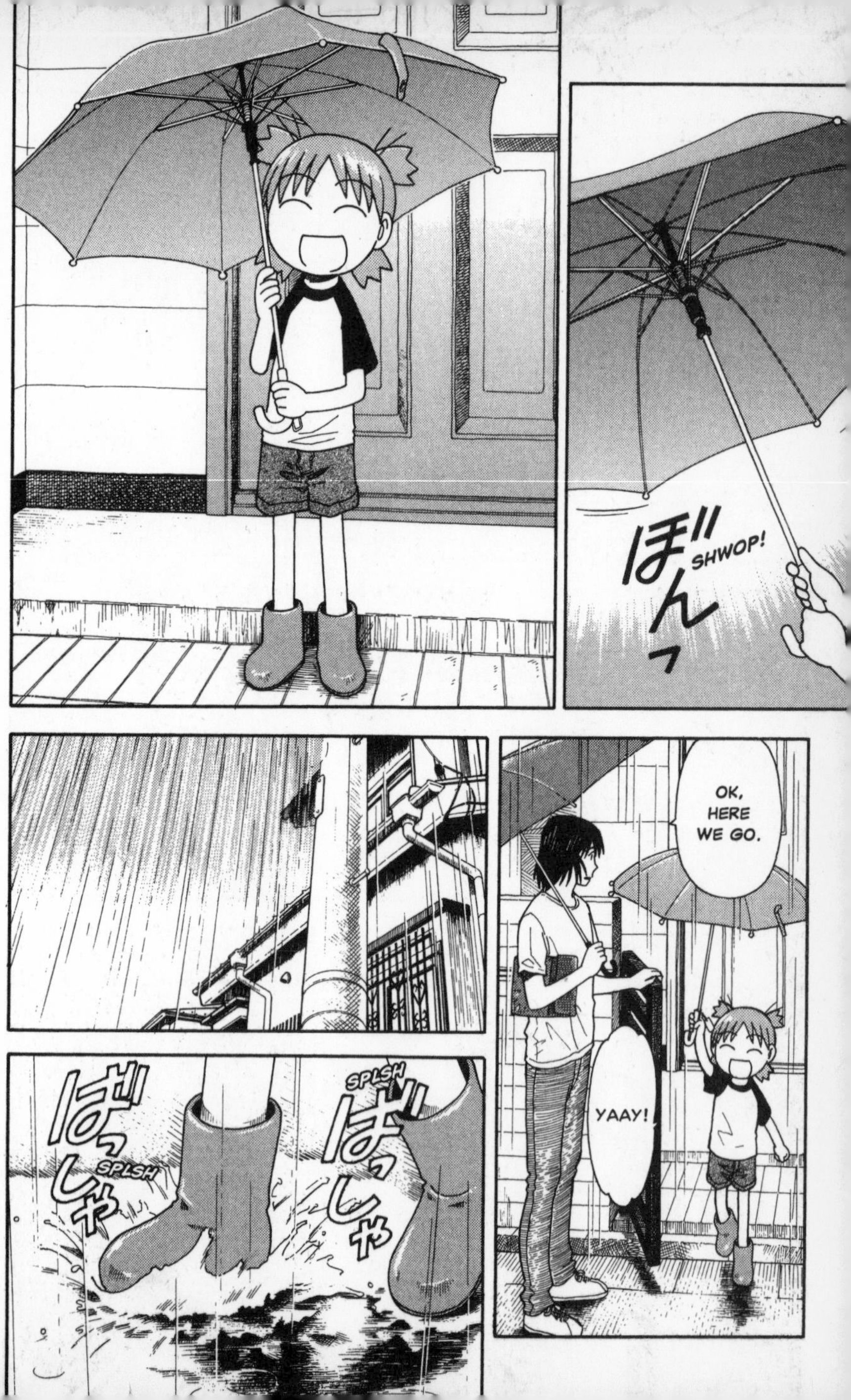
ぼんっ
SHWOP!
OK, HERE WE GO.
YAAY!
ばっしゃ
SPLSH
ばっしゃ
SPLSH

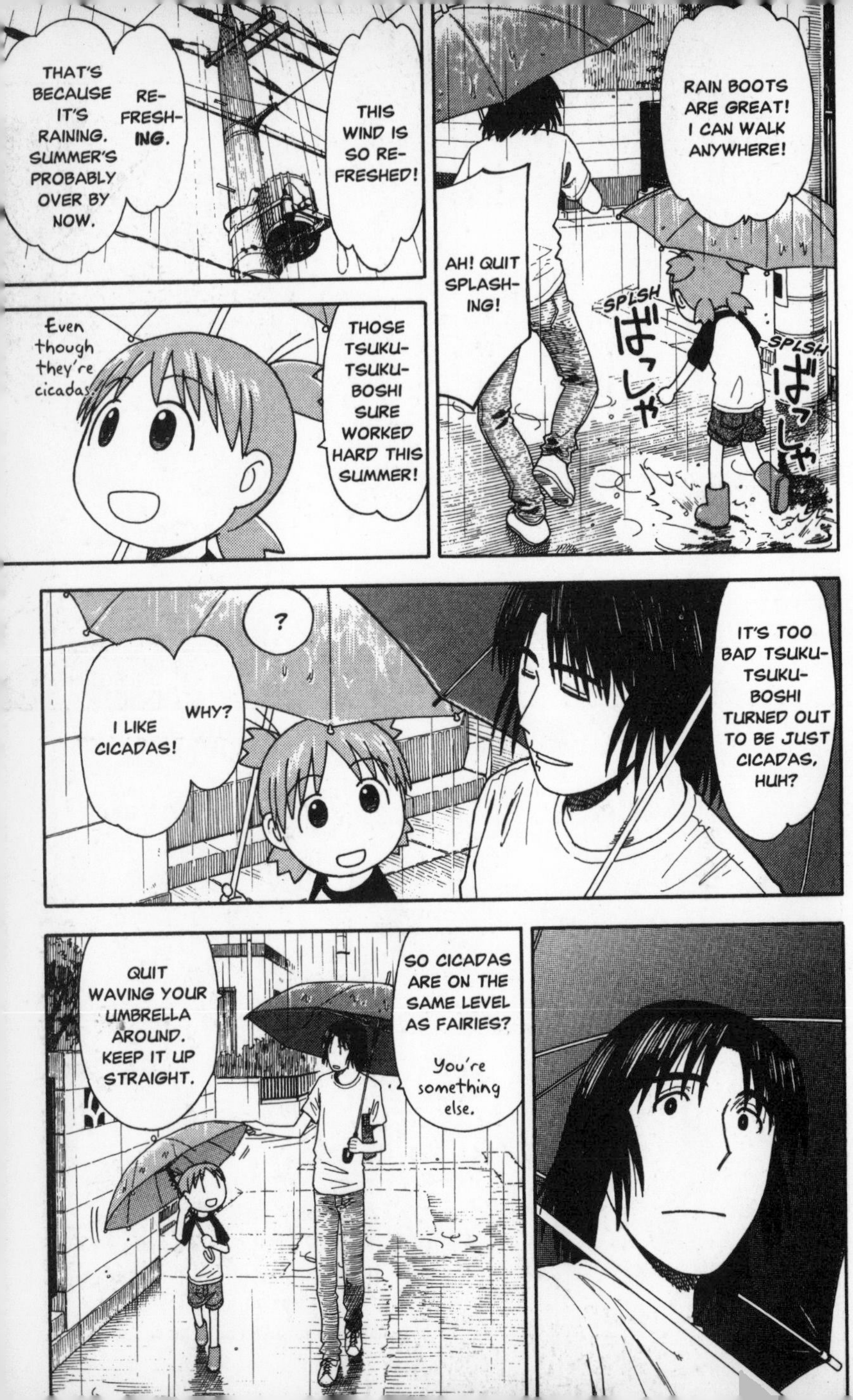
RAIN BOOTS ARE GREAT! I CAN WALK ANYWHERE!
SPLSH ばっしゃ
SPLSH ばっしゃ
AH! QUIT SPLASHING!
THIS WIND IS SO REFRESHED!
REFRESHING.
THAT'S BECAUSE IT'S RAINING. SUMMER'S PROBABLY OVER BY NOW.
THOSE TSUKUTSUKUBOSHI SURE WORKED HARD THIS SUMMER!
Even though they're cicadas.
IT'S TOO BAD TSUKUTSUKUBOSHI TURNED OUT TO BE JUST CICADAS, HUH?
?
WHY? I LIKE CICADAS!
SO CICADAS ARE ON THE SAME LEVEL AS FAIRIES?
You're something else.
QUIT WAVING YOUR UMBRELLA AROUND. KEEP IT UP STRAIGHT.

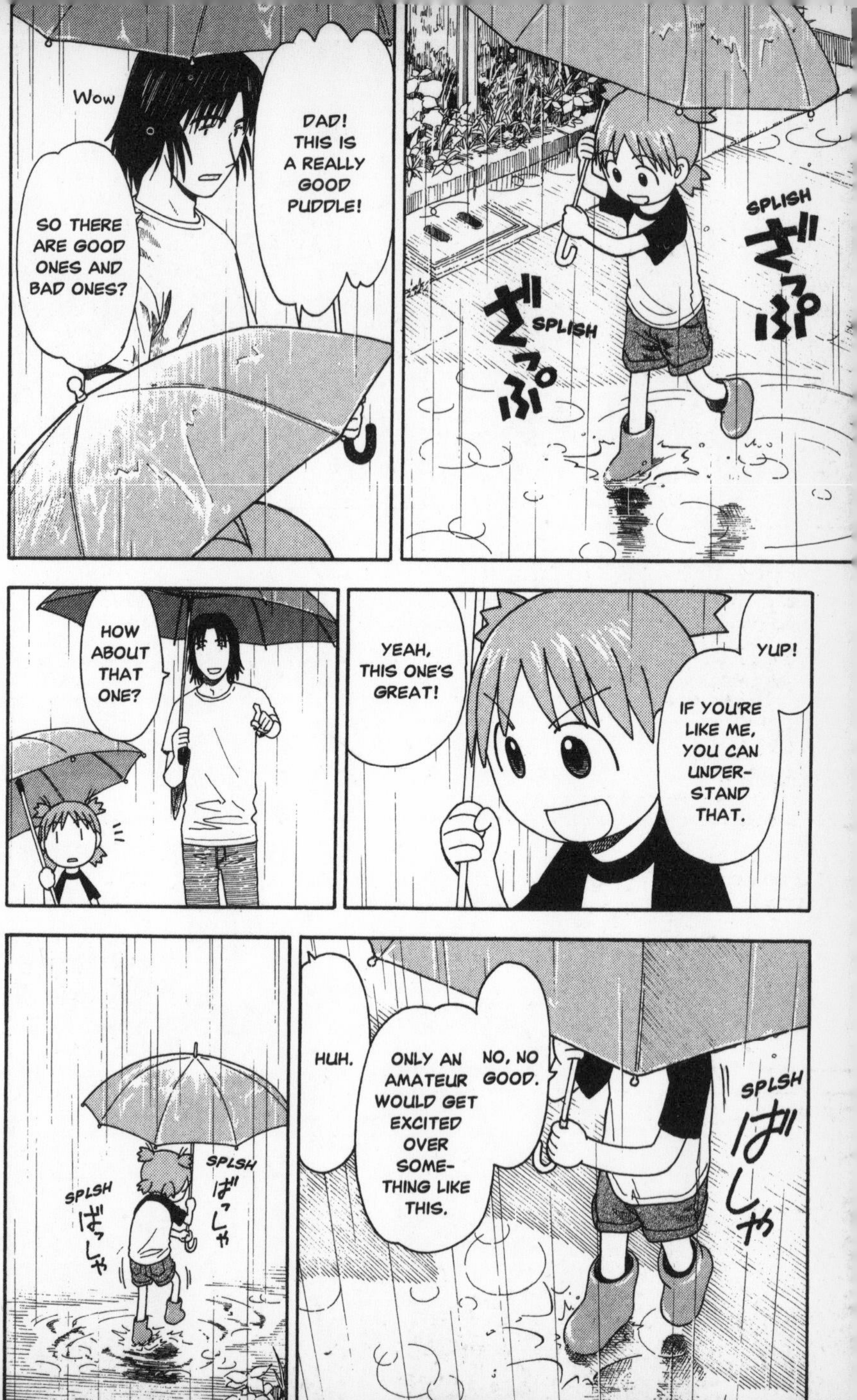
SPLISH
ざっぷ
SPLISH
ざっぷ
DAD! THIS IS A REALLY GOOD PUDDLE!
Wow
SO THERE ARE GOOD ONES AND BAD ONES?
YUP!
IF YOU'RE LIKE ME, YOU CAN UNDER-STAND THAT.
YEAH, THIS ONE'S GREAT!
HOW ABOUT THAT ONE?
SPLSH
ぱしゃ
NO, NO GOOD.
ONLY AN AMATEUR WOULD GET EXCITED OVER SOME-THING LIKE THIS.
HUH.
SPLSH
ぱっしゃ
SPLSH
ぱっしゃ

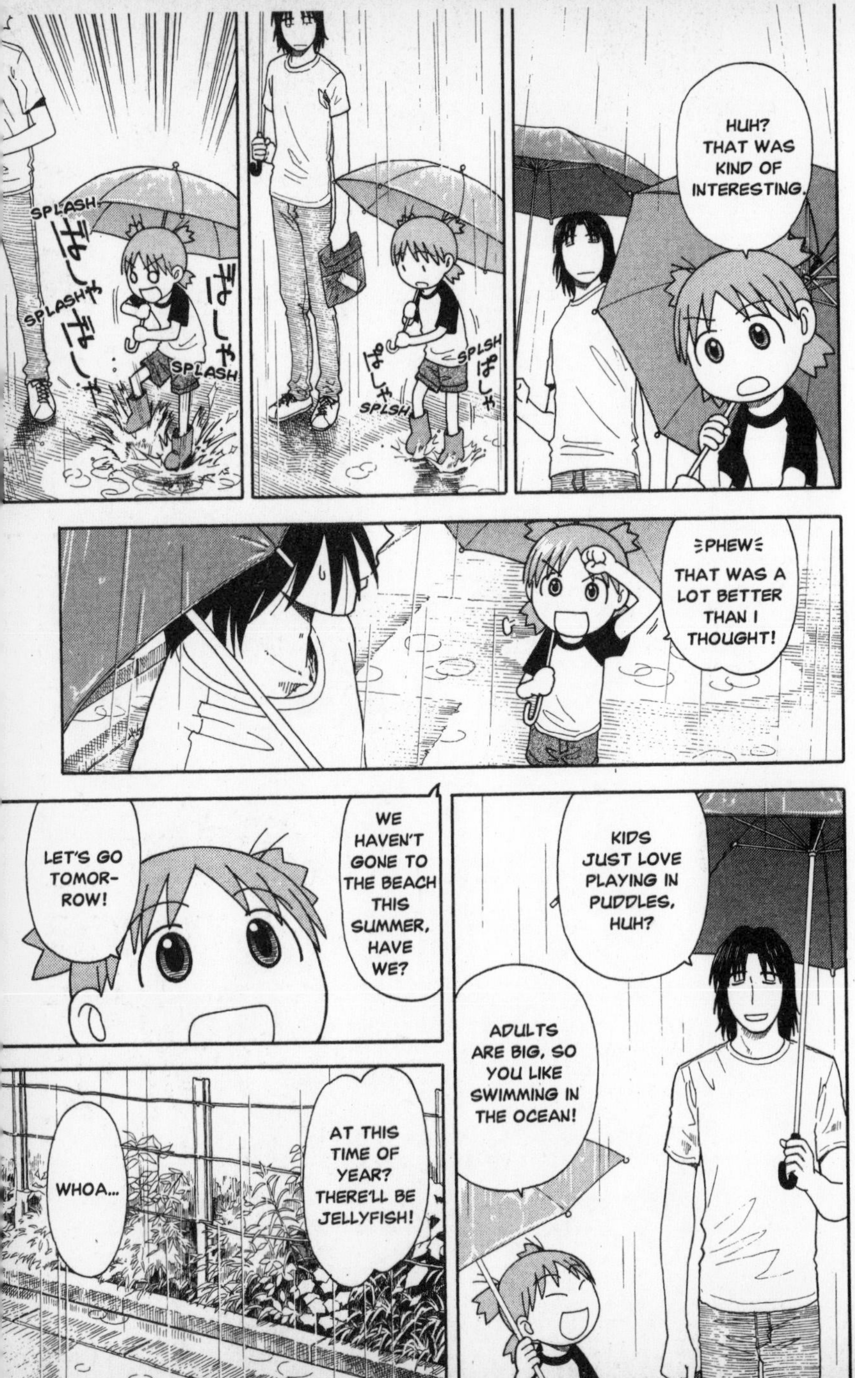
HUH? THAT WAS KIND OF INTERESTING.
SPLSH
ぱしゃ
SPLSH
ぱしゃ
SPLASH
ばしゃ
SPLASH
ばしゃ
SPLASH
≡PHEW≡
THAT WAS A LOT BETTER THAN I THOUGHT!
KIDS JUST LOVE PLAYING IN PUDDLES, HUH?
ADULTS ARE BIG, SO YOU LIKE SWIMMING IN THE OCEAN!
WE HAVEN'T GONE TO THE BEACH THIS SUMMER, HAVE WE?
LET'S GO TOMOR-ROW!
AT THIS TIME OF YEAR? THERE'LL BE JELLYFISH!
WHOA...

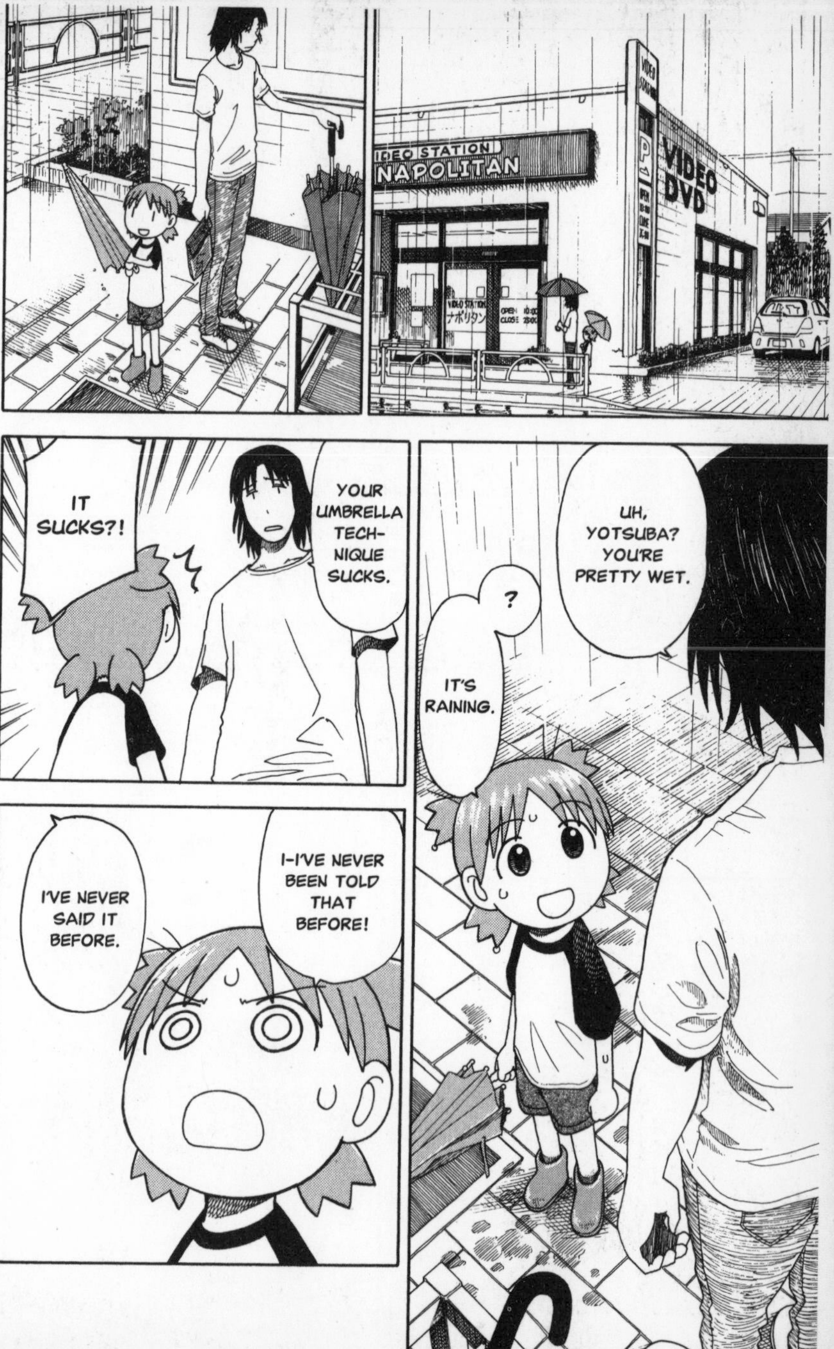
NAPOLITAN
VIDEO DVD
VIDEO STATION ナポリタン
OPEN 10:00 CLOSE 25:00
UH, YOTSUBA? YOU'RE PRETTY WET.
?
IT'S RAINING.
YOUR UMBRELLA TECH- NIQUE SUCKS.
IT SUCKS?!
I-I'VE NEVER BEEN TOLD THAT BEFORE!
I'VE NEVER SAID IT BEFORE.

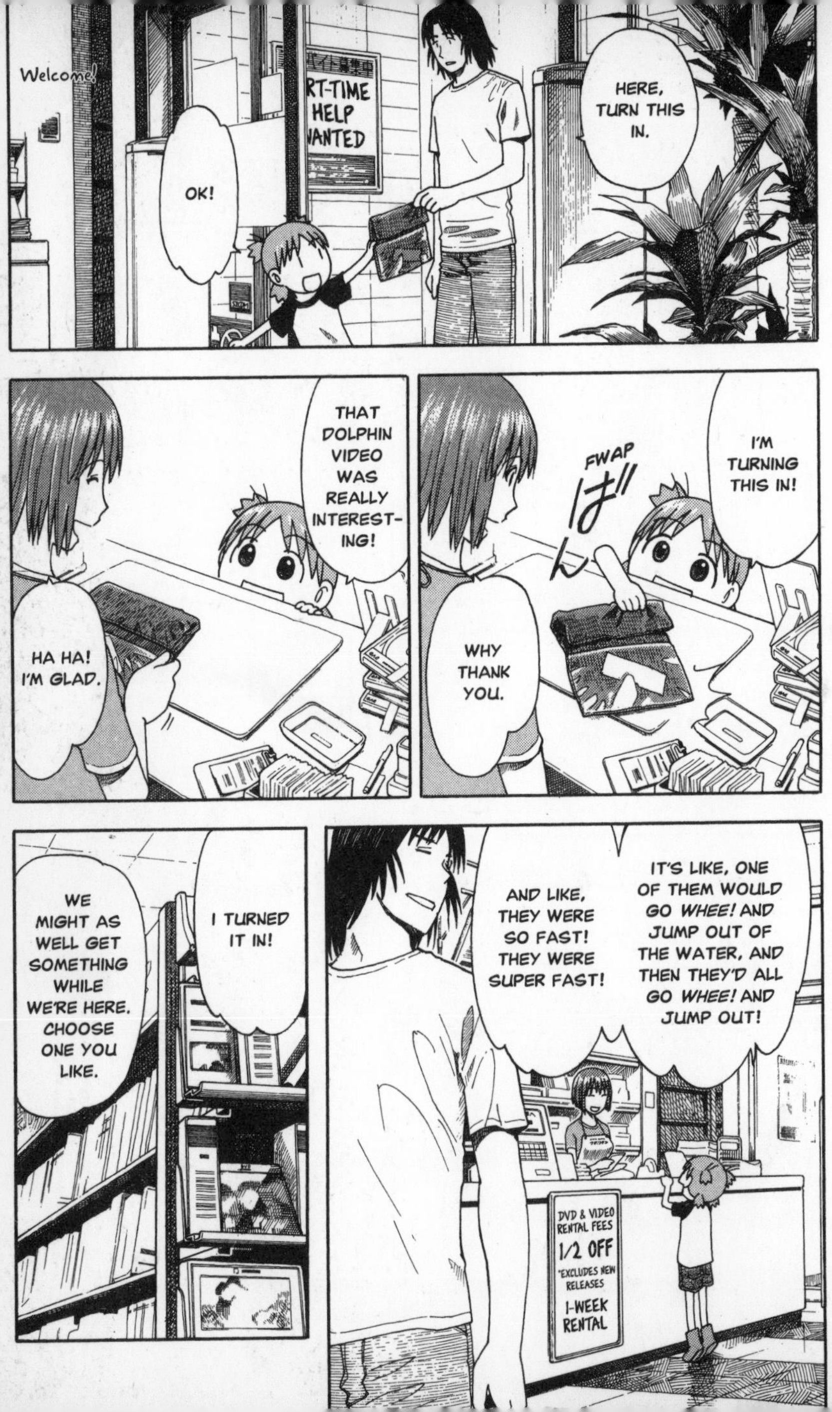
HERE, TURN THIS IN.
RT-TIME HELP WANTED
Welcome!
OK!
I'M TURNING THIS IN!
FWAP
ばん
WHY THANK YOU.
THAT DOLPHIN VIDEO WAS REALLY INTERESTING!
HA HA! I'M GLAD.
IT'S LIKE, ONE OF THEM WOULD GO *WHEE!* AND JUMP OUT OF THE WATER, AND THEN THEY'D ALL GO *WHEE!* AND JUMP OUT!
AND LIKE, THEY WERE SO FAST! THEY WERE SUPER FAST!
DVD & VIDEO RENTAL FEES 1/2 OFF *EXCLUDES NEW RELEASES 1-WEEK RENTAL
I TURNED IT IN!
WE MIGHT AS WELL GET SOMETHING WHILE WE'RE HERE. CHOOSE ONE YOU LIKE.

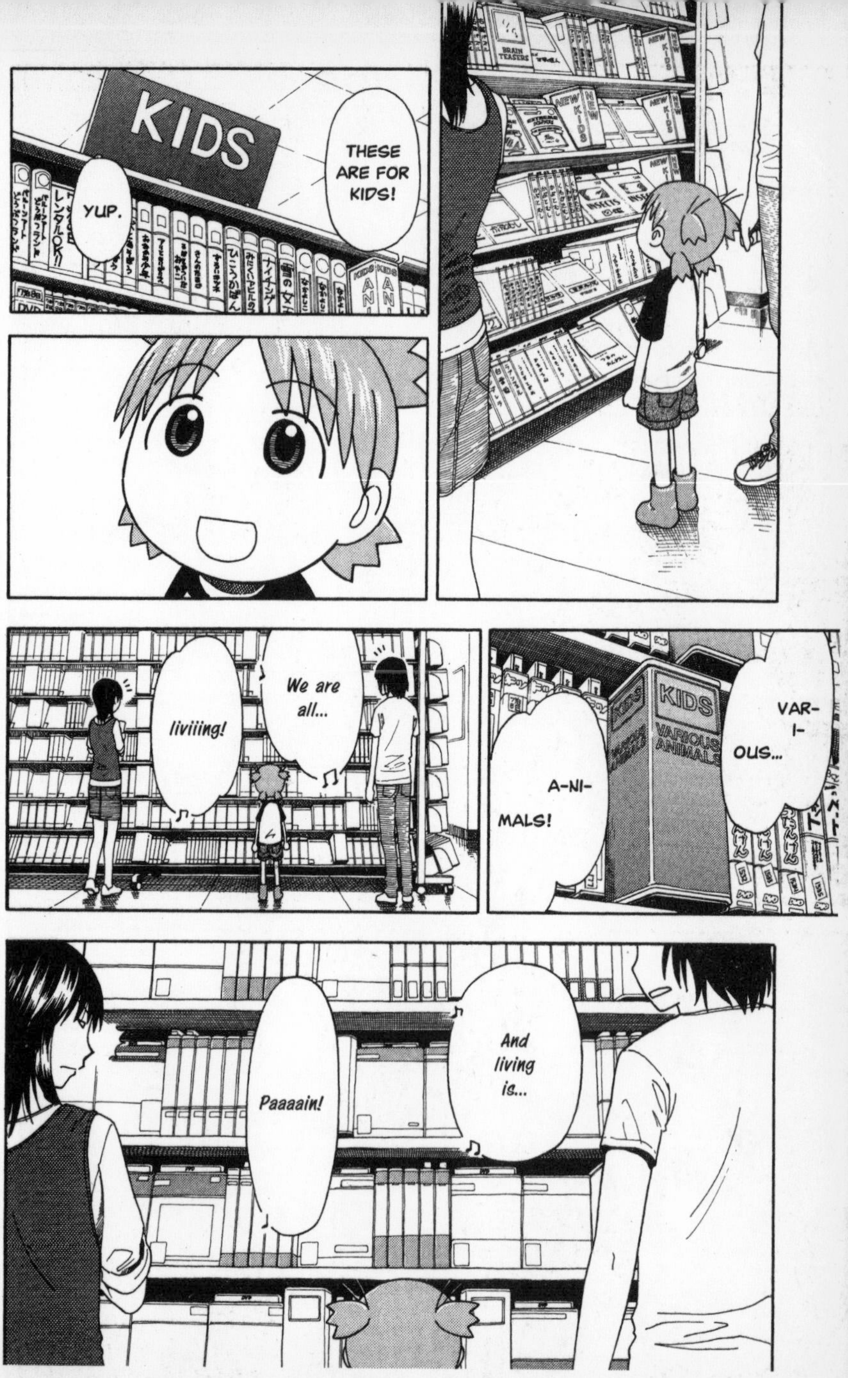
BRAIN TEASERS
NEW KIDS
INSECTS
KIDS
THESE ARE FOR KIDS!
YUP.
KIDS VARIOUS ANIMALS
VAR-I-OUS...
A-NI-MALS!
We are all...
liviiing!
And living is...
Paaaain!

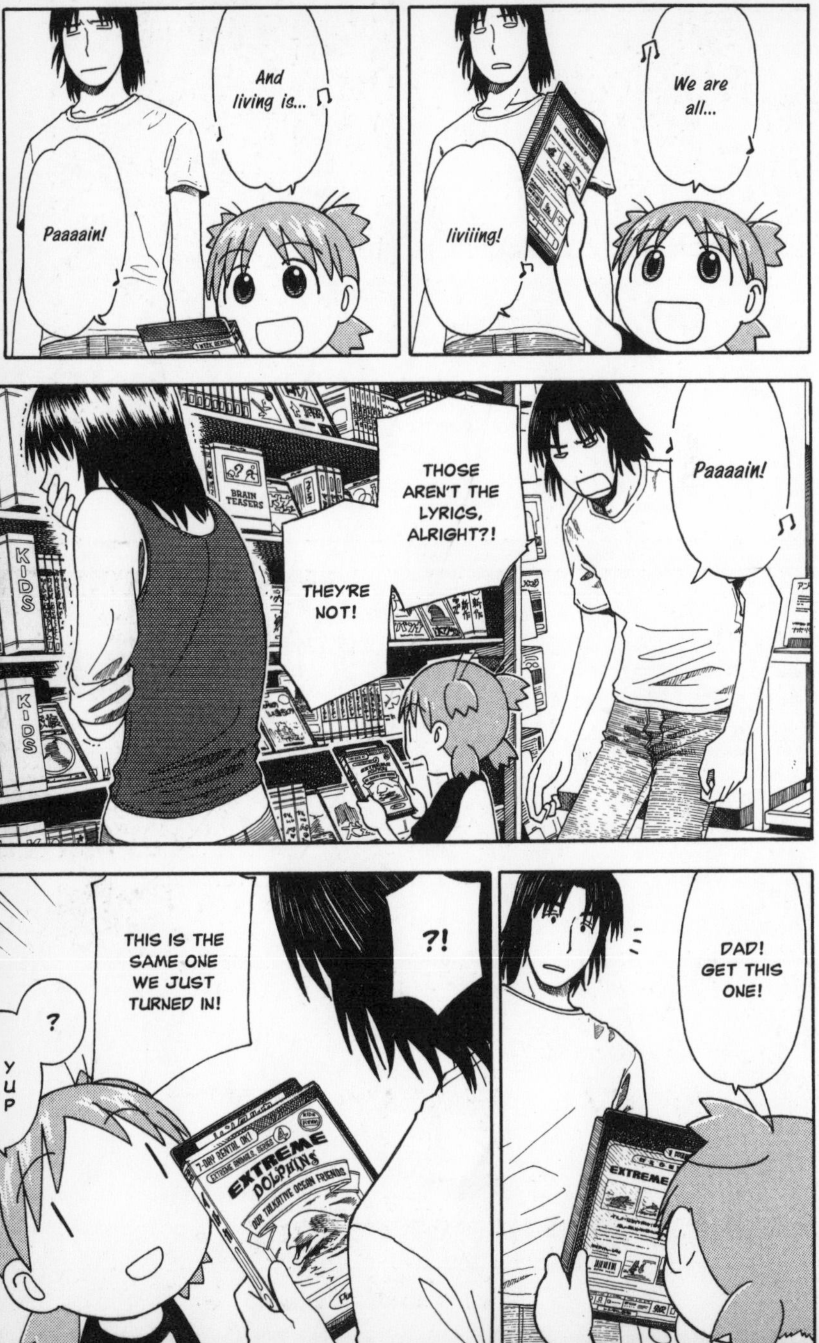
We are all...
liviiing!
And living is...
Paaaain!
Paaaain!
THOSE AREN'T THE LYRICS, ALRIGHT?!
THEY'RE NOT!
BRAIN TEASERS
KIDS
KIDS
DAD! GET THIS ONE!
EXTREME
?!
THIS IS THE SAME ONE WE JUST TURNED IN!
?
YUP
7-DAY RENTAL OK!
EXTREME ANIMALS, SERIES 4
EXTREME DOLPHINS
OUR TALKATIVE OCEAN FRIENDS

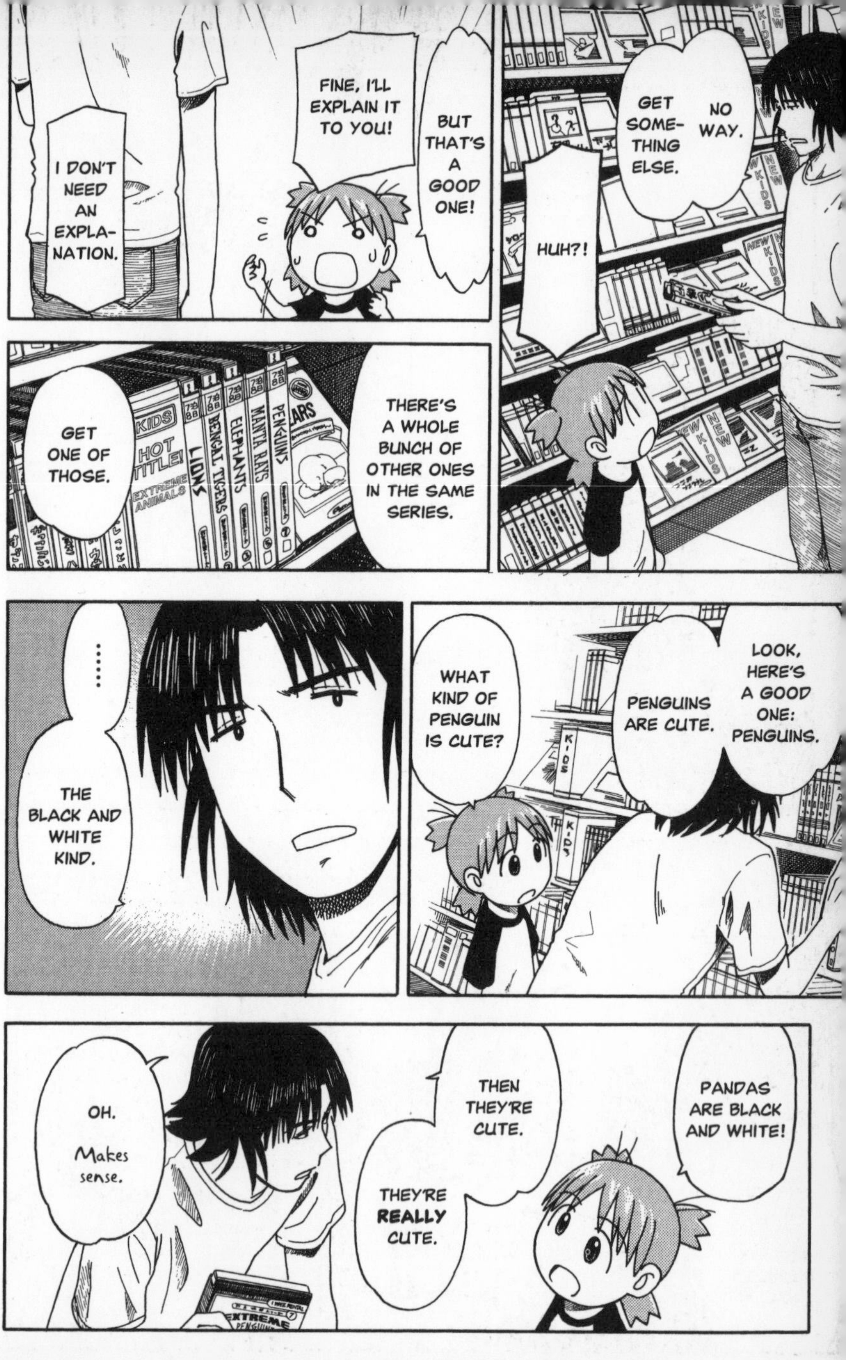
NO WAY.
GET SOME-THING ELSE.
HUH?!
BUT THAT'S A GOOD ONE!
FINE, I'LL EXPLAIN IT TO YOU!
I DON'T NEED AN EXPLA-NATION.
THERE'S A WHOLE BUNCH OF OTHER ONES IN THE SAME SERIES.
PENGUINS
MANTA RAYS
ELEPHANTS
BENGAL TIGERS
LIONS
KIDS
HOT TITLE!
EXTREME ANIMALS
GET ONE OF THOSE.
LOOK, HERE'S A GOOD ONE: PENGUINS.
PENGUINS ARE CUTE.
WHAT KIND OF PENGUIN IS CUTE?
......
THE BLACK AND WHITE KIND.
PANDAS ARE BLACK AND WHITE!
THEN THEY'RE CUTE.
THEY'RE REALLY CUTE.
EXTREME PENGUINS
OH.
Makes sense.

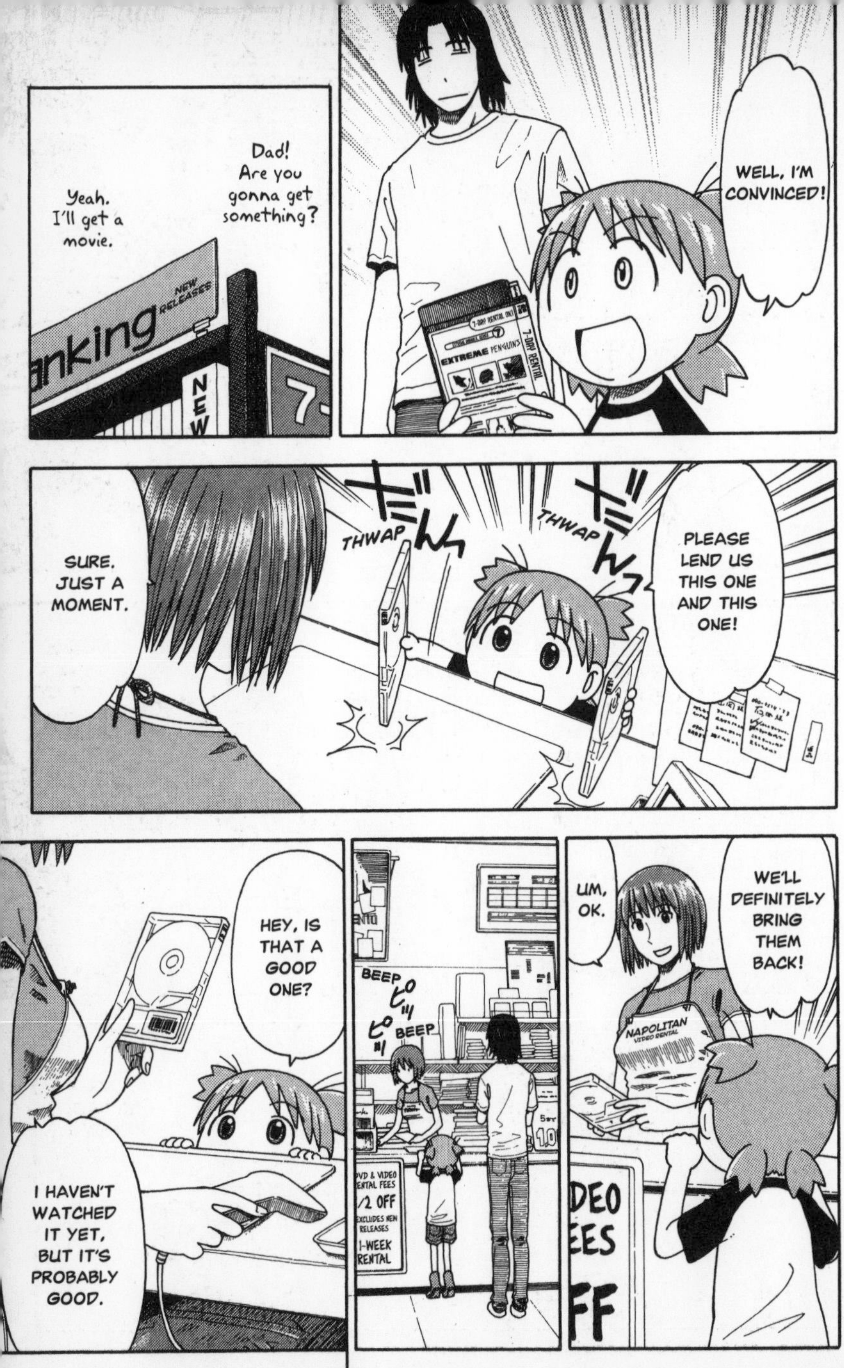
WELL, I'M CONVINCED!
7-DAY RENTAL
EXTREME PENGUINS
Dad! Are you gonna get something?
Yeah. I'll get a movie.
NEW RELEASES
THWAP
THWAP
PLEASE LEND US THIS ONE AND THIS ONE!
SURE. JUST A MOMENT.
WE'LL DEFINITELY BRING THEM BACK!
UM, OK.
NAPOLITAN VIDEO RENTAL
BEEP
BEEP
HEY, IS THAT A GOOD ONE?
I HAVEN'T WATCHED IT YET, BUT IT'S PROBABLY GOOD.

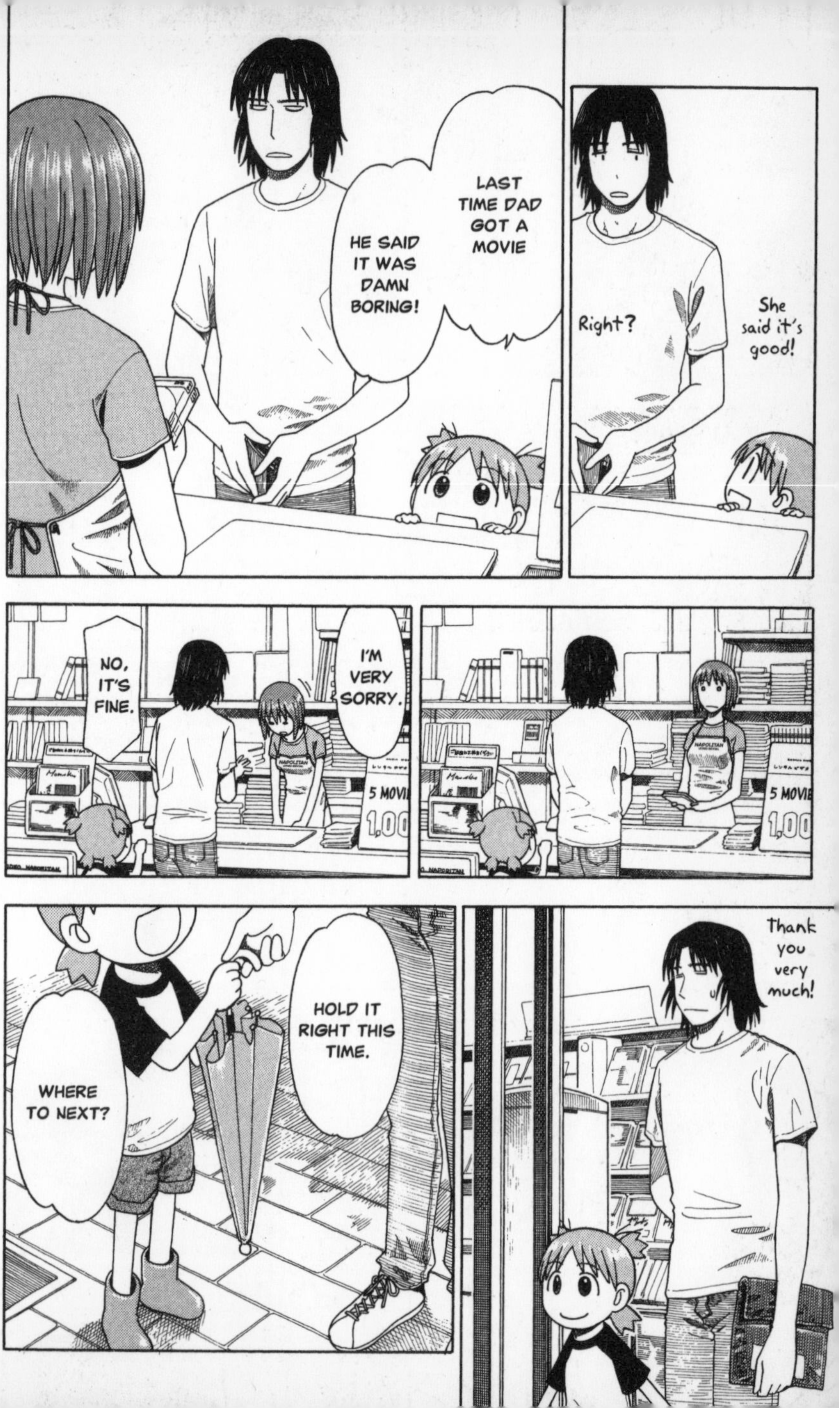
Right?
She said it's good!
LAST TIME DAD GOT A MOVIE
HE SAID IT WAS DAMN BORING!
I'M VERY SORRY.
NO, IT'S FINE.
Thank you very much!
HOLD IT RIGHT THIS TIME.
WHERE TO NEXT?

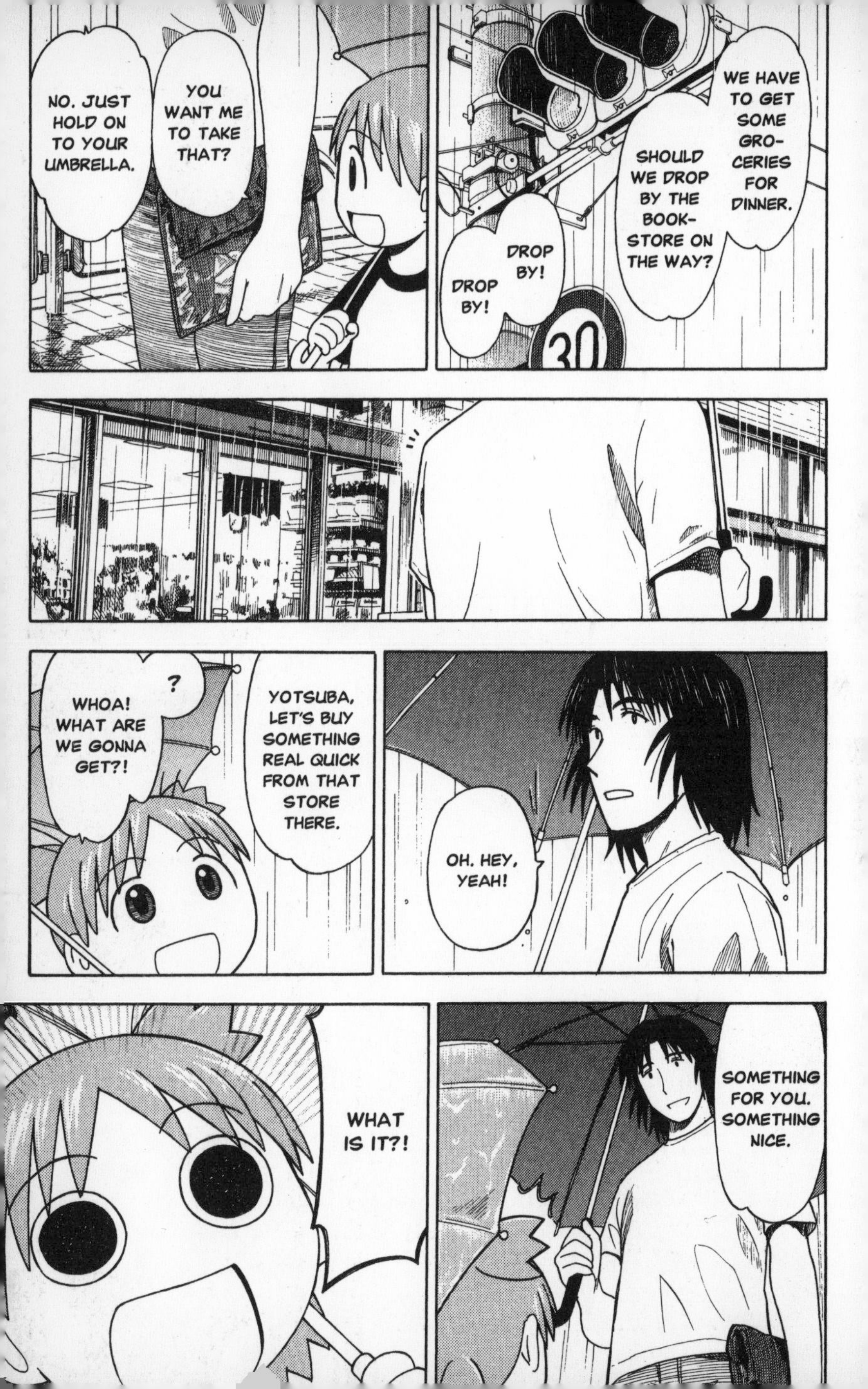
WE HAVE TO GET SOME GRO-CERIES FOR DINNER.
SHOULD WE DROP BY THE BOOK-STORE ON THE WAY?
DROP BY!
DROP BY!
YOU WANT ME TO TAKE THAT?
NO. JUST HOLD ON TO YOUR UMBRELLA.
OH. HEY, YEAH!
YOTSUBA, LET'S BUY SOMETHING REAL QUICK FROM THAT STORE THERE.
?
WHOA! WHAT ARE WE GONNA GET?!
SOMETHING FOR YOU. SOMETHING NICE.
WHAT IS IT?!

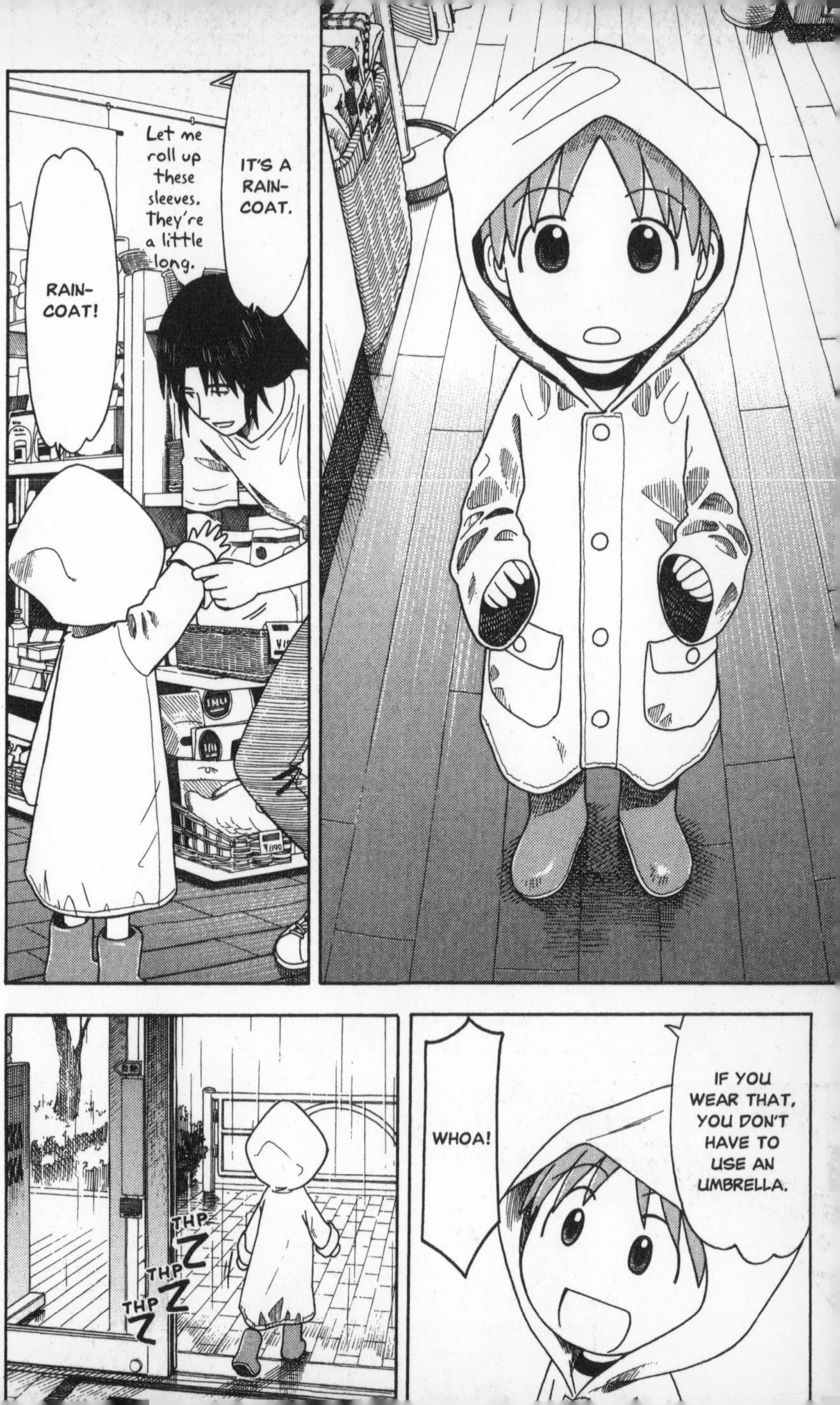
IT'S A RAIN-COAT.
Let me roll up these sleeves. They're a little long.
RAIN-COAT!
IF YOU WEAR THAT, YOU DON'T HAVE TO USE AN UMBRELLA.
WHOA!
THP Z
THP Z
THP Z

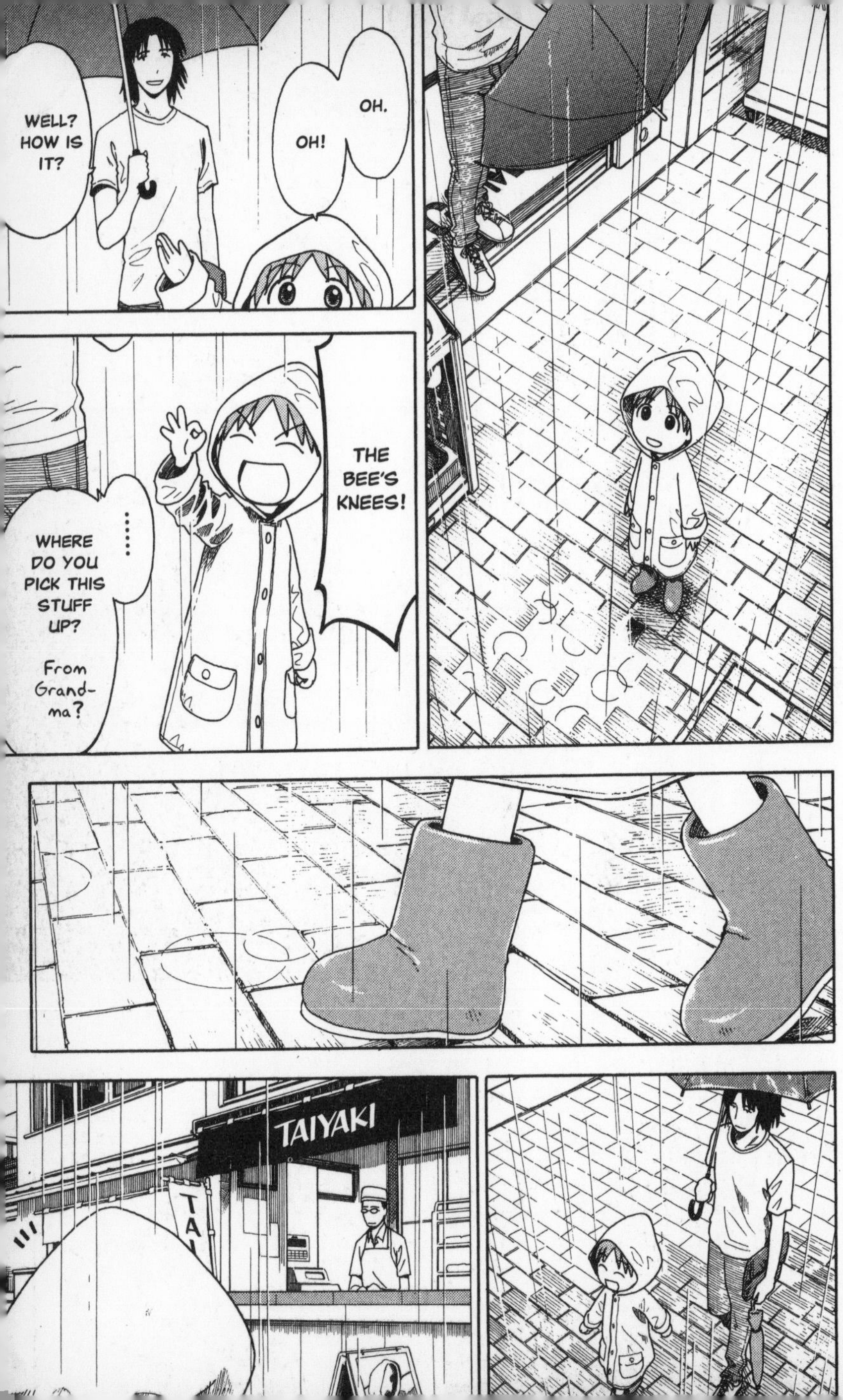
OH.
OH!
WELL? HOW IS IT?
THE BEE'S KNEES!
......
WHERE DO YOU PICK THIS STUFF UP?
From Grand-ma?
TAIYAKI
TAI

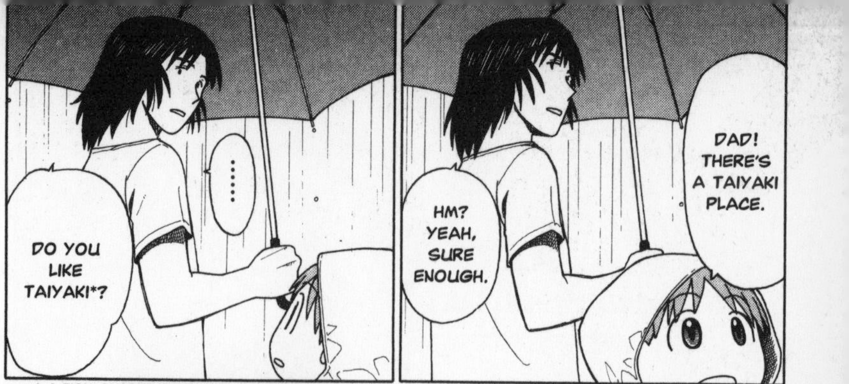
DAD! THERE'S A TAIYAKI PLACE.
HM? YEAH, SURE ENOUGH.
......
DO YOU LIKE TAIYAKI*?

* A FISH-SHAPED CAKE WITH A SWEET FILLING.

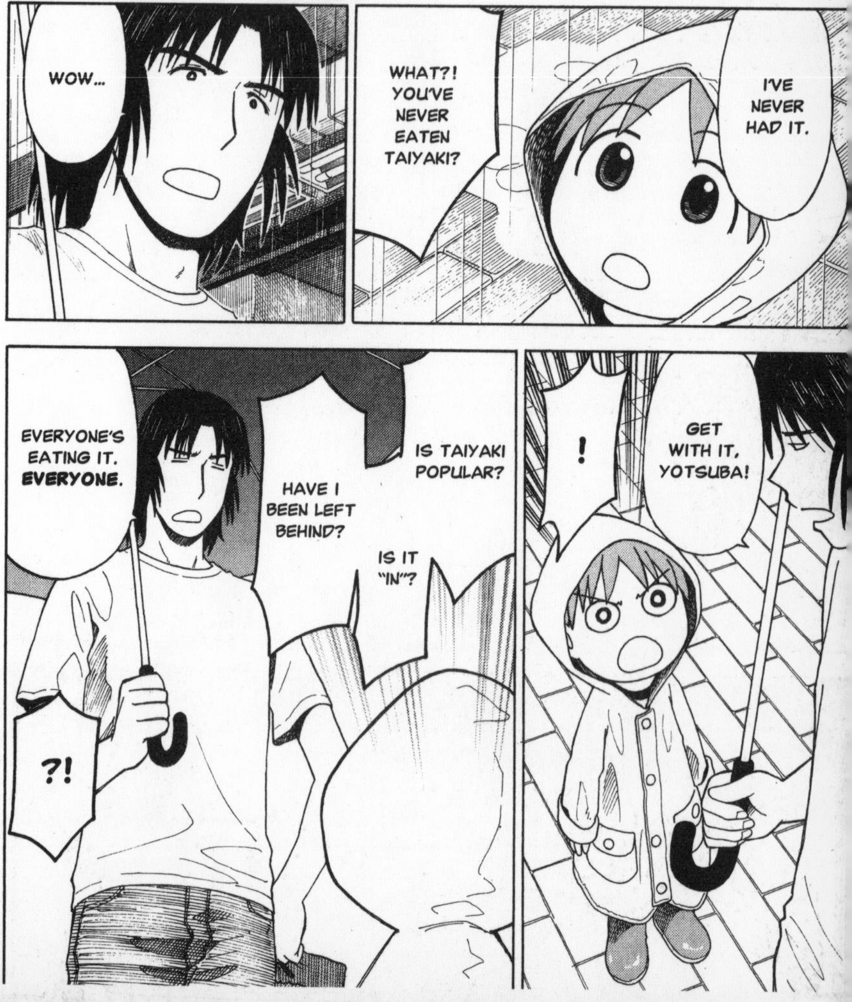
I'VE NEVER HAD IT.
WHAT?! YOU'VE NEVER EATEN TAIYAKI?
WOW...
GET WITH IT, YOTSUBA!
!
IS TAIYAKI POPULAR?
HAVE I BEEN LEFT BEHIND?
IS IT "IN"?
EVERYONE'S EATING IT. **EVERYONE**.
?!

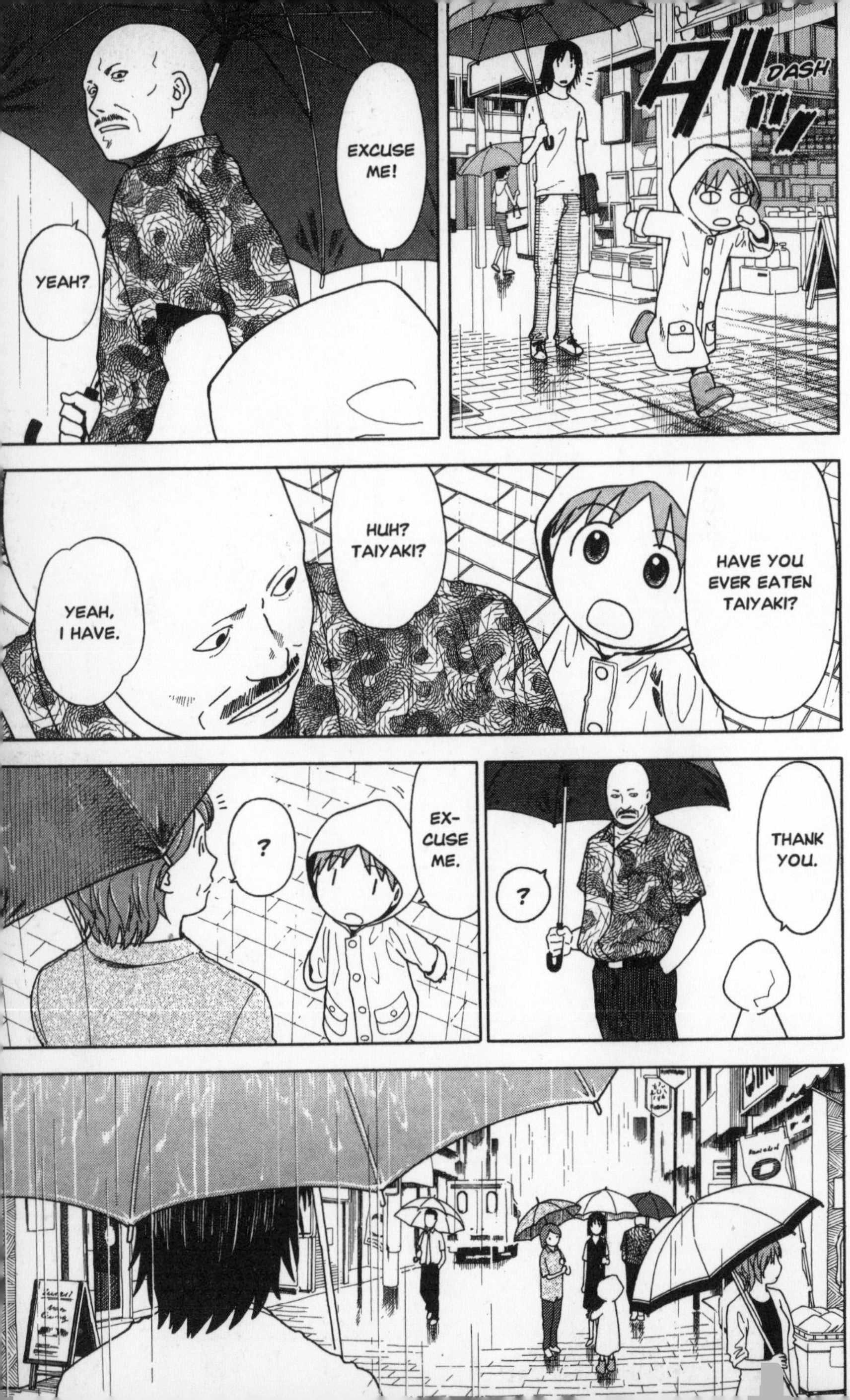
DASH
EXCUSE ME!
YEAH?
HAVE YOU EVER EATEN TAIYAKI?
HUH? TAIYAKI?
YEAH, I HAVE.
THANK YOU.
?
EX-CUSE ME.
?

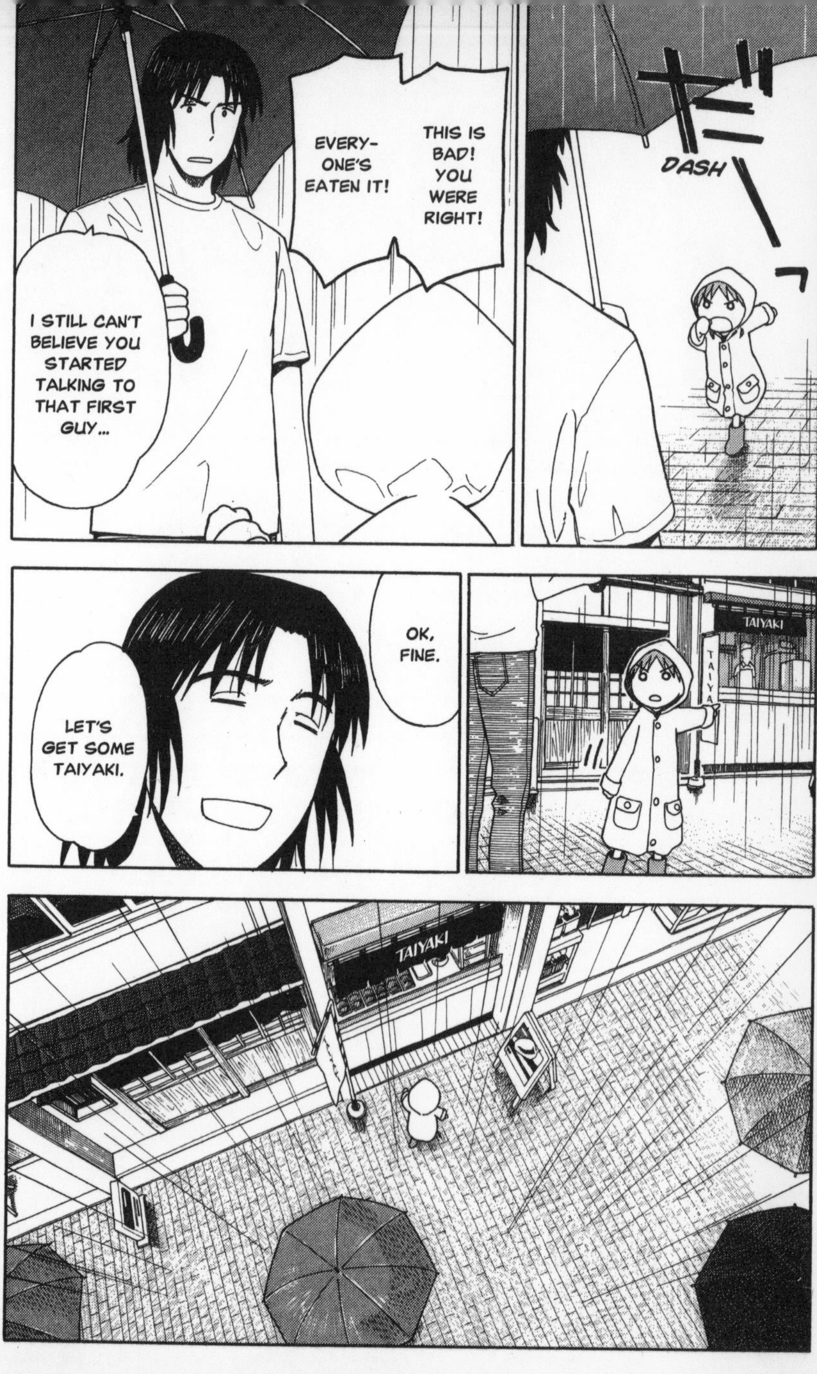
DASH
THIS IS BAD! YOU WERE RIGHT!
EVERY-ONE'S EATEN IT!
I STILL CAN'T BELIEVE YOU STARTED TALKING TO THAT FIRST GUY...
TAIYAKI
OK, FINE.
LET'S GET SOME TAIYAKI.
TAIYAKI

YOTSUBA&!

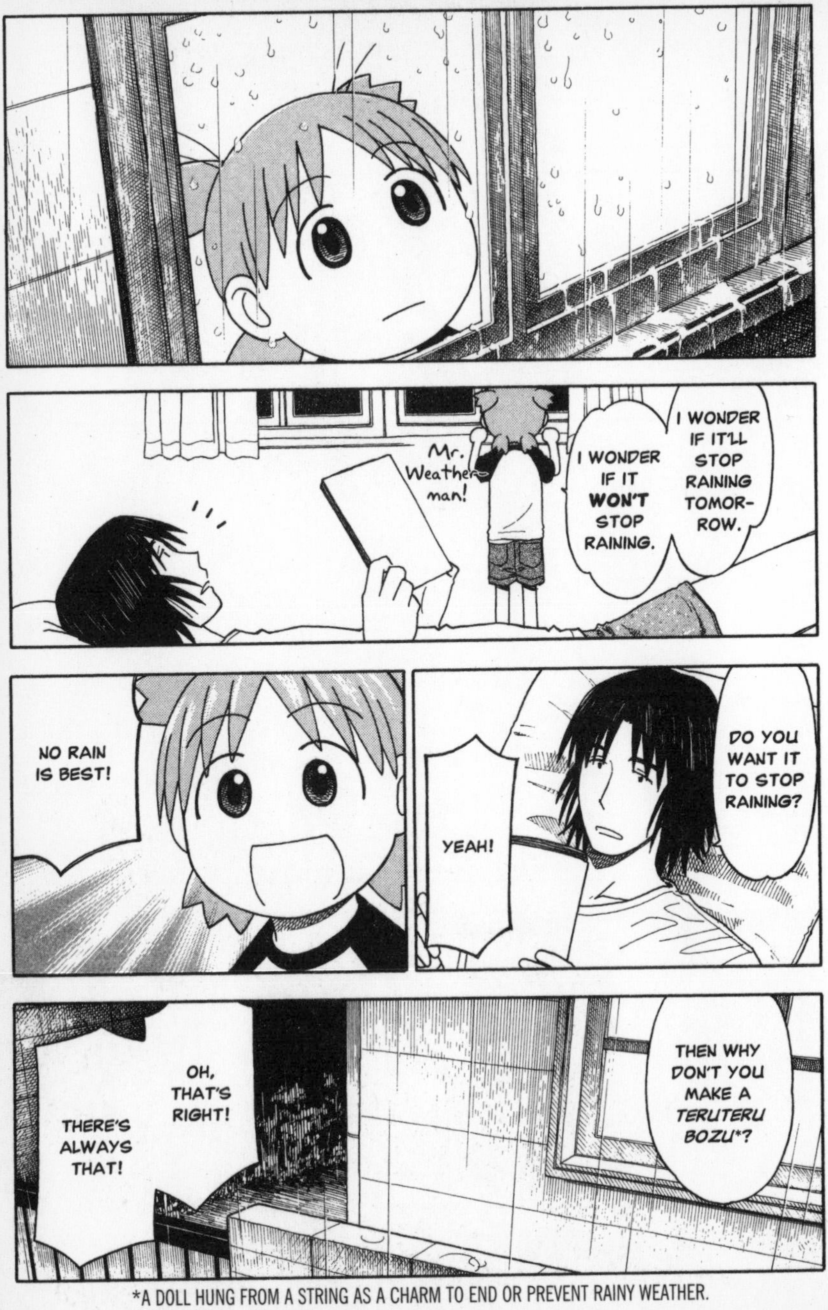
I WONDER IF IT'LL STOP RAINING TOMORROW.
I WONDER IF IT WON'T STOP RAINING.
Mr. Weatherman!
DO YOU WANT IT TO STOP RAINING?
YEAH!
NO RAIN IS BEST!
THEN WHY DON'T YOU MAKE A TERUTERU BOZU*?
OH, THAT'S RIGHT!
THERE'S ALWAYS THAT!

*A DOLL HUNG FROM A STRING AS A CHARM TO END OR PREVENT RAINY WEATHER.

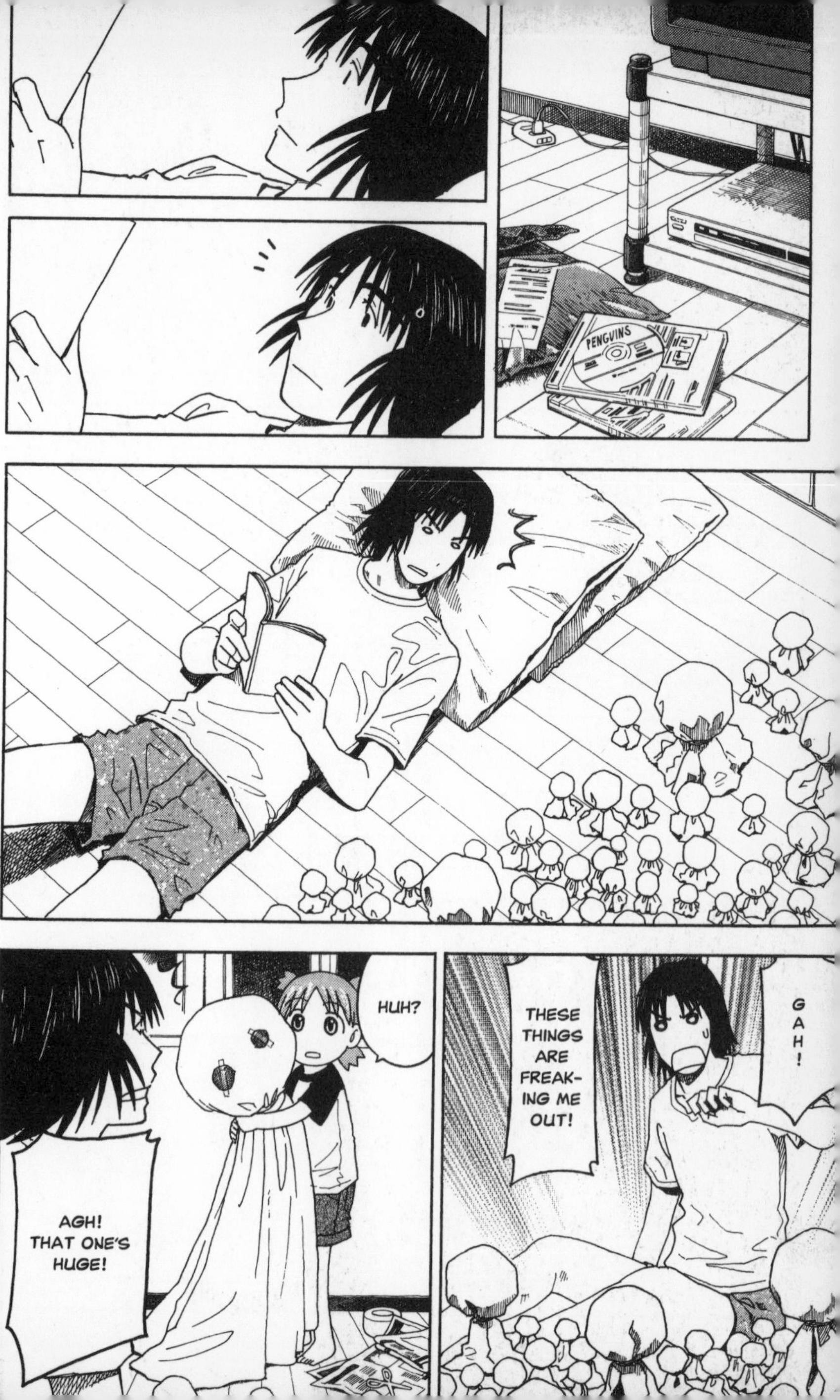
GAH!
THESE THINGS ARE FREAK-ING ME OUT!
HUH?
AGH! THAT ONE'S HUGE!

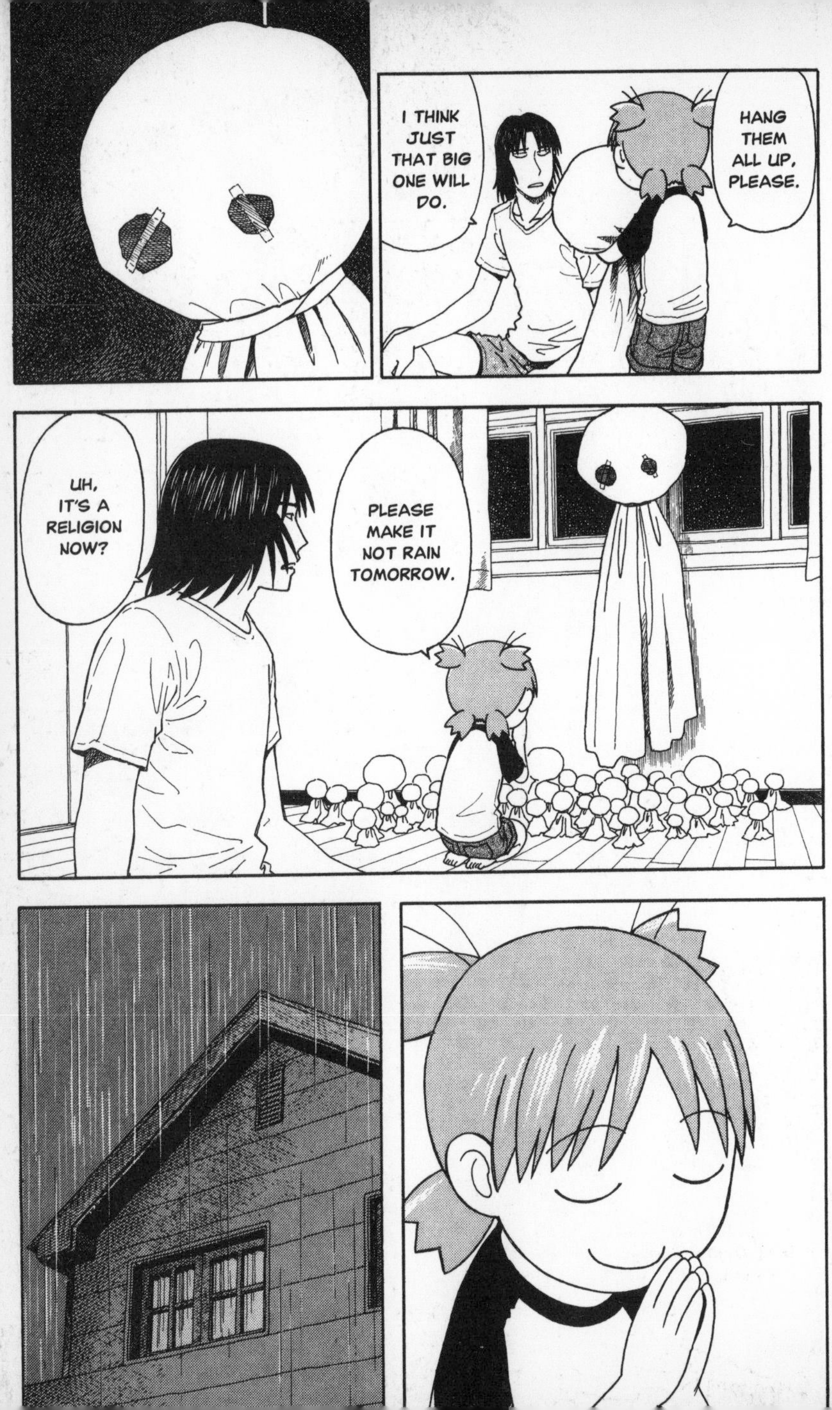
HANG THEM ALL UP, PLEASE.
I THINK JUST THAT BIG ONE WILL DO.
PLEASE MAKE IT NOT RAIN TOMORROW.
UH, IT'S A RELIGION NOW?

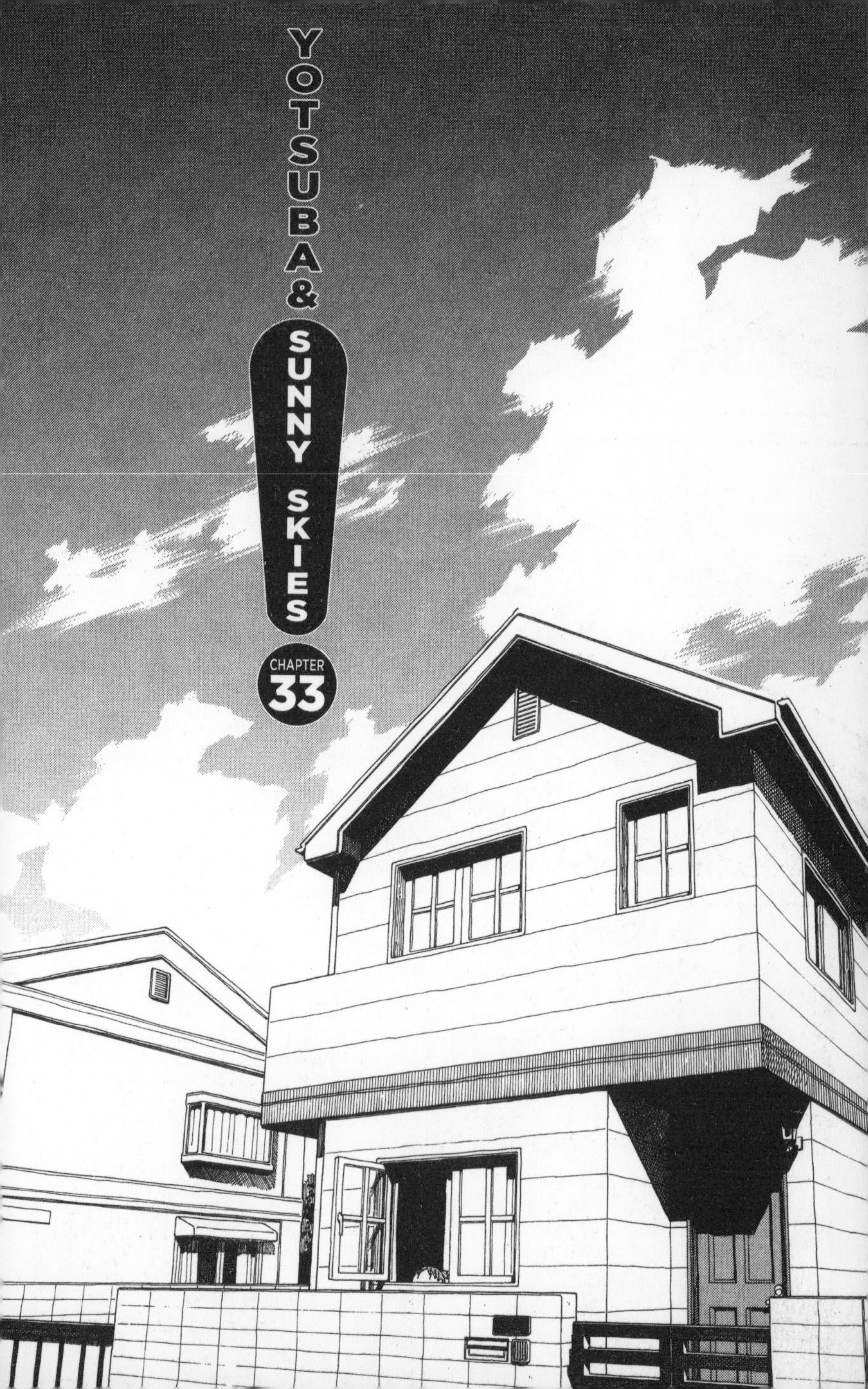
YOTSUBA&!
SUNNY SKIES
CHAPTER 33

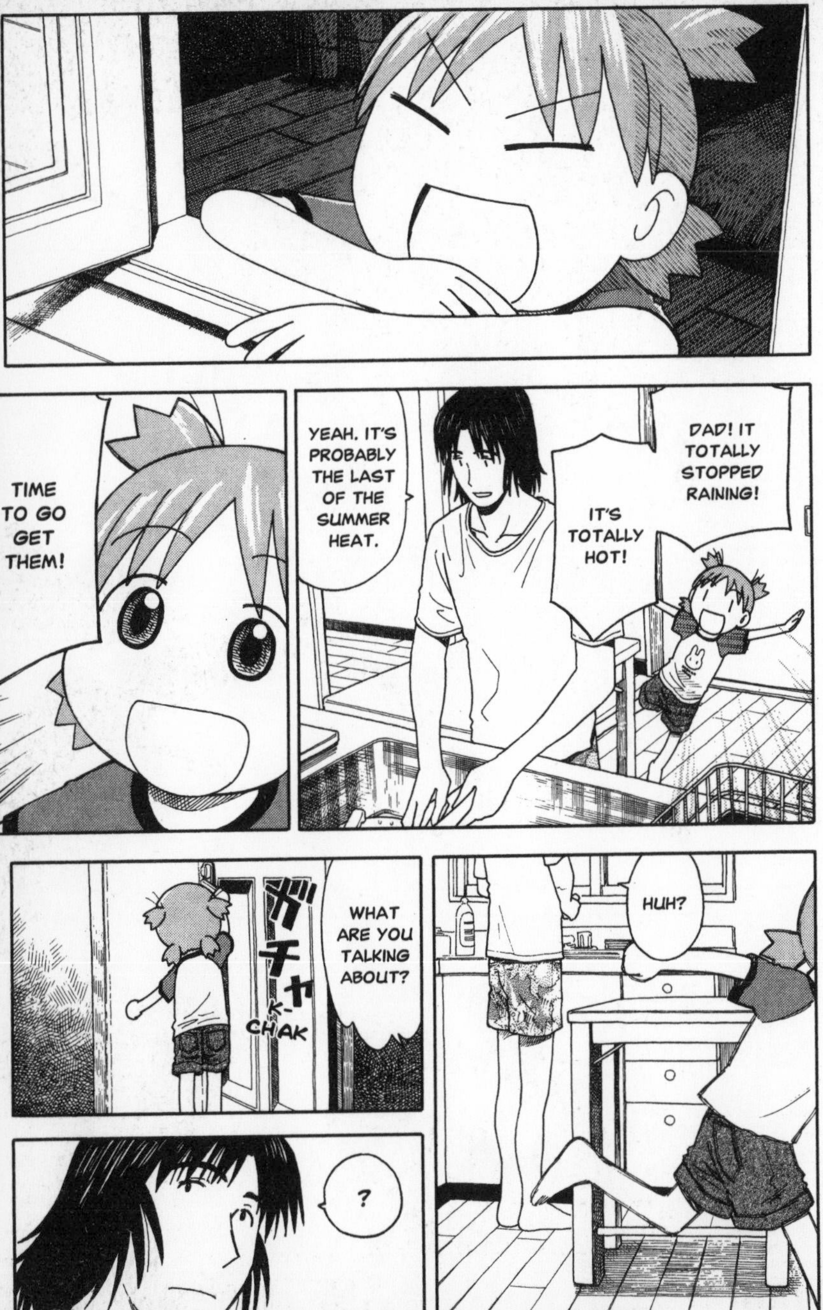
DAD! IT TOTALLY STOPPED RAINING!
IT'S TOTALLY HOT!
YEAH. IT'S PROBABLY THE LAST OF THE SUMMER HEAT.
TIME TO GO GET THEM!
HUH?
WHAT ARE YOU TALKING ABOUT?
K-CHAK
?

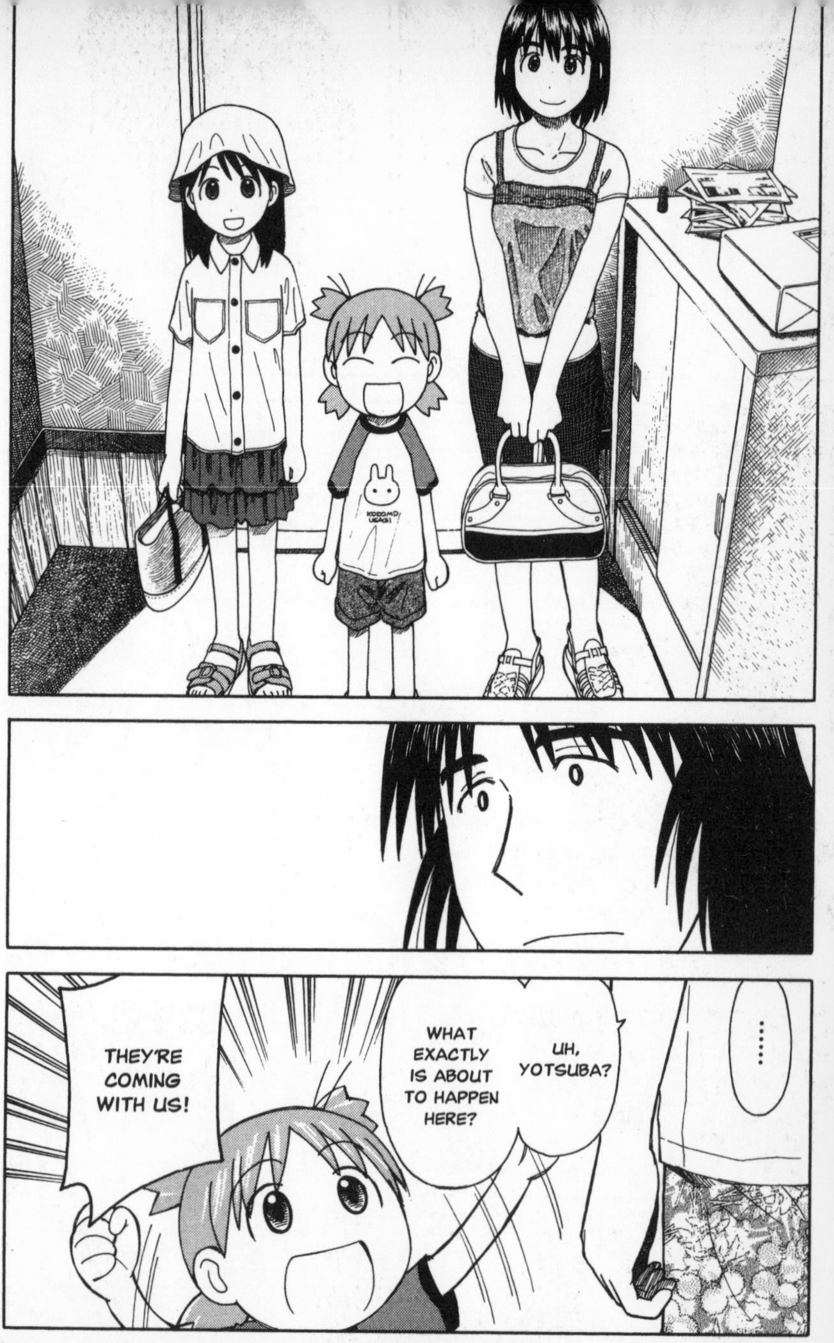
......
UH, YOTSUBA?
WHAT EXACTLY IS ABOUT TO HAPPEN HERE?
THEY'RE COMING WITH US!

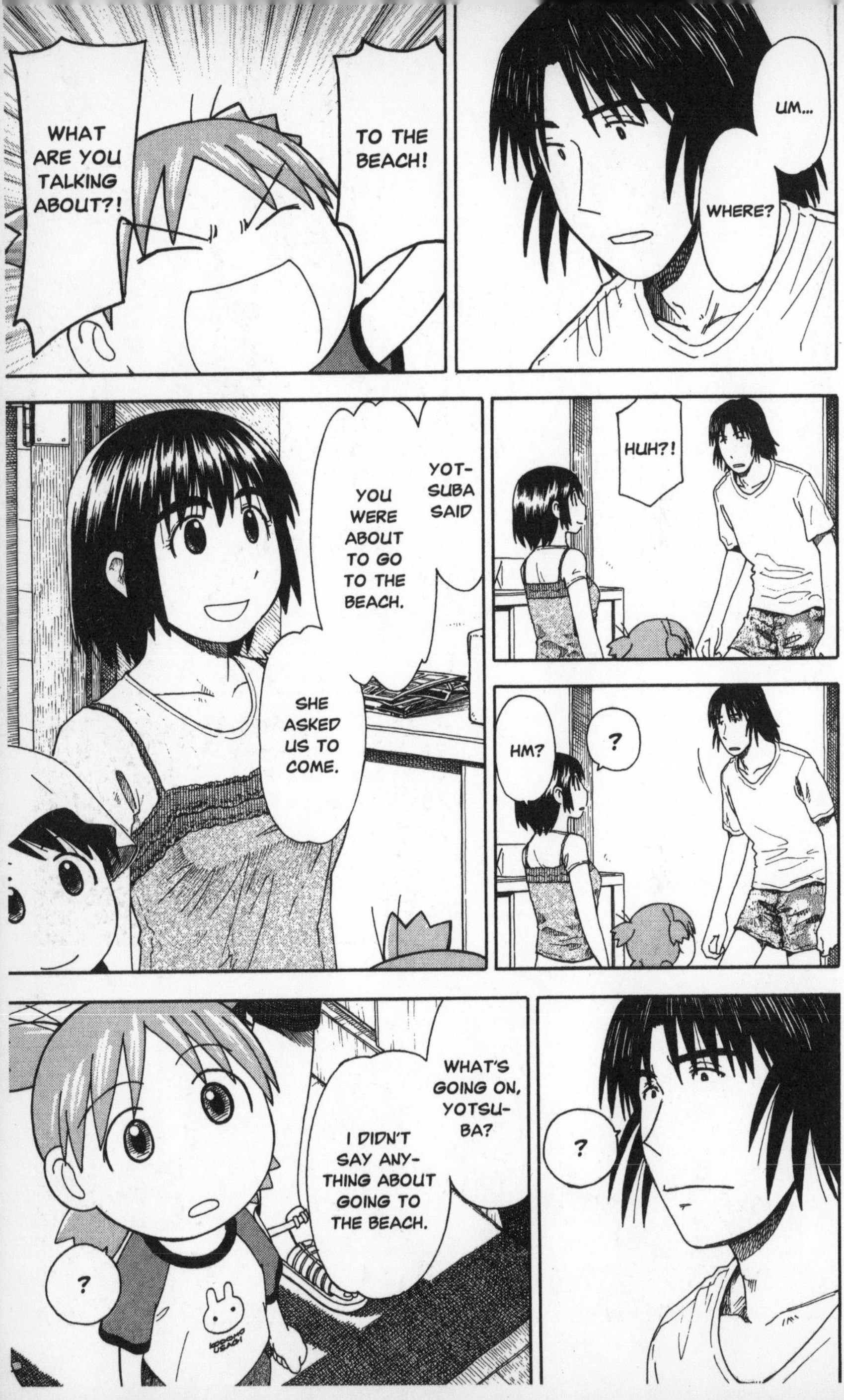
UM...
WHERE?
TO THE BEACH!
WHAT ARE YOU TALKING ABOUT?!
HUH?!
?
HM?
YOTSUBA SAID YOU WERE ABOUT TO GO TO THE BEACH.
SHE ASKED US TO COME.
?
WHAT'S GOING ON, YOTSUBA?
I DIDN'T SAY ANYTHING ABOUT GOING TO THE BEACH.
?

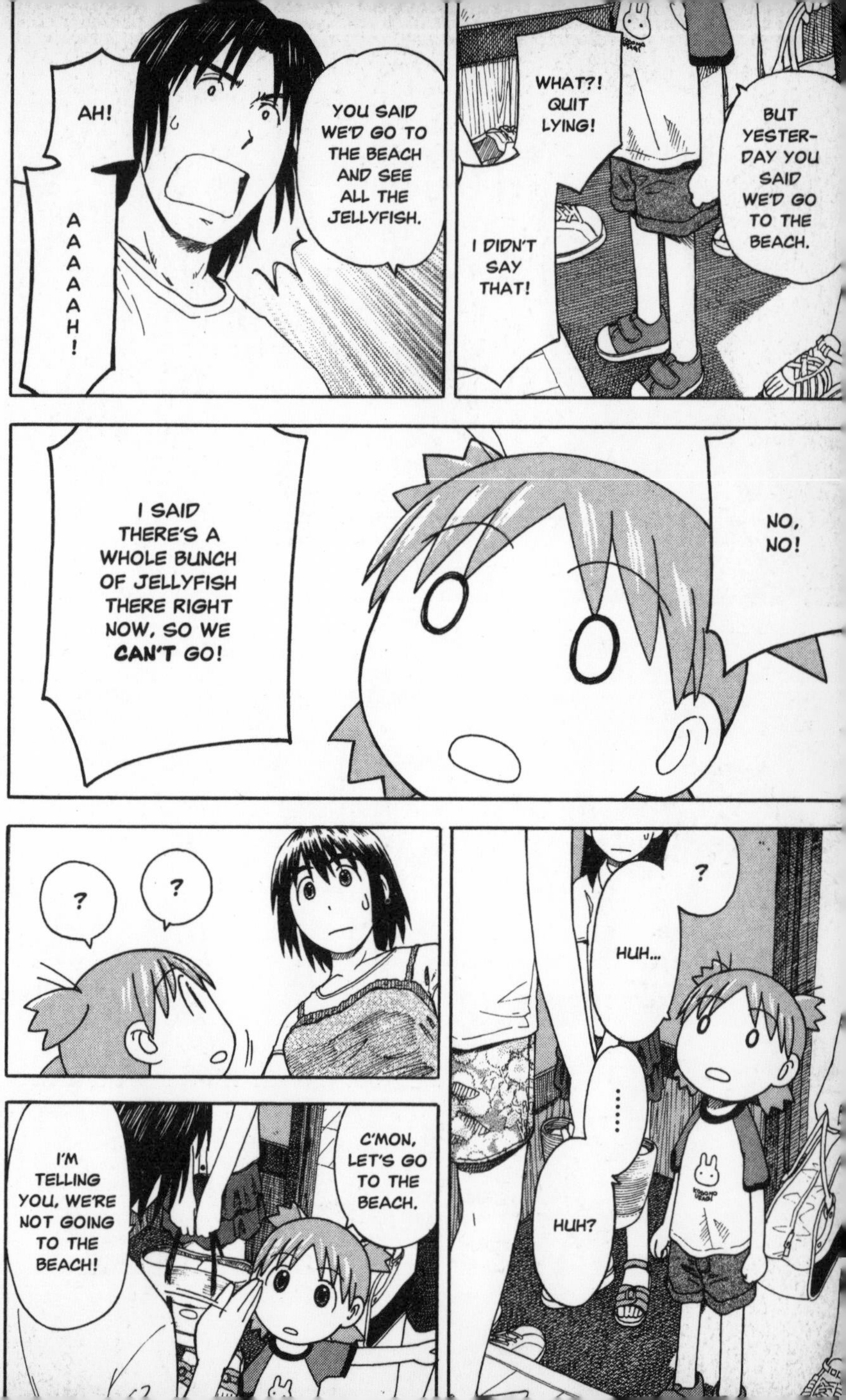
BUT YESTER-DAY YOU SAID WE'D GO TO THE BEACH.
WHAT?! QUIT LYING!
I DIDN'T SAY THAT!
YOU SAID WE'D GO TO THE BEACH AND SEE ALL THE JELLYFISH.
AH!
AAAAAH!
NO, NO!
I SAID THERE'S A WHOLE BUNCH OF JELLYFISH THERE RIGHT NOW, SO WE **CAN'T** GO!
?
HUH...
......
HUH?
?
?
C'MON, LET'S GO TO THE BEACH.
I'M TELLING YOU, WE'RE NOT GOING TO THE BEACH!

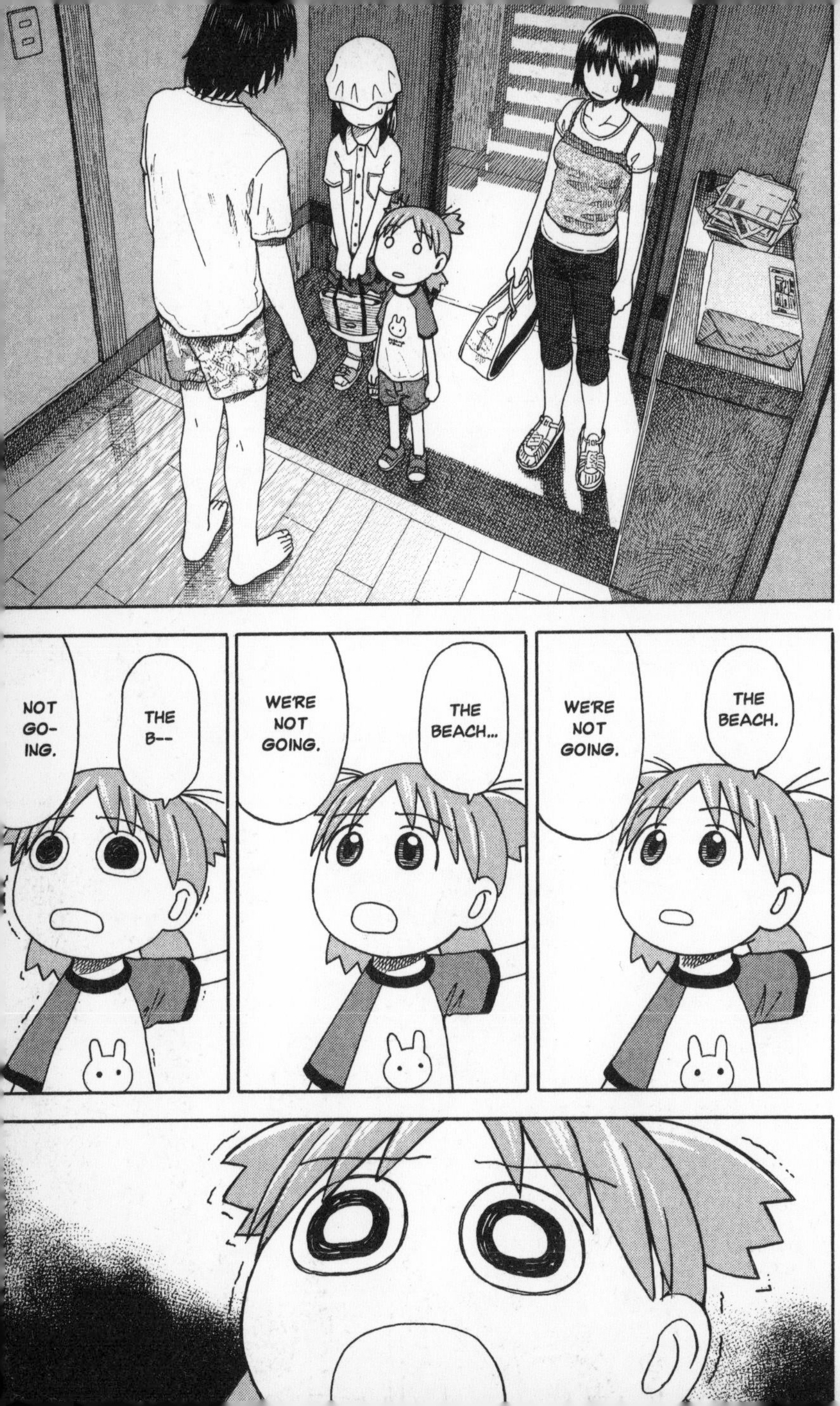
THE BEACH.
WE'RE NOT GOING.
THE BEACH...
WE'RE NOT GOING.
THE B--
NOT GO-ING.

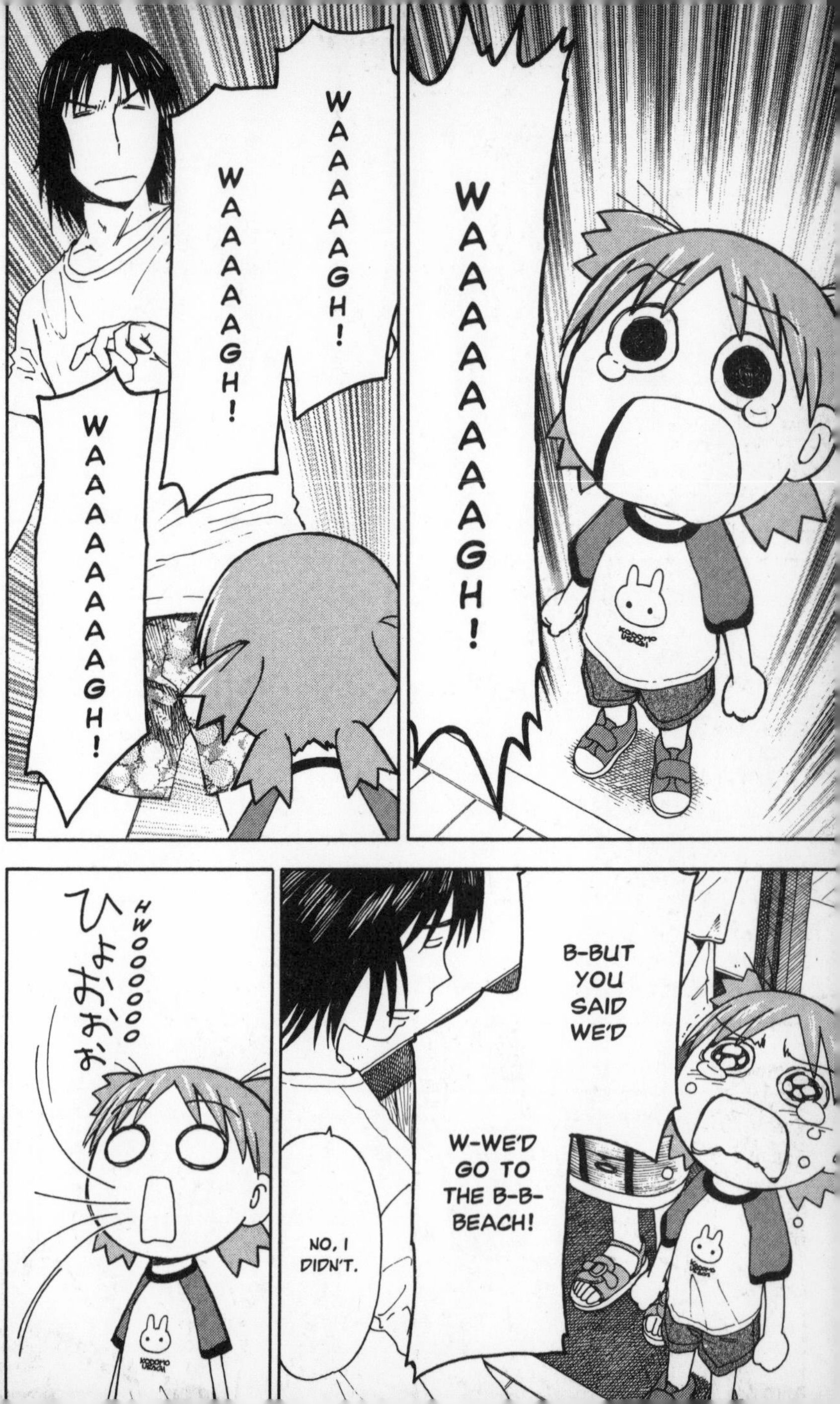
WAAAAAAAAAAAGH!
WAAAAAGH!
WAAAAAAGH!
WAAAAAAAAAGH!
B-BUT YOU SAID WE'D
W-WE'D GO TO THE B-B-BEACH!
NO, I DIDN'T.
HWOOOOOO
ひょぉぉぉ

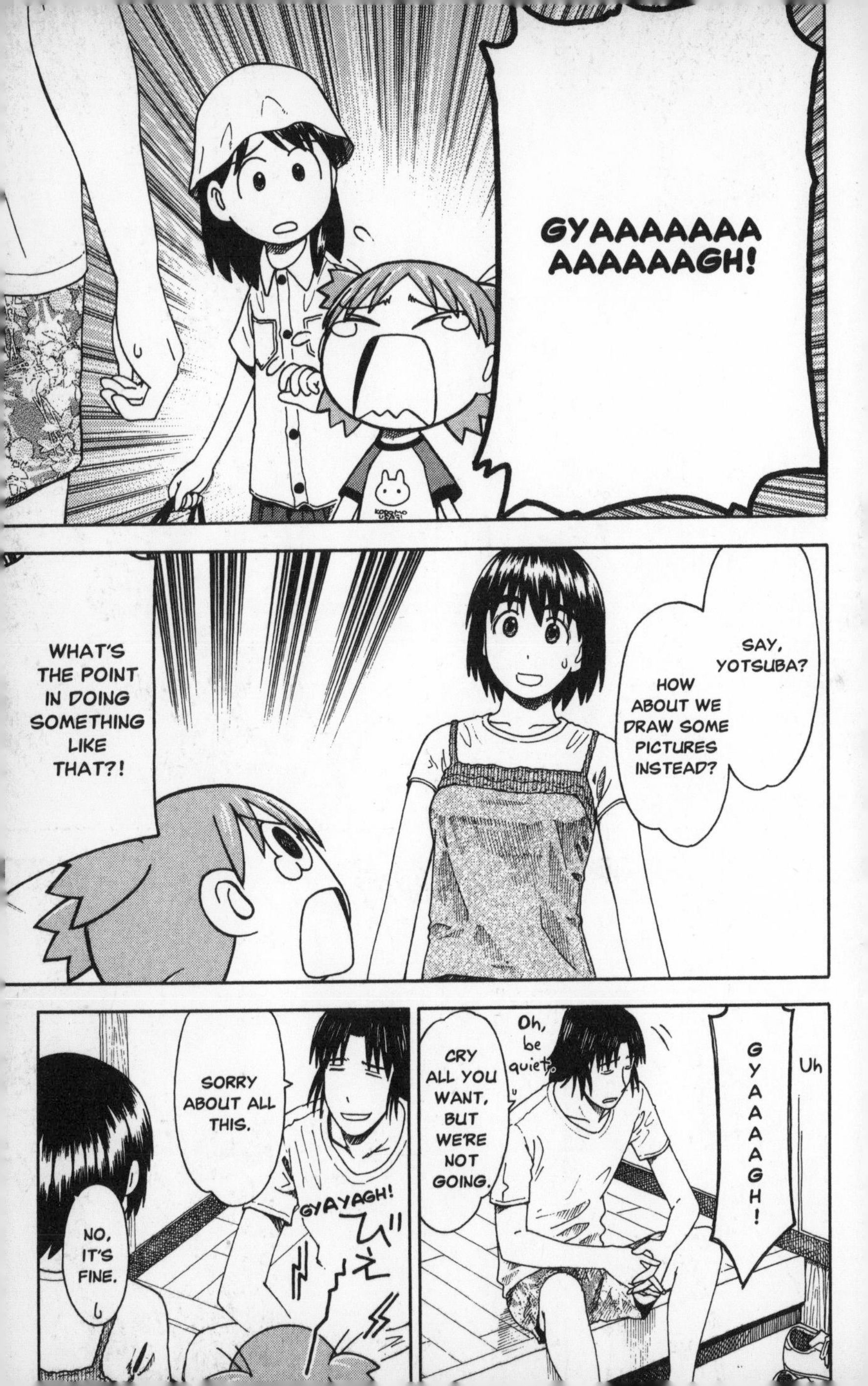
GYAAAAAAA
AAAAAAGH!
SAY, YOTSUBA? HOW ABOUT WE DRAW SOME PICTURES INSTEAD?
WHAT'S THE POINT IN DOING SOMETHING LIKE THAT?!
Uh
GYAAAAGH!
Oh, be quiet.
CRY ALL YOU WANT, BUT WE'RE NOT GOING.
GYAYAGH!
SORRY ABOUT ALL THIS.
NO, IT'S FINE.

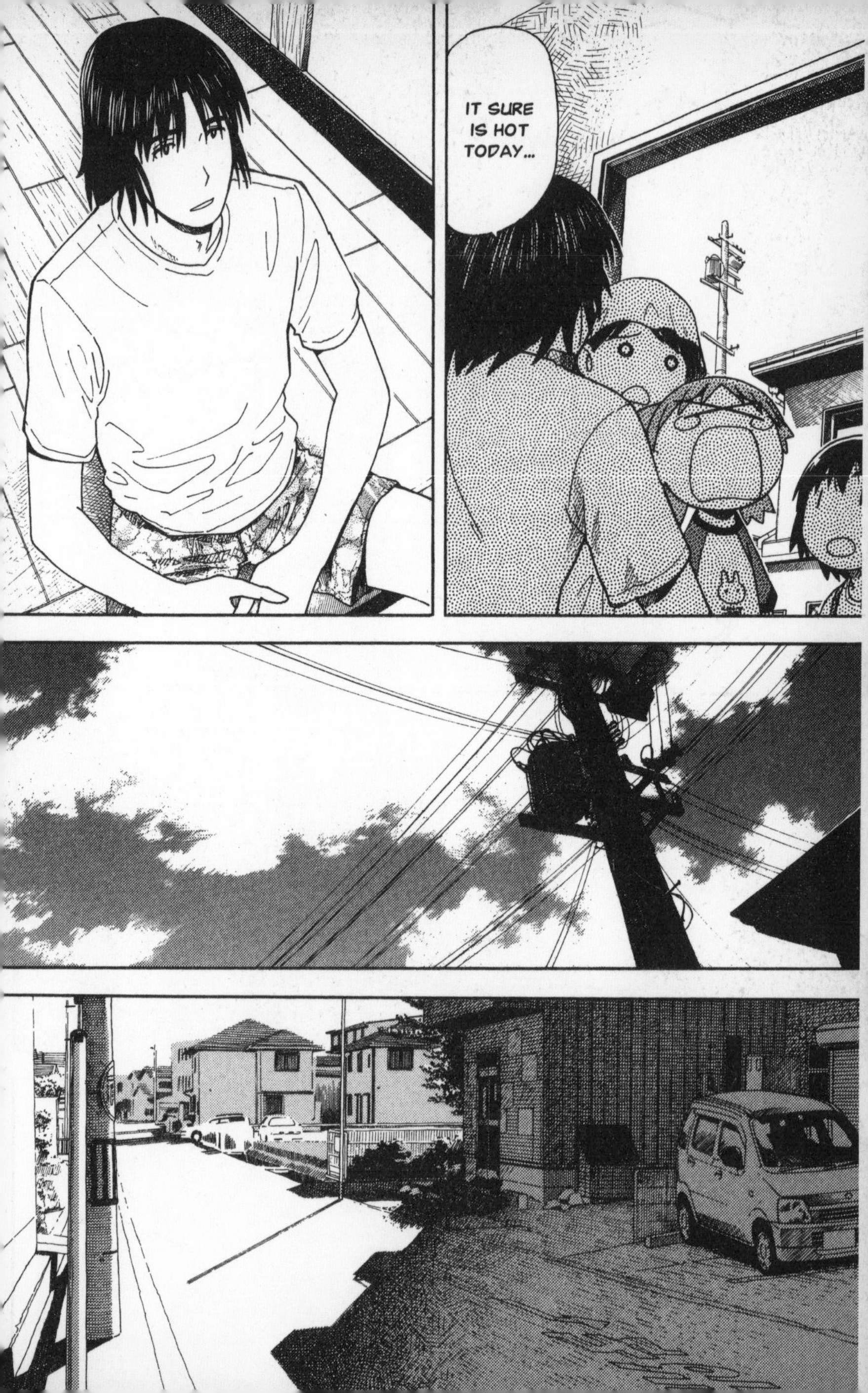
IT SURE IS HOT TODAY...

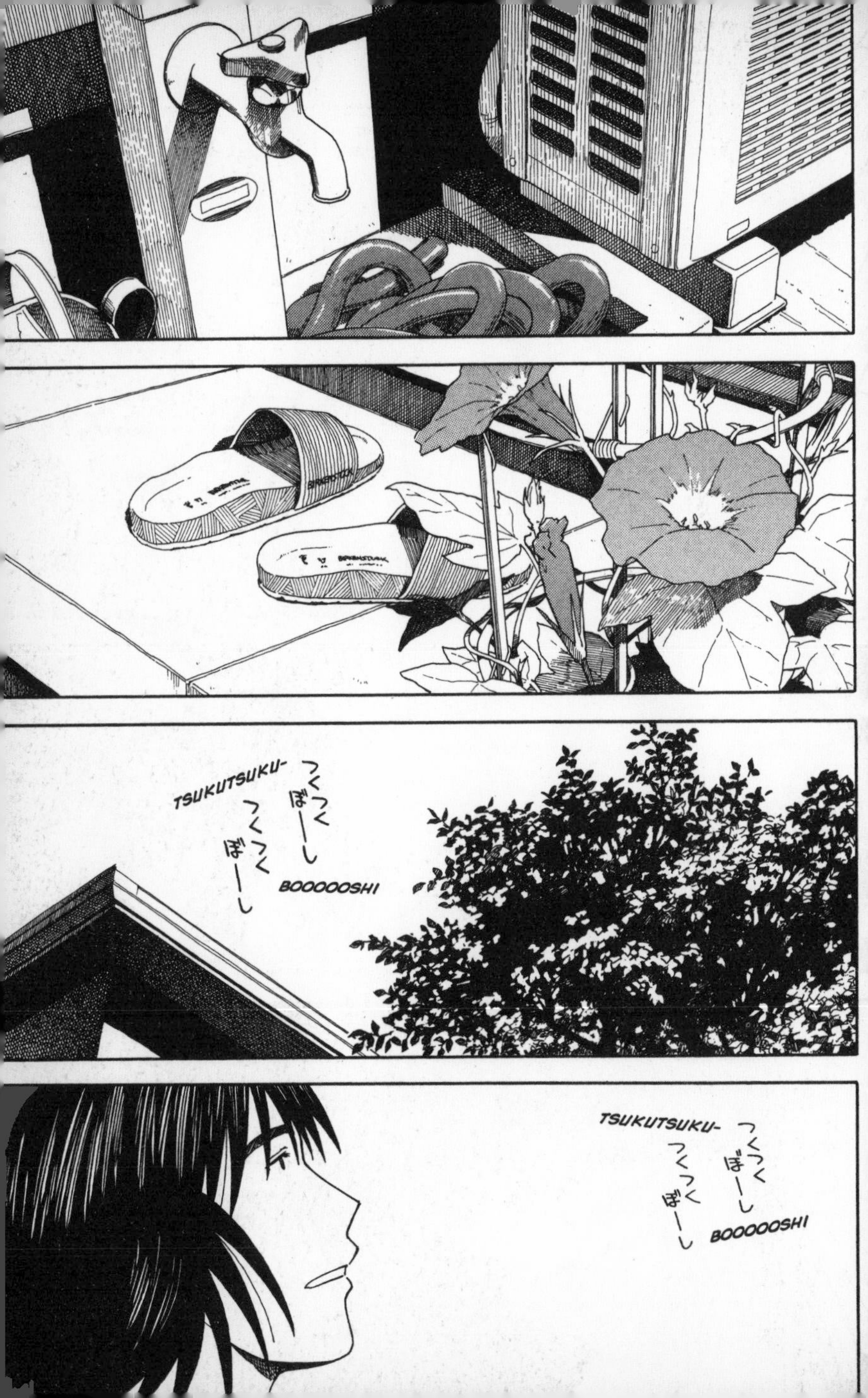
つくつく ぼーーし
TSUKUTSUKU-
つくつく ぼーーし
BOOOOOSHI
つくつく ぼーーし
TSUKUTSUKU-
つくつく ぼーーし
BOOOOOSHI

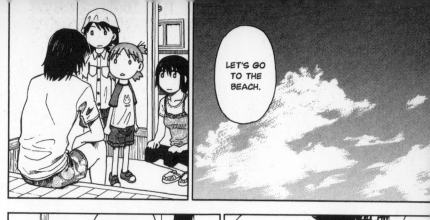

LET'S GO TO THE BEACH.
IT'S HOT AND IT'S THE END OF AU-GUST.
YOTSUBA, HURRY UP AND GET YOUR THINGS READY.
Step on it!
COME ON, YOTSUBA. YOU HAVE TO GET READY!
WE'RE GOING TO THE BEACH!
THMP
THMP
THMP
THMP

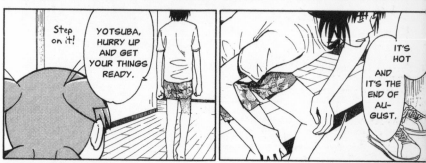

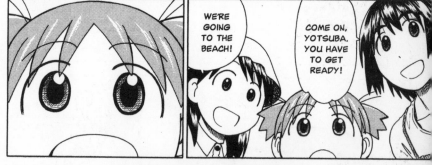

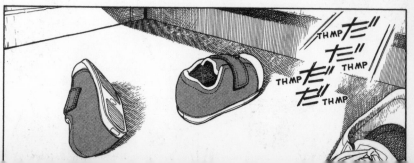

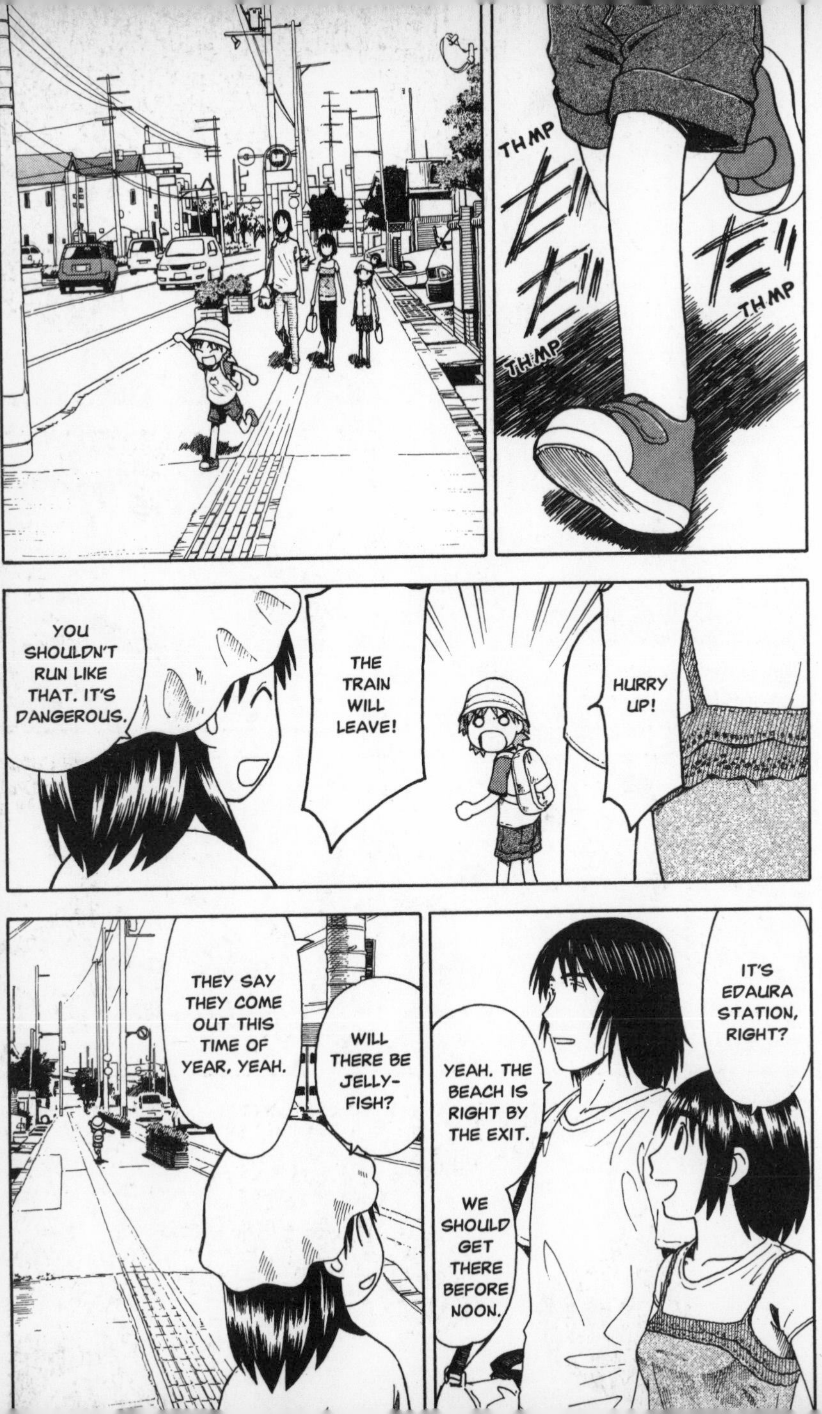
THMP
THMP
THMP
HURRY UP!
THE TRAIN WILL LEAVE!
YOU SHOULDN'T RUN LIKE THAT. IT'S DANGEROUS.
IT'S EDAURA STATION, RIGHT?
YEAH. THE BEACH IS RIGHT BY THE EXIT.
WE SHOULD GET THERE BEFORE NOON.
WILL THERE BE JELLY-FISH?
THEY SAY THEY COME OUT THIS TIME OF YEAR, YEAH.

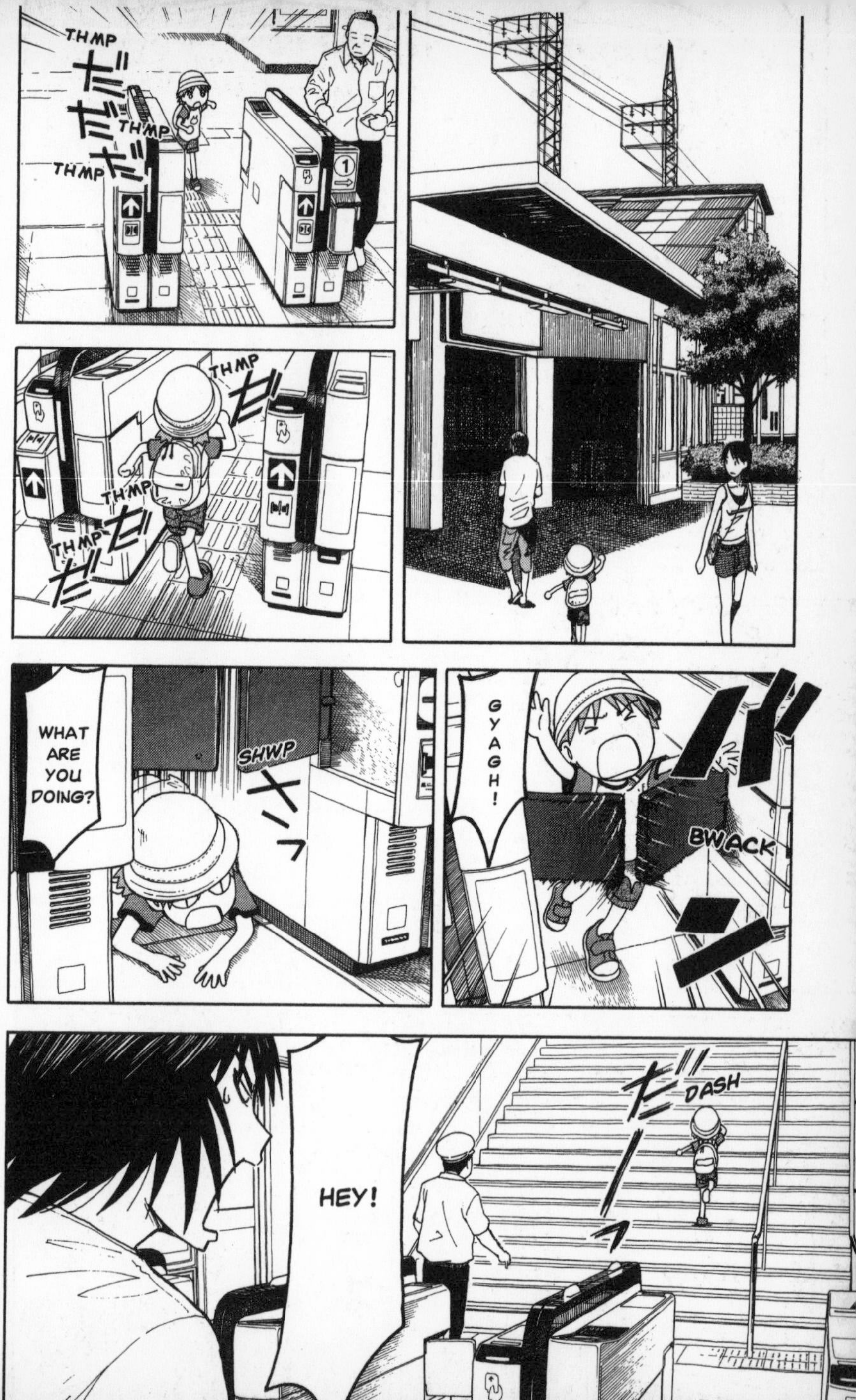
THMP
だ
THMP
だ
THMP
だ
THMP
だ
THMP
だ
THMP
だ
GYAGH!
BWACK
SHWP
WHAT ARE YOU DOING?
DASH
HEY!

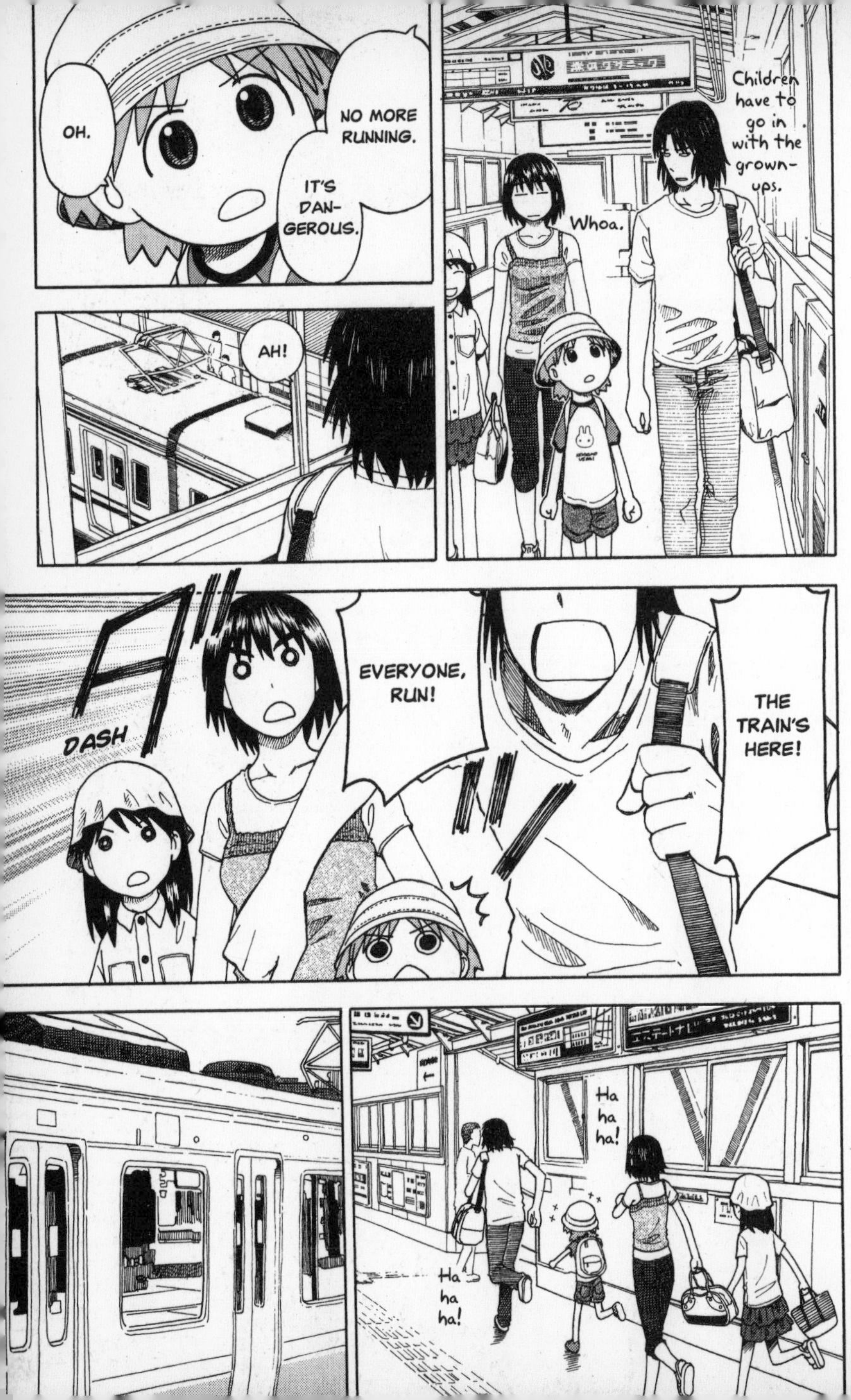
Children have to go in with the grown-ups.
Whoa.
NO MORE RUNNING.
IT'S DANGEROUS.
OH.
AH!
THE TRAIN'S HERE!
EVERYONE, RUN!
DASH
Ha ha ha!
Ha ha ha!

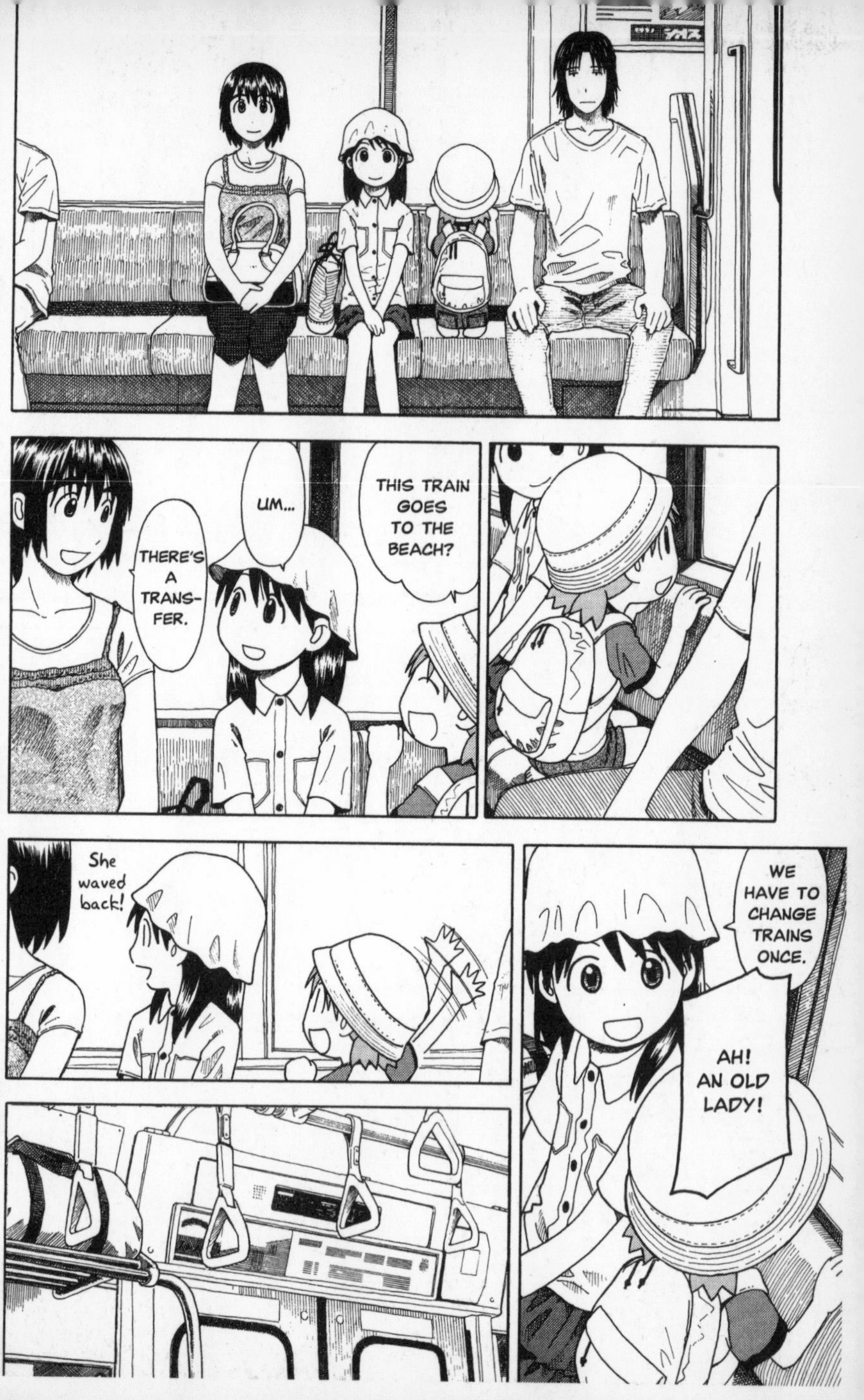
THIS TRAIN GOES TO THE BEACH?
UM...
THERE'S A TRANS-FER.
WE HAVE TO CHANGE TRAINS ONCE.
AH! AN OLD LADY!
She waved back!

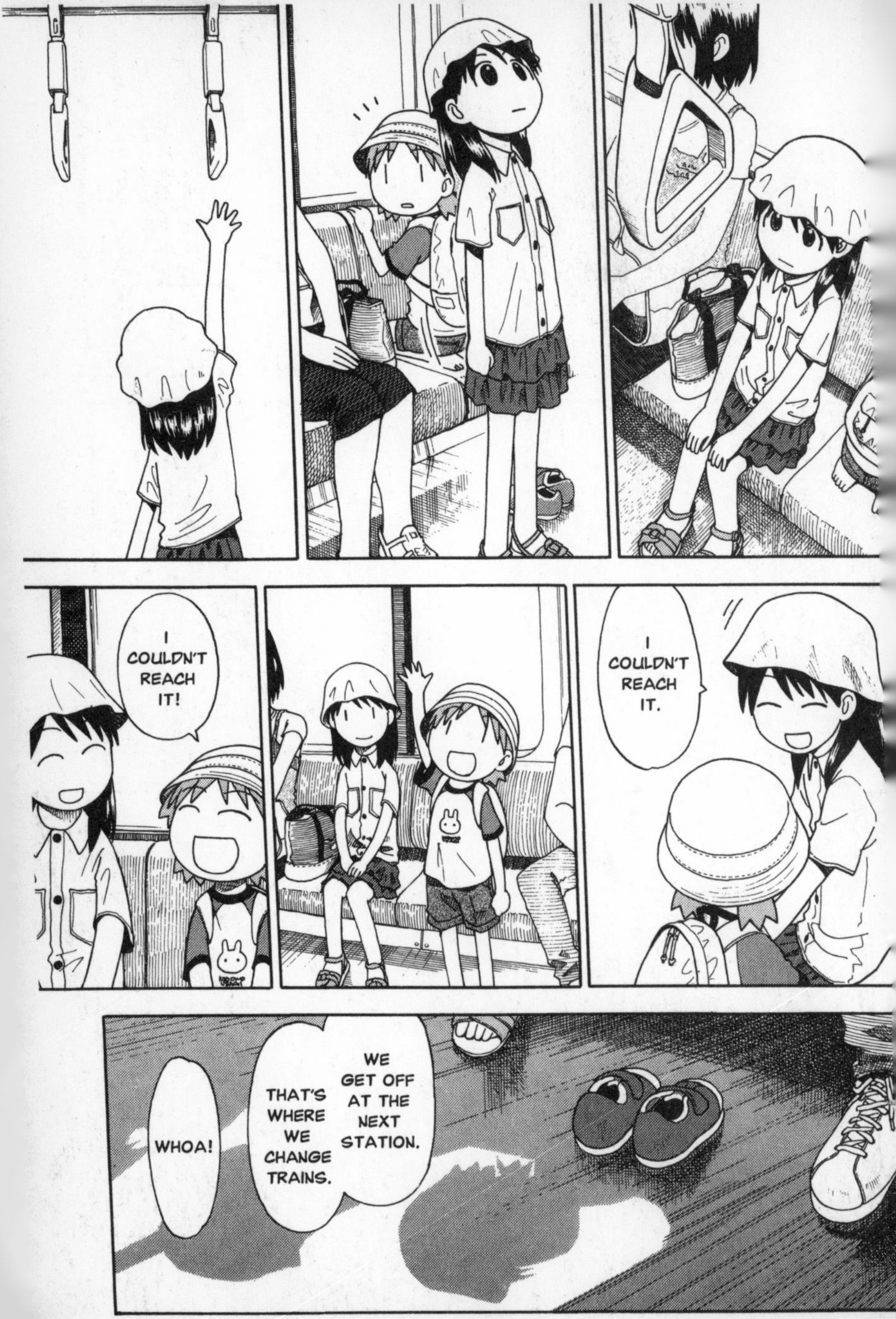
I COULDN'T REACH IT.
I COULDN'T REACH IT!
WE GET OFF AT THE NEXT STATION.
THAT'S WHERE WE CHANGE TRAINS.
WHOA!

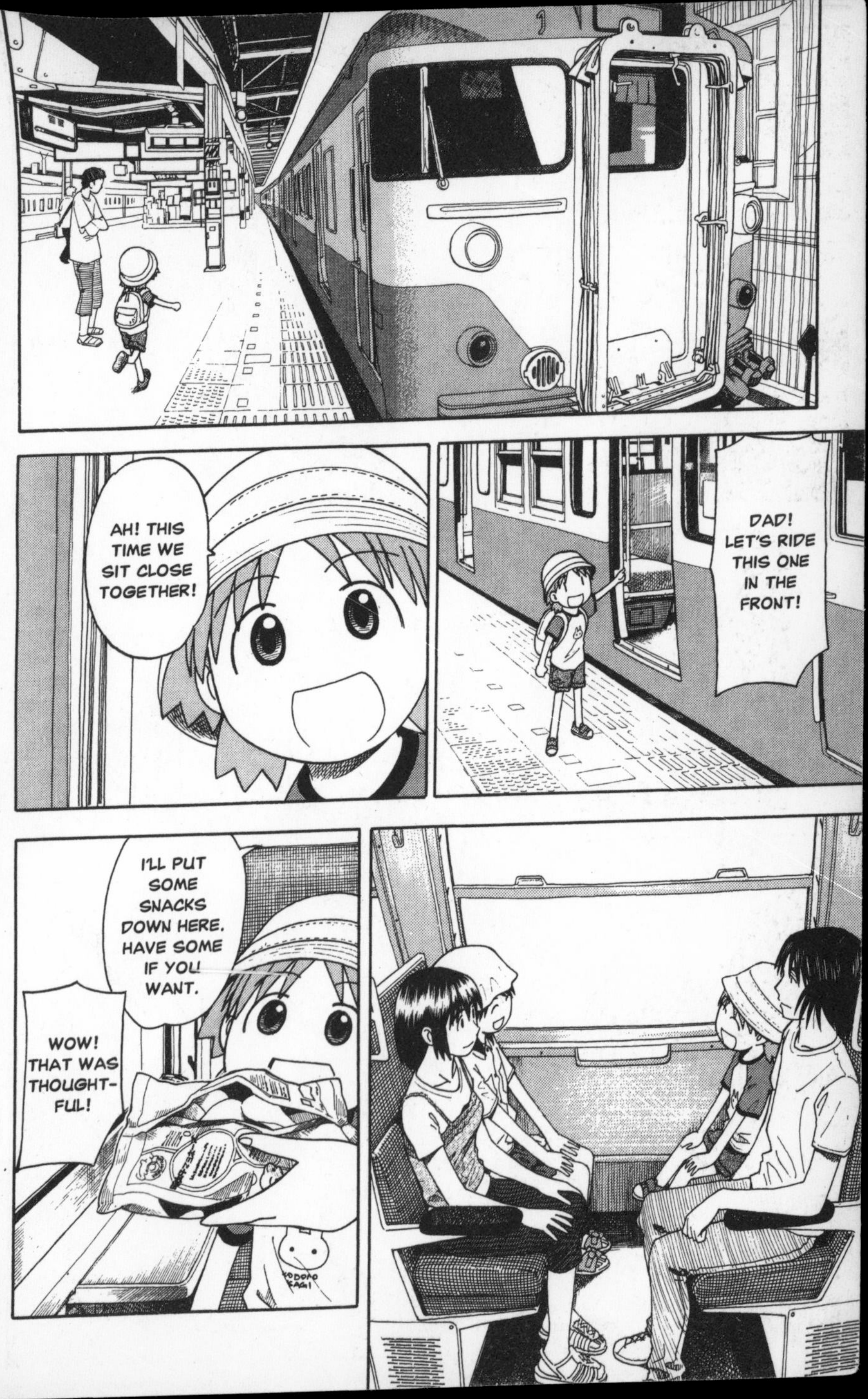
DAD! LET'S RIDE THIS ONE IN THE FRONT!
AH! THIS TIME WE SIT CLOSE TOGETHER!
I'LL PUT SOME SNACKS DOWN HERE. HAVE SOME IF YOU WANT.
WOW! THAT WAS THOUGHT-FUL!

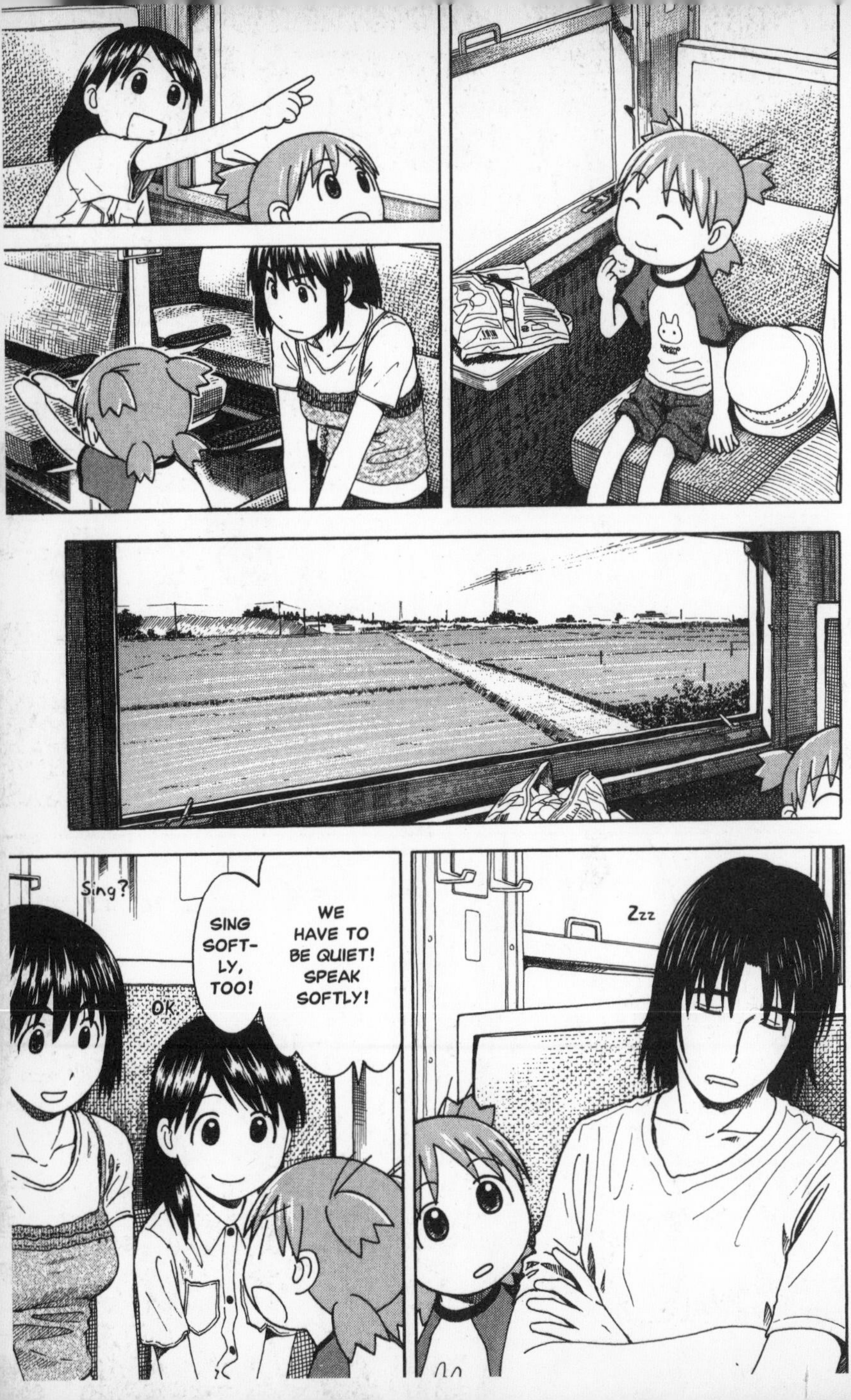
Zzz
WE HAVE TO BE QUIET! SPEAK SOFTLY!
Sing?
SING SOFT-LY, TOO!
OK

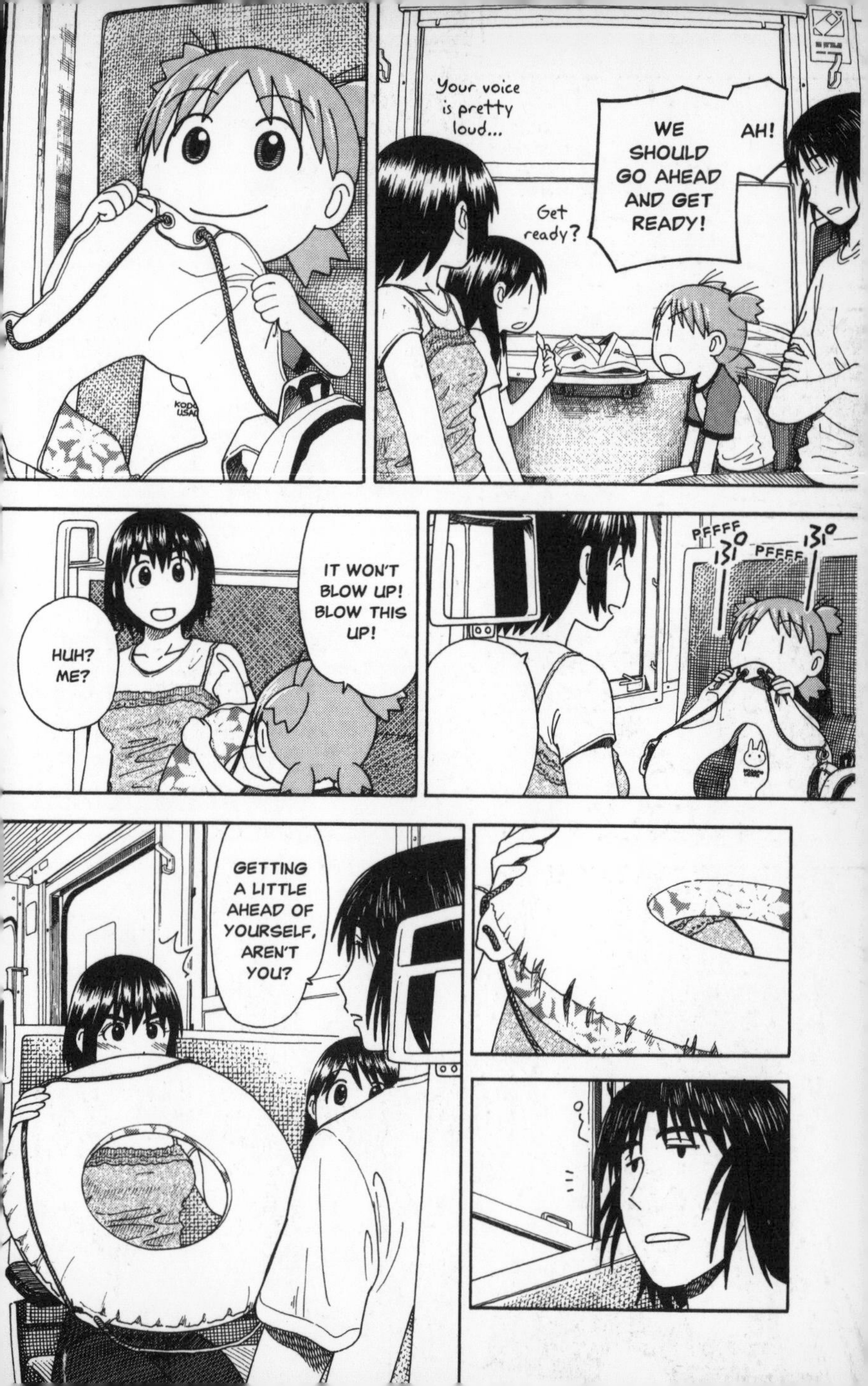
AH!
WE SHOULD GO AHEAD AND GET READY!
Get ready?
Your voice is pretty loud...
PFFFF
PFFFF
IT WON'T BLOW UP! BLOW THIS UP!
HUH? ME?
GETTING A LITTLE AHEAD OF YOURSELF, AREN'T YOU?

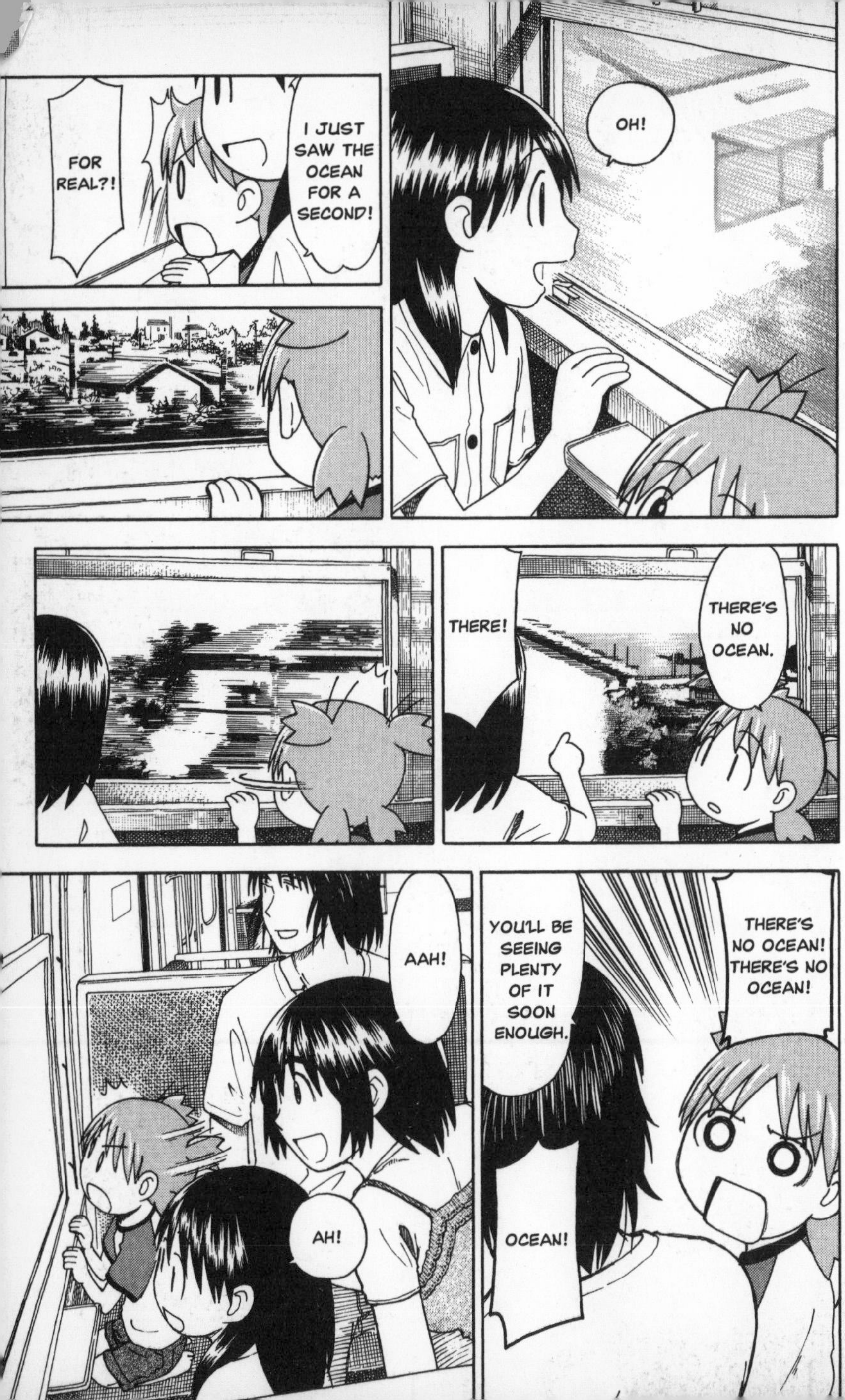
OH!
I JUST SAW THE OCEAN FOR A SECOND!
FOR REAL?!
THERE'S NO OCEAN.
THERE!
THERE'S NO OCEAN! THERE'S NO OCEAN!
YOU'LL BE SEEING PLENTY OF IT SOON ENOUGH.
OCEAN!
AAH!
AH!

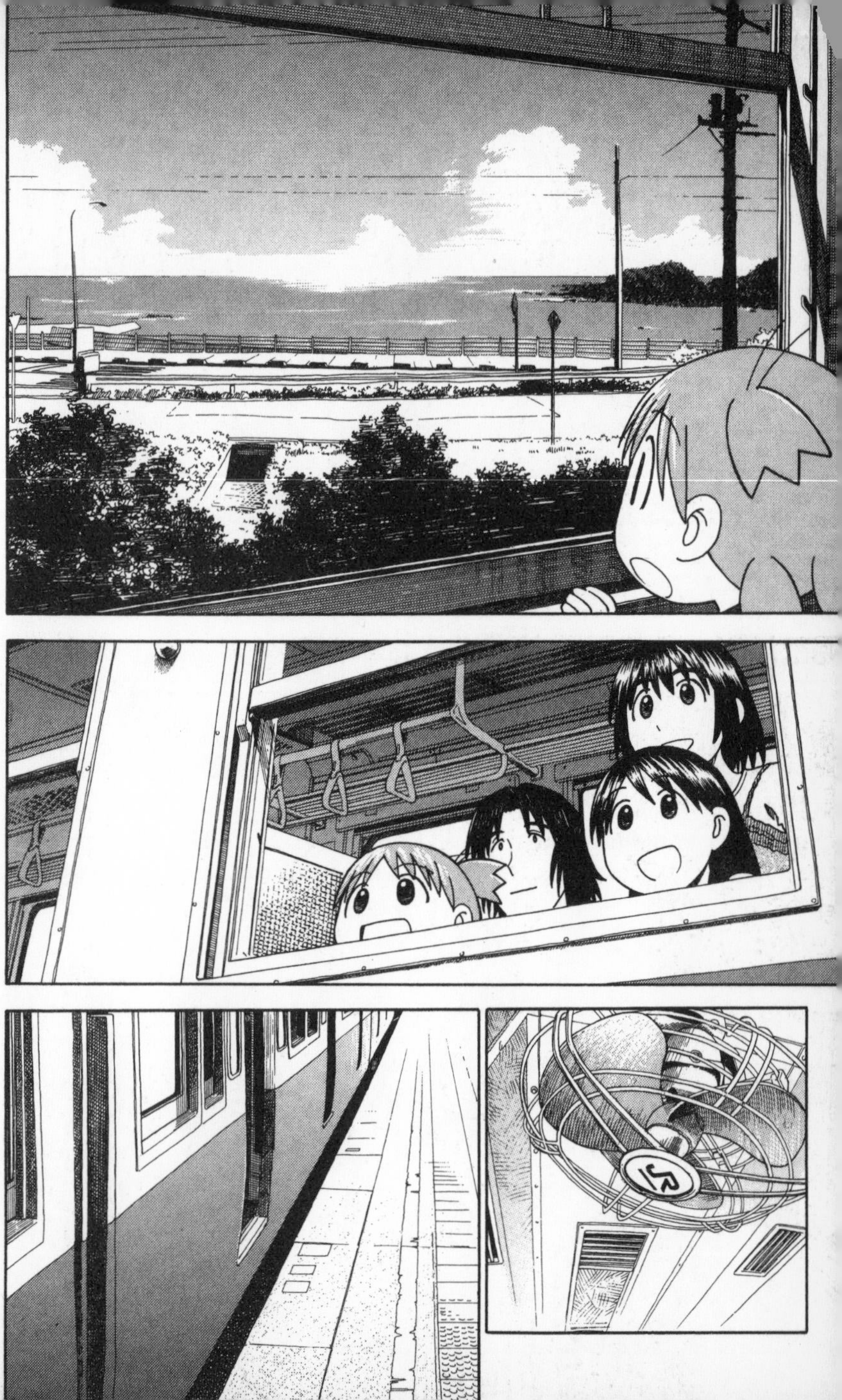

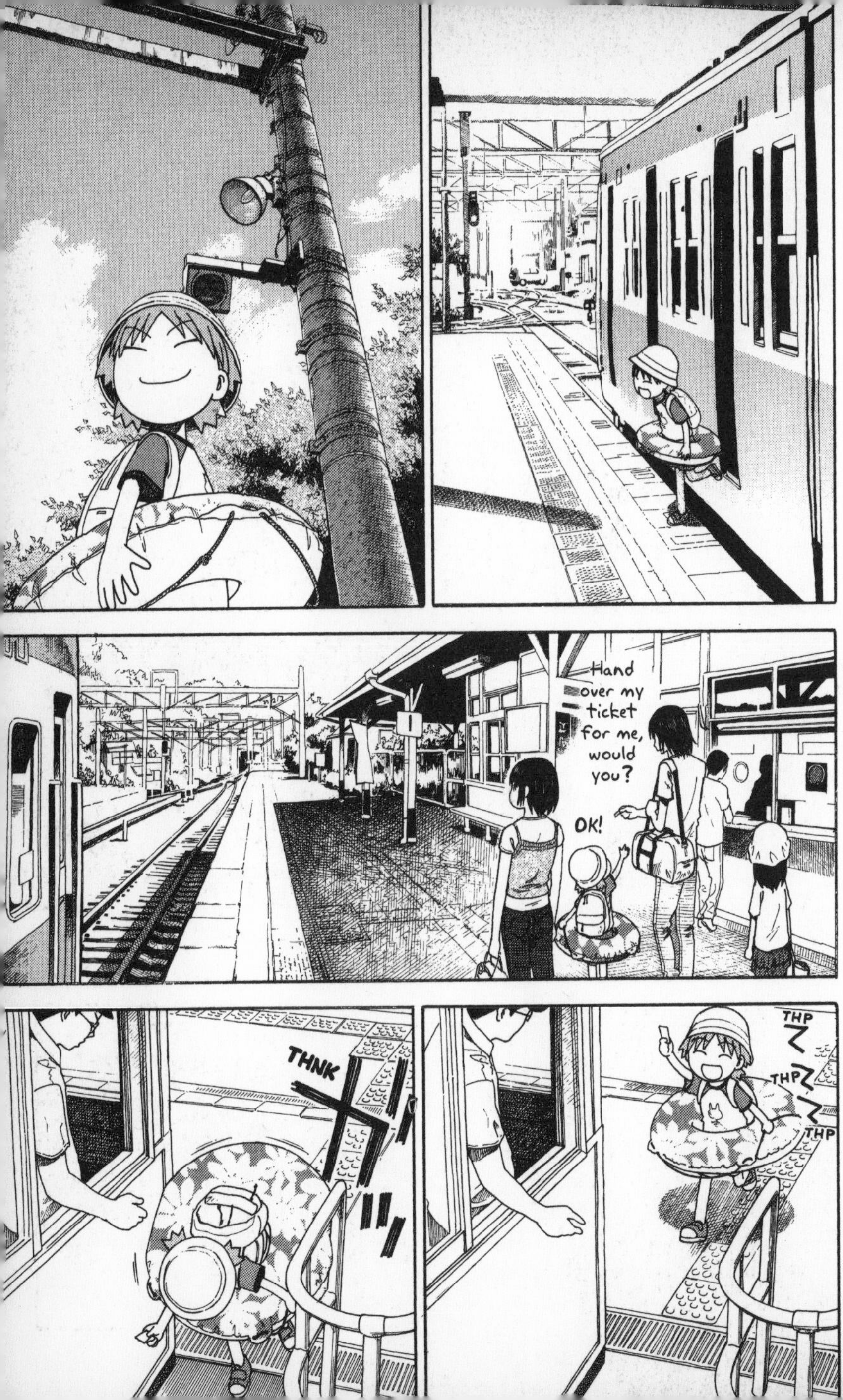
Hand over my ticket for me, would you?
OK!
THP
THP
THP
THNK

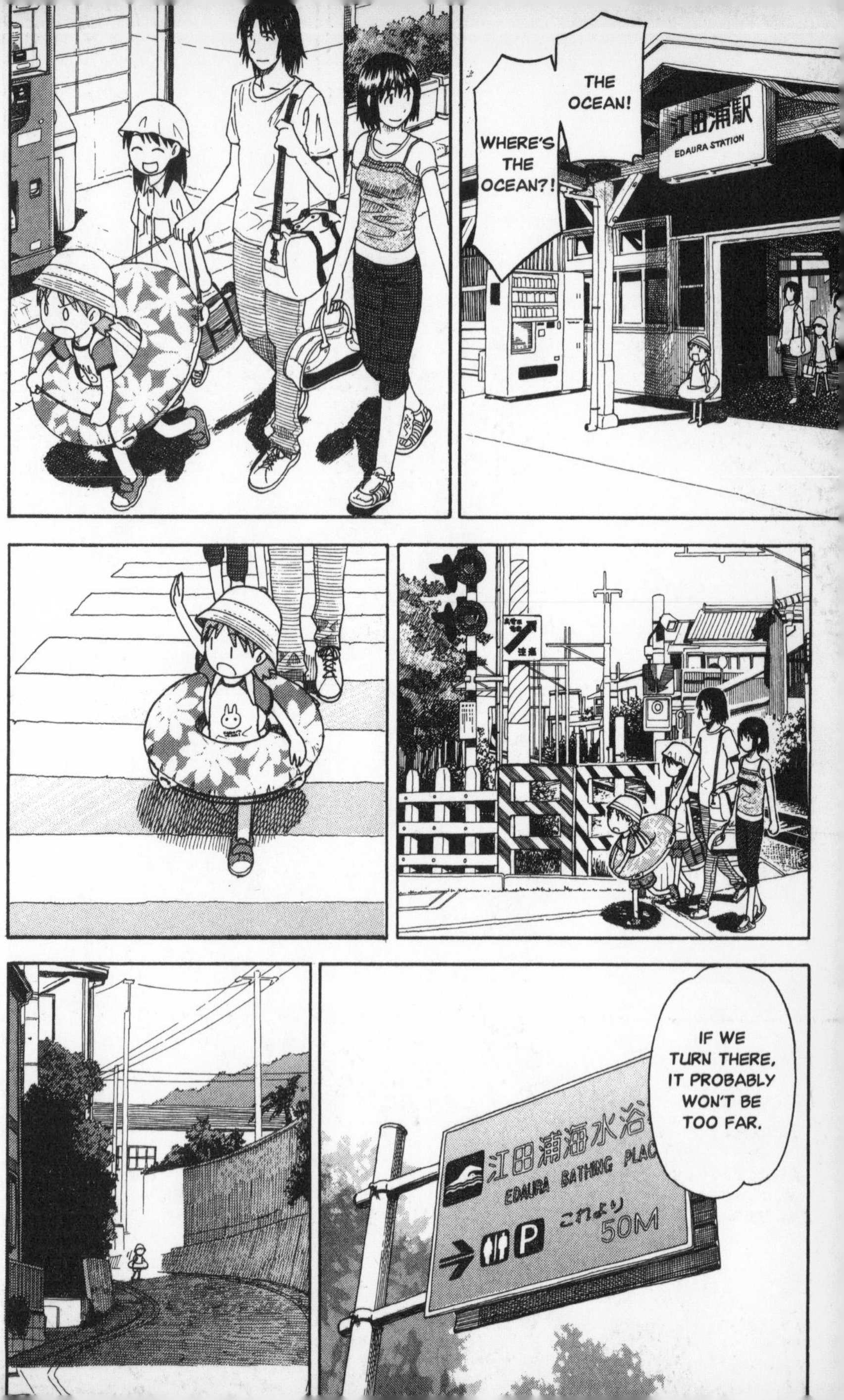
THE OCEAN!
WHERE'S THE OCEAN?!
江田浦駅
EDAURA STATION
IF WE TURN THERE, IT PROBABLY WON'T BE TOO FAR.
江田浦海水浴
EDAURA BATHING PLAC
これより 50M

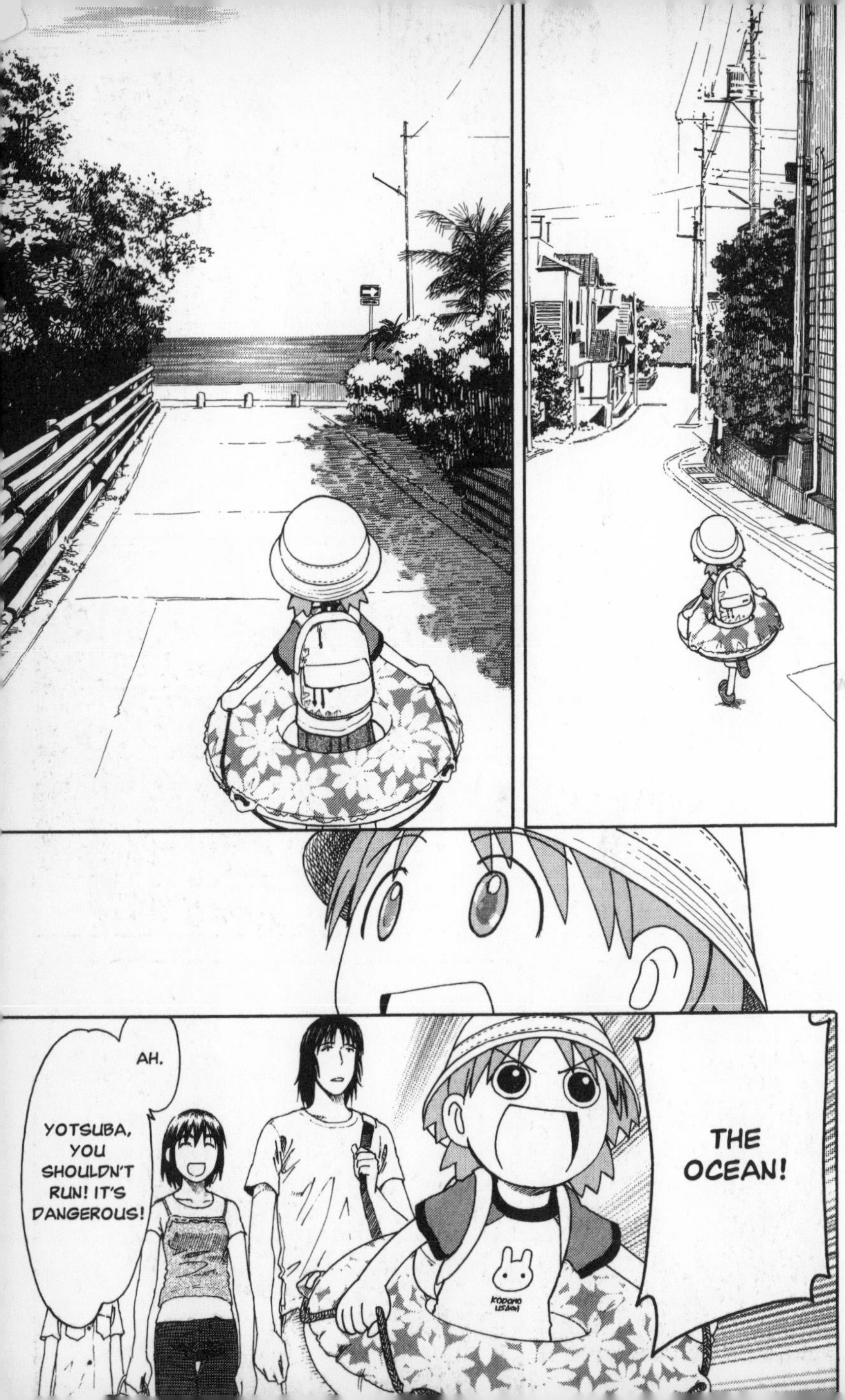
THE OCEAN!
AH.
YOTSUBA, YOU SHOULDN'T RUN! IT'S DANGEROUS!

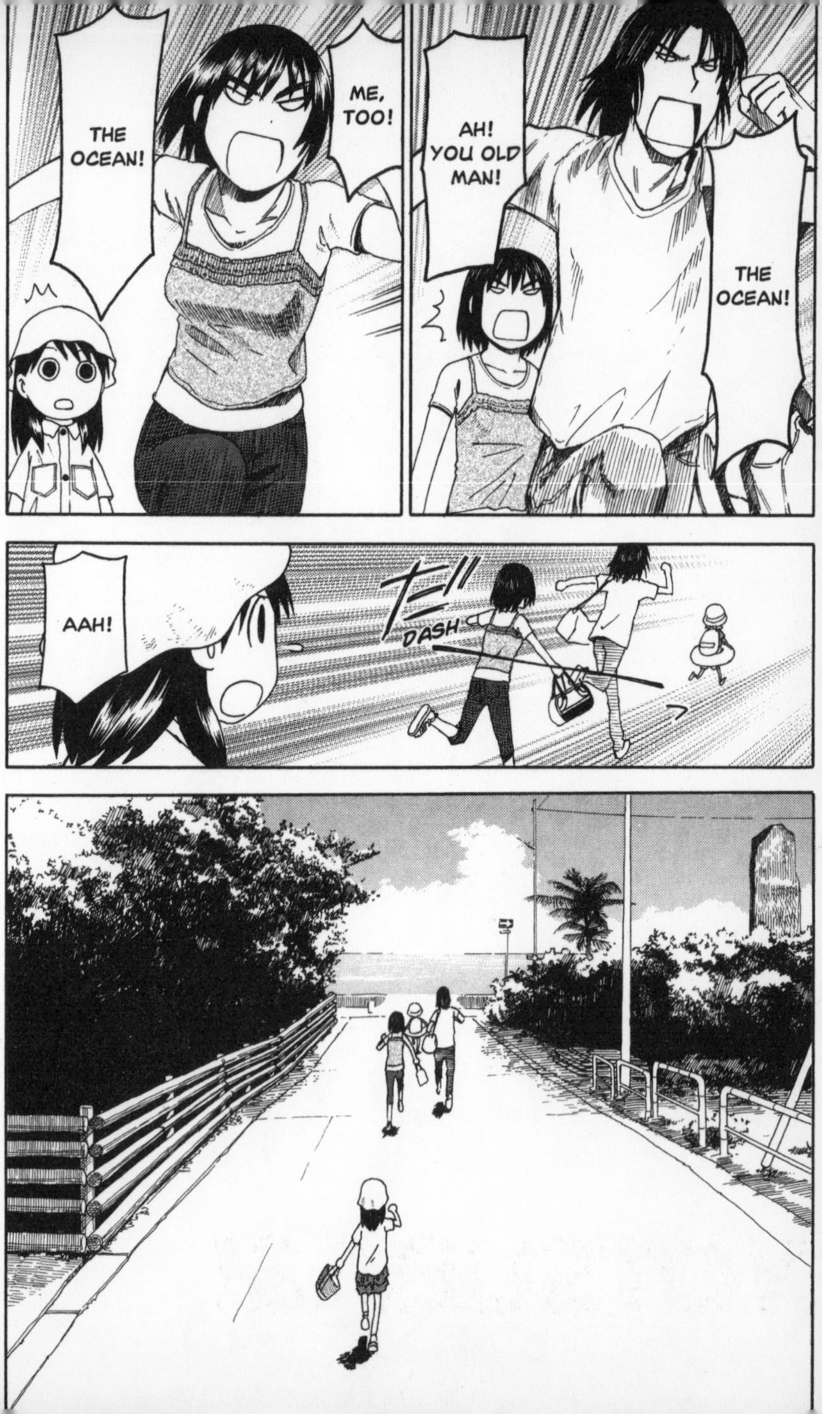
THE OCEAN!
AH! YOU OLD MAN!
ME, TOO!
THE OCEAN!
DASH
AAH!

YOTSUBA&!

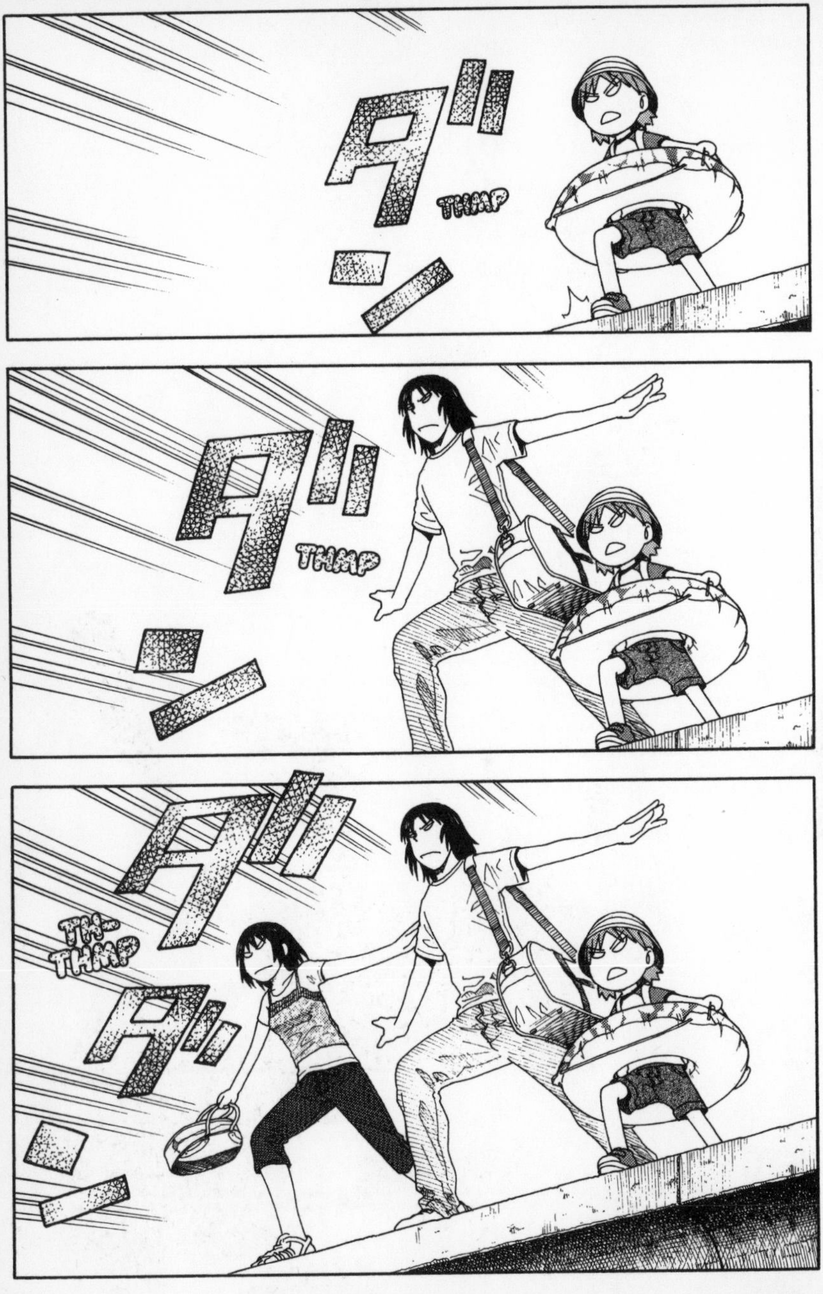

THMP
ダン
THMP
ダン
ダダン
TH-THMP

YOTSUBA & THE BEACH

CHAPTER 34

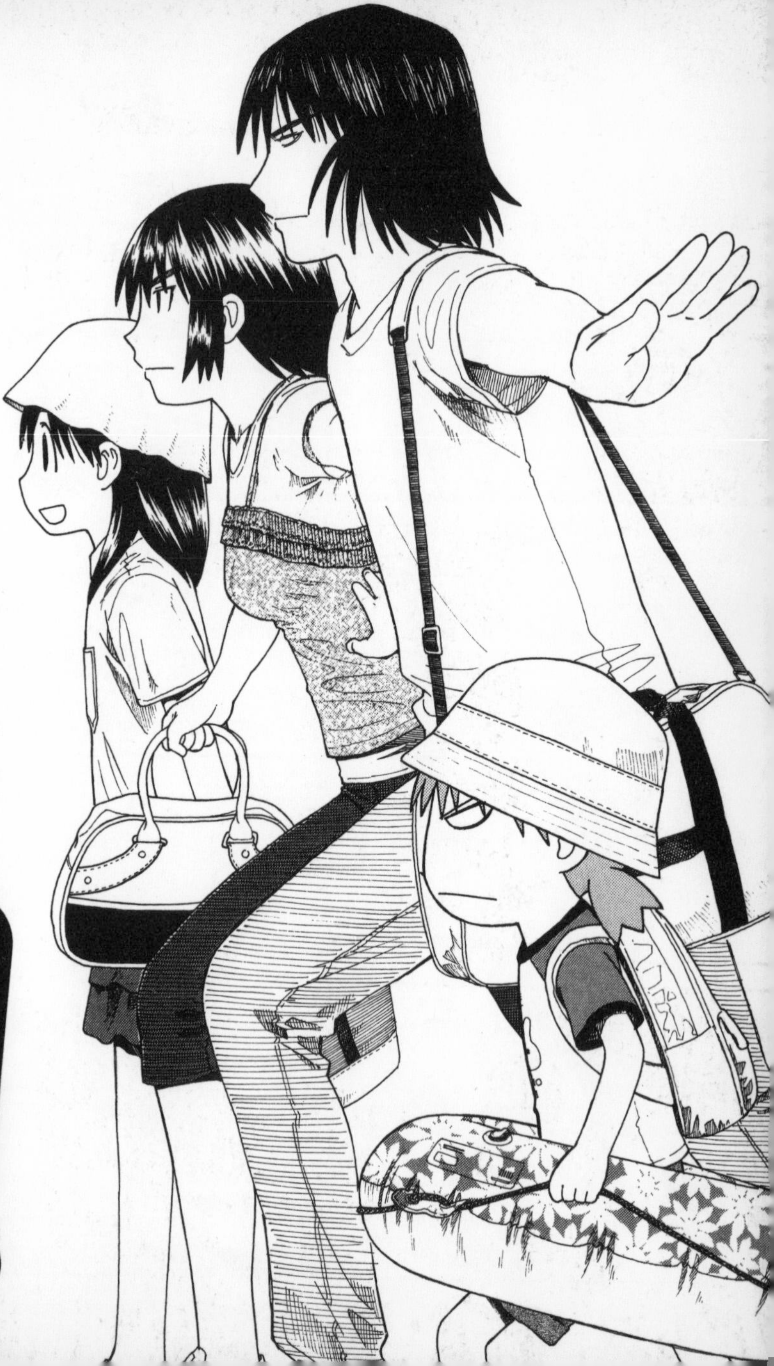

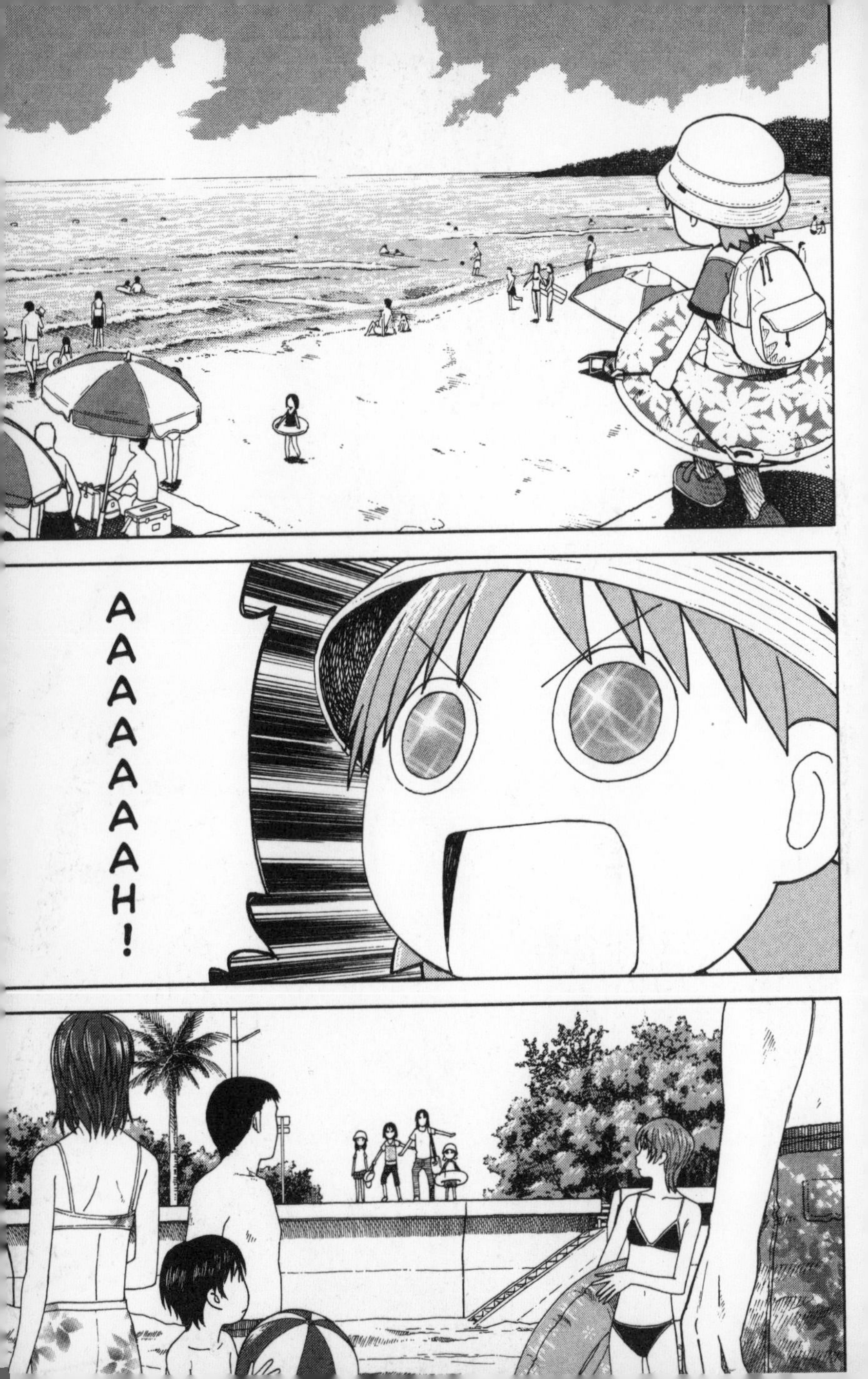
AAAAAAAAH!

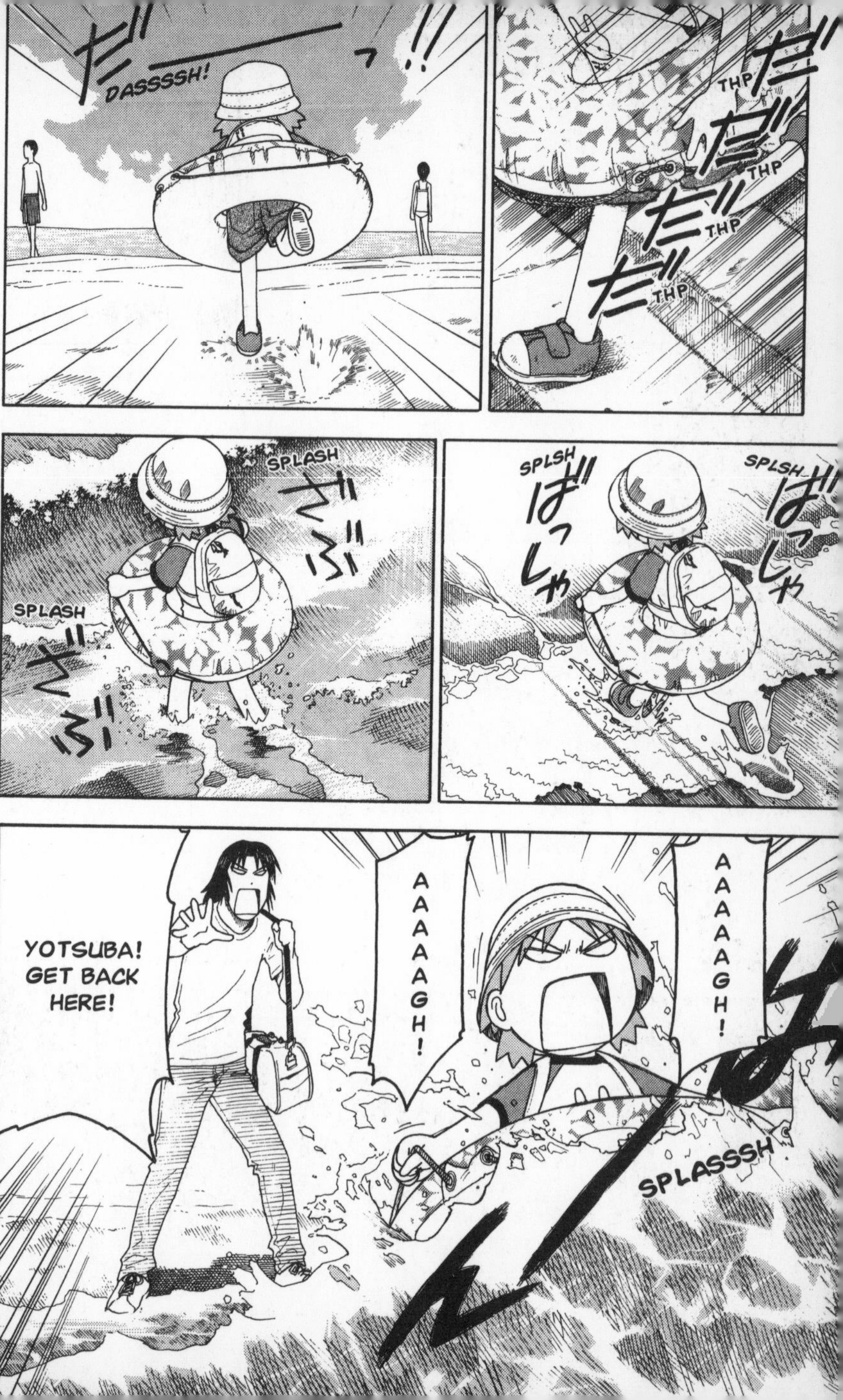

だ THP
だ THP
だ THP
だ THP
だ——っ!!
DASSSSH!
SPLSH ばっしゃ
SPLSH ばっしゃ
SPLASH ざぶ
SPLASH ざぶ
AAAAAAGH!
AAAAAGH!
YOTSUBA! GET BACK HERE!
SPLASSSH

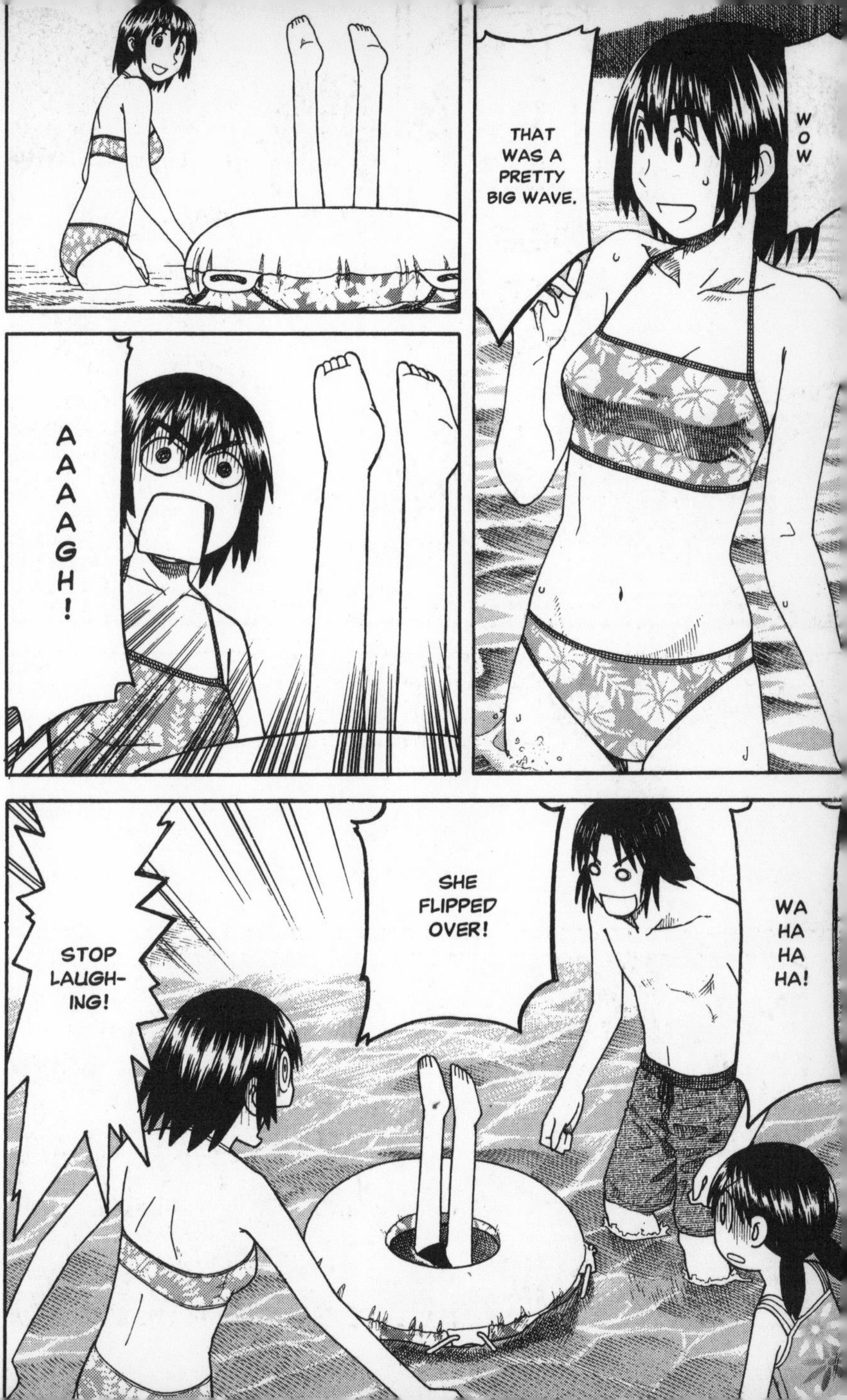
WOW
THAT WAS A PRETTY BIG WAVE.
AAAAAGH!
WA HA HA HA!
SHE FLIPPED OVER!
STOP LAUGHING!

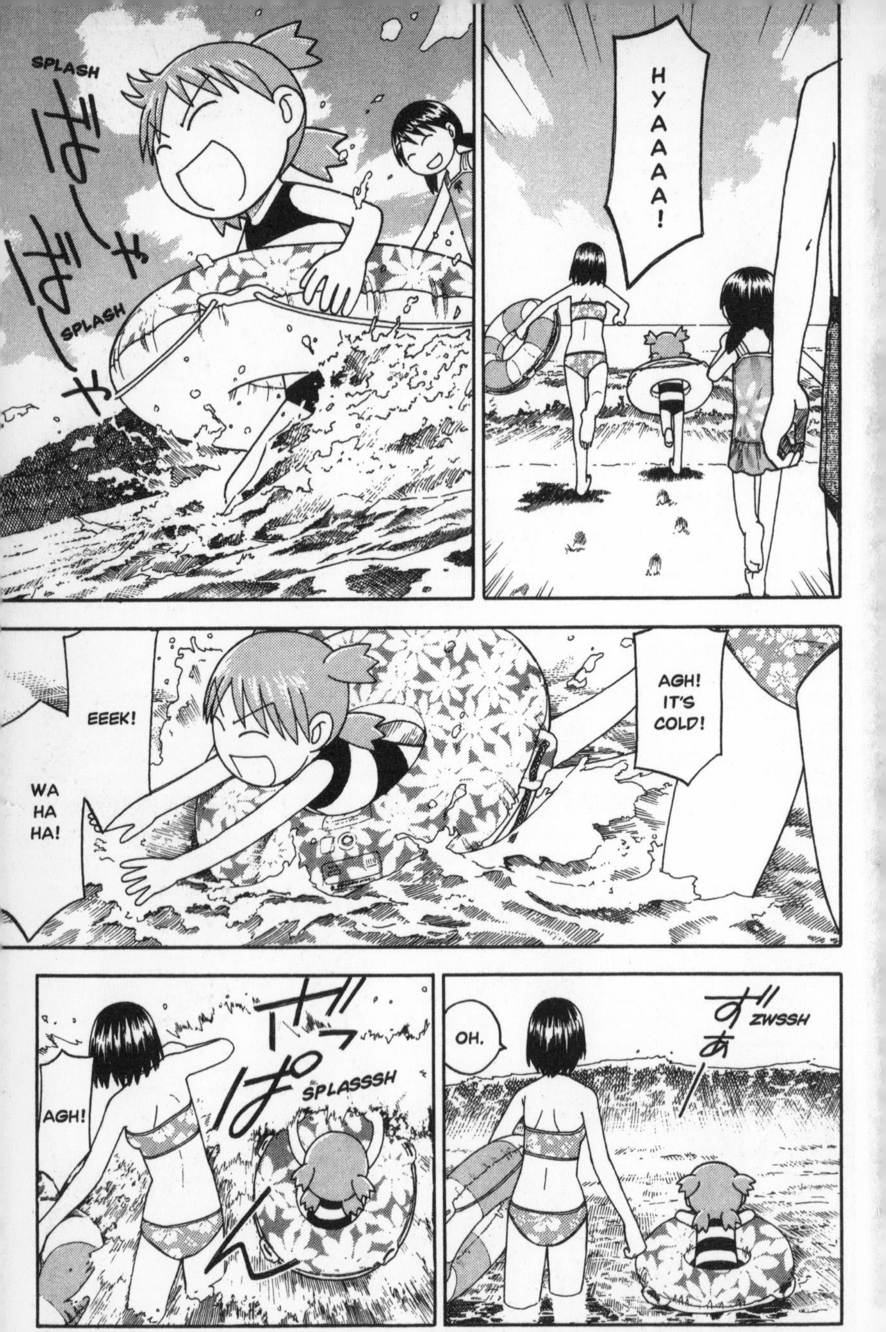
HYAAAAA!
SPLASH
SPLASH
AGH! IT'S COLD!
EEEK!
WA HA HA!
ZWSSH
OH.
SPLASSSH
AGH!

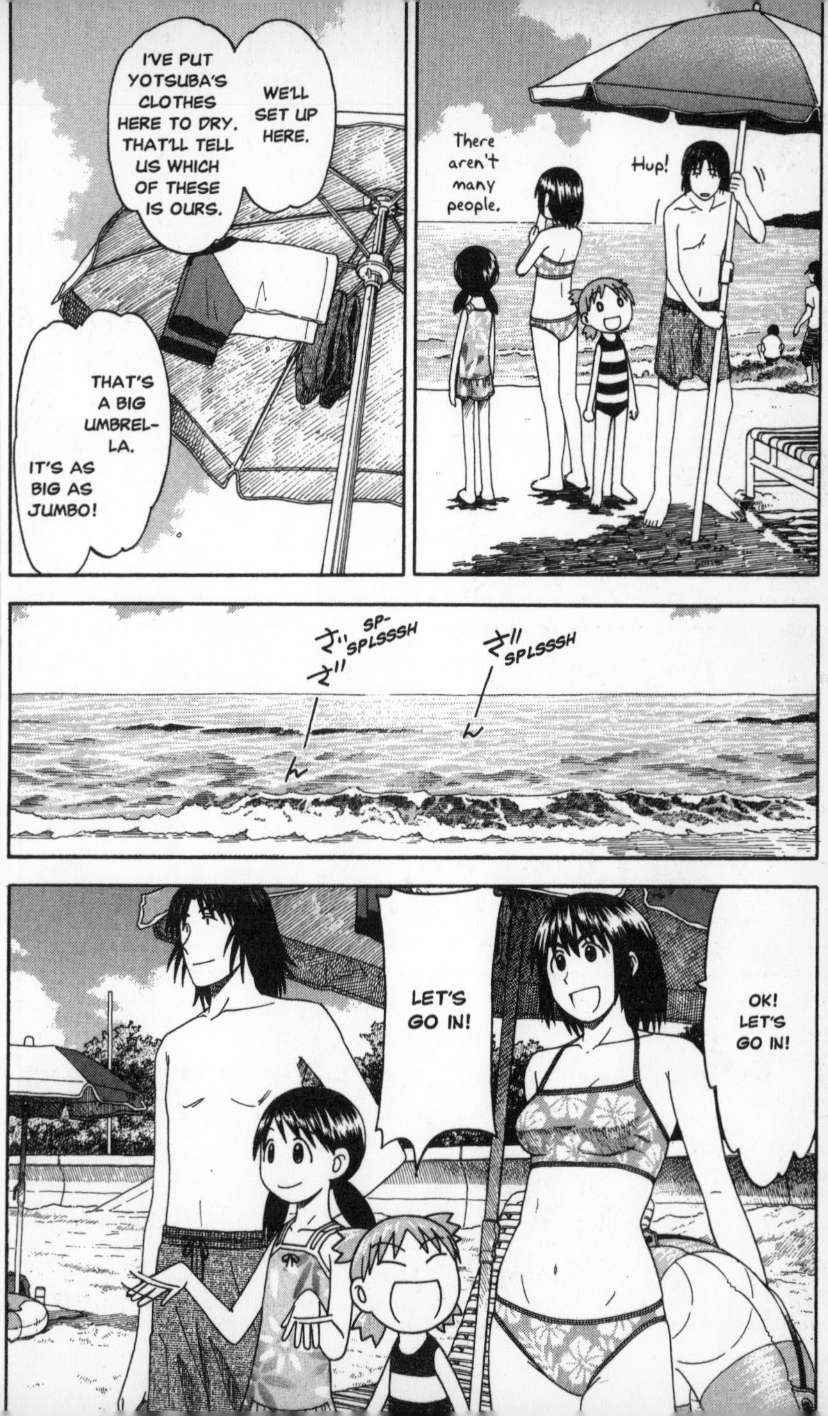
Hup!
There aren't many people.
WE'LL SET UP HERE.
I'VE PUT YOTSUBA'S CLOTHES HERE TO DRY. THAT'LL TELL US WHICH OF THESE IS OURS.
THAT'S A BIG UMBREL-LA.
IT'S AS BIG AS JUMBO!
ざーん
SPLSSSH
ざざーん
SP-SPLSSSH
OK! LET'S GO IN!
LET'S GO IN!

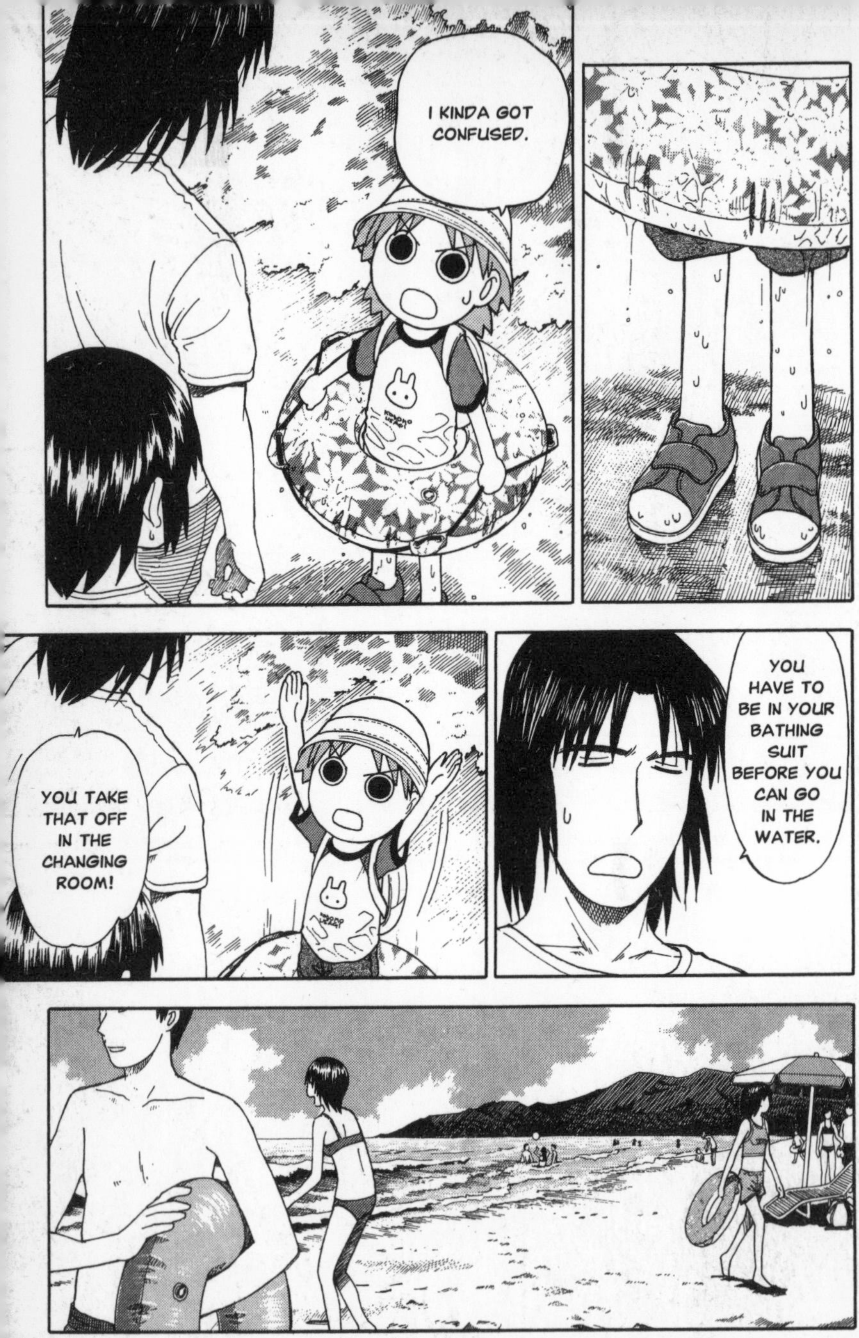
I KINDA GOT CONFUSED.
YOU HAVE TO BE IN YOUR BATHING SUIT BEFORE YOU CAN GO IN THE WATER.
YOU TAKE THAT OFF IN THE CHANGING ROOM!

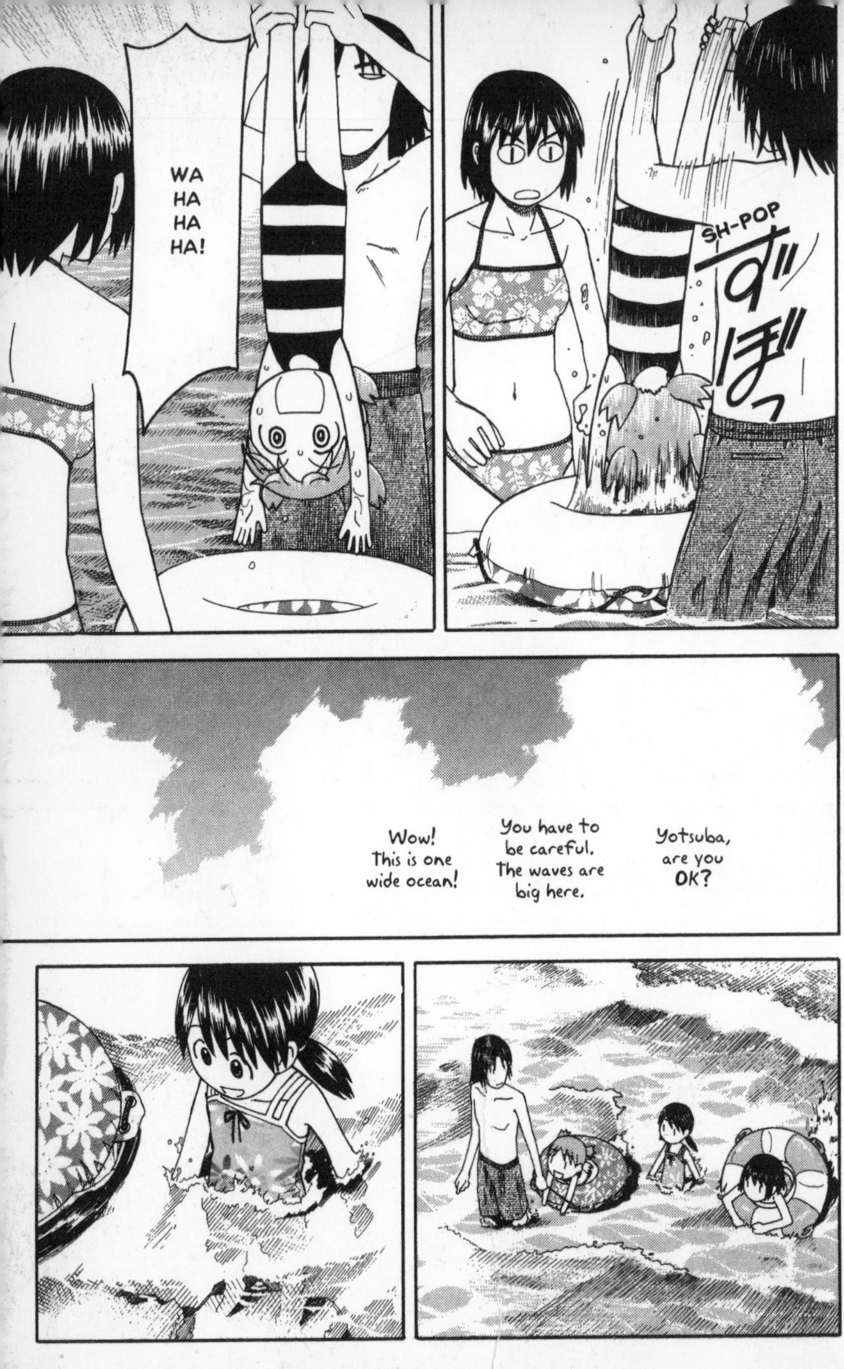
SH-POP
ずぼっ
WA HA HA HA!
Yotsuba, are you OK?
You have to be careful. The waves are big here.
Wow! This is one wide ocean!

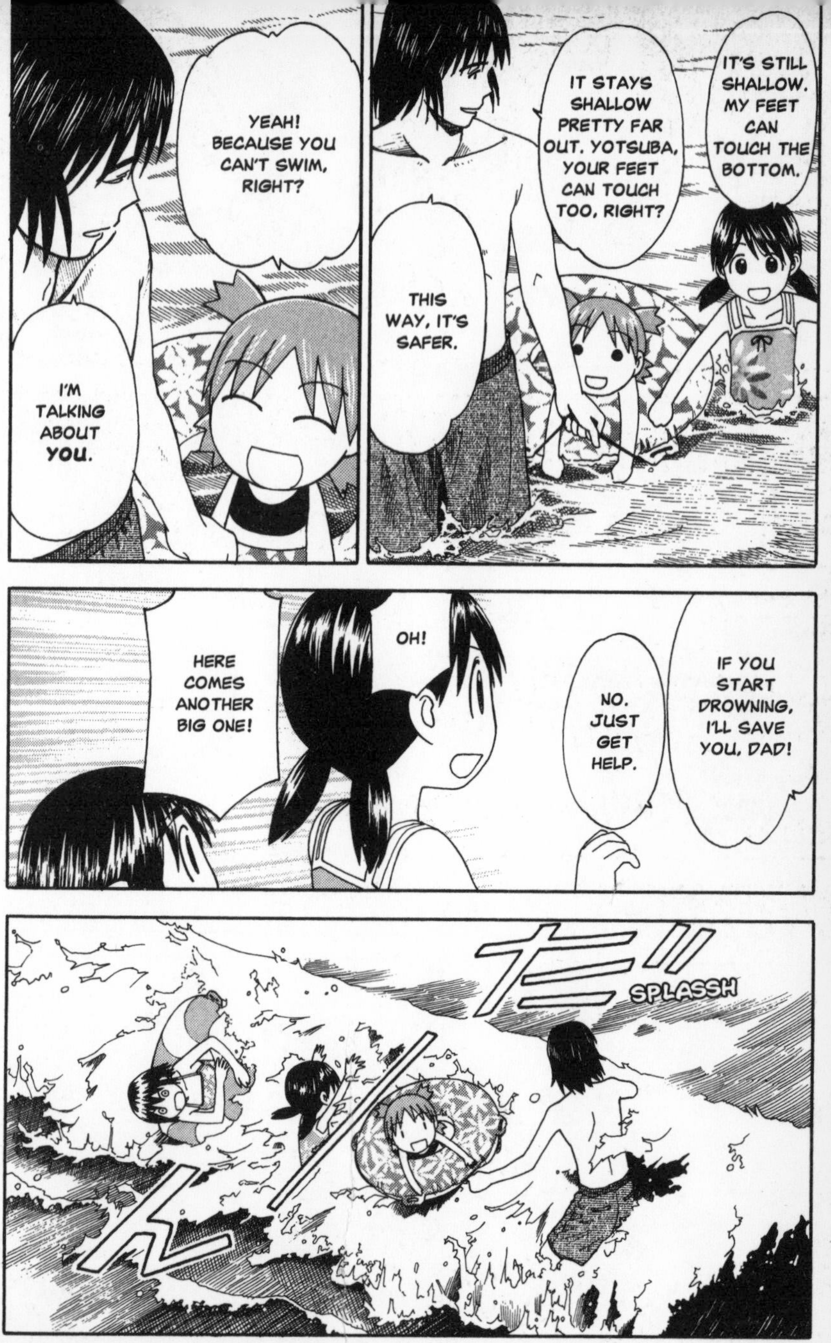
IT'S STILL SHALLOW. MY FEET CAN TOUCH THE BOTTOM.
IT STAYS SHALLOW PRETTY FAR OUT. YOTSUBA, YOUR FEET CAN TOUCH TOO, RIGHT?
THIS WAY, IT'S SAFER.
YEAH! BECAUSE YOU CAN'T SWIM, RIGHT?
I'M TALKING ABOUT **YOU**.
IF YOU START DROWNING, I'LL SAVE YOU, DAD!
NO. JUST GET HELP.
OH!
HERE COMES ANOTHER BIG ONE!
SPLASSH

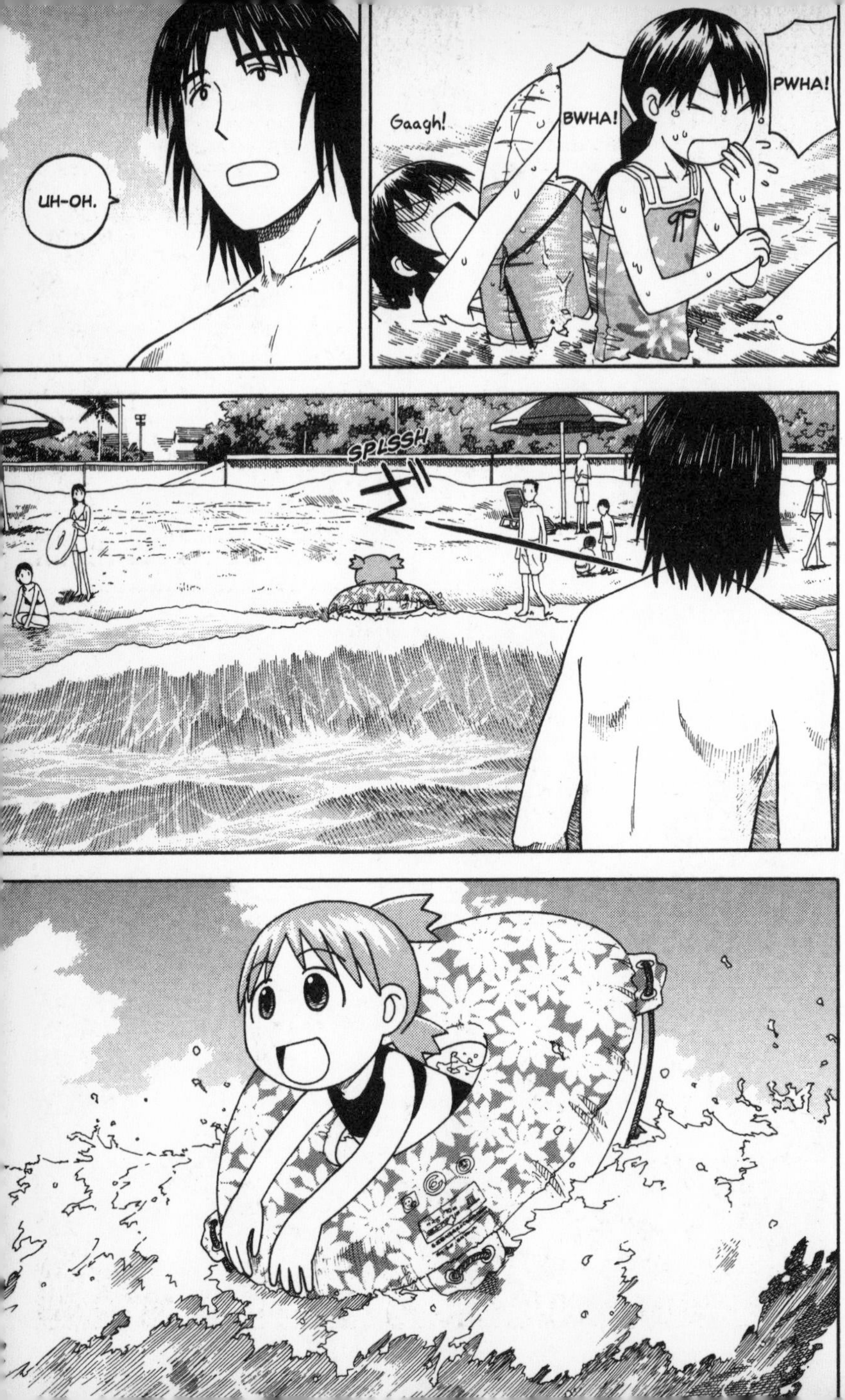
PWHA!
BWHA!
Gaagh!
UH-OH.
SPLSSH

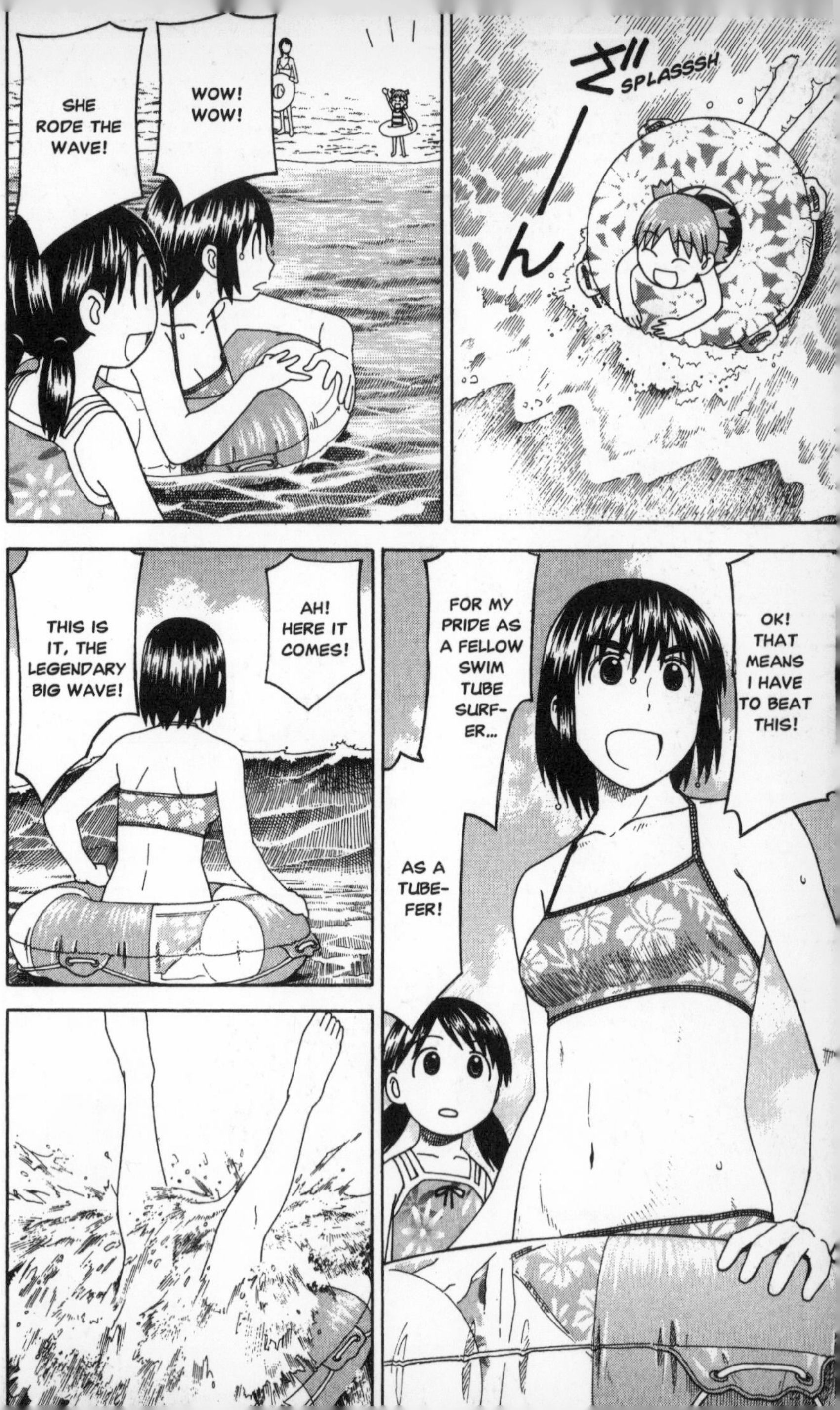

SPLASSSH
WOW! WOW!
SHE RODE THE WAVE!
OK! THAT MEANS I HAVE TO BEAT THIS!
FOR MY PRIDE AS A FELLOW SWIM TUBE SURF-ER...
AS A TUBE-FER!
AH! HERE IT COMES!
THIS IS IT, THE LEGENDARY BIG WAVE!

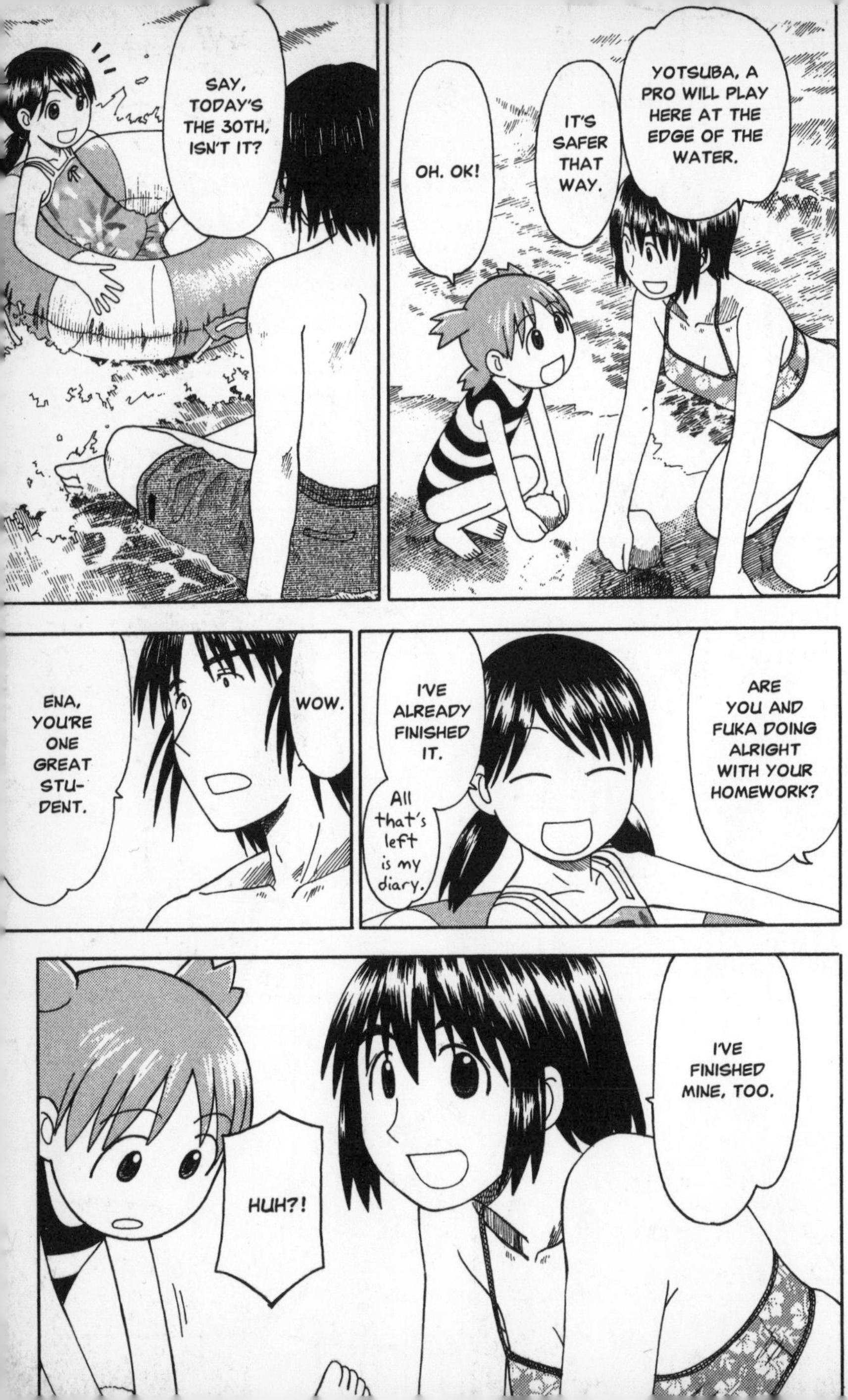

YOTSUBA, A PRO WILL PLAY HERE AT THE EDGE OF THE WATER.
IT'S SAFER THAT WAY.
OH. OK!
SAY, TODAY'S THE 30TH, ISN'T IT?
ARE YOU AND FUKA DOING ALRIGHT WITH YOUR HOMEWORK?
I'VE ALREADY FINISHED IT.
All that's left is my diary.
WOW.
ENA, YOU'RE ONE GREAT STU-DENT.
I'VE FINISHED MINE, TOO.
HUH?!

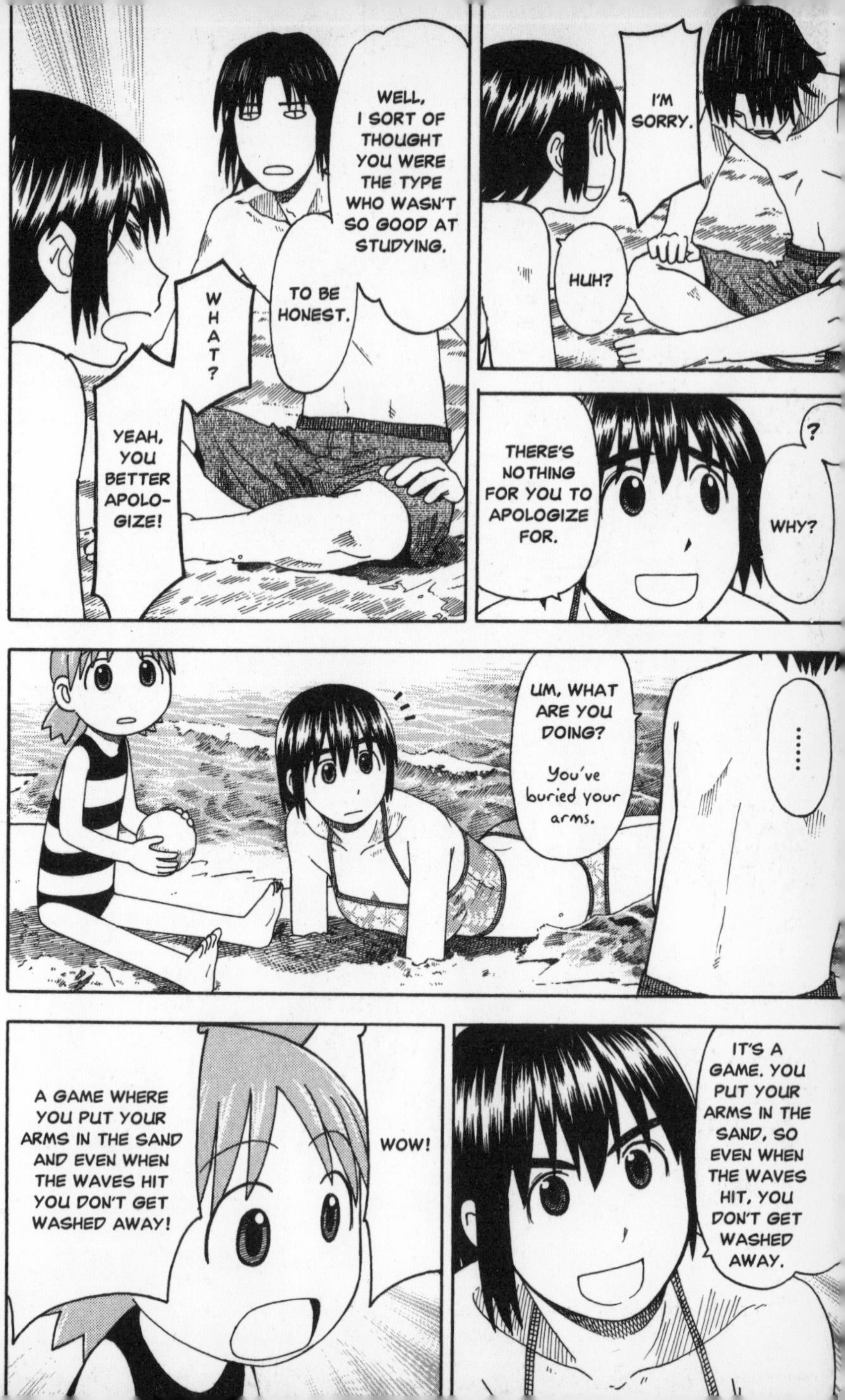
I'M SORRY.
HUH?
? WHY?
THERE'S NOTHING FOR YOU TO APOLOGIZE FOR.
WELL, I SORT OF THOUGHT YOU WERE THE TYPE WHO WASN'T SO GOOD AT STUDYING.
TO BE HONEST.
WHAT?
YEAH, YOU BETTER APOLO-GIZE!
......
UM, WHAT ARE YOU DOING?
You've buried your arms.
IT'S A GAME. YOU PUT YOUR ARMS IN THE SAND, SO EVEN WHEN THE WAVES HIT, YOU DON'T GET WASHED AWAY.
WOW!
A GAME WHERE YOU PUT YOUR ARMS IN THE SAND AND EVEN WHEN THE WAVES HIT YOU DON'T GET WASHED AWAY!

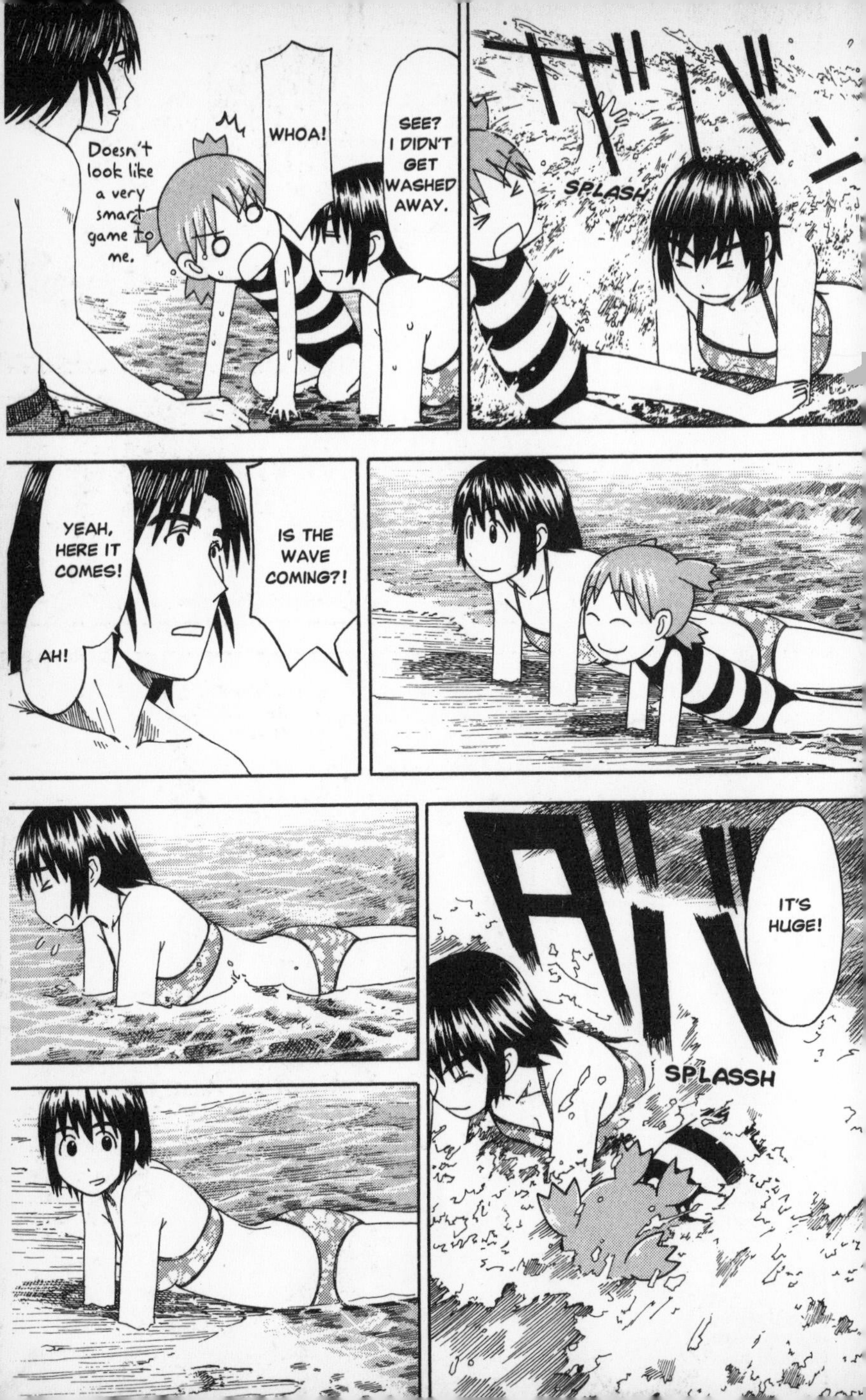
SPLASH
SEE? I DIDN'T GET WASHED AWAY.
WHOA!
Doesn't look like a very smart game to me.
IS THE WAVE COMING?!
YEAH, HERE IT COMES!
AH!
IT'S HUGE!
SPLASSH

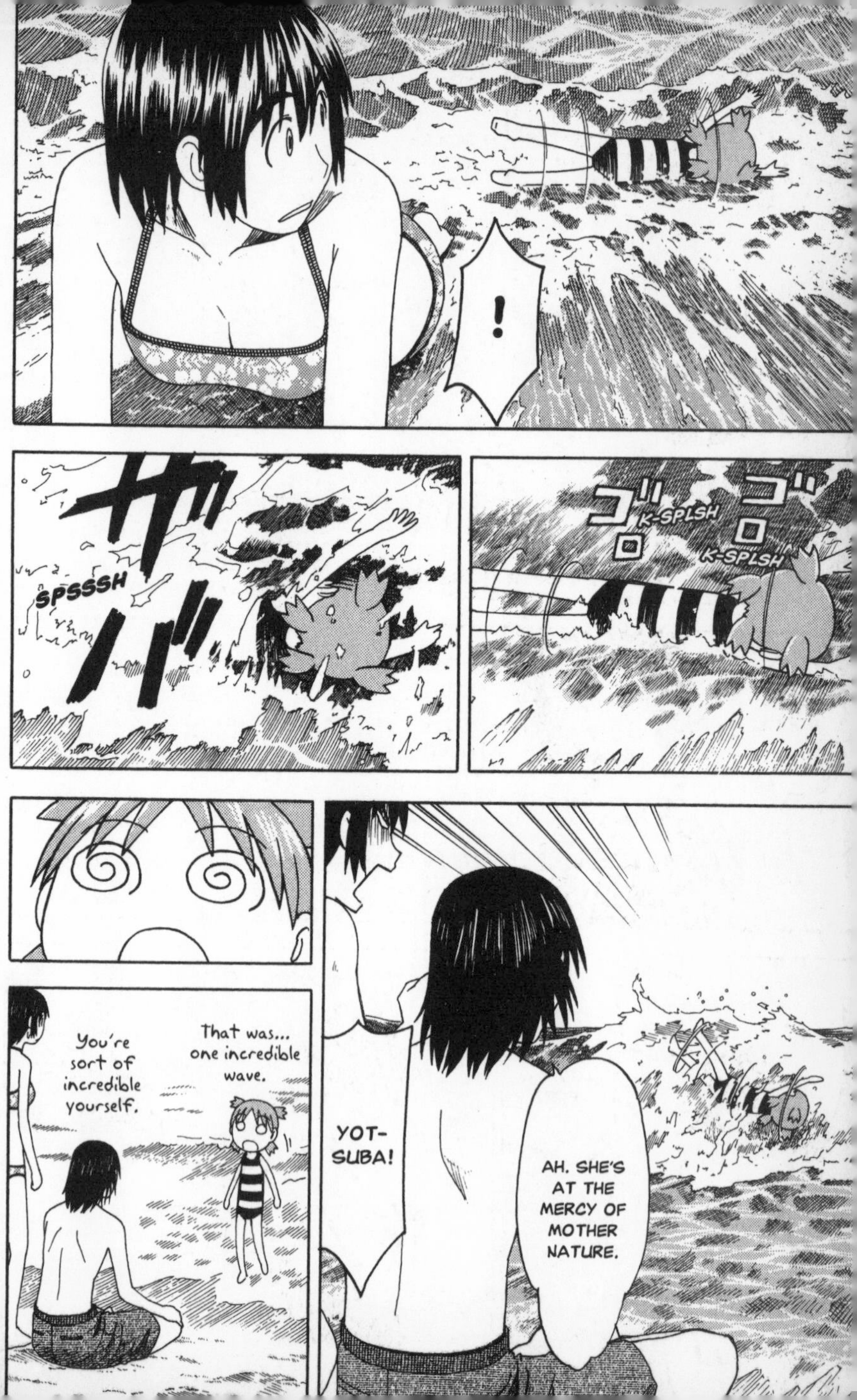
!
ゴロ
K-SPLSH
ゴロ
K-SPLSH
ザバ
SPSSSH
YOT-SUBA!
AH. SHE'S AT THE MERCY OF MOTHER NATURE.
That was... one incredible wave.
You're sort of incredible yourself.

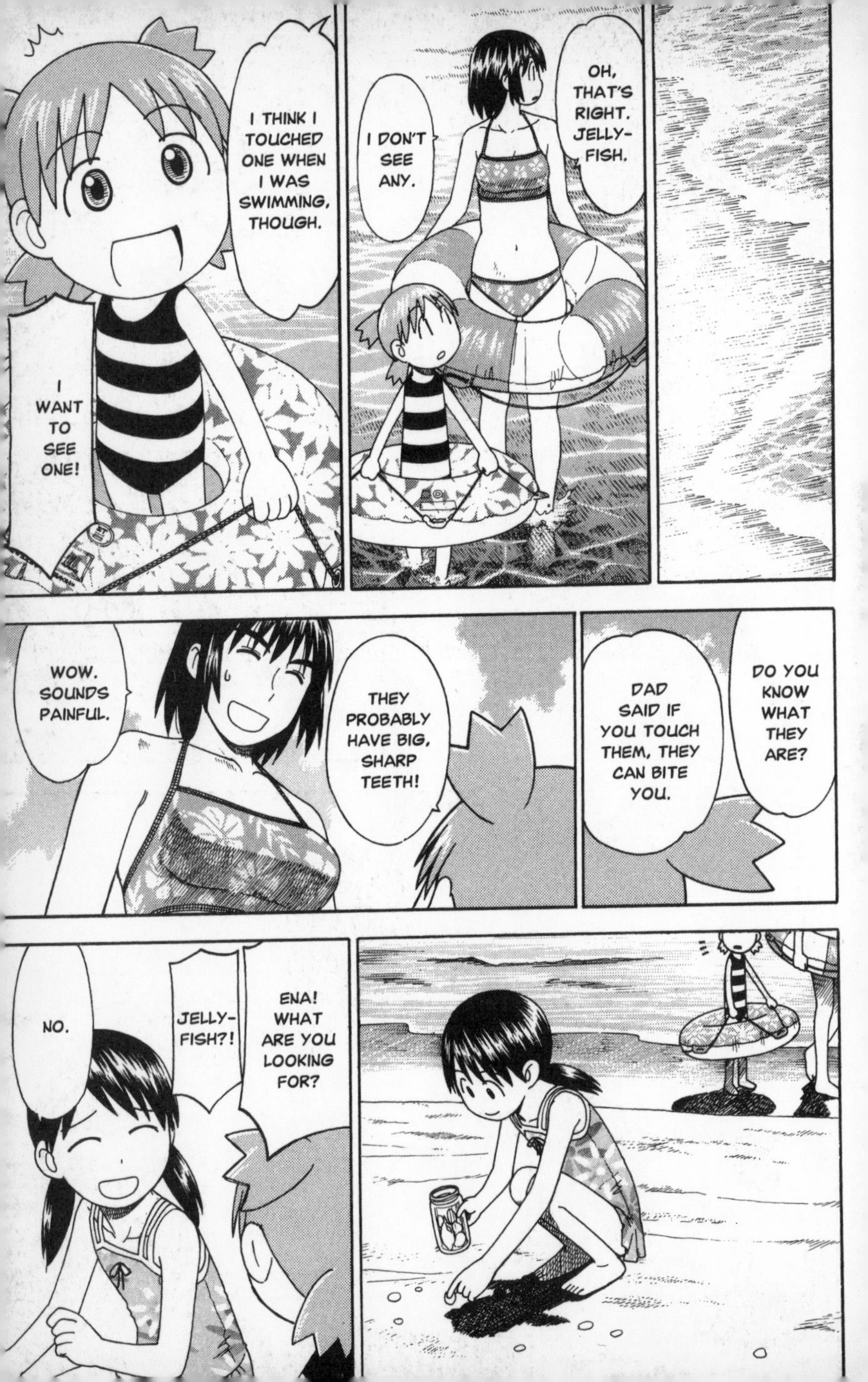
OH, THAT'S RIGHT. JELLY-FISH.
I DON'T SEE ANY.
I THINK I TOUCHED ONE WHEN I WAS SWIMMING, THOUGH.
I WANT TO SEE ONE!
DO YOU KNOW WHAT THEY ARE?
DAD SAID IF YOU TOUCH THEM, THEY CAN BITE YOU.
THEY PROBABLY HAVE BIG, SHARP TEETH!
WOW. SOUNDS PAINFUL.
ENA! WHAT ARE YOU LOOKING FOR?
JELLY-FISH?!
NO.

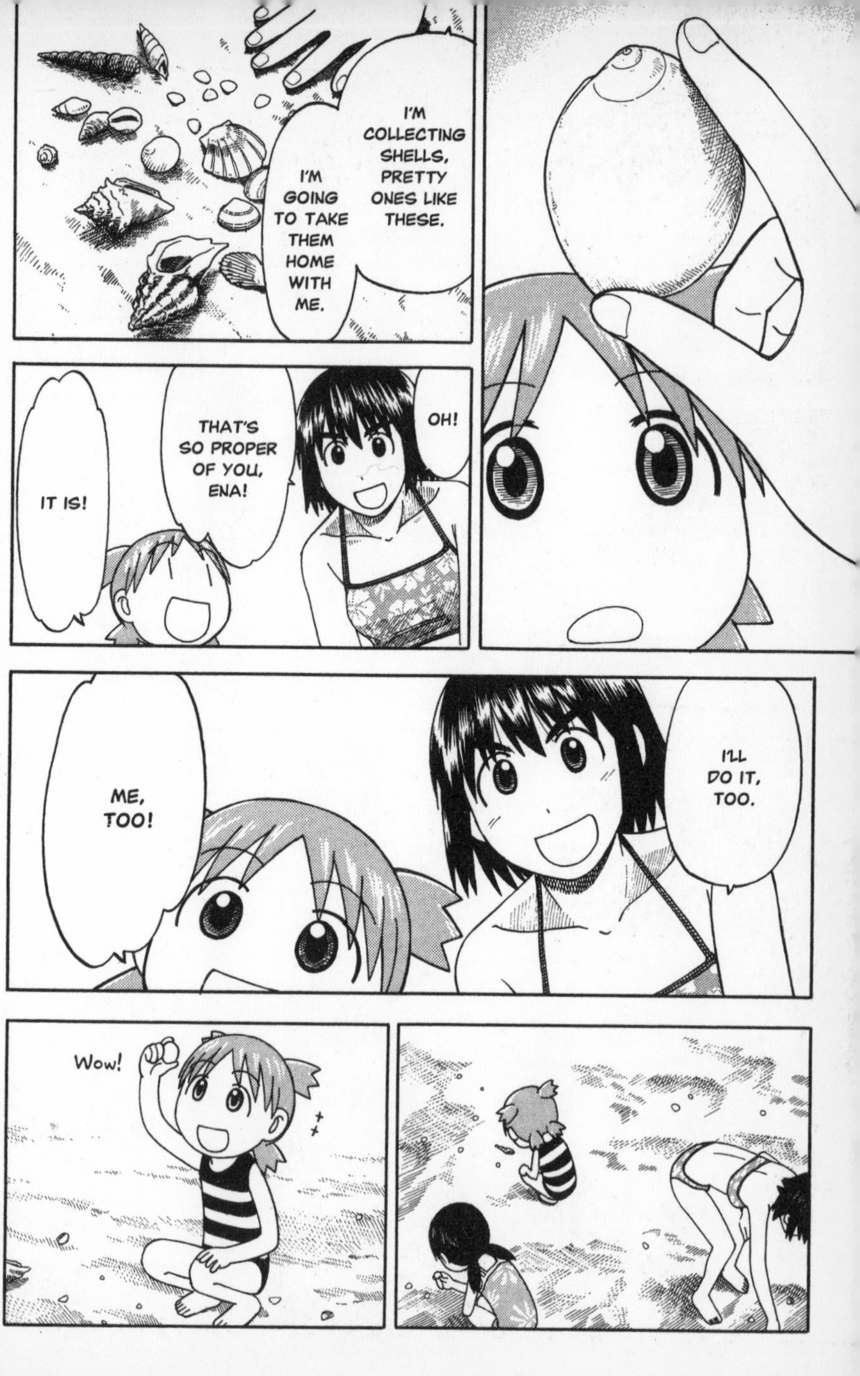
I'M COLLECTING SHELLS, PRETTY ONES LIKE THESE.
I'M GOING TO TAKE THEM HOME WITH ME.
OH!
THAT'S SO PROPER OF YOU, ENA!
IT IS!
I'LL DO IT, TOO.
ME, TOO!
Wow!

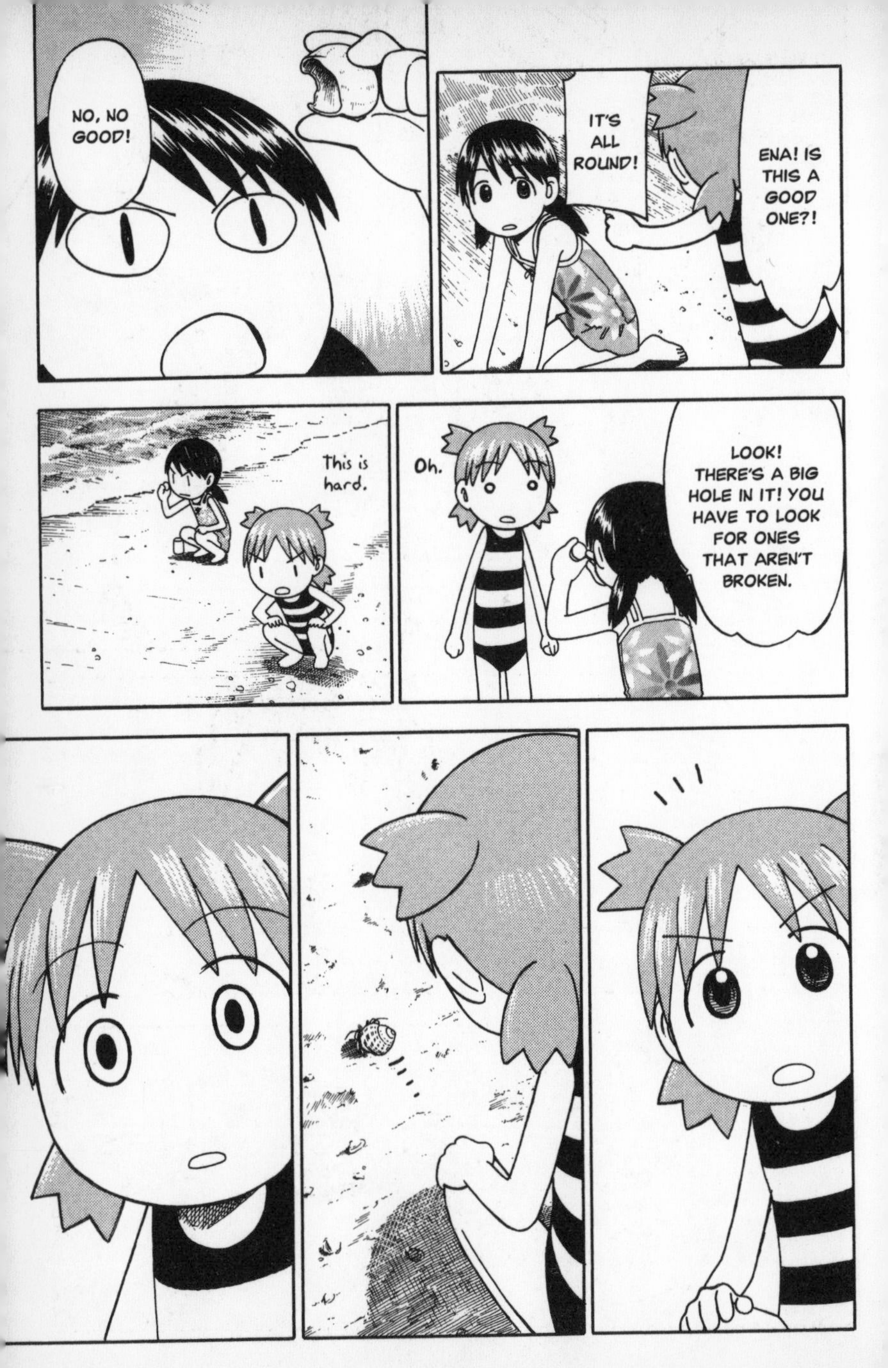
ENA! IS THIS A GOOD ONE?!
IT'S ALL ROUND!
NO, NO GOOD!
LOOK! THERE'S A BIG HOLE IN IT! YOU HAVE TO LOOK FOR ONES THAT AREN'T BROKEN.
Oh.
This is hard.

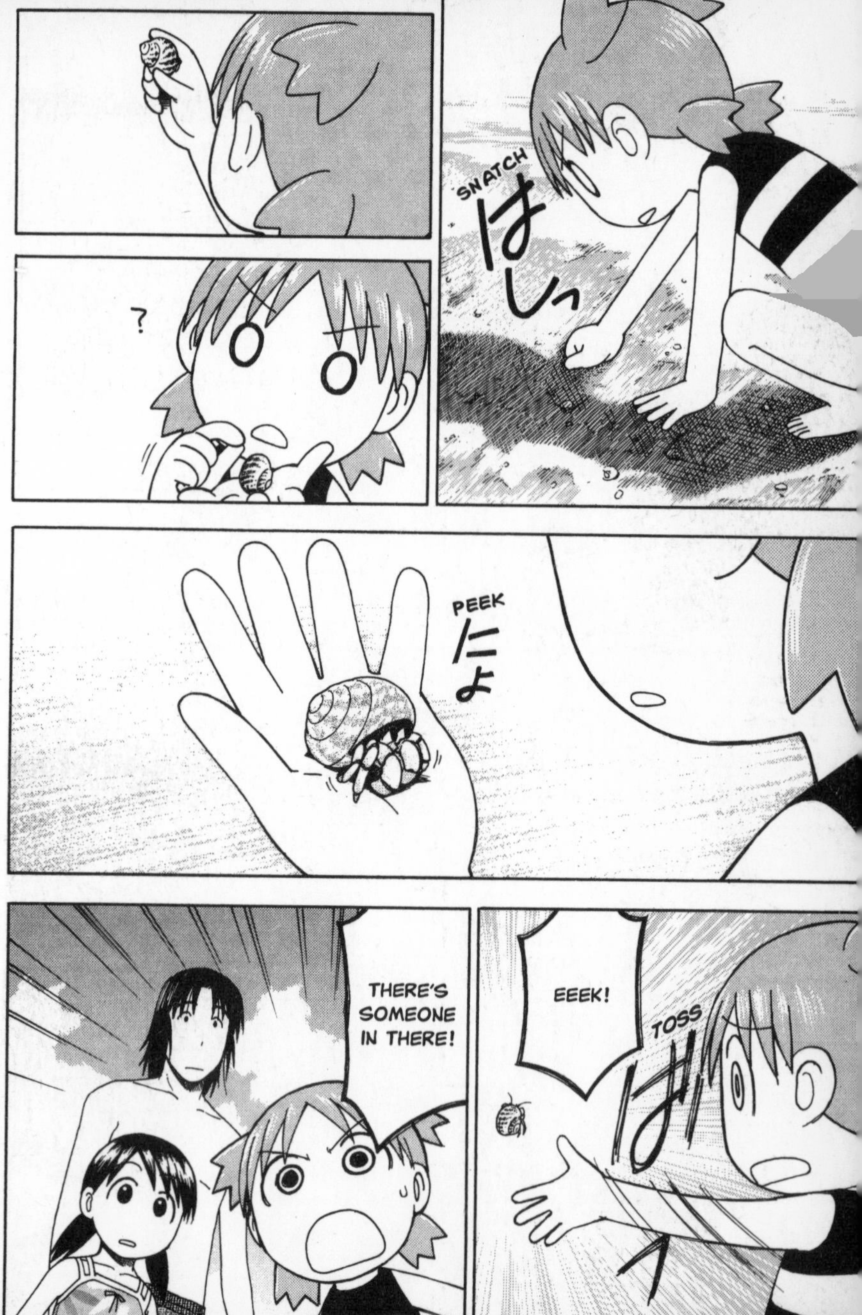
SNATCH
はしっ
?
PEEK
にょ
EEEK!
TOSS
THERE'S SOMEONE IN THERE!

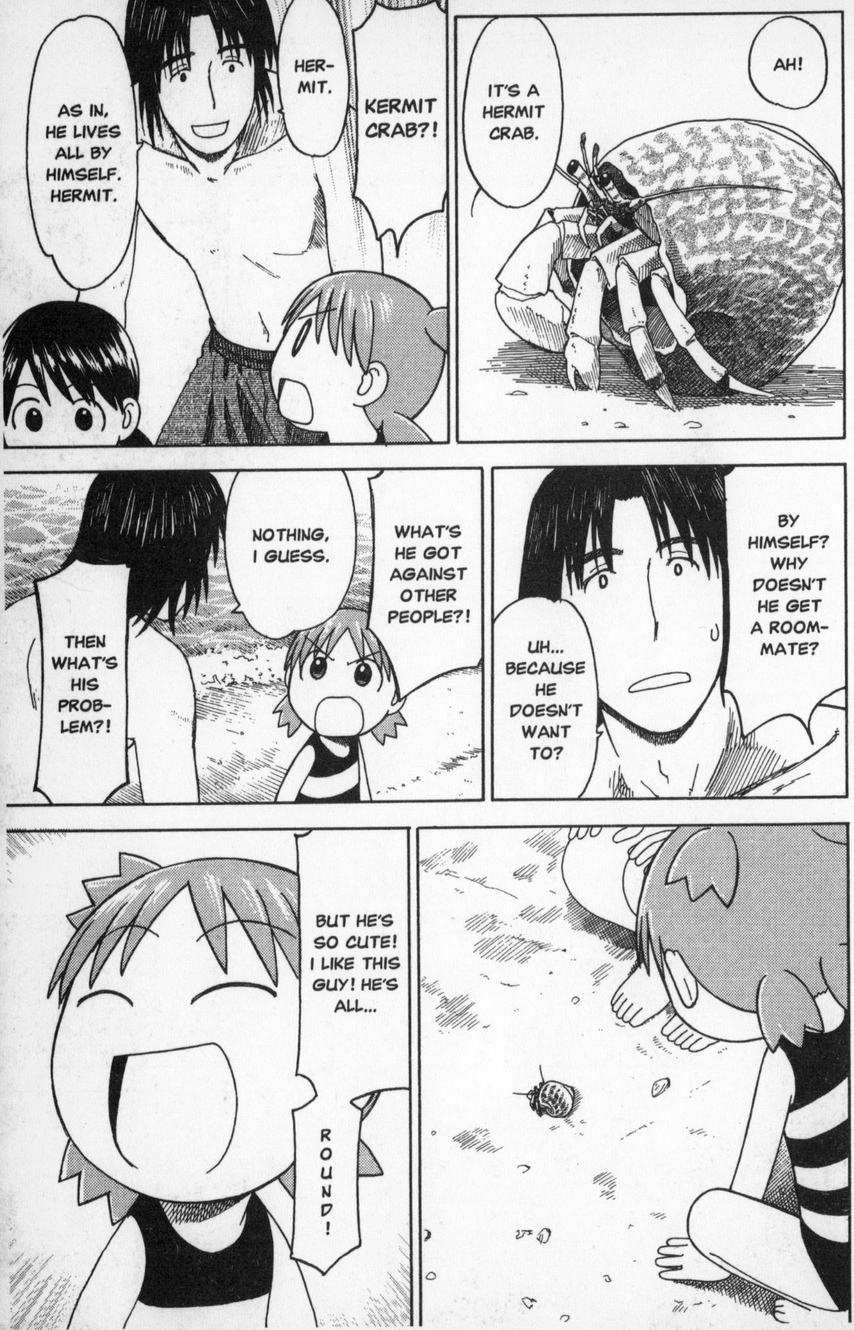
AH!
IT'S A HERMIT CRAB.
KERMIT CRAB?!
HER-MIT.
AS IN, HE LIVES ALL BY HIMSELF. HERMIT.
BY HIMSELF? WHY DOESN'T HE GET A ROOM-MATE?
UH... BECAUSE HE DOESN'T WANT TO?
WHAT'S HE GOT AGAINST OTHER PEOPLE?!
NOTHING, I GUESS.
THEN WHAT'S HIS PROB-LEM?!
BUT HE'S SO CUTE! I LIKE THIS GUY! HE'S ALL...
ROUND!

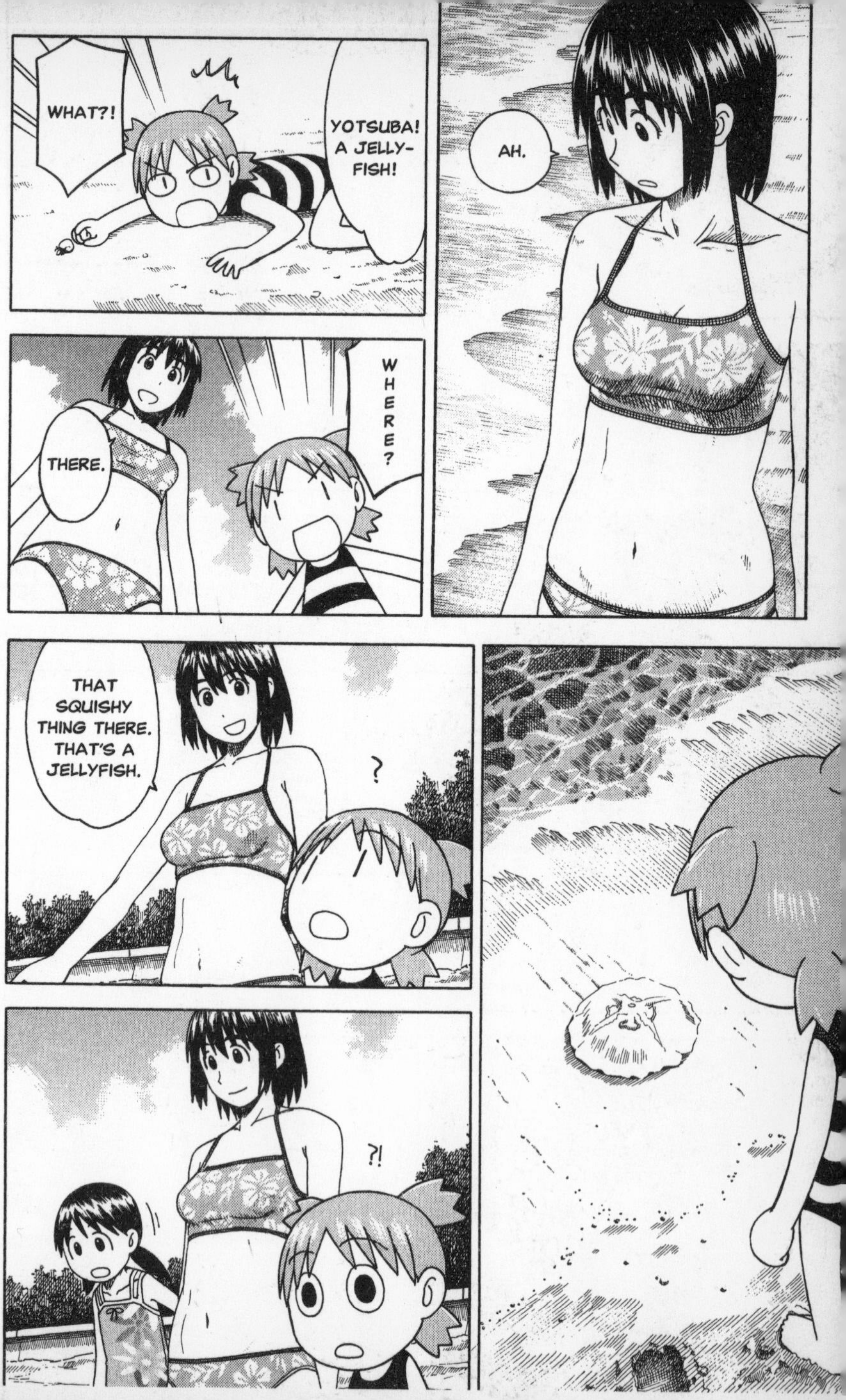
AH.
YOTSUBA! A JELLY-FISH!
WHAT?!
WHERE?
THERE.
THAT SQUISHY THING THERE. THAT'S A JELLYFISH.
?
?!

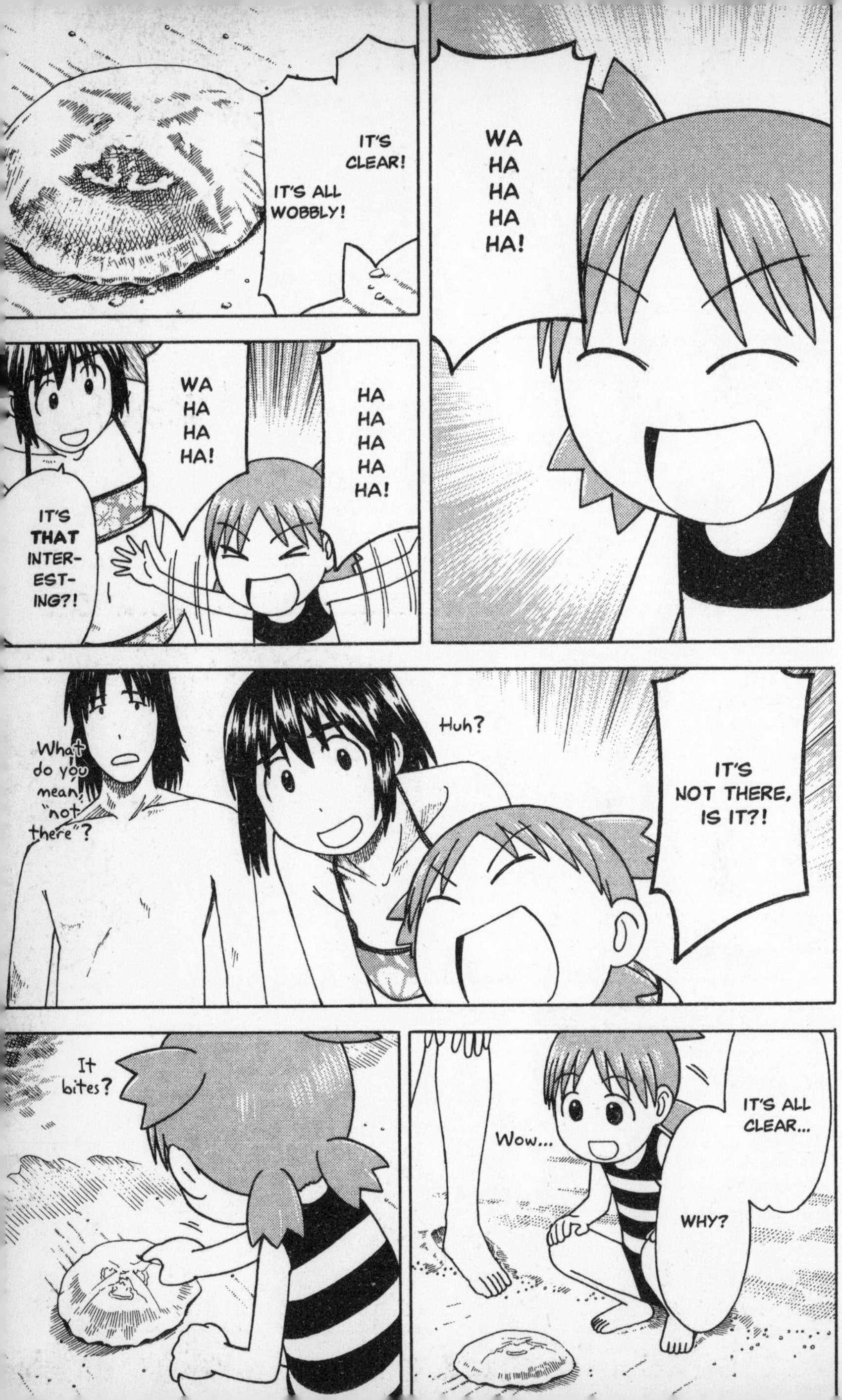
WA HA HA HA HA!
IT'S CLEAR!
IT'S ALL WOBBLY!
HA HA HA HA HA!
WA HA HA HA!
IT'S **THAT** INTER-EST-ING?!
IT'S NOT THERE, IS IT?!
Huh?
What do you mean, "not there"?
IT'S ALL CLEAR...
Wow...
WHY?
It bites?

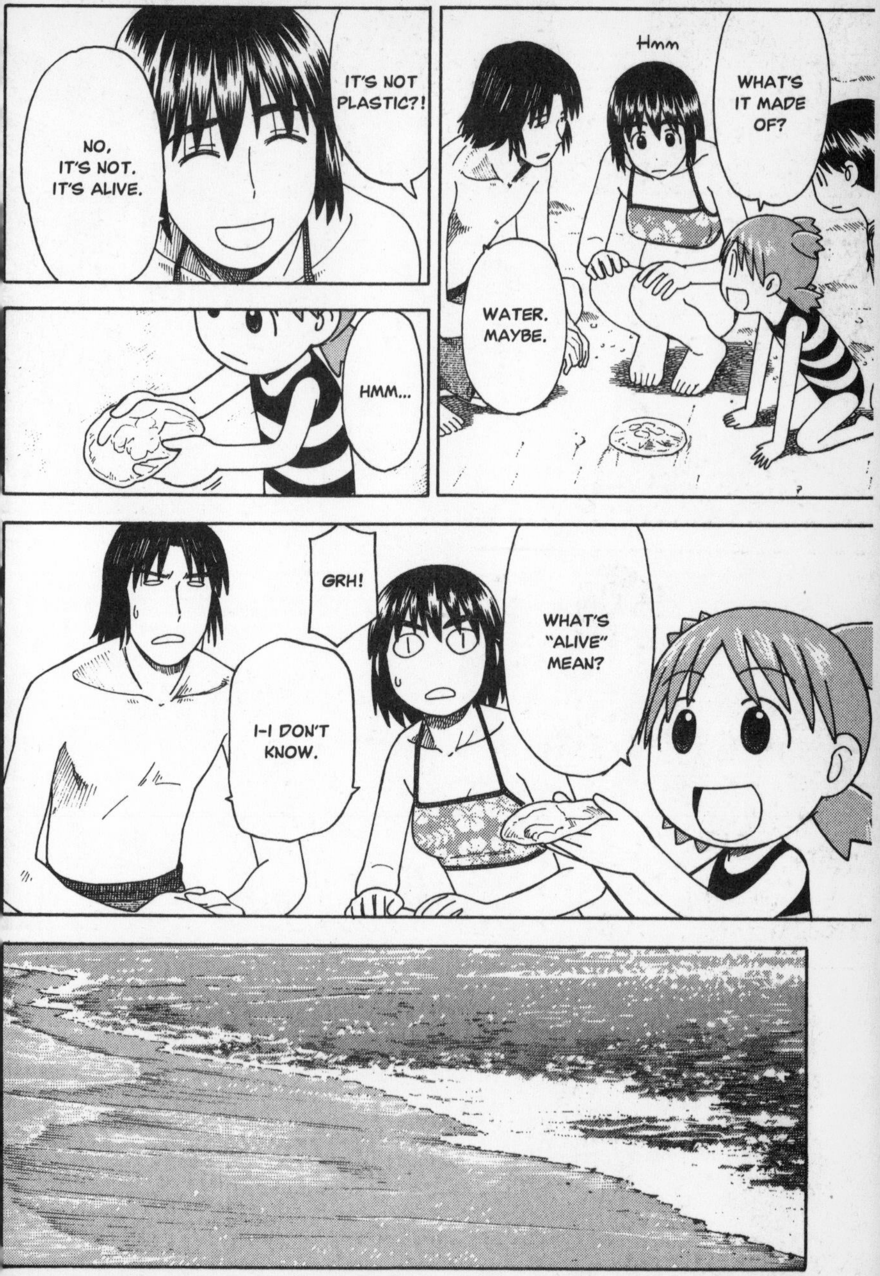
WHAT'S IT MADE OF?
Hmm
WATER. MAYBE.
IT'S NOT PLASTIC?!
NO, IT'S NOT. IT'S ALIVE.
HMM...
WHAT'S "ALIVE" MEAN?
GRH!
I-I DON'T KNOW.

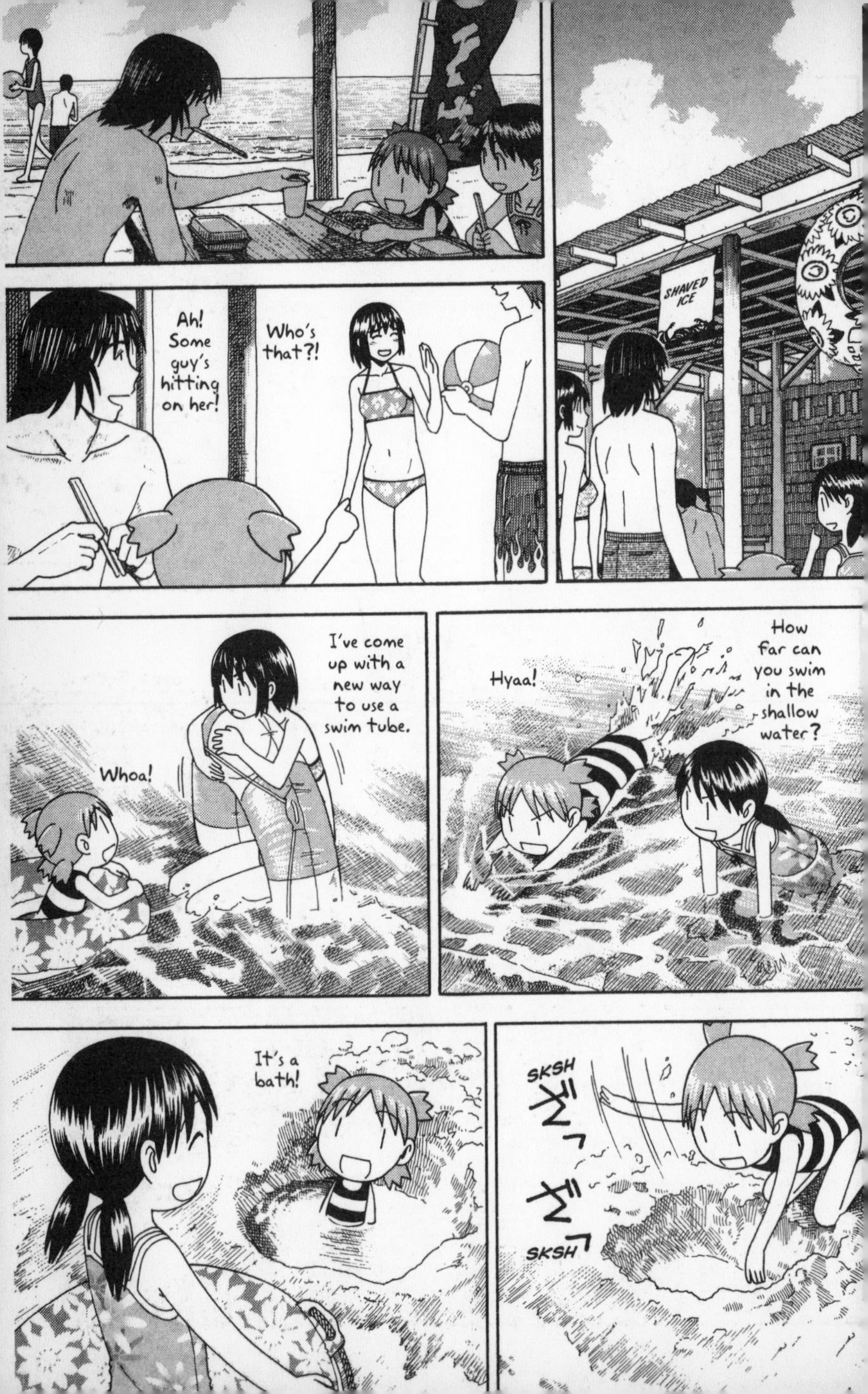
SHAVED ICE
Who's that?!
Ah! Some guy's hitting on her!
How far can you swim in the shallow water?
Hyaa!
I've come up with a new way to use a swim tube.
Whoa!
SKSH
SKSH
It's a bath!

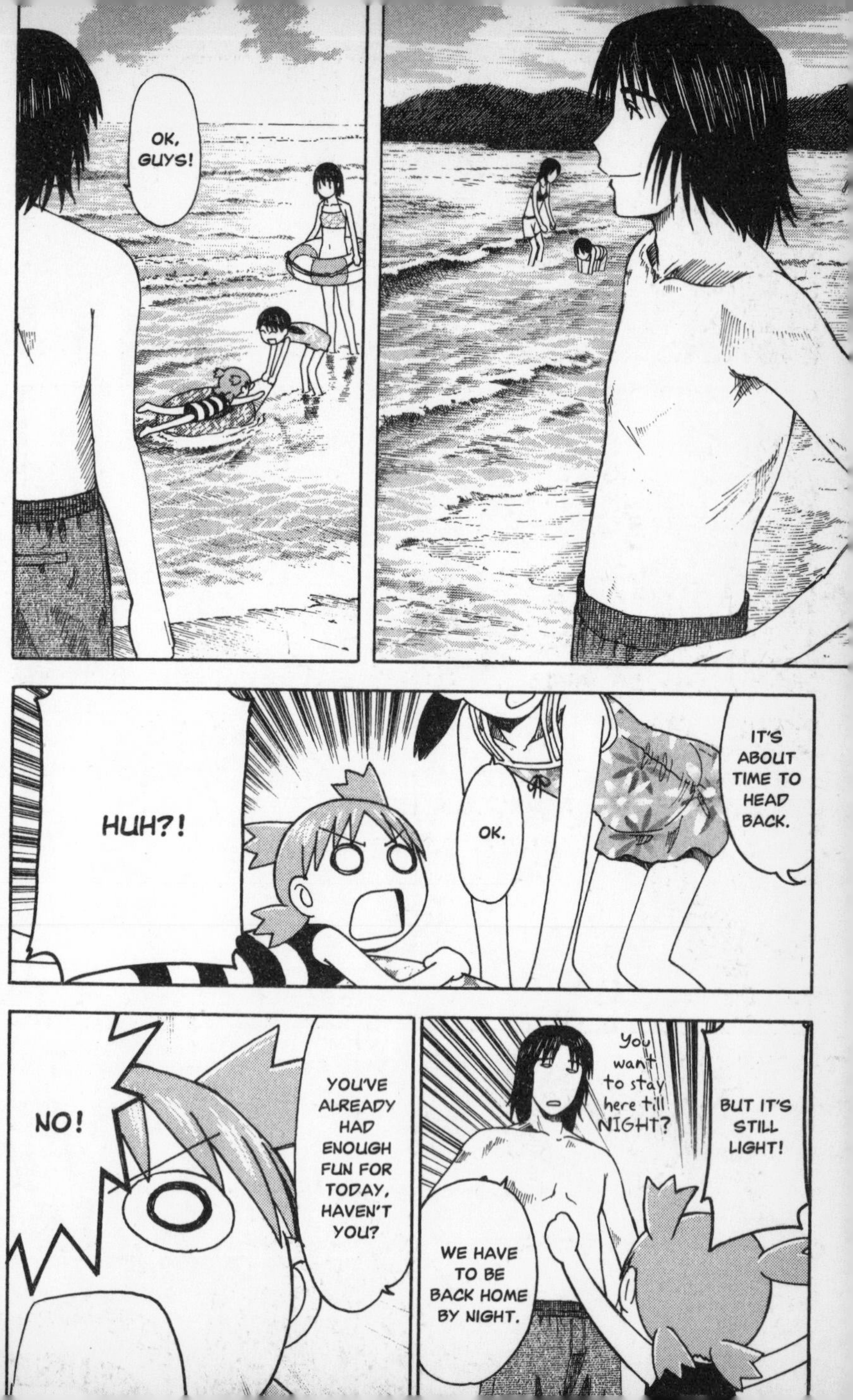
OK, GUYS!
IT'S ABOUT TIME TO HEAD BACK.
OK.
HUH?!
BUT IT'S STILL LIGHT!
You want to stay here till NIGHT?
WE HAVE TO BE BACK HOME BY NIGHT.
YOU'VE ALREADY HAD ENOUGH FUN FOR TODAY, HAVEN'T YOU?
NO!

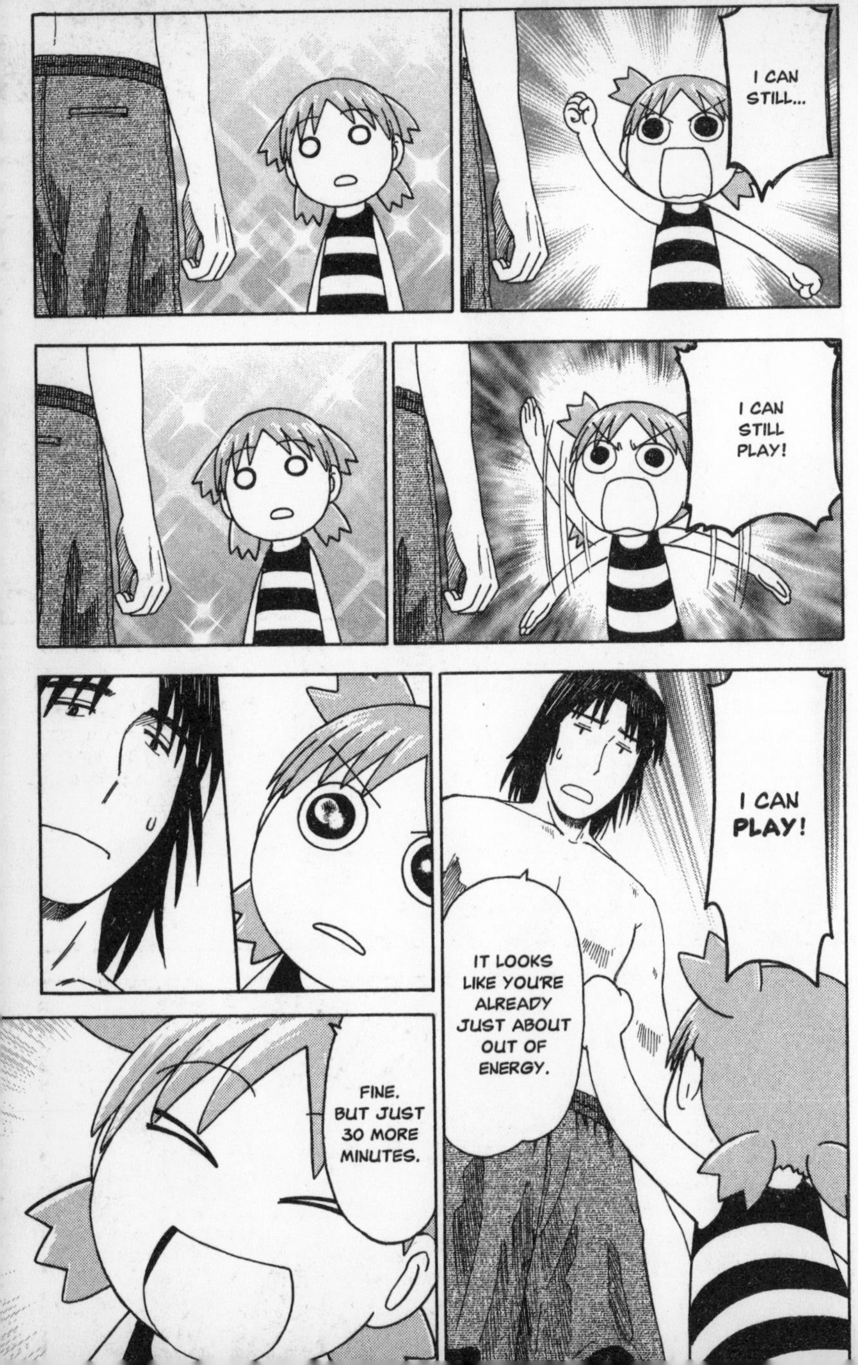
I CAN STILL...
I CAN STILL PLAY!
I CAN PLAY!
IT LOOKS LIKE YOU'RE ALREADY JUST ABOUT OUT OF ENERGY.
FINE. BUT JUST 30 MORE MINUTES.

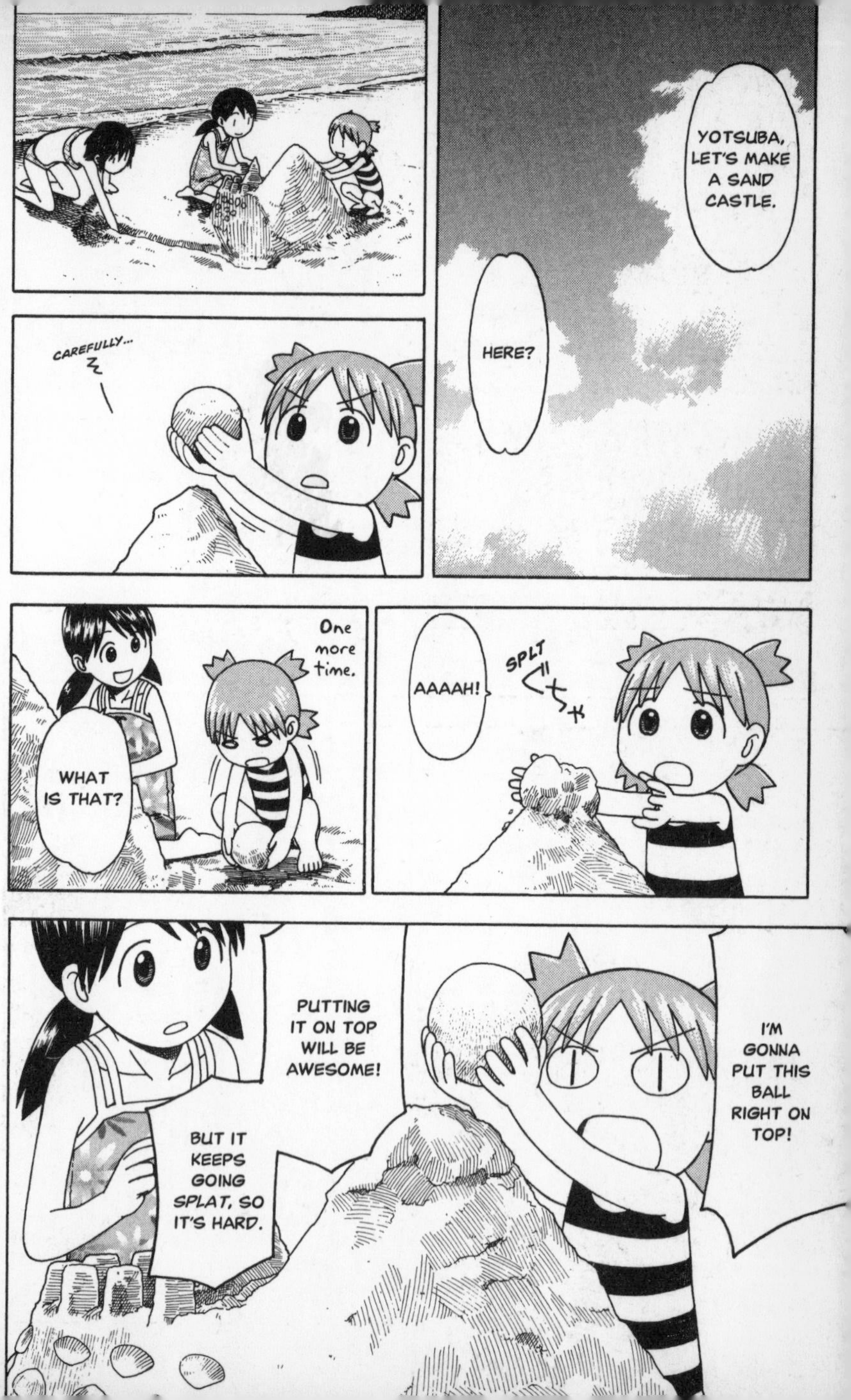
YOTSUBA, LET'S MAKE A SAND CASTLE.
HERE?
CAREFULLY...
SPLT
AAAAH!
One more time.
WHAT IS THAT?
I'M GONNA PUT THIS BALL RIGHT ON TOP!
PUTTING IT ON TOP WILL BE AWESOME!
BUT IT KEEPS GOING SPLAT, SO IT'S HARD.

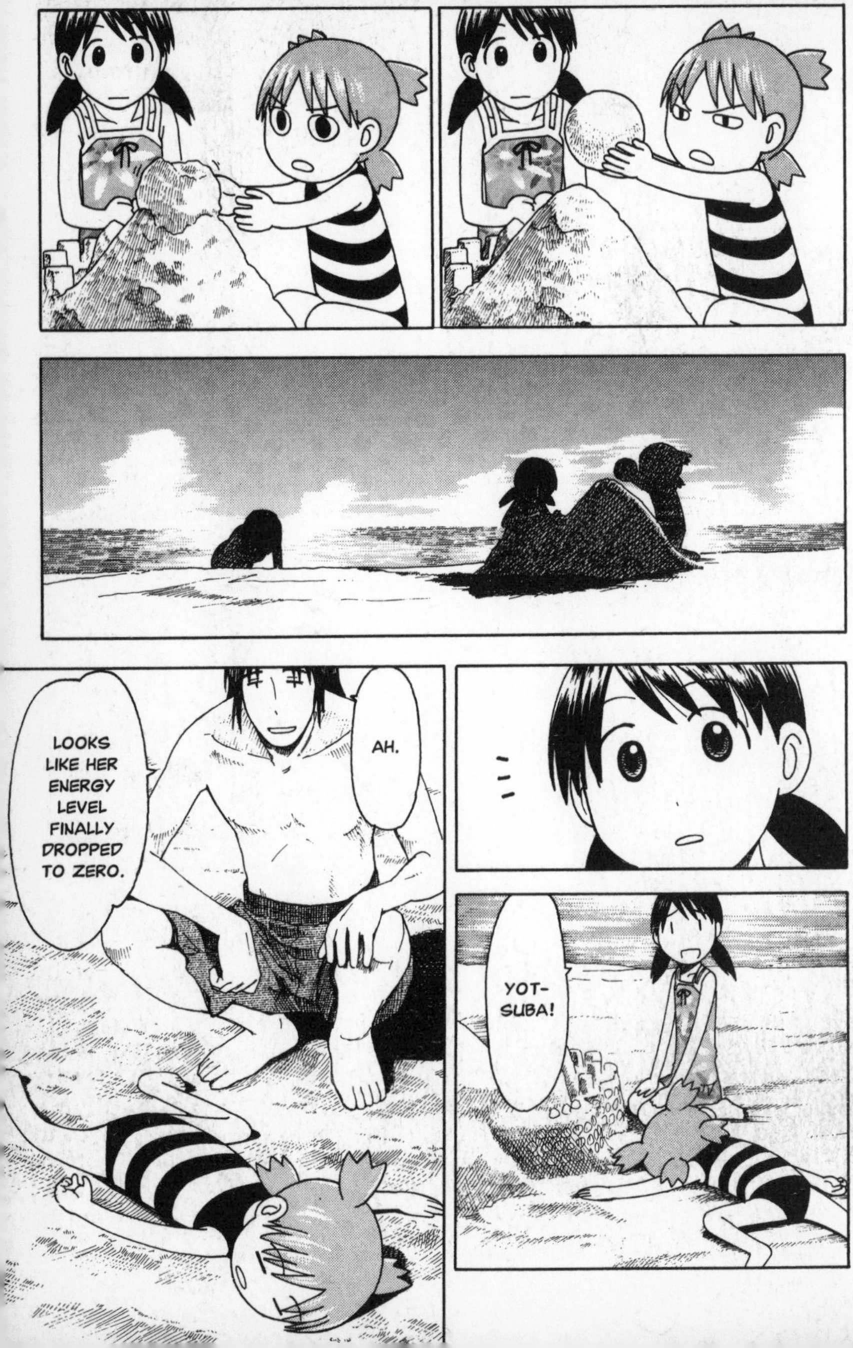
YOT-SUBA!
AH.
LOOKS LIKE HER ENERGY LEVEL FINALLY DROPPED TO ZERO.

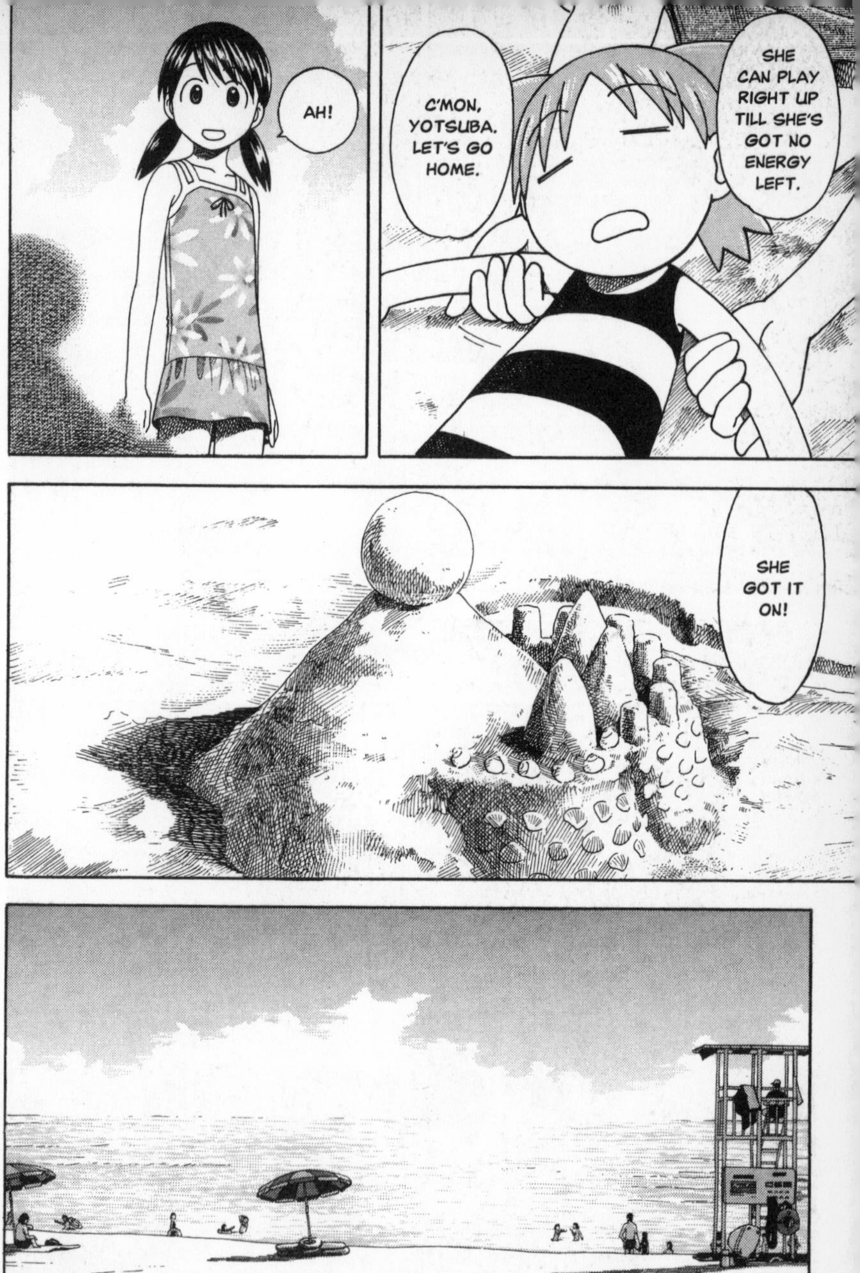
SHE CAN PLAY RIGHT UP TILL SHE'S GOT NO ENERGY LEFT.
C'MON, YOTSUBA. LET'S GO HOME.
AH!
SHE GOT IT ON!

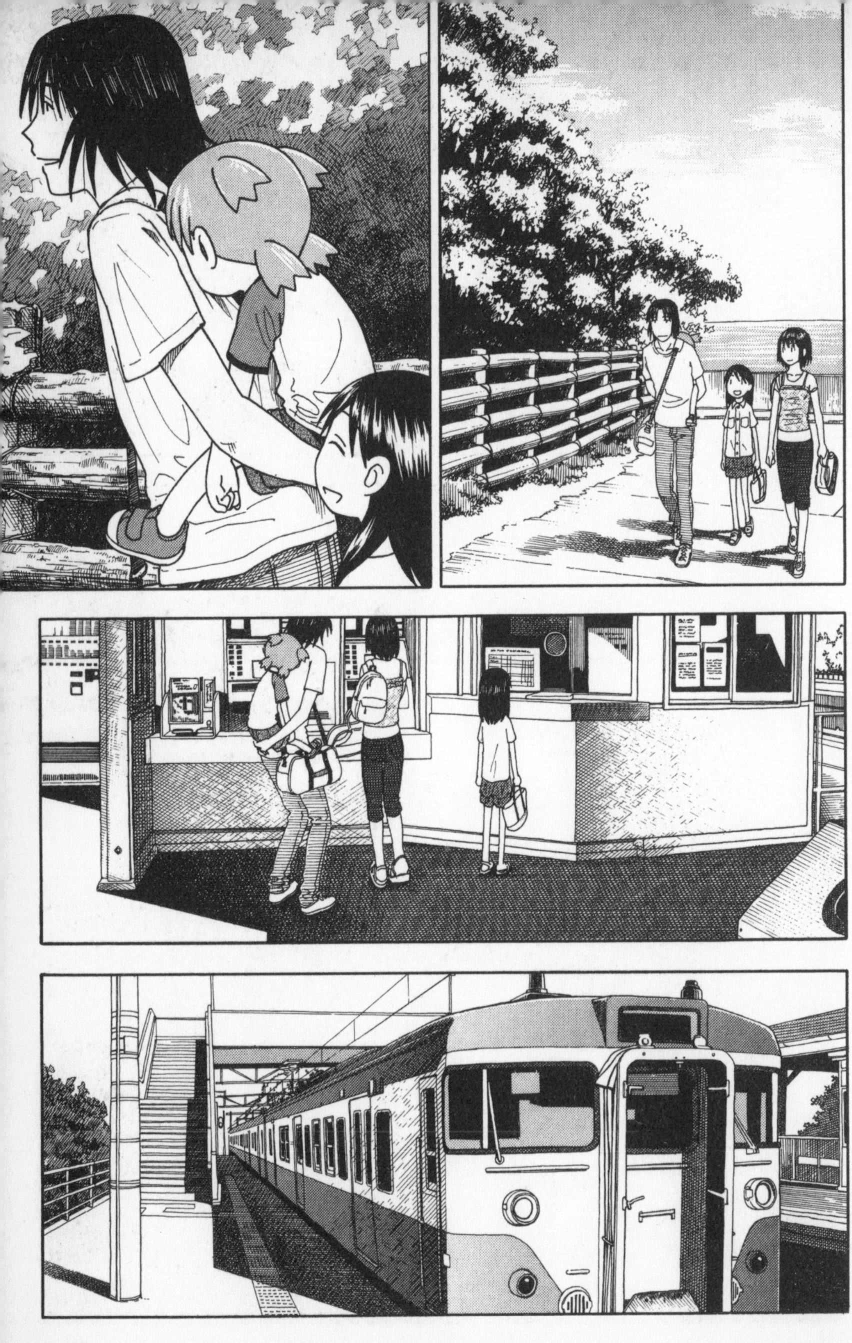

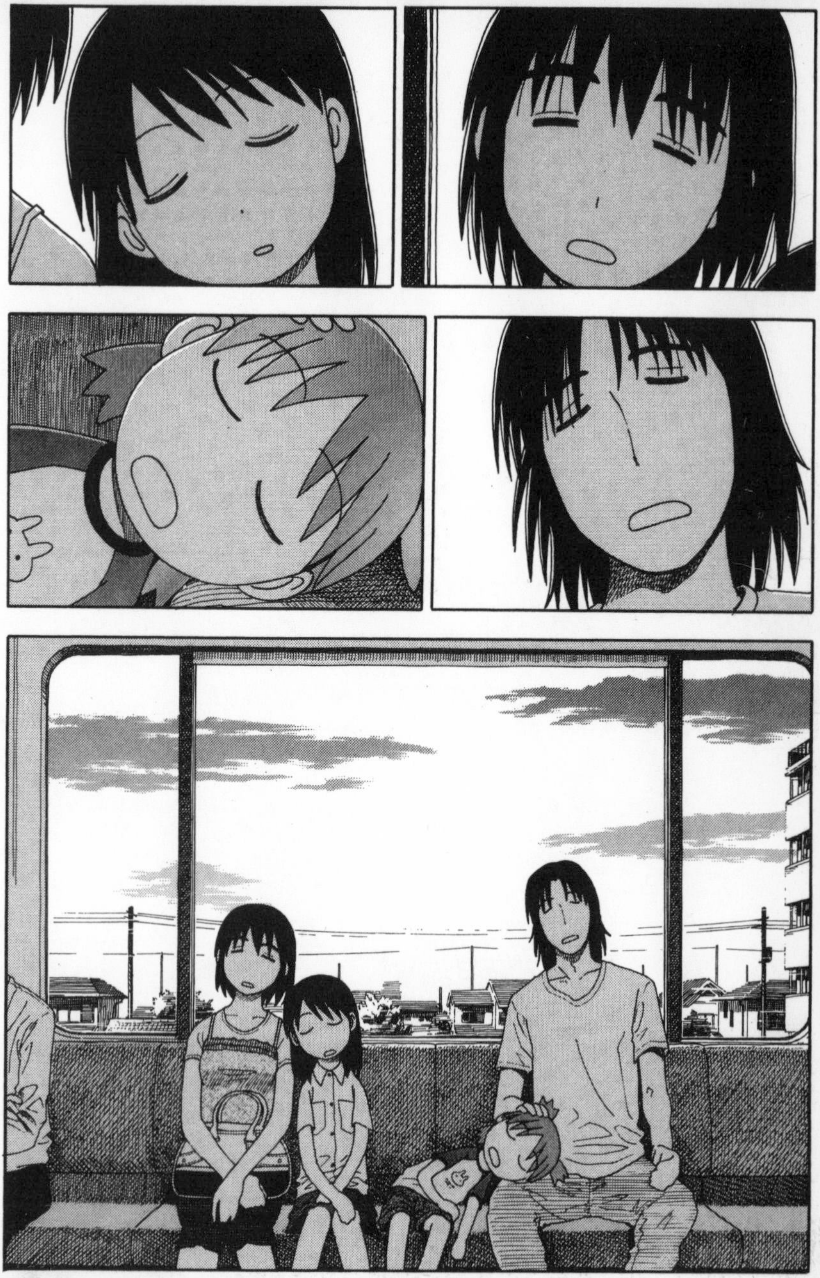

YOTSUBA&!

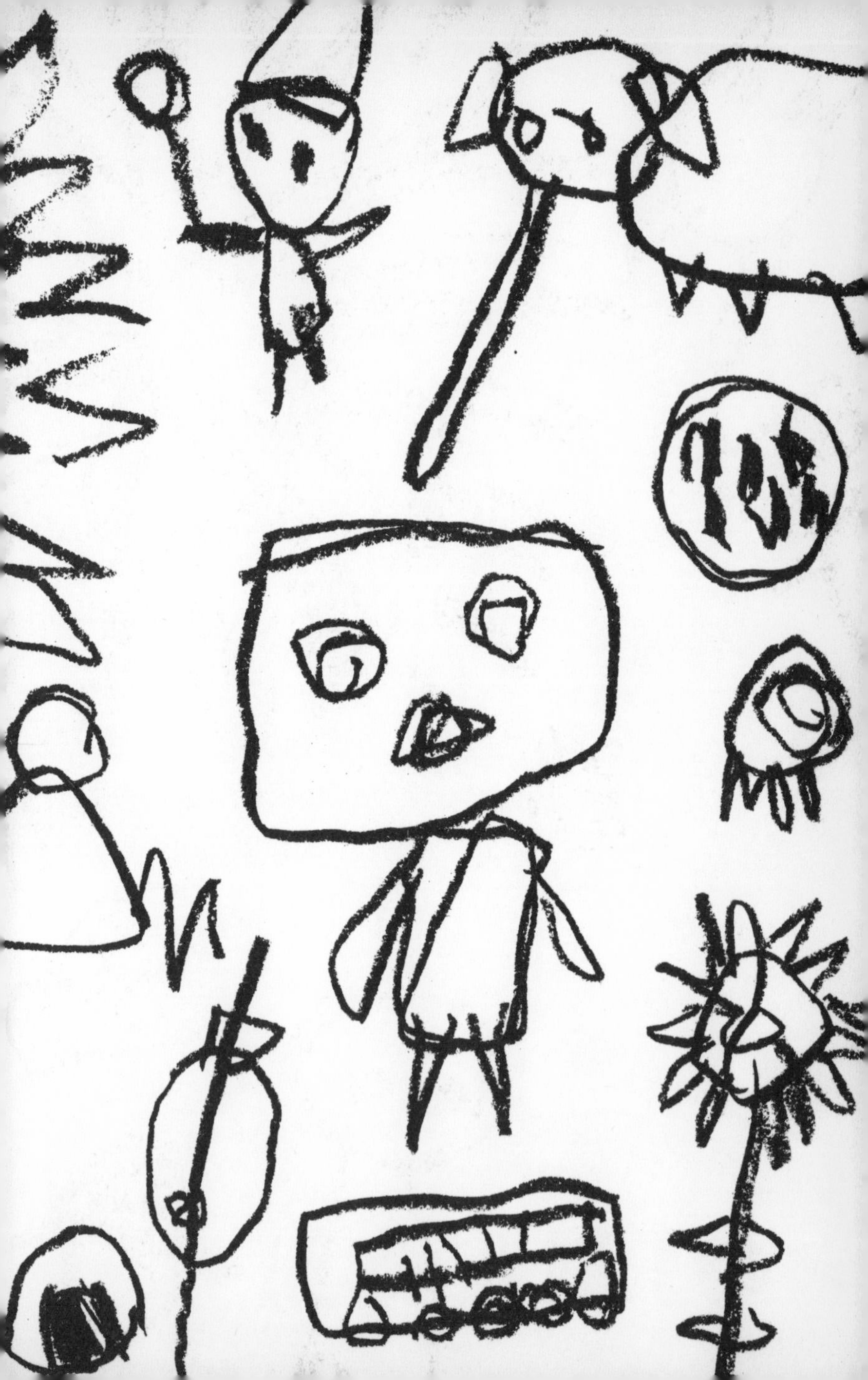

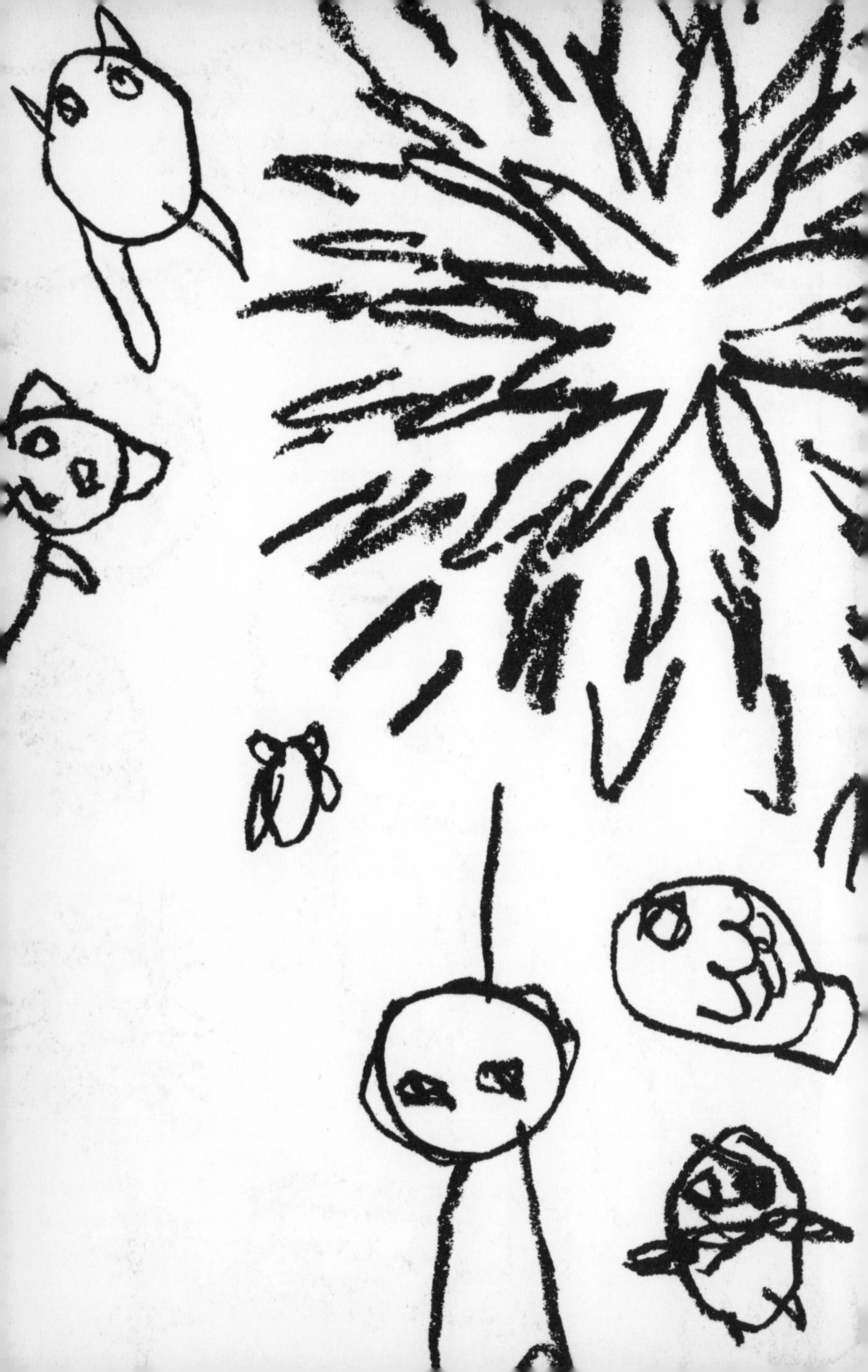

© KIYOHIKO AZUMA/YOTUBA SUTAZIO 2006
First published in 2006 by Media Works Inc., Tokyo, Japan.
English translation rights arranged with Media Works Inc.

Translator/Editor **JAVIER LOPEZ**
Graphic Artist **SCOTT HOWARD**
Copy Editor **SHERIDAN SCOTT**

Editorial Director **GARY STEINMAN**
Print Production Manager **BRIDGETT JANOTA**
Production Coordinator **MARISA KREITZ**

International Coordinators **MIYUKI KAMIYA & TORU IWAKAMI**

President, CEO & Publisher **JOHN LEDFORD**

Email: editor@adv-manga.com
www.adv-manga.com
www.advfilms.com

For sales and distribution inquiries please call 1.800.282.7202

ADV MANGA™ is a division of A.D. Vision, Inc.
5750 Bintliff Drive, Suite 210, Houston, Texas 77036
English text © 2007 published by A.D. Vision, Inc. under exclusive license.
ADV MANGA is a trademark of A.D. Vision, Inc.

ISBN: 978-1-4139-0349-2
First printing, October 2007
10 9 8 7 6 5 4 3 2 1
Printed in Canada

ENJOY EVERYTHING.

CROSSTOWN TRAFFIC!

Who needs to recycle when you can be cycling instead! After a brief (and misguided) experiment with conservation, Yotsuba sets her sights on a brand-new bike—and she certainly won't let a few tumbles keep her down. But things really get out of hand when Dad gets some top-shelf milk, and Yotsuba is determined to let Fuka have a taste... even if she has to pedal across town to do it!

6

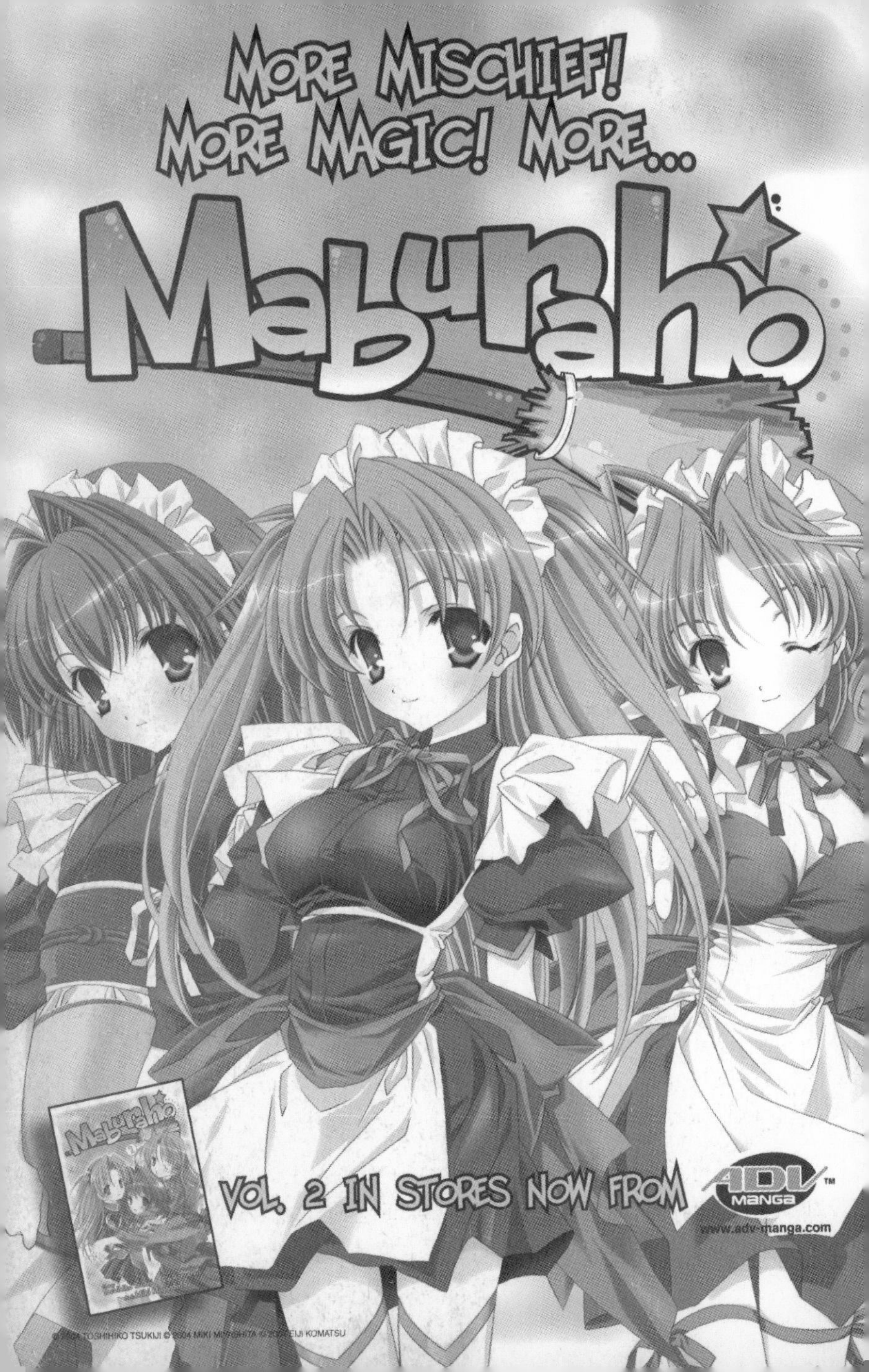
MORE MISCHIEF!
MORE MAGIC! MORE...
Maburaho
VOL. 2 IN STORES NOW FROM
ADV MANGA ™
www.adv-manga.com
TOSHIHIKO TSUKIJI © 2004 MIKI
EIJI KOMATSU

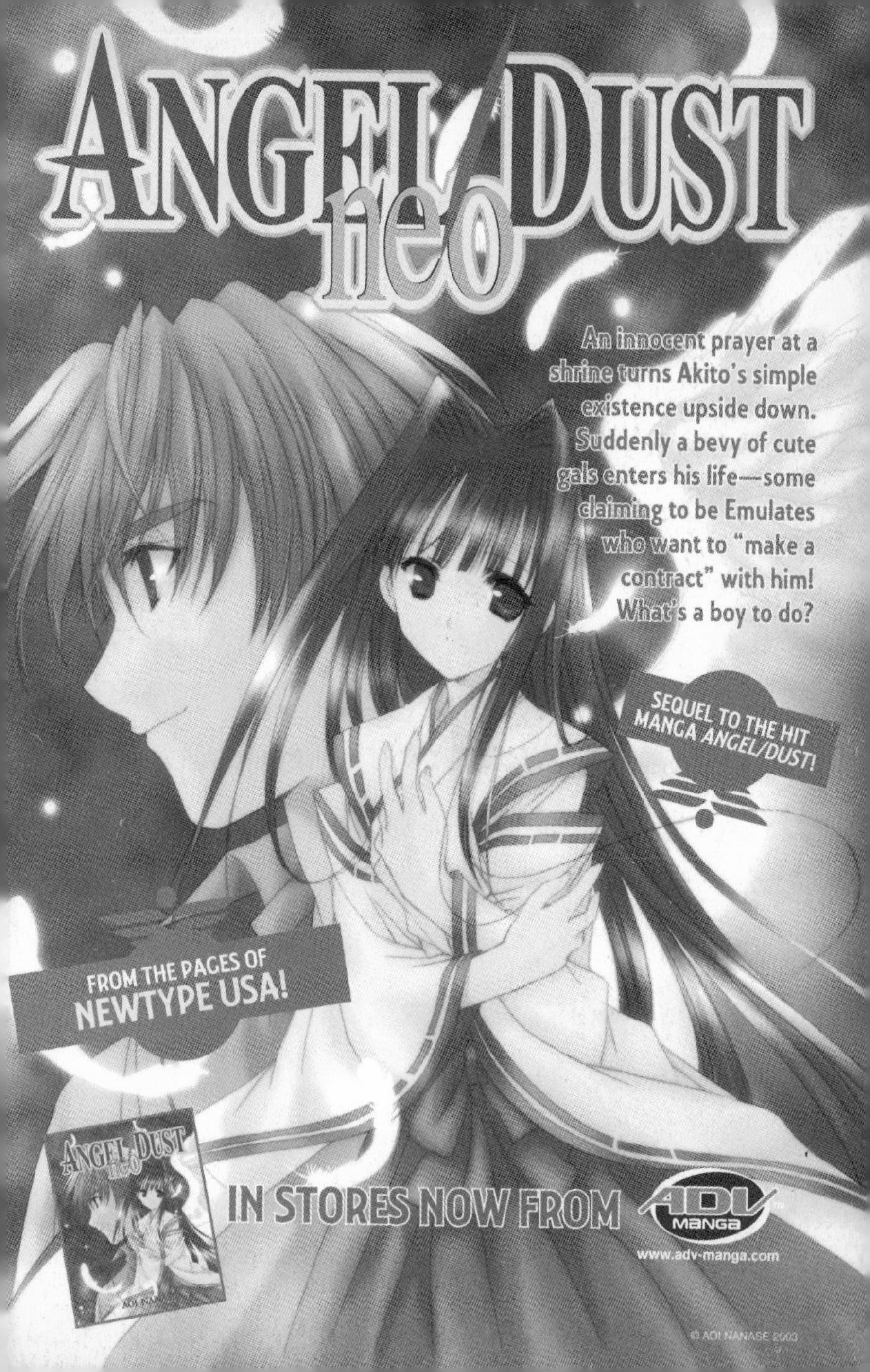

ANGEL/DUST neo
An innocent prayer at a shrine turns Akito's simple existence upside down. Suddenly a bevy of cute gals enters his life—some claiming to be Emulates who want to "make a contract" with him! What's a boy to do?
SEQUEL TO THE HIT MANGA ANGEL/DUST!
FROM THE PAGES OF NEWTYPE USA!
ANGEL/DUST neo
IN STORES NOW FROM ADV Manga
www.adv-manga.com
© AOI NANASE 2003